I0815108

Rebellious Saints

Rebellious Saints

Inspiring Stories for Young People

Christian Linker
Illustrated by Julia Dürr

PAULIST PRESS
New York / Mahwah, NJ

Cover art by Julia Dürr
Cover design by Sharyn Banks
Book design by Lynn Else

Christian Linker, *Der kleine Rebell. Legenden von Drachenkämpfern, Kräuterhexen und anderen Heiligen* illustrated by Julia Dürr © 2021 Verlag Herder GmbH, Freiburg im Breisgau

English translation copyright © 2023 by Paulist Press

All rights reserved. No part of this publication may be reproduced, stored in a retrieval system, or transmitted in any form or by any means, electronic, mechanical, photocopying, recording, scanning, or otherwise, without either the prior written permission of the Publisher, or authorization through payment of the appropriate per-copy fee to the Copyright Clearance Center, Inc., www.copyright.com. Requests to the Publisher for permission should be addressed to the Permissions Department, Paulist Press, permissions@paulistpress.com.

Library of Congress Cataloging-in-Publication Data
Names: Linker, Christian, 1975– author. | Dürr, Julia, 1981– illustrator.
Title: Rebellious saints : inspiring stories for young people / Christian Linker ; illustrated by Julia Dürr.
Description: New York : Paulist Press, 2023. | Audience: Grades 4–6 | Summary: "Twenty-two saints tell their own exciting story of how they found that desiring God and living for bold truth took them places they never expected to go and empowered them to do remarkable, sometimes very quirky, things"—Provided by publisher.
Identifiers: LCCN 2023002425 (print) | LCCN 2023002426 (ebook) | ISBN 9780809168057 (paperback) | ISBN 9780809187997 (ebook)
Subjects:
Classification: LCC BX4658 .L53 2023 (print) | LCC BX4658 (ebook) | DDC 282.092/2—dc23/eng/20230602
LC record available at https://lccn.loc.gov/2023002425
LC ebook record available at https://lccn.loc.gov/2023002426

ISBN 978-0-8091-6805-7 (paperback)
ISBN 978-0-8091-8799-7 (e-book)

Published by Paulist Press
997 Macarthur Boulevard
Mahwah, New Jersey 07430
www.paulistpress.com

Printed and bound in the
United States of America

Contents

Patrons and Rebels

"*Expecto Patronum!*"

Anyone who has read the Harry Potter books or seen the films knows these magic words. In an emergency, you can use them to bring magical aid to your rescue—if you have magical powers yourself. But the idea for this spell comes from the Christian faith. We have relied on patron saints for a long time. They are the holy men and women—sometimes even holy boys and girls—from two thousand years of Church history. Each one has their own area: a city or country, or a group of people. Unfortunately, they don't work the same way as in Harry Potter—they don't show up on command. They prefer to stay in the background.

But they can still work by inspiring us with their lives and their deeds. There are plenty to choose from because the Church celebrates thousands of saints. Not all were always pious, gentle people who walked around with halos around their heads, even as children. The lives of the saints are varied. Sometimes they had great adventures, and sometimes they went astray.

And very often the saints were people who rebelled against something—against injustice and slavery, against brutal kings and cruel laws, against evil "dragons," and sometimes even against their own parents.

We asked some of them to tell you a little bit about themselves. Here are their stories....

Mary, Mother of God

"Mother of God?" How can God have a mother? I didn't understand that at first either.

Back then, of course, no one called me "God's Mother." I wasn't even called Mary, but Mariam. That's what my name sounds like in my native language, Aramaic. As a girl, I lived in the Jewish village of Nazareth and never thought that an angel would appear to *me* of all people. What he said was absolutely unbelievable! God wants to become human! He wants to be born, and—I'll be his mother!

I was still very young, and I wasn't even married yet. I just had a boyfriend, Joseph. We wanted to get married—but how could I explain this to him?

Somehow, in spite of all these questions, I felt deep trust. God had a plan for me, even if I didn't understand it. I said yes, just like that. Because I knew everything would be fine if I let happen what God wanted.

Unfortunately, not everything turned out well at first. In the end it was all okay, but it wasn't always easy. Honestly, when you

are the mother of a child who is supposed to save the world from sin, very confusing things happen! When Joseph noticed I was pregnant, he wanted to break up with me. But then he realized how important it was that we have the child and raise him together. He stayed with me. The birth was a huge event. You know the story:

Jesus was born in a stable, and it seemed as if the whole world came to visit. Shepherds came to worship him, and later even some wise men from the East came with valuable gifts. But soon after Jesus was born, we had to flee the country because King Herod wanted to kill him. A few years later, when Jesus was twelve, he disappeared while we were on our way home from a trip to Jerusalem. It seemed like we looked for him for ages! At last we found him in the temple, where he was discussing religion with the important teachers. That boy really kept us guessing!

As you can imagine, the worst of all was my boy's death. One of his friends betrayed him, and the Roman governor Pilate had him crucified. I watched everything—it was so horrible. Not until he rose from the dead on the third day did I begin to understand how it all made sense.

Sometimes I think that if I were that young girl Mariam again, back in Nazareth, and if I knew what I know now, if the angel came—I would say yes again, even though it seems crazy. But the really crazy thing that's easy to forget is that God *asked*! He didn't order me or force me, but he asked. And I could have said no.

But I didn't.

In my story, I mentioned wise men from the East...

No saint is loved as much as Mary. As the mother of Jesus, Mary is often called "Mother of God." Sometimes she's called "Madonna," which means "My Lady." This name is so well-known that even a famous pop singer is called by it. Many artists have painted Mary as our protector, wearing a long cloak under which all people—rich and poor, young and old—can find safety.

The Three Wise Men

We are the wise men from the East. There are many legends and exciting stories about us. And because they are all so beautiful, we don't want to tell you too much about ourselves here. For example, we won't reveal how many of us there really were!

Now you might think, "Very funny—it says THREE KINGS!"

But if you look in the Bible, it doesn't *actually* say three. And it doesn't say kings. It just says that some "magicians" came from the East to see the newborn king. Back then, "magician" could also mean "astrologer." And that's exactly what we were—we watched and interpreted the movements of the stars.

One day we spotted a special new star, and we knew right away that something important was happening. Somewhere far away a new king had been born, mightier and more splendid than any before him. We *had* to see him, we thought, and so we picked out and wrapped some beautiful presents: gold, frankincense, and myrrh, the most valuable things we could pack. Gifts like these are only given to the most important kings.

So we followed the star and came to the land of King Herod. We immediately went to see him and asked where the new king was born. We thought Herod should know, king to king. But he had no idea. When we found the child, we understood why: This newborn king was not lying in a fancy crib in a big palace but in a little stable on the straw.

When we found him, we knelt and worshipped him. We must have looked funny kneeling in our fancy clothes with our expensive gifts in front of a poor little baby as if he was something special.

But in that moment, we understood something important. This baby really was the greatest of all—in the way God imagines real greatness. It has nothing to do with power and violence or money and bossing around. The greatness of God is love as shown in a little child, because every child that is born into this world should be treated like a king or a queen.

Unfortunately, this does not always happen. Many children are treated badly. They grow up poor and even have to work instead of going to school. To change that, there is a custom in some countries that you may already know about. At the beginning of each year, children dress up as kings and queens and parade through the streets of the villages and towns carrying a big star. They wear homemade crowns on their heads and rattle coins in a can, collecting money to help other children all over the world, because all children on earth are royal children whom God loves. The children bless the houses and apartments of the people, because it's not just priests in the Church who can bless—anyone who is good can do that!

Speaking of "all over the world..."

Legend has given names to the Three Kings: Melchior, Caspar, and Balthasar. Because they had to travel such a long way to get to the manger, the three are considered the patron saints of travelers and pilgrims. Some traditions show Melchior as an old man bearing gold, Caspar as a middle-aged man with dark skin bearing frankincense, and Balthazar as the youngest, bearing myrrh. But no one really knows for sure!

Saint Josephine Bakhita

My name is Josephine, but that's not my real name. I picked it later. I forgot what my parents called me. Sounds crazy, I know. Very bad things happened to me when I was little—maybe I forgot my name because I just wanted to forget all the bad things. Unfortunately, I can't forget everything. Especially not the time I was kidnapped from my village as a child. That's what the slave traders did.

Do you know what slaves are? They are people who are forced to work by people who "own" them as possessions, like you might own a teddy bear or an action figure. The slave traders stole me from my village and sold me in a market like I was just a thing. That was almost 150 years ago now. Back then it was still considered normal in some countries for people to buy and sell other human beings, especially people like me—people with black skin. They said that if you had black skin, you weren't as good as people with white skin.

My first owner resold me, and then that owner resold me, and by the time I was sixteen I had been owned by four different people. The last person who bought me was Italian. At that time, in Italy, as everywhere in Europe, slavery was already forbidden. That's why a court decided that I should be set free.

So I stayed in Italy, where I worked as a nanny for a while. And I was baptized because I heard the stories about Jesus and was fascinated by them. As a child and as a teenager, I experienced so much evil that my heart should have been filled with hate forever. But Jesus also experienced a lot of evil, yet he simply loved people more and more. Perhaps only love can set a person truly free. I mean, if you're full of hate and you long for revenge, then your soul is trapped. But I have found freedom, not just on the outside, because I finally belonged to myself and to no one else, but also on the inside, because I tried to love people.

Today, thank God, it is strictly forbidden to kidnap and sell people in most places in the world, at least officially. But in some countries, it happens anyway. Children, especially, suffer secretly. Pope Francis thinks that we should all fight against slavery and selling people, so he made me the patron saint of all enslaved people—and also for those who help them escape. God wants all people to be free. As long as someone is still in chains somewhere in the world, we cannot rest.

Speaking of a hard childhood...

Even today, many people are treated like slaves without rights. Some even wear chains. There are many human rights organizations, such as Amnesty International, and Church aid organizations as well. All of these organizations rely on us to support them in their work with our help or donations.

Saint Bernadette Soubirous

Somewhere in the farthest corner of France, at the foot of the mountains, lies the little town of Lourdes. No one ever expected anything exciting to happen there! At least not me. I was born in 1844 and my childhood there was very poor and ragged. My father had a mill that we used to earn our living, but it didn't do well. Sometimes I had to live with a foster family because my parents couldn't take care of me. I was sick a lot and, most of all, I was hungry because there was often not enough to eat. I didn't go to school at all. I couldn't read or write. Instead, I had to work in a pub, look after sheep, or collect firewood because there was no electric heating back then.

The very first time it happened, I was fourteen and gathering wood near a grotto when I suddenly saw her—the beautiful white lady! Nobody could see her but me. And, of course, nobody believed me at first. Everyone thought I was crazy, that I was just imagining it, or that I just made it up so I would have something to brag about.

I saw the lady a few more times over the following months, and then she stopped appearing to me. I didn't tell many people about it, but the story soon spread all over the country and all over the world. More and more people were convinced that Mary, the Mother of God, had appeared to me. They wanted to visit the grotto where I saw her, and some sick people who came were suddenly cured in that very place. I had to keep talking about my experiences—to the priest and the bishop and the people from the newspaper—and more and more people came to the grotto—hundreds, thousands. It was really scary.

That's why I finally left and went to another city, Nevers. There I became a nun and took care of sick children, just as I might have wished someone would have taken care of me. At my old home in Lourdes, a place of pilgrimage was created—that's what it's called when people come from all over to pray at a place, and maybe hope for a miracle.

Actually, miracles, or whatever you want to call them, happen all the time. Sometimes a person can be very sick and then is suddenly healthy, and the doctors can't explain how it happened. But I think the greatest miracle of all is hope itself. Hope means you don't accept the way the world is. That you don't just think, "That's the way it is; there's nothing you can do about it."

It also doesn't matter whether I really saw Mary back in the grotto. What's more important is that we keep our eyes open for the unexpected everywhere and never give up hope. That is why people see me as the patroness of the poor and of all those who are laughed at for their faith.

Speaking of the unexpected...

The fact that Mary appeared to a poor peasant girl shows that God is interested in all people, not just the rich and powerful. And the fact that Bernadette saw the apparition while she was gathering wood is a reminder that God not only wants to meet us in church or at solemn events but also in our normal everyday life: through other people, through special events, in nature, at school, or at work.

Saint Kateri Tekakwitha

Yes, that's my name: Kateri Tekakwitha. It's a Native American name, so it might not be easy for you to pronounce. I am a Native American, and my father was a chief of the Mohawks. The area where I grew up is now part of Canada. There wasn't a country called Canada back then, just forests and mountains and lakes and a few fair-skinned people who had come from across the ocean. They called themselves Europeans. Some of them were soldiers who wanted to steal the forests and mountains and lakes from us, but there were also other people who just lived with us. They told us of their God, who had a son named Jesus.

My mother believed in this Jesus, but not my father. He still worshipped the old gods and spirits. My mother wasn't a Mohawk; she was of the Algonquin tribe. And so, even as a child, I was always a bit torn between the different religions and cultures in my family.

Smallpox swept over our tribe when I was very young, and my parents died. It was a terrible disease, and back then there were no vaccines. I ended up getting smallpox myself, but I survived and went to live with my uncle.

Back then, we were often at war with the Europeans. Our people fought back as best they could, but eventually we had to give up and submit. Now, the Europeans wanted all of us to believe in Jesus too. That was really difficult for me—I mean, I liked Jesus, the stories about him touched my heart and I wanted to be a Christian—but because I *wanted* to, and not because I was forced, just because the Europeans said so.

Anyway, my family was against my being baptized. They wanted me to get married and have a normal life among the tribe. But I insisted on going my own way, living with my friends instead of just any man. Jesus, he was enough for me. And I thought: it must be possible for me to be all three—Mohawk, Algonquin, and Christian—at the same time. People thought you had to make a decision, and after baptism, give up all the old customs. But I didn't do that. I became a Christian and still continued to hunt in the woods with the others. The fact is that God created all people, no matter what they look like and whether they wear a hat or feather headdress or a

headscarf. You can stand by Jesus just as you are. If going to church in your Sunday dress or your best pants isn't your thing, go in your old jeans. Or with feathers on your head!

Speaking of dressing up...

Many Europeans used to think that anyone who wanted to become a Christian should act and dress like a European. It took a long time to understand that the customs of people from other continents also have value: the Native Americans, those of the Māori in New Zealand, those of the people in Africa, and so many more. Even today, many people find it difficult to imagine that one can be a Christian and still maintain their other traditions.

Saint George

Who wouldn't like to be a shining knight, blameless and without fear, bravely wielding his spear on horseback? Someone like me, a real hero who defeated an evil dragon and saved a princess!

But to be honest, there really weren't any knights in my day, because that was long, long before the Middle Ages. And who knows if there ever really were dragons?

But that doesn't matter here. Because even if you have never personally met a fire-breathing monster with huge wings, you have certainly had a similar encounter: You know the feeling of suddenly being very afraid. You know moments when an injustice makes you really angry. You know what it's like when you face an almost impossible problem. Everyone has experienced this.

That's why people all over the world have been telling horrible stories about monstrous, evil dragons for thousands of years. Dragons are a symbol of dark powers. With their mighty wings, they inspire our imaginations. Just like us knights. In the old stories, we not only rescue princesses, we also protect widows and orphans, defeat evil, and only use our swords to bring about justice.

Sounds good anyway. The truth was probably different. Knights were soldiers too, and soldiers fight in wars, and wars are never bright or heroic; they just bring suffering to people. Still, it's nice to tell legends. I think the legends are less about how it really used to be. They don't say much about people like me, but they tell something about people like you. Namely, about how you might like to be yourself and how you see yourself in your dreams. When you dress up, you can be someone else in your fantasy, for example, a knight; or even an evil dragon, if you want, because we humans always have both sides within us, the good and the bad.

It helps if you have good friends who will help you in battle. Maybe that's why those who mess with dragons today call me their patron. Modern dragons are environmental destruction or egoism or hatred of certain groups of people. Together we can find courage

and face these dragons wherever people stand up against injustice and stand by the weakest.

And speaking of knights...

Because in legend Saint George is a noble dragon slayer in shining armor, nobles and kings often saw him as their role model. So George is the national patron of many countries. For example, he is the patron saint of England. One country is even named after him: Georgia in southeastern Europe. And he is also the patron saint of some of the Boy Scouts in Europe. That fits because the Scouts often go on long journeys together to experience adventures. And above all, they have set themselves one goal: to do at least one good deed every day. If you take that seriously, you can certainly kill some dragons—figuratively, of course.

Saint Joan of Arc

Hello, I'm Joan. Or actually, Jeanne—that's what my name sounds like in French, because I'm from Domrémy in France. And the fact that France exists at all has a bit to do with me!

Hundreds of years ago, at the time of the knights, large parts of France were ruled by the English. The king of England thought that he should be king of France at the same time. We didn't have our own king back then, just a prince whose name was Charles. Charles should have become king of France himself, but he couldn't because the English were about to conquer the country. They ruled the capital, Paris, and were going to attack the important city of Orléans. Charles had no money—and not many friends either. Most of our own knights didn't stand by him. Things were looking really grim for him and for France.

I didn't really know much about any of these things at first because I was just a farm girl. In the Middle Ages peasants had nothing to do with politics—and girls certainly didn't. But when I was thirteen, I felt for the first time that I had to do something to end this terrible war. The feeling grew stronger and stronger—I was sure that God wanted me to save France.

When I was seventeen, I left home to go to Chinon, where the prince was staying. Somehow I managed to convince him that God sent me, and shortly after that, I really was a knight with sword and armor, a girl with short hair and in boy's clothes—unthinkable at that time. But I just felt that it was right. I felt strong and brave, and that spread to the other knights. I was just a teenager, but suddenly I was the leader of the French army, and we managed to liberate the city of Orléans.

Such stories are mostly about the brave knight coming to save the young princess. Here it was the other way around. I was the brave knight who saved the prince.

The king of England hated me for it. As we fought on, I was captured by the English in a battle and sentenced to death. They claimed I was a witch. Back then, people really believed that witches existed, mostly because they thought that girls and women shouldn't be strong and brave and smart. If we were, the devil must be behind it.

Unfortunately, Charles didn't save me from the English.

Years later, I was canonized. This should remind us today that brave girls have the power to change the world.

By the way, there are more interesting people named Charles...

In about 1930, five hundred years after Joan's death, the German playwright Bertolt Brecht wrote a play in which he put Joan in the twentieth century. He called the play *Saint Joan of the Stockyards*. It is about the exploitation of poor workers by a rich boss. Joan helps the workers fight their selfish boss. There have also been several plays and movies about Joan of Arc, a person who continues to fascinate us.

Saint Charles Lwanga and Companions

"So," said the king, "everyone who will stop praying in the future stand next to me. And those who want to continue praying go over to the wall...."

That sounded like a death sentence. And it was.

By the way, my name is Charles. I come from Uganda, a country in Africa. My friends and I lived at the king's court a long time ago. We were pages. That's what they called boys who worked as servants for the king. I was even their leader.

Back then, people from another country came to us in Uganda and told us the stories of Jesus. My friends and I couldn't get enough of them. It felt like Jesus himself was speaking to us and calling us to follow him.

So we were baptized and became Christians. And not only us but also our king, Mutesa, liked Jesus and supported all people who spread the faith. But Mutesa died and his son Mwanga became the new king. Mwanga's counselors and officials felt that believing in Jesus would not be good for our country because it is a foreign religion and the people who spoke about Jesus were probably spies for other countries.

Of course, that wasn't true. And it wasn't the only lie. One day my friends and I found out that the chief minister was plotting to remove Mwanga from the throne and make himself king. Like detectives, we uncovered the conspiracy, and the minister even went to jail. But the king released him because the minister claimed that it was not he, but that my friends and I were the ones planning something against Mwanga. Who do you think the king believed? His highest minister or some boys? He even allowed himself to be persuaded that our faith was bad. That's why he forbade us to continue praying to Jesus.

Sure, orders are orders, and you must do what the king says, especially when you're the leader of the royal pages. But Jesus is our King too. And I realized that Jesus is more important to me than all the kings of the earth. I didn't want to stop praying. I just couldn't.

So King Mwanga summoned us all. Those who would never pray again should stand next to him. And those who still wanted to continue praying to Jesus should stand against the wall.

I went to the wall without hesitation. Of course, I was very scared. I knew that anyone who stood against the wall would be killed. But I wasn't alone. Jesus was with me. And so were my friends. One by one they stood next to me, sixteen boys who refused to obey the king.

We died on June 3—our memorial day on the Church calendar. And because courageous children always need role models, my friends and I are considered the patron saints of young people in Africa.

Standing by Jesus isn't always easy...

It's always horrible to see people killing other people because they disagree with them or believe in something else. Burning people to death is especially cruel. Often it was not just about inflicting physical torture. Some thought that burning a person would destroy their personality and soul.

Saints Peter and Paul

"Hey, Paul!"

"What, Peter?"

"Why do we both have the same feast day? Don't you think that the two of us are totally different?"

"So what, Peter? We were even enemies. How did that happen again?"

"Well, I used to be a fisherman. Everyone called me Simon then. My brother Andrew and I were just about to throw the nets from our boat to catch a few fish when suddenly a man on the lake shore appeared in front of us: Jesus of Nazareth. We just left our boat and the nets and followed him across the country. We even witnessed his miracles.

"When our friend Judas betrayed him, I was sure that no matter what people said, I would always stand by Jesus."

"But then you denied him, didn't you, Peter?"

"Yes, well, the night they arrested him, I was recognized three times by three different people. They knew I was a friend of Jesus. But I was so afraid of being arrested that I said I didn't even know Jesus. Unfortunately, I have to admit that I had a big mouth before but later got scared. For example, when Jesus walked on water, I really wanted to be able to do that too, but I didn't have enough faith. I would have drowned if Jesus hadn't saved me. Despite all of this, Jesus chose me of all people to lead our community. I shall be the rock, he said to me, on which he builds his Church. He didn't mean a building, but the people, the community. In the language back then, *Peter* meant 'rock.' And then one day you showed up, Paul."

"Yes, and that certainly was not a heroic appearance. I never met Jesus. I just heard how after his death you were all saying that he rose from the dead. I thought that was bad because I thought you would destroy belief in God with these stories. That's why I fought you and put many of your friends in jail. By the way, back then my name was Saul. But one day Jesus himself appeared to me, and I realized that Jesus really lives and that he is the Son of God. From then on I called myself Paul, and I traveled halfway across the world to continue telling the story of Jesus. As a result, many new communities formed. And sometimes there were fights between these new churches and the church in Jerusalem, and with you, Peter."

"Yes, that was a tough fight. But the fact that we worked it out was important for the Church. That's how we were able to solve the problems and move the community forward."

"That's right. But our successors, the bishops, sometimes act as if quarrels in the Church are a bad thing. We need discussions and different opinions, because otherwise we would learn nothing new."

Speaking of different opinions...

For many centuries, Peter has been shown in pictures with keys. In the Gospel of Matthew, Jesus says to Peter, "I will give you the keys of the kingdom of heaven" (Matt 16:19). Of course, he did not mean this literally. But people kept telling each other stories about Peter standing as a kind of guard at the gate of heaven with a large key. In olden times some people believed that water collected in big lakes in the sky, and that the lakes had to be opened for it to rain. Some stories said that Peter opens the "locks of heaven" with his big key and thought he caused the weather. Paul made many journeys to tell people about Jesus and to plant new churches. He often wrote long letters to them. In them he scolded if he thought something went wrong, and encouraged when something went well. Sometimes Paul's thoughts in his letters are quite complicated because he was a very wise man. That is why he is often shown in pictures with a book or a scroll.

Saint Thomas More

I lived a long time ago in London and was part of the court of the king of England. As Lord Chancellor, I looked after all the lawyers and judges in the country on behalf of King Henry and was something like the highest judge myself—after the king, mind you, who was of course higher than me.

At that time there was no democracy, where everyone could have a say. The king could decide everything all by himself. Well, not *all* by himself, because there was still the pope in Rome. One day King Henry got into a big argument with the pope. He wanted to marry another woman, even though he was already married, and according to the rules of the Church, that was not possible. So Henry came up with the idea of founding his own church. Then the pope would no longer be the boss, but he himself, King Henry.

I didn't think that was right, so I told the king that I could no longer work for him. I didn't want to be Lord Chancellor anymore. I had enough to do anyway, because besides working for the king, I really liked writing books. One of my books is called *Utopia* and is about an island where all people live in freedom and peace and friendship with one another, where everyone is treated fairly and there is no injustice.

Unfortunately, this island doesn't actually exist, I just made it up. It is the island of my dreams because the search for justice has moved me all my life. For example, I always found it unfair that boys were considered more important than girls and got better education. I have four children myself, and I made sure that my three daughters were able to study as much as my son.

Once I quit, the king left me alone for a while, so he didn't really care what I thought about him. But then Parliament passed a law for the king. It said that only he and no one else could rule over the Church in England. And Henry wanted to force everyone to swear to it.

That might not have been so bad, I sometimes think. A little cheating, just raise your hand and swear, that's all I'd have to do, no matter what I really think. And then I could have a nice life as

a grandpa with my children and grandchildren. Nobody would have been angry with me. Just myself maybe. Because there was this thing with conscience. So I refused—and the king had me executed as a traitor.

I was ahead of my time, educating my daughters and working for fairness between boys and girls, men and women.

Speaking of men and women...

As the English Lord Chancellor, Thomas More was a powerful, wealthy man. The most famous picture of him was painted by a famous artist named Hans Holbein. Thomas More is dressed in a splendid robe made of velvet and trimmed with valuable fur. Very few people could afford that back then. He also wears an important sign of his power around his neck: his gold chain of office, which only the Lord Chancellor was allowed to wear. But although he was so rich and powerful, Thomas More never forgot the many who were less fortunate.

Saint Mary Magdalene

You might have noticed that in the stories of Jesus there are several women named Mary. It was a very popular name back then and still is today. Sometimes I'm called Magdalene, after my hometown, Magdala, although teachers are not always sure where it was. But was I the woman Jesus cast out seven demons from? Was I the "sinner" who wiped Jesus's feet with her own hair? How many Marys were there, anyway?

Maybe that's not important. What's important is that I was with Jesus when it really mattered. I was there when he died on the cross. Of course, it was a horrific experience; that's why all the men from our group ran away and hid. Only John stayed by the cross with us women so that Jesus didn't have to be all alone.

When Jesus died, I felt I had lost my best friend and all my hope. We all thought he was the Messiah who would redeem the world. None of us expected such a horrible ending. We were all in shock and had completely forgotten that Jesus once told us that he would rise from the dead. We buried him quickly without preparing his body with fragrant ointments, as was our custom. That's why I went to the grave with the other women the day after to make up for it. The tomb was not in the ground; it was in a cave in a garden, with a heavy stone blocking the entrance. The stone should have been there, but when we got there early in the morning, the stone had been rolled away. And Jesus was gone!

Who took his body and where did they put it? We wondered. A man appeared. That must be the gardener, I thought. I spoke to him and asked if he had noticed anything. But he just looked at me and said my name: Mary. That's when I recognized him. It was him!

Jesus!

Of course, I immediately told the men, that is, Peter and John and the others. At first, they didn't believe it, and they treated me like I was crazy. They had to see for themselves.

Although I was the first to meet Jesus after his resurrection, I never had much to say in our group. After Jesus returned to heaven, the men took charge, mostly Peter, James, and John. None of them took us women seriously. It was like that everywhere back then, not

just in our community. That's just how it was. And it remains this way in the Church to this day. Only men are allowed to become priests or bishops because the bishops are the successors of the twelve apostles, and they were all men.

But not long ago, Pope Francis officially declared that I am an apostle too. Maybe someday more people will listen to women in the Church.

As I said, I was the first to see Jesus after the resurrection. But after me, many, many others have also experienced him in different ways.

You will meet one of them now...

The Bible tells of a woman rubbing a precious ointment on the feet of an exhausted Jesus. It probably wasn't Mary Magdalene, but people have told the story this way for centuries. That is why Mary Magdalene is often shown in pictures with a jar of ointment. Some of Jesus's friends scolded her. They thought it would have been better to sell the expensive ointment and the jar and use the money to help the poor. But Jesus tells them no. It's good to remind ourselves that it's important to help other people and to try to make the world a little better.

Saint Christopher

We're always carrying something around with us: book bag, gym bag, mobile phone; or, if you're really nice, you might carry your neighbor's shopping bags. If you're tall and strong, you can carry more than other people. And that's what my legend is about. When I was alive, I was very tall and strong as an ox. I could be helpful, but

only if you were as big and strong as I was. I thought I should only serve the most powerful ruler.

That's why I went to work for the king. But one time someone in the palace was talking about the devil. The king was so afraid he went white with fright. I thought that if the king was scared just by hearing the devil's name, he must be much more powerful than the king. So, I left to become a servant of the devil. One day, the devil and I were walking along a road that had a cross with the figure of Jesus hanging on it. And the devil got scared and went out of his way to avoid the cross. I realized that Jesus must be bigger and more powerful than all the kings in the world and even the devil. I wanted to serve him.

But I couldn't find him anywhere. Someone told me to wait and see if Jesus would find me instead. While I waited, I decided to make myself useful. There was a raging river that didn't have a bridge. It was so wild that no boat could cross it safely. It was too deep and fast for anyone to wade through—except for me, so I started working as a porter. Whenever someone wanted to cross the river, I would take them on my shoulder and carry them from one side to the other. Even the biggest people were no problem for me. Until one day, this little boy stood on the shore.

This should be easy, I thought, lifting him onto my shoulder and stepping into the river. But the further I went, the heavier the child became. I thought I was going to fall. With the last of my strength, I reached the other side. I felt as if I had carried the whole world across the river on my shoulders. Indeed I had, for the little boy was Jesus, who carries the whole world. He called me Christopher, which means "Christ-bearer."

Is the legend true? Who knows. But I can tell you that whenever you carry a burden for another person, you are carrying Christ. It doesn't matter whether that means taking out the trash, helping a child in a wheelchair over a curb, or comforting someone who is sad. Because grief is a burden that's easier to carry when you have help. We are all Christ-bearers because we went through the water with him at our baptism.

Some people aren't baptized until they're adults...

According to the legend, the boy Christopher carried gave him a sign afterward to convince him that it was indeed Christ he had been carrying. He told Christopher to take his walking stick, a dead branch, and put it in the ground outside of his hut. When he awoke the next morning, it was covered with leaves and growing. Christopher's walking stick became like Christ, awakened from the dead.

Saint Edith Stein

My hometown is Breslau. When I was growing up it was in Germany, but today it is called Wrocław and is in Poland because the terrible Second World War that destroyed half of Europe also changed many borders. My fate was shaped by what happened back then in Germany, when Adolf Hitler and the Nazis were in power.

When I was growing up, I had no idea of that. I grew up in a Jewish family with lots of brothers and sisters, and I did well in school. My parents were religious people, like Jesus and his friends. While Christians believe that Jesus is the Messiah, Jews believe that the Messiah hasn't come yet. Belief in Jesus developed from Judaism, just as Islam did later. However, I wasn't interested in religion but in philosophy. I didn't even believe God existed. I thought the world must have some other meaning. I wrote a lot of essays about it, and my professors thought they were pretty good.

It was a sad time for me because I was unlucky in love. I felt rejected and alone. I felt nothing but dead silence. But precisely at this time, when I was feeling bad, I started thinking about God and his son, Jesus. I realized that I could believe in him, and so I was baptized. A few years later I even became a Carmelite nun and changed my name to Sr. Teresa Benedicta of the Cross.

Terrible things were happening in our country back then. Adolf Hitler and his Nazi party were in power. They claimed that they were the only ones who could say who was German and who was not, and they thought Germany should invade and rule other countries. Anyone who spoke out against them went to prison. But most of all, the Nazis hated the Jews. I was a Christian by then, but I was still a Jew at my roots.

Jews were banned from more and more things. We were no longer allowed to go to the swimming pool or even just shopping; we were not allowed to go to school or to work. Some time after the war began, the Nazis started what we now call the Holocaust or Shoah. Jews were arrested everywhere, taken away by train and murdered in huge death camps.

This is what happened to my sister and me.

Today people honor me as "Patron of Europe." I pray with you that there will be peace in Europe and that these terrible things will never happen again. Some even think I'm an important enough teacher that I should be called a "doctor of the Church."

You will learn about another teacher on the next page...

In some religious orders, new members take a new name. Edith Stein was given the name Sr. Teresa Benedicta of the Cross when she joined the Carmelites. The cross and suffering of Jesus were very important to her. Until the day she was arrested, she was working on a major book, *The Science of the Cross*, which was about the work of Saint John of the Cross. It is also about how we humans can meet God even in suffering. Edith Stein believed that God was with her even in deepest sorrow. Maybe that's why she found the strength to comfort and help others even in the brutal world of the concentration camp.

September 17

Saint Hildegard of Bingen

What did you do today? Where did you go? Who did you meet? Did you see trees, flowers, and animals? Maybe you saw a bird flying away from you. Did you see the sky and clouds passing overhead? Did you ever think that all this has something to do with you? Every pebble and earthworm, every star in the sky has something to do with you because everything in the universe is connected to everything else. Can you imagine it?

No one can wrap their mind around this. Logic doesn't help. But you can feel it—in your heart. Try it!

That's what happened to me. Suddenly I felt as if a sparkling light from the open heavens streamed through my brain, my heart, my whole body. And I realized what it all means: the stories in the Bible about God and Jesus, about creation.

Everything is filled with God's love.

I admit, it's easy to say. Believing so much in love comes at a cost. Sometimes it means a fight. When I was alive, no one listened to women, except in monasteries. I started one myself, actually two, and I was in charge—the abbess. One time, a man died who had been expelled from the Church. According to the rules, he should not have been buried in a Catholic cemetery. But I did it anyway, and I got in a lot of trouble with the bishop for doing it. He thought God didn't love the dead man and wanted him buried someplace else. But I did it anyway because I know that God's love embraces everyone.

Because everything alive is connected to everything else, I also realized that nature interacts with us and with our bodies in a special way. There are herbs and other natural things that can heal us from many diseases.

I wrote a lot about it. That's why I'm not only a saint, but an herbalist. Some people thought I was a witch. Back then some were afraid of smart women and called them witches. I knew I wasn't a witch, but some people were afraid of me anyway. For example, once I had to scold our emperor, Frederick Barbarossa, because he thought

he could decide by himself who would be the pope. I also preached to religious men and told them to take care of the poor instead of making themselves rich, because that's also part of love—keeping things from happening that harm love.

On the next page, you will meet someone else who felt this way...

The crozier is a special staff carried by bishops. It is a sign of his pastoral function and is a reminder of the staff used by shepherds. But bishops aren't the only people who carry croziers as "spiritual shepherds." Abbots and abbesses do as well, as shepherds of the monks and nuns in their communities. Saint Hildegard was abbess of an important monastery. Powerful people asked for and took her advice, even though the Church was usually dominated by only men. She's often shown in pictures with a crozier.

Saint Andrew Kim Taegon

When Jesus told his friends, "Go to all people and make disciples of everyone," he certainly wasn't thinking of using warships, cannons, and soldiers!

Nevertheless, in the past, people often used violence to spread faith in Jesus. Back then, men would sail from Europe to America, or to Africa or Asia and say, "From now on this is our land! You have to do what we say! And because we are Christians, you have to be baptized!"

Or something like that.

Sometimes, however, people from Europe would come peacefully to tell people in distant countries about Jesus—they are called missionaries. They almost always came from Europe, as if believing in Jesus was a European thing and not for all humanity.

Missionaries arrived in my homeland of Korea over two hundred years ago. They were amazed to see that we had already had Christians here for a long time! Some people from Korea had learned about the Christian faith when they visited other places, and when they got home, they told other Koreans about it. This knowledge was passed from one generation to the next without priests to help out. I was the first native Korean to become a priest.

My parents were also Christians, but it was forbidden back then. That's why we didn't have a seminary. But there was one in Macau, China, not far from Korea. I studied there when I was a teenager and was later ordained the first Korean priest in Shanghai. I came home to Korea and secretly worked in the capital, Seoul. And I tried to smuggle other Christians into Korea with the help of fishermen. The ships were supposed to leave them on the coast at night so I could sneak them into the city, but I was caught, arrested, and killed. So were thousands of other Korean Christians.

Today we have freedom of religion. At least we do in South Korea. Several million people here believe in Jesus, more than I would have dared hope.

We have our own Korean songs and customs and our own way of worshipping. That's the beauty of a worldwide Church—it's a little different in every country, colorful and diverse!

Or sometimes it can be dark and gloomy...

That's the thing about missions: On the one hand, Jesus gave his friends the job of taking his message to people in all countries. Christians today agree that this should not be done with violence or force. Those who have experienced Christianity as a good and healing thing will tell others about their experiences and show them the way. That is understandable. It's only a problem if we just talk and don't listen. After all, can't Christians learn things from anyone else?

Saint Thérèse of Lisieux

Can you be holy if you can't believe in God? Or at least not all the time? Or not the way others think you should?

I dreamed of becoming a saint, but I didn't think I was great at all. Even some of the other nuns in my convent didn't think much of me. They thought I was overconfident and proud, but really I was very scared. Most of all, I was sad and lonely.

Maybe that's why I wanted with all my heart to enter a monastery and join a community, even when I was a child. At first, no one accepted me because they said I was too young. I was not allowed to join until I was fifteen. I have no idea what I had in mind or what I hoped for—but I knew it would be a difficult year. You know the feeling when nobody understands you, when you talk but others don't get what's going on inside you?

Everyone around me seemed to have a clear idea of God, the creator of the world, the severe judge of good and evil, but somehow that didn't work for me. I thought Jesus showed us a different side of God, the merciful God who loves all people unconditionally, even sinners because they need love the most. That's what I wanted to do—to love other people unconditionally, without fanfare, just by doing small things that are part of everyday life. I called it the "Little Way."

I did not have a long or wide path through life, especially if you look at it on a map. I never left the small part of France where I'd been born and grew up. I had wanted to travel to Vietnam to work for my order in the missions there and take care of people. But I never got to go. Before I could, I got very sick with tuberculosis, a disease that used to kill many people. It makes it hard to breath, you cough constantly, you have a high fever, and from there it just gets worse and worse. At the time, one of my older sisters was the prioress, the head of the monastery, and she told me to write down my story and my thoughts—so I did. I wrote about my life and how I realized that I was called just to love God and everyone in my small way.

The end of my story is very dark. The sicker I got, the emptier I felt inside. I couldn't even imagine that God exists and that there is a heaven after death. The only thing I could imagine was love. I stuck with that to the end.

People must have seen something in me because, after I died, my story was published and people started asking me for help in their prayers. My little way of love inspired them.

And speaking of helping others...

In pictures, Thérèse of Lisieux is often shown with a bouquet of roses. Just before she died, she said that when she went to heaven, she would rain roses on the earth. Of course, this didn't happen literally, but she has scattered roses by encouraging people through her writing and example, helping them to not lose courage and to trust in God even in the worst times.

Saint Francis of Assisi

We all have stressful times with our parents. It happens in every family. Sometimes your parents' views are just very different than yours. You just hope that in the end, you'll get along anyway.

It was different for me. At first, I was a typical teenager. My father sold expensive cloth, and my family was pretty rich. Any time I went to a party, I could share treats with my friends, and we had a lot of fun.

But what I *really* wanted was to become a knight. Back then, cities in Italy used to go to war with each other, and when my hometown of Assisi went to war with the neighboring town of Perugia, I was excited to join in the fight. At least I was in the beginning. But I quickly learned that war is terrible. I was captured and put in prison. After a year I was released, but when I got home, nothing seemed the same as before. I was tired of parties; my dream of being a knight was gone. I felt best when I was alone or with poor people. I started giving them things from my father's shop. Even though we could afford it, he got very angry about it.

One day I was praying to Jesus in a half-ruined church when I thought I heard him ask me to rebuild his church. So I did—with my father's money, of course! He wanted me to stop and took me to court. The hearing was in public, in the middle of the cathedral square. I took off all my clothes because I didn't want anything from my father. I threw them all at his feet and left.

From then on, I owned nothing. I was poor, but I felt completely free. I wanted to live a simple life, in harmony with people and with the animals. Nature is a miracle, and God expects us to treat all his creatures well and protect our environment.

By the way, when I heard Jesus say I should rebuild his church, I didn't realize that he didn't mean that one building, but the Church as a community. At first, people laughed at me, but some admired my courage and eventually many joined me. We became a big religious order, the Franciscans.

Hundreds of years later, the Church needed a new pope, and Jorge Bergoglio, a bishop from Argentina, was elected. He did not want to forget the poor, so he took my name, Francis, as a sign that the Church must always be there for the poorest among us, especially children.

On the next page, you'll meet a holy child...

Living in harmony with nature was very important to Francis. In his famous "Song of the Sun," he praises nature and thanks God for it. This closeness to nature is also in many legends about him. He is said to have been able to speak with animals and to preach to them.

Saint Justin

Did you know that the city of St. Petersburg in Russia is named after a tsar, Peter the Great? Or that the capital of the United States is named Washington after George Washington? There are many cities all over the world that are named after famous people, mostly powerful kings and rulers.

But in the north of France, there is a little town that's named after a ten-year-old boy. It's called Saint-Just-en-Chaussée. That boy is me: Saint Just, or Justin in English!

When I was ten years old, something happened to my uncle. My father's brother, my uncle Justinian, had been kidnapped and sold into slavery many years before. Our family never heard from him. But one day, I had an inspiration. I just knew that Uncle Justinian was in Amiens, a town in the south, so on the spur of the moment, my father and I went to see if we could find him and rescue him. And somehow, we managed to find him and escape from Amiens with him.

Unfortunately, we weren't happy for long. We realized we were being followed by soldiers of a cruel prefect, Rictius Varus. He hated us because we rescued my uncle and because we were Christians. Suddenly, I had another inspiration and found a cave. I sent my father and uncle there to hide and promised to follow. But I didn't make it. I was caught by Rictius Varus. He said he'd let me live if I told him where my father and uncle were hiding, and if I promised him I'd stop being a Christian. But I said no, and so I had to die.

That sounds pretty brave. It's not what I wanted. I was only ten, and I wanted to live a long time, play with my friends, be with my family. But Rictius forced me to make a choice.

We all have moments like that. Maybe you already have. Most of the time it's not a matter of life and death. But sometimes you need the courage to stand by your convictions. Especially when you're fighting against injustice.

By the way, that's what my name means: the just one!

Speaking of Amiens, a different story happened there a few years later. Maybe you know it...

As a martyr, Justin is often shown holding a palm tree or palm branch. We see this in pictures of almost all the saints who were killed for being Christians. The palm tree with its fruit has long been considered a symbol of victory and of life in the Mediterranean region. If the martyrs in the old pictures have palm trees with them, this is to show that they triumphed in the end and gained eternal life.

November 11

Saint Martin of Tours

Today, most children probably think of a sword as a toy. Back in my day, it was a deadly weapon. But if you want, you can also use it to do good—like cutting your own cloak in two and giving half to a freezing beggar.

In pictures I am shown riding on horseback and wearing the shiny helmet of a Roman soldier on my head. Actually, I didn't want to be a soldier at all, but in our family it was expected. My father was an officer in the Roman army, and the emperor had ordered that officers' sons also had to become soldiers. When I was only fifteen, I was given a sword, a helmet, and a horse, and I had to fight. I fought in all kinds of countries because the Roman Empire was enormous. But it had also existed for a very long time. Eventually Roman rule weakened and the borders of the empire began to crumble.

At one time, we horsemen of the Imperial Guard were stationed in Gaul—that's what we called France—and there, in front of the gates of the city of Amiens, sat a beggar in the deep snow. The beggar was so poor that he didn't even have proper clothes, only a few rags, and that in the middle of winter. So I shared my cloak with this man so he could at least wrap himself in something warm.

Later on, some said I could have given him the whole cloak, not just half. Others claim the story is just made up. But that's not the point. The point is that it's important to do something when you see other people suffering. And the thing about the cloak was kind of tricky because it didn't belong to me personally. These cloaks were part of our uniform as the Emperor's best soldiers. Unlike the way it's shown in most pictures, the cloak was white with sheepskin on the collar and not red. When I severed this cloak, in a way I also severed the power of the Roman army.

The next night, I had a dream. I saw the missing part of the cloak again, and the beggar was wearing it on his body, but he was no longer the beggar at the city gate, he was Jesus, as if somehow I had personally given him half the cloak. This is because Jesus himself says

in the Bible: Whenever we do something for the weakest and poorest people, we do it for him.

After that, I left the army and the soldier's life as soon as I could. I would have loved to grow old alone somewhere in a lonely place. But the people needed a bishop, and they really wanted me, so I gave in to them. That's what really matters: that you're there when you're needed. Today I am considered the patron saint of the poor and of refugees.

Whenever you feel poor yourself or are on the run or wherever you stand up for poor or refugee people, I am with you. And speaking of helping the poor...

According to legend, Saint Martin was too modest to assume the office of bishop. When the people wanted to make him bishop anyway, he ran away and hid with the geese. But the geese chattered and honked so loudly that they betrayed Martin. He was discovered and eventually took the office of bishop. Because of this story, geese are sometimes shown in paintings of Saint Martin. In some places it is customary to eat roast goose on November 11, Saint Martin's feast day. Some even call it "Martin's goose."

Saint Elizabeth of Hungary

"You shall not bear false witness." You shouldn't lie. Don't do it. That's clear, isn't it?

But there *is* such a thing as a white lie. Imagine you are the wife of an important ruler, let's call him Louis. Because he is very rich and powerful, of course you are also very rich. But you are not powerful because it is the Middle Ages and you are a woman. Most of the time they didn't rule countries, the men did that. A woman's job was to take care of the poor—a little bit at a time, just so they'd have something to eat. But they weren't to help the poor too much, because it was important for the powerful that nothing change, that the poor stay poor and the rich stay rich. Otherwise, too much might change, and in the end the powerful would lose their power.

Louis thinks that you are giving away far too much money and goods to the poor, and he tells you to stop. But, of course, you go on anyway and keep sneaking out of the castle with baskets full of bread for the poor. You spread a blanket over it so no one sees the bread. But suddenly your husband comes around the corner. He was waiting for you, it was a trap!

"What's in the basket?" he asks. And you say, without thinking, "There's no bread in the basket, just a bouquet of roses." Now of course he wants to see it. So you take away the cloth and prepare yourself to be punished because you were trying to bring bread to the poor. But what's in the basket? Roses! A miracle!

It might not have really happened that way. My husband wasn't as mean as the legend says. Still, it's a beautiful story about right and wrong. If you have a basket full of bread and you claim there are roses in it, then of course that is wrong. And if some people are incredibly rich and other people are terribly poor—is that right or wrong? It is wrong! Even worse than lying about bread and roses.

Sometimes the truth is more complicated than it appears at first. This also applies to the story of my life. After my husband had died, I swore to myself that I would live in poverty. And I let myself be bossed around by my spiritual advisor, Conrad, who was not like Louis at all. Conrad was mean to me, and I don't know why I didn't fight back.

It's true that the lives of the saints are anything but perfect. But there are certain things people talk about even after many hundreds of years. For me it's the story of the miracle of the roses.

Maybe it shows that in certain situations we just have to listen to our heart before we decide what we should or shouldn't do.

And speaking of what we should do...

The bread in Elizabeth's basket turns into roses as her hard-hearted, suspicious husband looks into the basket. When Elizabeth got to the poor with the basket, the bread was there again. This legend of the miracle of the roses is probably the best-known of the stories about Saint Elizabeth and has been depicted in many paintings.

December 4

Saint Barbara

A young girl is locked in a tower—does that sound familiar? Of course—Rapunzel. The girl with the endless braid. She let her hair down so that a prince could climb up and free her. But I didn't have a prince. I didn't even want one. I was locked up in the tower, not by a wicked witch, but by my own father.

Before he locked me in the tower, he had always treated me well. He cared for me and spoiled me, and he tried to grant my every wish. He was a wealthy merchant and would have done anything for me—except let me choose how I wanted to live.

In our day, belief in Jesus was strictly forbidden throughout the Roman Empire. But I still knew a few young people who were Christians. They met secretly, and sometimes I was with them. Eventually I wanted to be baptized myself, but my father wanted to prevent that. He ordered me to marry a rich young man and forget about Christianity. When I refused, he locked me in the tower. He treated me like I was his property and could do with me as he pleased.

But I would not obey him, and eventually I managed to escape. My father chased after me and almost caught up to kill me, when suddenly a cave where I could hide miraculously appeared. At least that's what the legend says. Unfortunately, I was betrayed by a shepherd who saw what happened. My father caught me, but instead of taking me back to the tower, he took me to prison. He said I had to tell everyone in town that I didn't believe in Jesus. But I refused. Then the mayor had me beaten and sentenced me to death. In the end it was my own father who killed me with a sword. On that very day, a branch from a cherry tree blossomed in my prison cell. The branch had gotten caught on my robe when my father dragged me to prison. The buds opened the day I was killed.

Because of this, a custom developed in some places: On my memorial day, December 4, people cut branches from fruit trees and place them in water. And at Christmas the buds of the branches open

and bloom. Maybe my story is just an ancient legend with little truth. But it's true about the branches. Try it. For me, the fact that these blossoms open in the middle of winter is a sign that nobody can lock life away for long. It doesn't matter whether it's in towers or dungeons or by using scare tactics or anything else. Life will eventually blossom again.

Speaking of which, in the middle of winter...

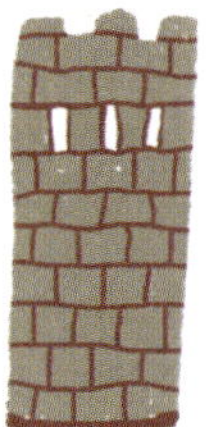

Pictures and figures of Saint Barbara almost always show the tower. It usually has three windows, symbolizing the triune God—God the Father, Son, and Holy Spirit. Incidentally, there are two other saints who are often mentioned along with Barbara: One is Saint Margaret of Antioch, who, according to legend, defeated a dragon (also called a "worm," in the old-fashioned way). The other is Saint Catherine of Alexandria, who is said to have been tortured for her faith by being tied to a spiked wheel and then beheaded. In southern Germany there's a verse that calls them "The three holy girls: Barbara with the tower, Margaret with the worm, Catherine with the wheel." The three are among the Fourteen Holy Helpers.

Saint Nicholas

No. I'm not him. I have nothing in common with Santa Claus—I repeat: nothing at all!

I'm Nicholas of Myra. If you want to eat a chocolate that's supposed to look like me, then please at least pick one where I'm wearing a miter on my head. That's what they call the bishop's hat. A long time ago, I was a bishop in Myra, Turkey.

I admit that back then, bishops didn't even wear miters. But this constant confusion with Santa Claus really annoys me because the chubby man with the bushy white beard and the red, fur-trimmed hat is only a tool to encourage consumerism. I don't care about that at all! I never cared about earning money. I preferred giving things away to others. After I received an inheritance, I gradually distributed it to all those in need. Maybe that's why people later thought that I'd be the one who brings presents to children.

Many of the legends told about me have to do with children: how I once prayed that God would bring a dead boy back to life. Or

how a child who had been taken away to Babylon by kidnappers was brought back to Myra by a storm after I prayed for him.

I think you can always tell how good or bad a place is by how it treats its children. Jesus said that children should be our example of how to get to heaven.

Over the years, many songs have been written about me, but unfortunately, life is not a Disney movie. Some children who already have much get more and those who have little get nothing. Sadly, I can't even change that from heaven. Not even Santa Claus can do that.

But maybe whenever you see things in your everyday life that are unfair or even cruel to children, maybe you can say something. See if you can find other children who will also speak up. It's good when children stick together. But be sure not to exclude any children, especially if they are the ones who don't have much.

"Fair trade chocolate"—that is, chocolate from cocoa beans that were bought from farmers at a fair price—also helps. It helps ensure that the children in the countries where the cocoa comes from do not have to work in the fields but can go to school.

By the way: This was about how to make the lives of disadvantaged children a little brighter—and the following story is also about a little light in the darkness...

Saint Nicholas is usually shown dressed as a bishop with a miter on his head—the tall bishop's hat—and a crosier in his hand. Sometimes Nicholas also has three bags of gold with him. According to legend, one night he secretly threw these three bags through the bedroom window of three sisters. They were so poor that without this they would have been destitute. Nicholas is also often shown with a sailing ship. He is considered the patron saint of seafarers because, according to legend, he once saved a ship that was caught in a storm.

Saint Lucy

In the northern part of the world, as the end of the year approaches, it is very dark. The sun rises a little later every morning and sets a little earlier every afternoon. No wonder people long for the warm light of the sun during this time. Of course, today you can just flip a switch and the lights go on. But candles are much cozier. The people who live in the far north, for example, in Sweden, know this, because for almost the whole of December it is dark practically all day. The sunlight lasts for just a few hours a day.

In Sweden there is a special custom: Girls dressed in white robes wear a wreath with candles on their heads. In many families, it's the eldest daughter's job. She puts on the wreath of candles early in the morning, and then she wakes her parents and siblings and brings them the first Christmas cookies of the season.

This happens on December 13, my memorial, because I too once wore a wreath of lights and brought people things to eat.

Here's how it happened: A very long time ago, belief in Jesus was strictly forbidden throughout the Roman Empire. Whenever Christians were caught, they were severely punished by order of the emperor. That's why they mostly hid in caves or secret underground passages for worship. Sometimes I secretly brought them food and drink. I could afford to give people presents because my father was a wealthy merchant, so I brought as much as I could carry. So that I could have both hands free and wouldn't need to grope my way through the caves and passages in the darkness, I braided a wreath, put a few candles in it, and put it on my head. That gave me enough light so I could see everything around me. It was the same for the people in the caves. Somehow it always gets brighter when we stand up for other people, even without candles or lamps, because the light is within you. You can't always see it, but you can feel it.

Jesus said of himself that he is the light of the world. You can't always see it shining, at least not from the outside. Still, it's always there. Just as you can light many other candles with the flame from a single candle, you can also pass on the light of Jesus. Sometimes a smile or a friendly look is enough. Because the moment you smile, you start to glow yourself, as if you had a wreath of lights on your head, just like me. Try it!

Speaking of being there for other people...

Saint Lucy's wreath of candles is one of many symbols in the pre-Christmas Advent period: Whether it's the candles on the Advent wreath, Saint Lucy's wreath of lights, or the lights on the Christmas tree—it's always about illuminating the darkness. Many prayers and songs also speak of the fact that light came into the world with the birth of Jesus. Light came to us when God redeemed the world by sending his son, Jesus.

Saint Stephen

After reading a few of the stories in this book, you've probably noticed one thing: Becoming a saint can be dangerous, even bloody. Many saints died violent deaths. Or maybe it's the other way around, maybe they were canonized precisely because bad things happened to them due to their belief in Jesus, even though it was forbidden in their countries.

By the way, I am considered the very first Christian to be killed for believing in Jesus. I lived in Jerusalem and belonged to the newly formed Church. It had only been a short time since Jesus ascended into heaven and sent the Holy Spirit to us, but our Church had grown quite large very quickly. Just like today in the Church, it was not just about telling the stories of Jesus and breaking bread together in the Eucharist. Believing in Jesus also means taking care of other people, especially the poor, the sick, the weak. That was the deacons' job—a role that still exists today. I was a deacon, one of the first.

Unfortunately, many in Jerusalem didn't like what we were doing. They didn't want us to talk about Jesus. I once had a heated argument with such people, and they reported me to the authorities. They claimed I said bad things about Moses. That was considered a serious crime, and I had to defend myself in court. I explained that what we do is exactly what Moses and the prophets said we should do. Actually, we were doing a lot better than the judges and people who reported me did!

The judges got extremely angry. They drove me out of town and killed me by throwing stones at me. That's how I became the first martyr. The word *martyr* means "witness," so a martyr is someone who tells about their faith. Many stories make it sound as if the martyrs died calmly because they knew that Jesus was with them. Of course, that's not always true. I was terrified! I am sure that every person in such a situation is scared. Jesus himself was terrified when he was arrested. That is why he is always particularly close to us when we are afraid. This helps us to stand by our convictions. Heroes are not those who are not afraid but those who face their fears.

Thank God it's not usually a matter of life and death. Sometimes you're just afraid of being laughed at when, for example, you stand up for an unpopular child in your class. Or if you intervene when someone is being teased or bullied. There are many situations in everyday life where you can do something that is important in the moment. Instead of "important" you could also say "holy." In any case, we saints in heaven are with you. We stay with you and look forward to all your ideas on how you can make the world a little bit better.

Saint Stephen's "attributes" remind us of how he died. Attributes are what we call the symbols assigned to a saint in statues or paintings. People used to know these very well, so they always knew immediately who was in a picture when they saw these symbols. The attributes of Saint Stephen are: A book of the Gospels, which has the biblical stories about Jesus, to remind us that Stephen was murdered because he professed his faith in Jesus and his "good news" (the literal translation of *gospel*). Because Stephen was killed with stones, he is shown with stones. Often there are three stones. And because he was a deacon, he often wears a dalmatic, the deacon's vestment.

Glossary

ANDREW KIM TAEGON, born August 21, 1821, in Dangjin, South Korea, died September 16, 1846, in Seoul; first Korean priest, martyr.

Memorial: September 20
Patron of: Korean clergy, Catholic Church in Korea.
Interesting fact: Andrew Kim Taegon was not the only Korean martyr in the nineteenth century. In the Jeoldusan district of Seoul, since 1967, there has been a shrine with a pilgrimage church, museum, and meeting place, where the Korean martyrs are honored.

BARBARA, second or third century in Nicomedia (present-day Turkey); martyr.

Memorial: December 4
Patron of: girls, miners, bricklayers, architects, roofers, prisoners, the dying, firefighters. Helper against plague and fever. One of the Fourteen Holy Helpers.
Attributes: tower with three windows, martyr's palm.
Meaning of name: Greek and Latin, "stranger, foreigner."
Interesting fact: According to legend, Barbara hid from her pursuers in a crevice in a rock. That is why to this day, miners consider her their patroness.

BERNADETTE SOUBIROUS, born January 7, 1844, in Lourdes (France), died April 16, 1879, in Nevers (France); seer (had visions of Saint Mary in a grotto near Lourdes), nun.

Memorial: April 16
Patron of: shepherds.
Attribute: roses.
Name meaning: Derived from Old High German, "strong like a bear."

Interesting fact: The Jewish poet Franz Werfel came to Lourdes in 1940 to escape from the Nazis. There he vowed to write a novel about Bernadette if he was rescued. This is how the famous novel *The Song of Bernadette* came about.

CHARLES LWANGA, born 1860 in Bulimu (Uganda), died on June 3, 1886, in Namugongo (Uganda).

Memorial: June 3
Patron of: youth of Africa.
Name meaning: Old High German, "man."
Interesting fact: It is likely that Charles Lwanga later adopted the European name Charles in addition to his traditional African name.

CHRISTOPHER, probably a legend; giant carrying a child across the river, who then revealed himself as Christ.

Memorial: July 24
Patron of: travelers, drivers, ferrymen, seafarers, gardeners, fruit growers. Protector against sudden death, one of the Fourteen Holy Helpers.
Attributes: pilgrim's staff blossoming into a tree. Usually depicted as a giant carrying a child across a river on his shoulder.
Name meaning: Derived from Greek, "Christ-bearer."
Interesting fact: Because Christopher is also considered the patron saint of motorists, many EMS helicopters used in Germany are called "Christoph."

DOCTOR OF THE CHURCH: a title given by the Catholic Church to saints whose contributions to theology and doctrine are considered especially important. Until the late twentieth century, only male saints were considered doctors of the Church.

EDITH STEIN, born on October 12, 1891, in Breslau (Silesia, today Wrocław in Poland), died on August 9, 1942, in the Auschwitz concentration camp; Jewish philosopher, scientist and—after her conversion to Christianity—Carmelite nun.

Memorial: August 9

Meaning of name: Old English, "wealthy fighter"; religious name: Teresa Benedicta of the Cross.

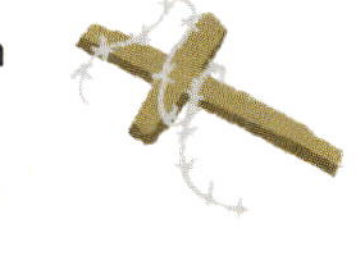

Interesting fact: In addition to her books, Edith Stein published many articles on philosophical and social issues. In them she also fought for women to be given more rights in Church and society.

ELIZABETH OF HUNGARY, born 1207 in northern Hungary or in Pressburg (today Bratislava in Slovakia), died November 17, 1231, in Marburg an der Lahn; daughter of a Hungarian king.

Memorial: November 19
Patron of: Third Order Franciscans, the poor and needy, the sick, persecuted innocents, bakers.
Attributes: basket with roses or with bread and roses; sometimes a model of the Gothic St. Elizabeth Church in Marburg.
Meaning of name: Hebrew, "God is abundance."
Interesting fact: Elizabeth was so loved that she was canonized just four years after her death and officially honored as a saint.

FOURTEEN HOLY HELPERS: A group of saints especially venerated in the Catholic Church because their intercession was thought to be very powerful, especially against disease. The list originated in Germany during the plague epidemic that was later known as the Black Death. Several saints in this book are in this group: Barbara, Catherine of Alexandria, Christopher, George, and Margaret of Antioch.

FRANCIS OF ASSISI, born 1181 or 1182 in Assisi (Italy), died October 3, 1226, in Assisi; founder of the Franciscans.

Memorial: October 4
Patron of: Italy, Assisi, the Franciscan Order, poor people, social workers, environmental protection, merchants, tailors, weavers, drapers.
Attributes: animals (especially birds and sometimes a wolf), lilies, book, skull.
Name meaning: Thought to have been named "Francis" because of his father's love for the country of France.
Interesting fact: The tradition of the Christmas crib originates with Francis of Assisi.

GEORGE, third or fourth century; Roman soldier, martyr; according to legend, dragon slayer.

Memorial: April 23
Patron of: England, Georgia (United States), merchants, knights and orders of knights, scouts, soldiers, saddlers, horseback riders, and horses.
Attributes: dragon, sword, armor.
Name meaning: Derived from the Greek for "farmer."
Interesting fact: George is one of the Fourteen Holy Helpers. They are often depicted together in art. Many churches and chapels are dedicated to them.

HILDEGARD OF BINGEN, born around 1098 in Bermersheim, died on September 17, 1179, in the Rupertsberg near Bingen am Rhein; doctor of the Church; mystic and author of numerous religious, scientific, and medical works, Benedictine nun, founder and abbess of three monasteries.

Memorial: September 17
Patron of: scientists, linguists, herbalists.
Attributes: nun's habit and crozier of abbess, three towers.
Name meaning: From Old High German, "fight and protection."
Interesting fact: Hildegard had such great influence in her time that bishops, princes, and kings consulted her. She even dared to criticize Emperor Friedrich Barbarossa.

JOAN OF ARC, born around 1412 in Domrémy (now Domrémy-la-Pucelle) on the Meuse, died May 30, 1431, in Rouen; peasant girl, fighter, martyr.

Memorial: May 30
Patron of: France, soldiers, broadcasting, and radio.
Attributes: sword, armor.
Name meaning: From Hebrew, "God is gracious."
Interesting fact: According to legend, Joan thought she heard the voices of Michael the Archangel, Saint Catherine, and Saint Margaret. Because of this, she was later made the patron saint of radio.

JOSEPHINE BAKHITA, born around 1870 in Sudan, died February 8, 1947, in Schio (Italy); former slave, nun.

Memorial: February 8
Patron of: captives, slaves.
Name meaning: From Hebrew, "God adds."
Interesting fact: When Josephine Bakhita died, thousands of people gathered to pay their respects and mourn her.

JUSTIN, third century in France (Burgundy), martyr.

Memorial: October 18
Attributes: martyr's palm, portrayed as a ten-year-old boy.
Name meaning: Latin, "the just one."
Interesting fact: There is another boy named Justin who was an early Christian martyr. According to tradition, this Justin was twelve years old when he and his companion Pastor were murdered under the Emperor Diocletian for being Christians in what is now Spain.

KATERI TEKAKWITHA, born 1656 in Ossernenon (now Auriesville, New York), died April 17, 1680, in Kahnawake or Caughnawaga (now a Mohawk reserve outside of Montreal, Canada)

Memorial: April 17
Patron of: Native Americans, Mohawks, Canada, environmentalists, exiles.
Name meaning: Kateri (from Katharina), derived from Greek, "pure."
Attributes: turtle, lily.
Interesting fact: Kateri Tekakwitha had three different names in her life: As a child, she was called Jorágode ("sunshine"); as an orphan she came to her uncle's tribe and was called "Tekakwitha" ("she who bumps into things"). When she was baptized, she took the name Kateri for Catherine of Siena.

LUCY, third or fourth century in Syracuse (Sicily), martyr.

Memorial: December 13
Patron of: the blind, sick children, notaries, lawyers, doorkeepers, servants.
Attributes: lamp, martyr's palm, sword, two eyes on a tray.

Name meaning: Latin, "the shining one."
Interesting fact: Saint Lucy is associated with light. Before the adoption of the Gregorian calendar, the shortest day of the year would fall on or around Saint Lucy's Day, after which the hours of light would increase.

MARTIN OF TOURS, born around 316 in Sabaria (today Szombathely in Hungary), died on November 8, 397, in Candes near Tours in today's France; soldier, benefactor, bishop.

Memorial: November 11
Patron of: City of Tours, Diocese of Mainz, Diocese of Rottenburg-Stuttgart, Burgenland, Canton of Schwyz, poor people, beggars, prisoners, soldiers, riders, horses, tailors, geese.
Attributes: beggar, sword, horse, geese, dressed as a soldier or bishop.
Name meaning: Latin, "one dedicated to Mars (the war god)."
Interesting fact: In the Middle Ages, children would go from house to house with lanterns on Saint Martin's Day, singing, and receiving small gifts. There are still such parades today. The encounter between Martin and the beggar is reenacted and the children are given sweet Martin's pretzels. At the end everyone gathers around a bonfire.

MARY, first century, biblical figure.

Solemnity: January 1
Patron of: Christianity, many nations and dioceses throughout the world including the United States under her title Immaculate Conception.
Attributes: crescent moon, lilies, roses, blue robe, baby Jesus.
Name meaning: Derived from the Hebrew name Mariam.
Interesting fact: As the mother of Jesus, Mary is especially revered. There are so many commemorations, patronages, and attributes that it is not possible to list them all here.

MARY MAGDALENE, first century, biblical figure.

Memorial: July 22
Patron of: women, repentant sinners, gardeners, barbers, perfumers, schoolchildren, students.
Attributes: ointment jar, red egg (symbol of the resurrection), depicted embracing Christ's feet after the resurrection.

Name meaning: Latin, "from Magdala" (a place on the Sea of Galilee).
Interesting fact: According to legend, Mary Magdalene later traveled across the Mediterranean to what is now southern France to spread the word about Jesus.

NICHOLAS, third or fourth century, Bishop of Myra (now Demre near Antalya in Turkey).

Memorial: December 6
Patron of: Russia, children, altar boys, sailors, merchants, bakers, butchers, brewers, innkeepers, prisoners.
Attributes: bishop's clothing with miter and crosier, sailing ship, three bags of gold.
Name meaning: Greek, "victor among the people."
Interesting fact: Saint Nicholas Day used to be the most important day of the year for children because in many places, they received gifts on this day, not on Christmas as today.

PAUL, first century, biblical figure, persecutor of Christians, later apostle, missionary, martyr.

Solemnity: June 29
Patron of: press and media, missions, theologians, pastors.
Attributes: sword, book.
Name meaning: From Latin, "little one."
Interesting fact: Paul's original name was Saul. Only after his conversion from a persecutor of Christians to a Christian was he called Paul ("little one"). Even today there is a saying that someone goes "from Saul to Paul" when they convert to Christianity.

PETER, first century, biblical figure, fisherman, disciple of Jesus, martyr.

Solemnity: June 29
Patron of: popes, fishermen, sailors, shipwrecked people, bricklayers, carpenters, watchmakers, locksmiths, penitents.
Attribute: keys.
Name meaning: Greek, "rock."
Interesting fact: Peter and Paul are shown together in many pictures. Peter almost always has a relatively broad head and a rounded beard. He

either has curly hair or is bald except for a forelock. Paul, on the other hand, wears a pointed beard and is completely bald.

STEPHEN, first century, biblical figure, first martyr, deacon.

Feast: December 26

Patron of: coachmen and horses, cattle, masons, tailors, weavers, carpenters, deacons.

Attributes: book with three stones. Also frequently shown is the vision of the dying Stephen who, according to Acts, saw "the heavens open" and Jesus at the right hand of God.

Name meaning: Derived from the Greek word *stephanos*, "crown or wreath of victory."

Interesting fact: Farmers used to pray on Saint Stephen's Day primarily for healthy cattle. There was a "consecration of oats" in which the fodder was symbolically blessed.

THÉRÈSE OF LISIEUX, born January 2, 1873, in Alençon (France), died September 30, 1897, in Lisieux, Carmelite nun, mystic.

Memorial: October 1

Patron of: florists, aviators, missionaries.

Attributes: Carmelite habit (brown habit, white mantle, black veil), roses.

Interesting fact: The book in which Thérèse told her life story and shared her thoughts is called *Story of a Soul*. In the first editions of this book, a large number of passages were deleted or changed, mostly by her own sisters, because Thérèse had also written about her insecurities and doubts about her faith. These passages did not fit the image of a "perfect" saint. It was not until the mid-twentieth century, over fifty years after the first edition, that an uncensored, complete edition appeared.

THOMAS MORE, born February 7, 1478, in London, died July 6, 1535; politician, English Lord Chancellor, writer.

Memorial: July 6

Patron of: politicians, statesmen, lawyers, civil servants.

Attributes: portrayed in the rich attire of the Lord Chancellor, sometimes also with a chalice, host, and papal cross, symbolizing his loyalty to the Catholic Church.

Name meaning: Hebrew, "the twin"; after the apostle Thomas.
Interesting fact: On June 22, shortly before Thomas More's execution, the English bishop John Fisher was also executed by order of Henry VIII. Both lost their lives resisting a violent, tyrannical ruler. They were canonized together in 1935.

THE THREE WISE MEN (THREE KINGS), first century, originally called the "wise men" in the Bible.

Memorial: January 6
Patrons of: travelers, pilgrims, playing card manufacturers, the city of Cologne (the relics of the Three Kings are said to be there in the cathedral).
Attributes: star, gifts, crowns.
Names and gifts: Caspar (Persian, "guardian of the treasure") with myrrh, Melchior (Hebrew, "king of light") with gold, Balthazar (derived from Babylonian and Hebrew, "God protects") with incense.
Interesting fact: In many illustrations, one king is depicted as a young man, one as a middle-aged man, and one as an old man. In addition, one king often looks African, one Asian, and one European. The three continents known at the time are thus represented and a signal is given: Jesus came into the world for everyone—for young and old, for people from all parts of the world.

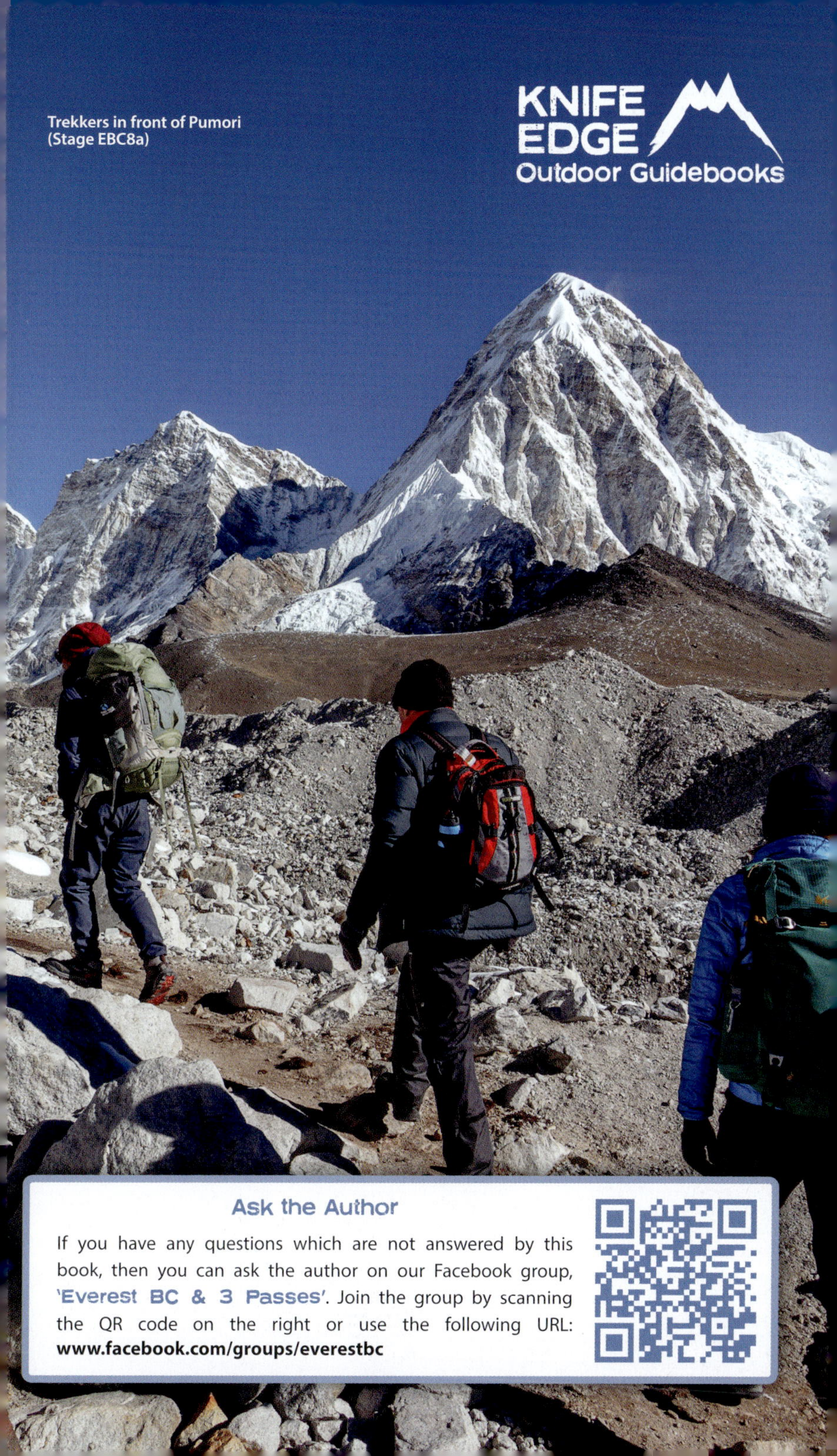

Trekkers in front of Pumori
(Stage EBC8a)

Ask the Author

If you have any questions which are not answered by this book, then you can ask the author on our Facebook group, **'Everest BC & 3 Passes'**. Join the group by scanning the QR code on the right or use the following URL: **www.facebook.com/groups/everestbc**

Publisher: Knife Edge Outdoor Limited (NI648568)
12 Torrent Business Centre, Donaghmore, County Tyrone, BT70 3BF, UK
www.knifeedgeoutdoor.com

©Andrew McCluggage 2025 except the following:
©Stuart Butler 2025: Yetis (p95)
©Stuart Butler & Andrew McCluggage 2025: 'How to organise a trek' (p34); 'Travel' (p58) excluding 'Visas'; 'Accommodation' (p62); 'Food' (p64); 'A Typical Trekking Day' (p66); 'Responsible Trekking' (p78); 'Safety' (p79) excluding 'Trekking safety'; 'Hypothermia/frostbite' (p82); 'Money' (p83); 'Culture & Etiquette' (p96); 'Buddhism (in a nutshell)' (p97); 'Gompas, Stupas and other Buddhist Monuments' (p98).

First edition 2025
ISBN: 978-1-912933-19-8

All images ©Andrew McCluggage 2025 except:
Images on pages p213, p216 & p223: ©Stuart Butler 2025
Images on pages p60, p61, p205, p207, p211, p214, p219, p222, p229 & p237: ©Adobe Stock

Mapping produced by Knife Edge Outdoor Limited:
©Knife Edge Outdoor Limited 2025.

Map data: ©OpenStreetMap contributors. Data available under the Open Data Commons Open Database License (ODbL).

A catalogue record for this book is available from the British Library.

All rights reserved. No part of this publication may be reproduced in any form without the prior written consent of the publisher.

Front cover: A brightly painted stupa at Dingboche
Back cover: Everest viewed from Stage EBC8b/8c
Title page: Mount Everest viewed from the CEBC trail (Stage EBC8b)
This page: Sunrise view from Kala Patthar
Back cover flap: Yaks near EBC

All routes described in this book have been recently walked by the authors and both the authors and publisher have made all reasonable efforts to ensure that all information is as accurate as possible. However, while a printed book remains constant for the life of an edition, things in the wild often change. Trails are subject to forces outside our control. For example, landslides, avalanches, tree-falls or other matters can result in damage to paths or route changes; waymarks and signposts may fade or be destroyed by wind, snow or the passage of time; or trails may not be maintained by the relevant authorities. If you notice any discrepancies between the contents of this guide and the facts on the ground, then please let us know by email (info@knifeedgeoutdoor.com).

Contents

Tengboche Gompa (EBC3)

Getting Help

Distress signal

The signal that you are in distress is six blasts on a whistle spaced over a minute, followed by a minute's silence. Then repeat. The acknowledgment that your signal has been received is three blasts of a whistle over a minute followed by a minute's silence. At night, flashes of a torch can also be used in the same sequences. Always carry a torch and whistle.

Signalling to a helicopter from the ground

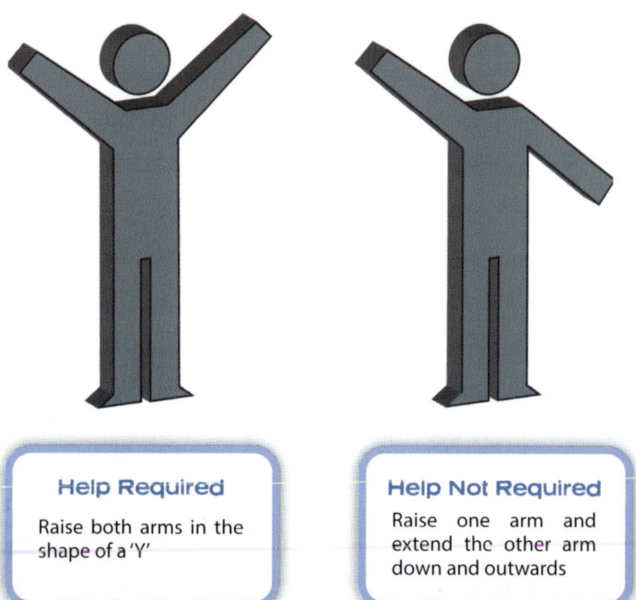

Help Required

Raise both arms in the shape of a 'Y'

Help Not Required

Raise one arm and extend the other arm down and outwards

WARNING

Hills, cliffs and mountains can be dangerous places and walking is a potentially dangerous activity. Some of the routes described in this guide cross potentially hazardous terrain at very high altitudes. You walk entirely at your own risk. It is solely your responsibility to ensure that you and all members of your group have adequate experience, fitness and equipment. Neither the author nor the publisher accepts any responsibility or liability whatsoever for death, injury, loss, damage or inconvenience resulting from use of this book, participation in the activity of mountain walking or otherwise.

Some land may be privately owned so we cannot guarantee that there is a legal right of entry to the land. Occasionally, routes change as a result of land disputes.

Introduction

The exquisite Ama Dablam (AR2)

Due to the powerful forces of human nature, we are drawn irresistibly towards the earth's superlatives: the longest river, the deepest canyon, the largest desert, for example. However, it is the tallest mountain that casts the most captivating spell upon us. Since Mount Everest (which lies on the border between Nepal and Tibet) was identified in the 19th century as the highest peak on earth, it has bewitched humankind. Its clearly-defined summit provides an obvious focal point for our desire and ambition: who would not want to gaze down from the roof of the planet? And since 1953, when Tenzing Norgay and Edmund Hillary proved that it was possible to experience that view, Everest has become the ultimate lodestone for mountaineers. However, it is not only climbers who find themselves spellbound because Everest is also a magnet for less experienced dreamers: those who simply desire to lay eyes upon the highest point on earth without setting their sights on reaching the summit. For many, merely catching a glimpse of Everest and its aristocratic neighbours would be the fulfilment of a life's dream and a trek in the Everest region enables that dream to become a reality.

Although reality is sometimes disappointing when compared to the dream, that is not the case with the Everest region (the Nepalese side of which is known as the Khumbu). Because so much emphasis is placed on one summit, it is easy to forget that it is surrounded by countless other snowy mountains which are also amongst the highest in the world. They are mountains that look like mountains should look: steep, jagged and unattainably high; swathed in vast blankets of the whitest snow and adorned with enormous sparkling glaciers. However, these huge summits do not blend together in anonymity like those in some other mountain ranges because each of these giants is distinctly recognisable and has its own unique character which you will learn to appreciate as the days go by: the 'horizontal' sawtooth ridge of Nuptse; the aesthetically flawless outline of Ama Dablam; the terrifyingly steep faces of Lhotse; the near-perfect pyramid shape of Pumori; the split summit of Thamserku; and the precariously leaning towers of Taboche and Cholatse, to name a few. Even without the drawcard of Everest, the extraordinary beauty and scale of the Khumbu's landscape would ensure its place on most trekkers' bucket lists.

Only a handful of decades ago, trekking to Everest was a significant, and prohibitively expensive, ordeal. However, the construction of the airfield at Lukla (1964) opened a convenient gateway into the Khumbu which trekkers were quick to make use of. These days, the numerous daily flights to Lukla from Kathmandu make access during the trekking season comparatively straightforward. From Lukla, the best-known and popular way to approach Everest (without using a helicopter) is to hike directly towards Everest Base Camp (EBC) on the Classic Everest Base Camp Trek (CEBC). It uses largely the same route to head to, and return from, EBC and unsurprisingly, it is the busiest trek in the region. EBC is a fascinating place where you can see the colourful tents of the climbers preparing to risk everything to scale the world's highest mountain and most trekkers want to visit it. However, it is not the only option. As an alternative, you could opt for the beautiful trek along the less-frequented paths of the upper Dudh Koshi valley to Gokyo and its magnificent lakes: Everest is visible from Gokyo's wonderful viewpoints too. Or, with a few extra days, you could see more of the region by visiting both EBC and Gokyo: they are connected by the icy Cho La pass.

With even more time, you could visit both EBC and Gokyo as part of a longer circumnavigation of the Khumbu on the incredible Three Passes Trek (TPT): this is the finest and most comprehensive trek in the region and it makes use of some more peaceful paths away from the busy CEBC trail. And there are many other possibilities too, the best of which are fully described in this book. Every one of the treks is extraordinary, providing views of some of the highest peaks and ridges on the planet, and, whichever one you choose, the experience will be unforgettable.

With such amazing sights to experience, it is hardly surprising that these treks are popular. The CEBC is the busiest and, in peak season, its lodges are full. However, the number of hikers on the trails is rarely oppressive and, if you start early, you will be alone for a good part of the day: you will pass, or be passed by, other trekkers but for most people, these fleeting interactions are no bad thing. At night, you will stay in one of the basic, but magnificently situated, lodges: there you will meet many of the people that you passed earlier in the day, making it easy to develop trail friendships. These are sociable treks and some of the bonds forged can last a lifetime.

Any multi-day trek is a challenge because each day you will need to hike for many hours and negotiate climbs and descents. However, in the Everest region, the challenge is complicated further by the impact of high altitude on your body: it makes hiking harder and can cause you to feel unwell. Occasionally, if symptoms are not recognised or heeded, the altitude can cause Acute Mountain Sickness (AMS) which, in extreme cases, can be fatal. This may sound intimidating but it is reassuring to note that many thousands of normal people undertake treks in the Khumbu each year without incident: with the right preparation, planning and approach, the treks are manageable for most people of reasonable fitness. The challenge is an achievable one and this book provides the information required to plan, and prepare for, an Everest trek. Furthermore, the routes themselves are fully described to guide you on the trail itself and, unlike some other books, this one contains real maps: for each stage, there are 1:40,000 scale maps to go with the accurate and concise route descriptions. Because we were unable to find commercially available maps that fulfilled our requirements, we commissioned our own maps with a larger scale than other available maps: we believe that these are the finest maps available for the Everest region. As well as including these maps in this book, we have also published a sheet map for the Everest region which is extremely helpful for planning and navigation: **'Trekking Map: Everest Base Camp' (ISBN 9781912933532)**.

We aim to ensure that you have the best chance possible of completing your trek. We place great importance on the correct preparation and we focus in detail on altitude acclimatisation and equipment. We also believe that it is crucial to match your itinerary to your experience, fitness and ability. Accordingly, we have included here an extraordinary level of detail on itinerary planning: our unique itinerary planner has 29 different itineraries to choose from. For each itinerary, we have completed for you all the difficult calculations of time, distance and altitude gain/loss. This makes it easy for you to design a manageable itinerary that suits your specific needs. Once on the trail, you will be able to relax and fully enjoy some of the world's best trekking.

Nepal: Basic facts

Although Nepal is sandwiched between two of the world's largest nations, it is not itself a huge country: occupying 147,516 km^2, it is only 70% of the size of Great Britain. However, what it lacks in surface area, it makes up for in height because it is home to eight of the ten highest mountains on the planet (including Mount Everest, the tallest of them all). Nepal is rectangular in shape and three of its sides form frontiers with India. However, the fourth side, to the N, borders Tibet (which was annexed by China in 1951): it is this N side which is of most interest to trekkers because its entire 1400km length runs along the line of the Himalaya, the highest range of mountains on earth.

- **Geographical regions:** Nepal can be divided into three key regions. Each of them is a strip running across the country from W to E: the Tarai region (17% of Nepal's surface area) is the strip to the S and it is low, flat and fertile; the Mid-hill region (68%) is the middle strip; and the mountainous Himalayan (or Himal) region is the N strip (15%). The Himal begins at around 3,000m above sea level.
- **Capital:** Kathmandu.
- **Population:** 29.7 million; 101 ethnic groups.
- **Language:** more than 90 languages are spoken. The official language is Nepali and most people speak or understand it. However, most ethnic groups also have their own local language. English is taught in schools and therefore many people speak or understand it too.
- **Religion:** the majority of Nepalese people practice either Hinduism or Buddhism. However, Islam, Christianity, Jainism, Sikhism, Bon, ancestor worship and animism are also practised. The different religious groups in Nepal co-exist largely peacefully. Nepal was the world's last Hindu monarchy before it became a secular republic in 2006.
- **Economy:** Nepal has few natural resources and poor infrastructure. It is one of the poorest countries in the world, with many people living in poverty. Its key industries include tourism, textiles, carpets, cement and brick. Agricultural produce includes cereals, potatoes, rice, sugar-cane and tobacco: agriculture employs around 75% of the population. Tourism employs a million people and is one of the fastest growing industries.

The Khumbu

The Everest region, known locally as the 'Khumbu', is located in NE Nepal along the border with Tibet. It is part of the larger Solukhumbu district of Nepal which comprises both the middle hills of the Solu region and the high mountains of the Khumbu. The Khumbu is fan shaped and comprises five main river valley systems (W to E):

- **Thame Khola** runs E from Tashi Laptsa La pass to Thame (where it joins the Bhote Koshi);
- **Bhote Koshi** runs S from the Nangpa Glacier (on the Tibet border) to Namche (where it joins the Dudh Koshi);
- **Dudh Koshi** runs S from Cho Oyu, passing Namche and Lukla before heading S out of the Khumbu. By the time the river leaves Namche, it has collected water from the other four systems;
- **Lobuche (Khumbu Khola)** runs S from the Khumbu Glacier to Pheriche/Dingboche (where it joins the Imja Khola); and
- **Imja Khola** runs SW from the glaciers around Island Peak to Phortse (where it joins the Dudh Koshi).

The Khumbu is a Sherpa heartland (see p94) but in the Solu, Rai people are the main inhabitants. The major villages in the Khumbu are Namche, Khumjung, Kunde, Thame, Phortse and Pangboche. The Khumbu has no roads: access is by air or on foot. Much of the Khumbu is protected within the Sagarmatha National Park (see p88) and a national park buffer zone between Lukla and Monjo.

Using this Book

There are many different treks in the Khumbu, with varying levels of difficulty: in this book, we describe the eight best Everest treks plus two additional treks for those who are interested in hiking into the region (rather than flying). To help you choose from the confusing array of possibilities, we have summarised and explained these ten routes in the 'Everest Treks' section of this book (p14) which also includes a summary map and elevation profile for each trek: we suggest that you start your planning by reading this part of the book.

Once you have chosen a trek, we recommend that you read our section on altitude acclimatisation (p9) which explains the risks that you will face at high altitude and how to trek safely. After you have processed this information, you are ready to select an itinerary: you should choose one which allows sufficient time for altitude acclimatisation and which matches your time-frame, experience, fitness and ability. To help you with this complicated process, our 'Itinerary Planner' section (p38) provides a range of different itineraries for the different treks (29 itineraries in total). For each itinerary, we have completed for you all the difficult calculations of time, distance and altitude gain/loss. This makes it easy for you to design a manageable itinerary that suits your specific needs.

When you have a rough idea for an itinerary for the trek that you have chosen, you are ready to work out how to arrange the trek and we explain in detail the different ways of doing that: see 'How to organise a trek' on p34. Elsewhere, we also explain almost everything else that you will need to know to prepare for the trek.

Finally, once you are on the trek, you can use the route description section of the book (p100-253) as your guide along the way. As well as fully describing the route, there are detailed maps, elevation profiles and orientation charts (to help you to identify peaks along the way).

Sections & Stages

This book is designed to be used by walkers of differing abilities. Many guidebooks for long-distance treks rigidly divide the treks into a fixed number of long day-stages, leaving it up to the hiker to break down those stages to design daily routes which suit his/her abilities. This book, however, has been laid out differently to give the trekker flexibility: it divides the treks into shorter stages which you can combine to design daily routes that meet your own specific needs.

We have divided each trek into 'Sections' and 'Stages' and labelled each with a combination of numbers and letters. The labelling is a simple system but requires a little bit of explanation. The first thing to appreciate is that the routes of the treks often overlap and a particular section of path could in fact be used by many different treks. We have sought to simplify matters by ensuring (for the most part) that each section of path has one name only, even though it is used for multiple treks.

Because the Classic Everest Base Camp Trek (CEBC) is the most popular trek and most of the other treks share many of the CEBC's paths, we have first labelled the parts of that trek. Firstly, we have divided the CEBC into 11 'Sections', labelled EBC1 to EBC11: each Section represents one trekking day of our median CEBC schedule (which has 11 trekking days plus 2 ADs).

Secondly, these Sections have been broken down into a number of smaller 'Stages'. In the Khumbu, most of the accommodation is located in small villages and each Stage covers the distance between one village and the subsequent one: this means that there is accommodation at both ends of the Stage. There are only a few exceptions to this: EBC, for example, is at the end of Stage EBC8b but has no accommodation. All significant settlements along the CEBC are the start/finish point of a Stage. You can choose how many of these Stages you wish to walk each day. Each Stage has its own walk description and is shown on the route maps. Stages are labelled with a number (representing the relevant Section that the Stage is part of) and a letter. So, for example, the first Stage in Section EBC3 is 'Stage EBC3a' and the second Stage is 'Stage EBC3b'. Take a look at the Itinerary Planner and all should become clear.

Next we continue the labelling with the Three Passes Trek (TPT). For the parts of the TPT which are shared with the CEBC, we continue to use the CEBC's labelling. However, Sections and

Stages which are not shared with the CEBC have a new label: the prefix is 'TP' and numbers and letters are used in the same way as for the CEBC; for example, 'TP9c'.

Next we label the Gokyo Lakes Trek (GLT): again, for the parts of the GLT which are shared with the CEBC, we continue to use the CEBC's labelling. Sections and Stages which are not shared with the CEBC have a new label: the prefix is 'GL' and numbers and letters are used in the same way as for the CEBC; for example 'GL4a'.

The other five main Everest treks all use different combinations of the Stages of the CEBC, the TPT and/or the GLT, so there is no need for further labelling. However, the two treks which allow you to walk into the Khumbu use completely separate trails: their prefix is 'W'. Finally, side-routes and alternative routes use prefixes 'SR' and 'AR' respectively.

The Itinerary Planner includes a range of tables summarising all 10 of the treks and suggesting itineraries for each: for many treks, we include itineraries for both clockwise (CW) and anti-clockwise (ACW) trekkers. In each table, the maths have been done for you so there is no need for you to waste time (and mental strength) working out daily distances, timings and altitude gain/loss.

Of course, the suggested itineraries are only suggestions. You can shorten or lengthen your day to suit yourself: just decide how many stages you want to walk that day. It is up to you. As there is accommodation at the end of most stages, it is easy to design your own bespoke itinerary and adjust it on the ground as you go (subject to accommodation availability and altitude acclimatisation considerations).

For example, day 1 of the 11-day CEBC itinerary involves walking Stages EBC1a and EBC1b. However, you could decide to extend your day by walking Stages 1a, 1b and 2a, all on the same day. Or you might be tired and decide to shorten your day by walking only Stage 1a. With some other guidebooks, you would have to work out how to split stages yourself, involving some complicated maths to plan distances, times and altitude gain/loss going forward. This book, however, does all the hard mental work for you. And significantly, it makes it easier for you to take altitude gain into account and make prudent acclimatisation decisions (which, in extreme cases, could be the difference between life and death).

In this book:

Timings: indicate the approximate time required by a reasonably fit hiker to complete a stage. Timings assume that the hiker is successfully undergoing the process of altitude acclimatisation and is walking at a slow and steady pace. However, they do not include stoppage time. Do not get frustrated if your own times do not match ours: everyone walks at different speeds and everyone reacts differently to changes in altitude. As you progress through the trek, you should learn how your own times compare with those given here and you can adjust your plans accordingly.

Walking distances: given in both miles and kilometres (km). One mile equates to approximately 1.6km.

Place names in brackets in the route descriptions: indicate the direction to be followed on signposts. For example, "('Namche')" would mean that you follow a sign for Namche.

Ascent/descent numbers: the aggregate of all the altitude gain or loss (measured in feet and metres) on the uphill or downhill sections of a stage. As a rule of thumb, a fit walker at sea level climbs 1000 to 1300 feet (300 to 400m) in an hour: however, at the Khumbu's high altitudes, your hourly altitude gain is likely to be much less than that. The ascent/descent numbers set out in the statistics tables in the route descriptions are based on the direction of travel indicated in the relevant table: trekkers walking in the opposite direction should simply swap the ascent and descent figures.

Elevation profiles: provided for each Section, indicating where the climbs and descents fall on the route. The profiles are based on the most common direction of travel: if you are travelling in the opposite direction, simply read them in reverse. To help you plan a sensible itinerary which allows sufficient acclimatisation time, each elevation profile also displays the relevant sleeping altitude increase/decrease (SA).

Maps: real mapping is provided for every part of every trek. These are extracts from 1:40,000 scale maps produced by Knife Edge Outdoor Guidebooks. We believe that these are the best maps available for the Khumbu. On the maps, we have marked the route of the treks (colour coded), stage numbers, and significant waypoints (colour coded). On each map, N is at the top of the page. As well as including these maps in this book, we have also published a sheet map for the Everest region which is extremely helpful for planning and navigation: 'Trekking Map: Everest Base Camp' (ISBN 9781912933532).

Orientation charts: show you which summits you should see in each direction from the most significant places/viewpoints on the treks. The numbers in the centre of the charts correspond to the numbered waypoints used on the maps and in the route descriptions.

The following abbreviations are used:

ACW	Anti-clockwise/counter-clockwise
AD	Acclimatisation day: a day where you sleep in the same place as the previous day. This effectively means that you will have slept at the same altitude for two nights. Others call this a 'rest day' but this is misleading because activity during the day can assist with acclimatisation (if you are not showing symptoms of AMS): during the AD, you can trek to higher altitudes as long as you return back down to sleep.
AMS	Acute Mountain Sickness
AR	Alternative route
BC	Base camp
BCE	Before the Common Era (a secular alternative to 'BC')
CE	The Common Era (a secular alternative to 'AD')
CEBC	Classic Everest Base Camp Trek
CW	Clockwise
EBC	Everest Base Camp
GLT	Gokyo Lakes Trek
GS	Gorak Shep
KP	Kala Patthar
OR	Off-route
SA	Sleeping Altitude
SNP	Sagarmatha National Park
SR	Side-route (day hike)
TPT	Three Passes Trek
8000ers	The 14 mountains that are taller than 8000m above sea level (see p93)

TL	Turn left
TR	Turn right
SH	Straight ahead

N, S, E and W, etc.	North, South, East and West, etc.
N-S	North to South
S-N	South to North
W-E	West to East
E-W	East to West

When to go

Lobuche: in the background, Taboche & Cholatse

Although Nepal's climate follows the typical northern hemisphere pattern of four seasons, there is one significant difference: the Indian Monsoon. The monsoon is a seasonal change in the direction of the region's prevailing winds which controls Nepal's climate and determines the best seasons for hiking. Each summer, the moisture-laden winds of the summer monsoon (which originate in the Indian Ocean) arrive and around 80% of the country's total annual rain falls in 105 days or so. The mountains of the Himalaya act as an enormous trap for the precipitation which falls as snow at higher altitudes, forming snowfields and glaciers (which help to sustain life in the region by releasing melt-water throughout the dryer seasons). Historically, the timing of the monsoon has been astonishingly regular: on average, it starts on 13 June and finishes on 23 September. However, with climate change, the monsoon has become less predictable in recent years and the end has tended to occur later.

Summer (June to September): monsoon season is the worst period for trekking. The sky is less clear and there is plenty of precipitation, falling as rain in the valleys and snow at altitude. However, it does not usually rain all day: early mornings are often clear but cloud typically builds rapidly covering the summits by noon. Damp mist forms in the valleys and rain falls in the afternoon or evening. Few trekkers visit the Khumbu in this season: paths are muddy; clear views are less frequent; flights to Lukla are often cancelled; and many lodges close.

Autumn (October to November): the most popular season for trekking. The end of the summer monsoon brings cool, dry weather and crystal-clear skies which last throughout October and November. Occasionally, there are snowfalls above Namche but these usually clear quickly. Daytime temperatures are manageable but it is cold at night. In recent years, the start of autumn has been less predictable with the summer monsoon ending later. With the best chance of clear views, this is the season that everyone wants to experience and accordingly, the trails are busy and many lodges are full.

Winter (December to February): although this is the coldest season, it is often the driest period too. In the first 2-3 weeks of December, skies are usually clear and the number of trekkers drops so, if you can tolerate the low temperatures, this is a great time for trekking. Towards the end of December, however, there can be heavy falls of snow and high passes will close for the winter. January and February are bitterly cold so trekking in the Khumbu is only for the brave and well-equipped: occasional snowfalls continue and, because the snow does not melt, hiking is more challenging. However, when it is not snowing, skies are often very clear. Night temperatures can creep down to -20 to 30°C: because the lodges have poor insulation, rooms can be bitterly cold. Fewer lodges open in winter but there will usually be something open in each village in the Khumbu.

Spring (March to May): this is the second most popular season for trekking. It is still very cold at the start of the period (particularly at night) but temperatures rise gradually throughout the season until the monsoon arrives in June. By April, the Khumbu has warmed significantly. Unfortunately, as the temperatures rise, the air becomes more hazy and more clouds build. In the middle hills, cloud and haze begin to obscure views. However, for most of spring, the high Khumbu still enjoys clear mornings (and far-reaching views) with clouds building during the day. In May, afternoon thunderstorms become increasingly common as the monsoon approaches. The lodges and trails are slightly less busy than in Autumn and, if you are lucky, your trip might coincide with the blooming of the rhododendrons which cover many of the slopes (March/April).

Season	Pros	Cons
Summer (June to September)	Warmest temperatures **Fewest trekkers**	Monsoon season: plenty of precipitation **Muddy trails** Frequently cloudy skies **Poor visibility** Lukla flights often cancelled
Autumn (October to November)	Crystal-clear skies **Dry weather** High passes accessible	Highest number of trekkers **Busier trails** Accommodation harder to find **Cold at night**
Winter (December to February)	In December, crystal-clear skies and dry weather **Fewer trekkers than autumn or spring**	Increasing risk of snow **From the end of December, heavy snow falls: high passes close** Very cold during day and night **Much accommodation closes as the season progresses** Fewer flights to Lukla
Spring (March to May)	Good visibility and dry weather for much of the season **Fewer visitors than autumn** Rhododendrons bloom **Beds are easier to find than in autumn**	Cold at the start of the season **In early season, snow covers the high passes (which may not be accessible)** Skies become increasingly hazy as the season progresses **Afternoon thunderstorms: increasingly common as season progresses**

Altitude acclimatisation

Makalu seen from Chukhung Ri (SR4)

The high altitudes of the Everest treks (up to 5600m) put great strain on your body. As you climb higher, the air becomes 'thinner': reducing air pressure makes air less dense and there is less oxygen in each breath of air that you take. As the oxygen in the air reduces, your body adapts and undergoes physiological changes (such as making more red blood cells to carry oxygen). However, these changes take time to implement and, in the meantime, you will breathe faster and more deeply and your heart will beat more quickly. The process of adaptation to increases in altitude is known as 'acclimatisation'. Most people start to notice changes in altitude above 2500m and above that level, it normally takes 1-3 days for your body to acclimatise to a modest altitude increase: however, everybody is different and the process takes longer for some than others.

If you climb too quickly, your body does not have time to acclimatise and you can develop acute mountain sickness (AMS): this could force you to abandon your trek or, in the worst case, develop into HAPE or HACE which can be fatal (see p10). Almost everyone feels the increases in altitude on an Everest trek (even guides and porters) but, for most people, symptoms are mild and/or pass quickly. However, you will probably hear stories along the trail of trekkers who had to descend before reaching EBC and occasionally, trekkers die of altitude related issues. Unfortunately, it is impossible to predict how each person will react to altitude and the ability to acclimatise is not related to level of fitness: some very fit people will struggle to acclimatise and some very unfit people will have no problems at all.

AMS symptoms

Because AMS is a significant risk on an Everest trek, you should be alert to its symptoms in both your own body and those of the other members of your group. The table below contains a list of possible symptoms, however, it is only a rough guide: because everyone is physiologically unique and symptoms vary, it is impossible to be precise for every person.

Most people develop the normal acclimatisation symptoms which usually simply indicate that your body is in the process of adaptation to altitude change. You will need to urinate more frequently and you should drink plenty of water. Symptoms usually abate as your body adapts: however, if mild symptoms continue to worsen, then you should treat them more seriously.

The problem with diagnosing AMS is that many of its symptoms are similar to those caused by other common issues: dehydration, for example, also causes severe headaches and is very common at high altitude because your body loses more moisture when acclimatising (see p69); nausea/vomiting can be caused by stomach upsets which again are common when trekking in Nepal; and coughs can be a simple Khumbu cough (see p82) rather than AMS. Accordingly, if you develop any symptoms that could conceivably be AMS, it is prudent to act on the basis that AMS is the cause (even if there is also a possibility that the cause is something else).

	Normal acclimatisation symptoms	Mild AMS symptoms	Severe AMS symptoms
	Normally OK to continue: monitor closely	Do not ascend until symptoms pass	Descend immediately & seek medical attention
Fast/deep breathing	↑		
Breathlessness	↑		
Sleeplessness	↑		
Loss of appetite	↑		
Food/drinks taste different	↑		
Vivid dreams	↑		
Dizziness		Slight dizziness ⊖	Very dizzy ↓
Headache		Mild/moderate headache that does not pass by morning ⊖	Severe headache that is not alleviated by painkillers ↓
Nausea		⊖	↓
Fatigue and weakness		⊖	↓
Vomiting			↓
Loss of coordination			↓
Confusion			↓
Loss of consciousness			↓
Persistent cough			↓
Extremely high heartbeat			↓
Coughing up blood or pink phlegm			↓
Difficulty breathing			↓
Fever			↓
Mild AMS symptoms getting worse quickly			↓

HACE/HAPE

If untreated, AMS can quickly develop into High Altitude Cerebral Edema (HACE) or High Altitude Pulmonary Edema (HAPE), both of which can be fatal. If you develop any of the symptoms of HACE or HAPE (see below), **descend immediately**, even if it is the middle of the night.

HACE/HAPE	Symptoms
HACE (Swelling of the brain)	Severe headache **Nausea/vomiting** Loss of coordination/confusion **Blurred/double vision** Loss of consciousness
HAPE (Fluid in lungs)	Persistent cough **Coughing up blood or pink phlegm** Difficulty breathing/breathless while at rest **Blue lips/tongue/fingers** Fever

How to prevent AMS

There is still much that we do not know about the effects of altitude on the human body and opinions vary on how best to prevent sickness at altitude, however, the following guidelines are generally accepted best practice:

Gradual increase in sleeping altitude: above 2500m, you should sleep no more than 500m higher than the previous night. **This is the most important rule** and, in fact, the cautious approach is to sleep no more than 300m higher each night: the more cautious the approach, the more effective it will be at preventing AMS. Most trekkers fly directly to Lukla (2840m) from Kathmandu (1400m) and head straight out on the trail the same day (without any prior acclimatisation). For this reason, Phakding (2610m) is a good place to spend the first night in the Khumbu: it is a good walk from Lukla and is only slightly above 2500m.

Planned acclimatisation days: after every 1000m of increase in sleeping altitude (every 2-3 days), you should spend two nights at the same altitude before sleeping higher. Traditionally, the day between the two nights was known as a 'rest day', however, we think that this term is misleading because activity during the day can aid acclimatisation (if you are not showing symptoms of AMS): accordingly, in this book, we refer to it as an 'acclimatisation day' (AD). During an AD, you can undertake a day hike to a higher altitude, as long as you return back down to sleep (at the same altitude as the previous night): climb high, sleep low is a commonly used maxim. That said, if you are feeling the effects of altitude then rest on the AD can be preferable.

Enforced acclimatisation days: due to the spacing and availability of accommodation, it is not always possible to adhere completely to guideline 1 above. If you have no choice but to break the rule and sleep more than 500m above your previous night's sleeping location, then you should take an AD and spend two nights (or possibly more) at your new location to allow your body more time to acclimatise.

Voluntary acclimatisation days: if you do not feel good in the morning, then do not proceed higher (even if the rest of your group is doing so). This is your body telling you that it has not sufficiently acclimatised. For minor symptoms, you could take an unplanned AD to see if the issue resolves: if it does, then you can proceed upwards the next day; if it does not resolve, or the issue deteriorates, then you should head down.

Hydrate, Hydrate, Hydrate: the process of acclimatisation requires your body to expel bicarbonate and it does this by increased urination which results in additional fluid loss. To replace lost fluids, you will have to drink much more than usual while your body is acclimatising: 4-5 litres is often recommended.

Avoid overexertion: if you walk slowly and steadily (especially when going uphill), and take regular breaks, this should aid acclimatisation.

Avoid alcohol: alcohol contributes to dehydration which will not help acclimatisation.

How to treat AMS/HAPE/HACE

The single most effective treatment for AMS and other altitude-related illnesses is descent: usually symptoms abate if you go down 300-1000m. Descending will never make AMS worse and, if in doubt, that is what you should do. With serious symptoms, you should descend immediately (day or night). You may have to abandon your trek but it is not worth risking your life just to complete a trek. It is worth pointing out that a high proportion of those who die from altitude-related illnesses, while trekking in Nepal, were members of a large guided group: there is a tendency for group members to hide their symptoms because they do not want to be left behind (becoming the only person in the group to fail).

Mild AMS	HACE	HAPE
Do not ascend any further until symptoms resolve: your body needs more time to acclimatise. If you go higher, symptoms will only get worse. An AD at the same altitude can be enough to settle the issue. Rest and drink plenty of fluids. Consider taking Acetazolamide (see below). If symptoms worsen, descend. Often 300m is enough for symptoms to resolve but you may need to descend further. If you descend and the AMS symptoms disappear, you may be able to ascend again (after a night or two at the lower altitude).	Immediate descent by at least 1000m Administer oxygen 8mg Dexamethasone immediately. Then 4mg every six hours for at least three days 250mg Acetazolamide twice daily Keep patient warm Give sugary drinks and food **Opinions on medication dosages can vary: always check with a medical professional**	Immediate descent by at least 1000m Administer oxygen 10mg Nifedipine immediately. Then 20mg every eight hours for three days 50mg Sildenafil (Viagra) every six hours Salbutamol/Salmeterol inhaler: two puffs every two hours Keep patient warm Give sugary drinks and food **Opinions on medication dosages can vary: always check with a medical professional**

Acetazolamide (Diamox)

Acetazolamide (brand name Diamox) is a diuretic prescription medication which is used by many trekkers to prevent and treat symptoms of AMS. It speeds up acclimatisation by increasing urination and the excretion of bicarbonate from the kidneys. It also increases the body's respiratory rate, improving oxygenation: in simple terms, it helps you breathe better. A common misconception is that it masks AMS symptoms: in fact, it treats the causes, not the symptoms. If you feel better after taking acetazolamide, it is because your condition has improved. Side effects are usually minor and include increased urination, loss of appetite, loss of taste and tingling in the fingers and toes.

Trekkers can take Acetazolamide either as a preventative (seeking to stop AMS symptoms from occurring in the first place and to aid acclimatisation) or as treatment for AMS (after AMS symptoms have already manifested themselves). Regarding its use as a preventative, opinions vary. Some trekkers understandably prefer not to take medication for an illness that might never occur, particularly those with sufficient time for a cautious itinerary. However, people with less time and faster itineraries often opt to take it. As a treatment though, the use of Acetazolamide is more universally welcomed and many trekkers carry it in their day-packs just in case: many people who were not taking it at the beginning of the trek, start taking it later simply to help them get a good night's sleep. Whether you take it as a preventative or for treatment, it is important to remember that it does not give you super powers: continue to follow the acclimatisation rules above and do not climb higher if you have AMS symptoms.

Opinion varies on the correct dosage but in the UK, for example, doctors often recommend 125mg every 12 hours as a preventative. However, to treat AMS (after symptoms start), 250mg every 12 hours may be appropriate. **Always check dosage with a medical professional.**

Taboche & Cholatse viewed from the ridge below Nangkar Tshang Peak (SR2)

The Everest Treks

Pangboche Gompa

For around 500 years, the Khumbu has been settled by Sherpas who migrated across the Himalaya from Tibet. They established settlements throughout the region, often high above the valleys, in places where there was flat ground for the grazing of yaks and the planting of crops. Trails were established to connect these settlements and to facilitate trading routes with Tibet. Many of these paths survive but Sherpas no longer use them for trading with Tibet (which was largely closed to the outside world after its annexation by China in 1951). Instead, tourism is the contemporary beneficiary of this legacy of trails and trekkers from all over the world use them to access the Khumbu's spectacular landscape. Because the network of trails and villages is extensive, and the scenery is fantastic everywhere, there is a wide variety of possible trekking routes and itineraries in the region. In this book, we describe the eight best Everest treks but there are countless other possibilities. In addition, we describe two further treks which enable you to walk into the Khumbu.

Starting point

The village of Lukla (which has an airstrip) is the gateway to the Khumbu and all of the Everest treks start there. Furthermore, geography has ordained that there is only one straightforward way to walk from Lukla into the high Khumbu: this involves climbing to Namche using the path along the Dudh Koshi river. In summary, all the treks start with the same hike from Lukla to Namche (Sections EBC1 & EBC2) and they must also use this same route to travel from Namche back to Lukla at the end. However, from Namche, there are a variety of route options (travelling three different valley systems) and the route that you take depends upon the trek selected.

How hard are the treks?

The level of difficulty of the treks varies and accordingly, we discuss this individually for each trek in the specific sections below. However, there are some general factors (affecting difficulty) that are relevant to all of the treks:

Altitude: on paper, the treks in the Everest region are not prohibitively difficult. Compared to many multi-day treks in the Alps, for example, the daily distance and altitude gain/loss are modest. However, in isolation, these bare statistics are misleading and trekking in the Khumbu can be harder than you might think. On these treks, you will climb to very high altitudes (4750-5600m above sea level) which have a significant impact on the human body. The higher you go, the less oxygen there is in the air that you breathe and hiking (in particular, climbing) becomes increasingly more difficult. Up to a point, your body can (with time) adjust to the lower oxygen levels by virtue of a process known as 'altitude acclimatisation'. However, during this process, activity can be hard work: minor climbs that would be easy at sea level can leave you struggling for breath; you will have to walk slower than normal and you will not be able to travel as far each day as you usually could. Because fitness is largely irrelevant to the process of acclimatisation and everyone's body adjusts differently to changes in altitude, you cannot predict how easily you will acclimatise unless you have previously hiked at high altitude. Consequently, hiking at high altitude should not be undertaken lightly and we recommend that you choose a cautious and sensible itinerary which allows plenty of time for acclimatisation. Do not try to rush the process: generally, the more time you take, the better you will feel, the easier you will find the trek and your chances of success will be greater.

Fitness level: on every trek, you will need to walk many miles each day. Furthermore, each route traverses remote landscapes of mountains, hills and valleys so you will need to climb/descend significantly, on a daily basis, to negotiate the undulating terrain: sometimes, the climbs and descents are steep and challenging. As the days go by, such exertions take their toll on your body, both physically and mentally, and this is exacerbated by the effects of high altitude. Accordingly, a reasonable level of fitness is required: the fitter you are at the start of the trek, the better your chances of success and the more you will enjoy it. It is sensible to train in advance: there is no substitute for training hikes. Although not essential, previous trekking experience will help. Note that the issues of fitness and altitude acclimatisation are separate and different: the ability to acclimatise to altitude increase is not generally related to level of fitness. Some very fit people will struggle to acclimatise and some very unfit people will have no problem doing so. However, at any given altitude, the fitter you are, the easier you will find hiking at that specific altitude: once you are acclimatised to that altitude, fitness (not altitude acclimatisation) will determine your performance at that altitude.

Pack weight: the more you carry in your pack, the greater the demand on your body and the more challenging your trek will be. Most trekkers will make use of a porter and only carry a small day-pack on the trail. However, trekking in the Khumbu without a guide/porter is still permitted and some trekkers carry their own gear: in addition to warm clothes and other necessities, you will have to bring a warm sleeping bag (which can be fairly heavy). Without prior experience of trekking, it can be difficult to decide what to bring and many trekkers set off carrying some equipment which is unnecessary or simply too heavy: this can contribute to injury and/or exhaustion, leading to abandonment. If carrying your own gear, you should give equipment choice careful consideration: it will be crucial to your enjoyment of the trek and the likelihood of success.

Temperatures: another factor to consider is the cold. As the altitude increases, air temperature decreases. Although the sun helps to make daytime temperatures more bearable, it can still be very chilly. And at night, the temperature rapidly plummets. This is exacerbated by the effects of high altitude on your body: the lack of oxygen in the blood makes you feel even colder. This takes its toll on your body (both physically and mentally) making the trekking more difficult than normal.

Trail condition and navigation: for the most part, the treks use clear paths which are straightforward to follow. However, occasionally paths are less obvious and are more difficult to navigate. Sometimes paths are steep, rocky and challenging underfoot. Some sections of the treks are exposed with steep drops. Occasionally, you might have to climb up or down a few boulders but fortunately, you will not require any technical scrambling or climbing skills. Detailed information on the trail conditions and navigation for each trek is set out below.

Trek Summary Table

Trek No.	Direction	Trek name	Overall Difficulty Level	Days	Total Time (hr:min)	Distance		Ascent		Descent		Max. Alt	
						km	miles	m	ft	m	ft	m	ft
1	N/A	Classic Everest Base Camp: including KP (p17)	Medium	11-15	53:15	116.0	72.1	6046	19837	6046	19837	5600	18374
2	ACW	Three Passes: including Chukhung Ri, KP & Gokyo Ri (p19)	Very hard	16-19	82:00	156.0	97.0	9817	32210	9817	32210	5600	18374
2	CW	Three Passes: including Gokyo R , KP & Chukhung Ri (p19)	Very hard	16-19	83:25	156.0	97.0	9817	32210	9817	32210	5600	18374
3	CW	Gokyo Lakes Trek (p22)	Medium	12	39:40	88.5	55.0	5003	16415	5003	16415	4750	15585
4	ACW	Gokyo Lakes and EBC (via Cho La): including KP & Gokyo Ri (p24)	Hard	14-18	63:50	136.9	85.1	7903	25930	7903	25930	5600	18374
4	CW	Gokyo Lakes and EBC (via Cho La): including Gokyo Ri & KP (p24)	Hard	14-18	68:05	136.9	85.1	7903	25930	7903	25930	5600	18374
5	CW	Gokyo Lakes and EBC (avoiding Cho La): including KP (p26)	Medium-Hard	16-18	68:25	147.2	91.5	7956	26104	7956	26104	5600	18374
6	ACW	Gokyo Lakes & Renjo La (p27)	Medium-Hard	11-13	43:00	92.0	57.2	5092	16707	5092	16707	5360	17586
7	ACW	EBC & Two Passes (Cho La & Renjc La): including KP & Gokyo Ri (p29)	Hard	15-18	71:15	141.2	87.8	8162	26780	8162	26780	5600	18374
8	CW	EBC & Two Passes (Cho La & Kongma La): including Gokyo Ri, KP & Chukhung Ri (p30)	Hard	16-18	80:10	151.8	94.3	9753	32000	9753	32000	5600	18374
9	W-E	Bhandar to Cheplung (p32)	Hard	5-6	32:55	80.5	50.0	5405	17734	5074	16648	3440	11287
9	W-E	Bhandar to Lukla (p32)	Hard	5-6	33:10	79.4	49.3	5593	18351	5082	16674	3440	11287
10	S-N	Phaplu to Cheplung (p33)	Medium-Hard	3	18:55	50.8	31.6	3108	10197	2997	9833	3080	10105

Trek 1: Classic Everest Base Camp Trek (CEBC)

Stages: EBC1 to 11 (plus KP)

Because the CEBC is the most direct route to EBC, it is the best-known trek and is the one on most hikers' bucket lists. It involves a magnificent journey from Lukla to EBC and back, using the Imja Khola valley between Namche and Pheriche/Dingboche and then the Lobuche valley from there to EBC. Along the way, it passes a series of beautifully situated villages including Tengboche and Pangboche with their fascinating monasteries. Such is the consistency of the sublime scenery that a myriad of locations along the trail vie with EBC itself for a place on the list of the region's finest viewpoints. Of course, Everest is regularly on display with the visible jet-stream battering its summit but, in fact, its slightly smaller neighbours, Nuptse and Lhotse (the world's 4th highest peak), often steal the show. Seemingly everywhere, there are 6000ers and 7000ers, none more beautiful than the aesthetically flawless Ama Dablam and the picture-perfect Pumori. And below the summits, there are countless dazzling glaciers.

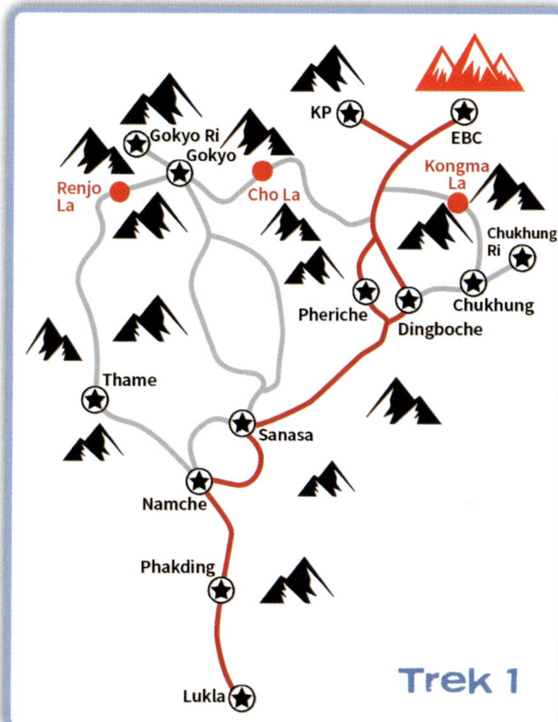

Although it is technically a side-route rather than part of the main trail, most people will want to add the climb of Kala Patthar to their itinerary: it is located on Pumori's S ridge and provides the best view of Everest on the CEBC. Furthermore, if you have time and energy, there are many other incredible side-routes that you can tackle along the way and they can significantly help with altitude acclimatisation.

However, do not expect to enjoy these delights in solitude because more people walk this route (in some shape or form) than any of the others and the trail can be very busy in peak seasons. CEBC trekkers share the paths with TPT hikers and most of the other treks also make use of parts of the CEBC. In the autumn season, competition for beds can be fierce but numbers usually reduce outside of this period. However, because the CEBC becomes more popular with each year that passes, the peak seasons are expanding and it is likely that some of the traditionally less busy months will become more popular in the future.

Difficulty: Medium. The CEBC is within the capabilities of most moderately fit people. In simple terms, the trek involves a climb from Lukla to EBC and a return down the same paths: of course, there are undulations along the way. Some of the climbs/descents are long and/or steep and the high altitude makes these more tiring. However, if you are following the recommended guidance for altitude acclimatisation, then your itinerary will limit daily altitude gain and the distance that you will travel each day. In fact, the distance travelled and height gained each day will be less than on many lower altitude treks elsewhere in the world, and you

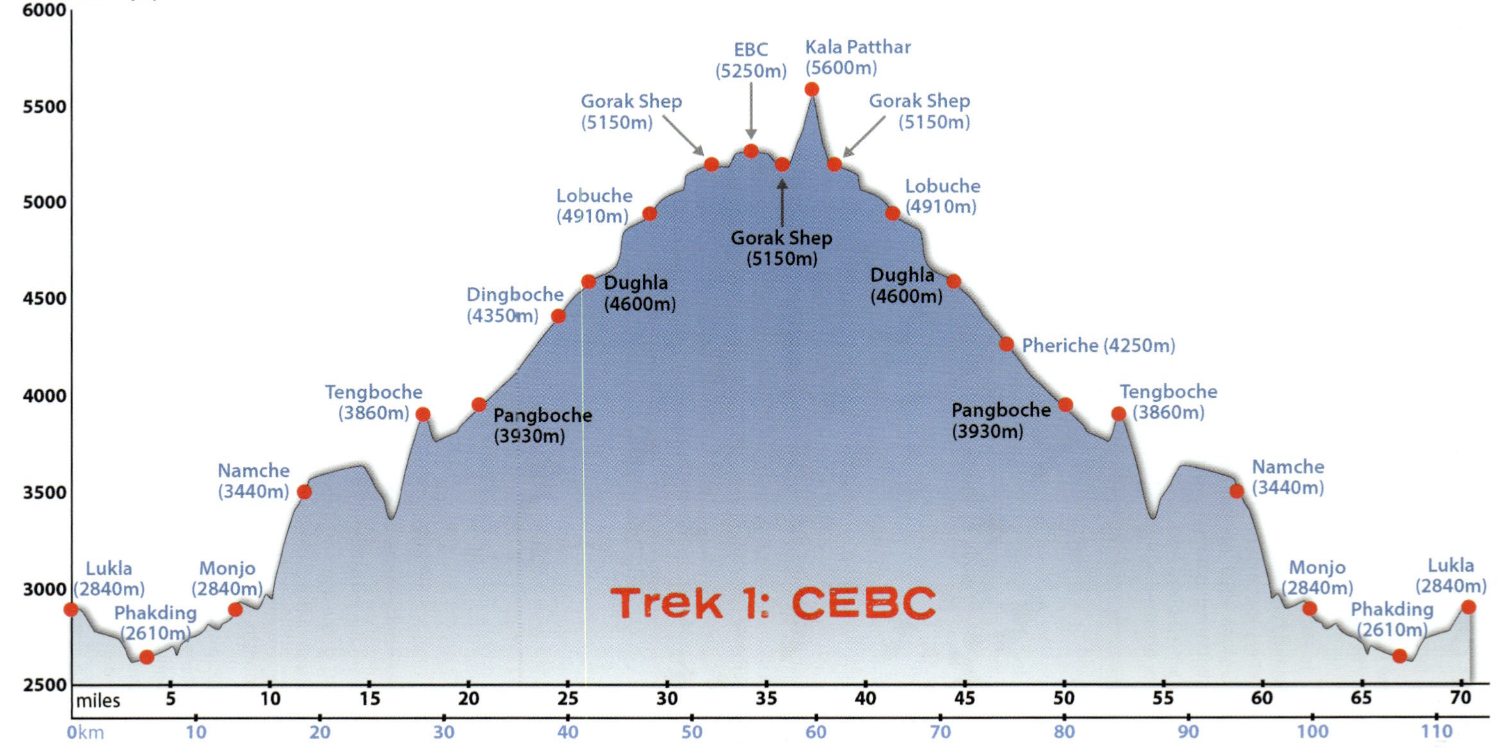
Elevation (m)
6000
5500
5000
4500
4000
3500
3000
2500
Lukla (2840m)
Phakding (2610m)
Monjo (2840m)
Namche (3440m)
Tengboche (3860m)
Pangboche (3930m)
Dingboche (4350m)
Dughla (4600m)
Lobuche (4910m)
Gorak Shep (5150m)
EBC (5250m)
Gorak Shep (5150m)
Kala Patthar (5600m)
Gorak Shep (5150m)
Lobuche (4910m)
Dughla (4600m)
Pheriche (4250m)
Pangboche (3930m)
Tengboche (3860m)
Namche (3440m)
Monjo (2840m)
Phakding (2610m)
Lukla (2840m)
Trek 1: CEBC
miles
5
10
15
20
25
30
35
40
45
50
55
60
65
70
0km
10
20
30
40
50
60
70
80
90
100
110

should have plenty of downtime for rest and recovery. Because so many people use the CEBC trail, the paths are well-trodden and route-finding is largely straightforward.

Trek 2: Three Passes Trek (TPT)

ACW: EBC1-5 » TP6-7 » EBC8 » EBC9a-9b » TP9c » TP10-13 » EBC11 (plus Chukhung Ri, KP & Gokyo Ri)

CW: EBC1-2 » TP13-10 » TP9c » EBC7b » EBC8 » EBC9a » TP7-6 » EBC5c » EBC10b-10h » EBC11 (plus Gokyo Ri, KP & Chukhung Ri)

This high-altitude circumnavigation of the Khumbu is the ultimate Everest trek, using the finest trekking routes the region has to offer. It crosses three passes above 5000m and the views are exceptional even by the Himalaya's exacting standards. Furthermore, because it also visits EBC and KP and shares the route of the CEBC between Lukla and Dingboche/Pheriche, TPT trekkers experience most of the CEBC too. For many people, however, the icing on the cake is the visit to Gokyo which is the staging point for hikes to the superlative viewpoint on Gokyo Ri and Gokyo's chain of beautiful lakes beneath Cho Oyu (the world's 6th highest peak). As you would expect, the paths that the TPT shares with the CEBC (the TPT's E side) are often busy. Elsewhere, however, the paths are much more peaceful and available beds are easier to find.

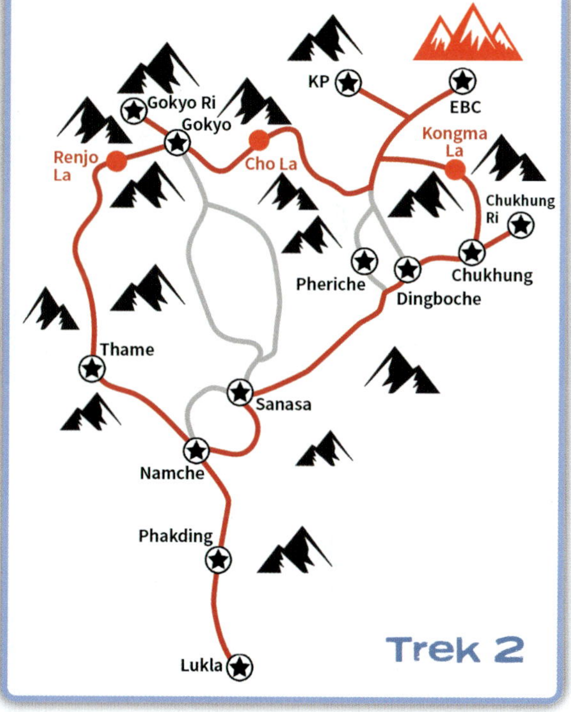

Difficulty: Very hard. The TPT is the longest and most challenging trek in the region with some long days and huge climbs. Nevertheless, it is within the capabilities of most fit hikers. The crossing of each of the three passes is long and challenging, requiring you to climb well above 5000m: you will need to be well-acclimatised before attempting the first pass. Snow falls on the passes in winter making them inaccessible into early spring. Usually, they open to hikers in the second half of March but in some years, access can be limited into April. In fact, because of the high altitude of the passes, snow can fall at any time of year and it is therefore wise to carry hiking crampons/spikes.

The paths shared with the CEBC are clear and route-finding is largely straightforward. Away from the CEBC, fewer people walk the paths and they are often narrower and rockier. Although the route is generally straightforward to follow, some sections are tricky to navigate particularly when there is snow/ice on the ground. In particular, route-finding E of each of Kongma La and Cho La can be tricky in snow or low visibility. Furthermore, on the E side of Cho La, you will have to cross the Cho La glacier: this is normally straightforward and the route is usually obvious but occasionally, it can be concealed by snow. The crossings of the Khumbu and Ngozumpa glaciers are also hard work although the altitude is lower and the ice is largely covered with rock. We recommend that you take a guide on the TPT.

Direction: from Namche, you can hike either CW or ACW. Most people walk ACW and there are some compelling reasons for this approach. Firstly, an ACW approach is better for acclimatisation: ACW trekkers, having spent a night at Chukhung (4730m), should be acclimatised to 4730m before attempting their first pass (Kongma La). In addition, most trekkers incorporate the climb of Chukhung Ri into their itineraries and this further aids acclimatisation. CW trekkers, on the other hand, tackle their first pass (Renjo La) after a night at Lumde (4370m) and will therefore only be acclimatised to 4370m before heading above 5000m.

Furthermore, Lumde is much closer to Namche than Chukhung and therefore CW trekkers tend to arrive at Lumde in less time than it takes ACW trekkers to get to Chukhung: this means that CW trekkers tend to have less acclimatisation time before the first pass. Of course, CW trekkers can solve the issue of time by taking extra ADs (in Thame and/or Lumde) but there is no way around having to start the climb to Renjo La from the lower altitude of 4370m. In summary, some CW trekkers may not be adequately acclimatised before attempting the first pass and this can lead to altitude-related issues later on.

Another consideration that is often overlooked is how you will spend your acclimatisation time. Obviously, you will have more spare time during your slow upwards journey than on the faster trip downwards. On the TPT's E side (between Namche and Chukhung), there is a wider variety of interesting sights, and acclimatisation hikes, than on the W side (between Namche and Lumde). Consequently, we prefer to climb slowly from Namche to Chukhung rather than rushing through that section on the way down. However, that is not to say that there is nothing to occupy spare time between Namche and Lumde: Thame, for example, is a highlight of anyone's trip to the Khumbu and the tranquil hike up the Bhote Koshi valley from Lumde is wonderful too.

Even ignoring acclimatisation issues, the TPT is probably more difficult when hiked CW. Renjo La and Cho La are both harder CW largely because the altitude gain (on crossing day) is greater in that direction. The terrain on the W side of Cho La is also exceptionally steep, making it a very tough climb for CW trekkers. With Kongma La, however, it is more difficult to determine which direction is easier: CW trekkers start higher and have less altitude gain but the climb in that direction is relentlessly steep.

Finally, to complicate matters further, the issue of relative difficulty of the passes rears its head. Most people agree that Kongma La (to the E) is the hardest of the three passes and that Renjo La (to the W) is the easiest. However, opinions vary on whether should you cross the hardest one first or leave it to last. ACW trekkers will undertake the hardest one first and the easiest one last. CW trekkers, start with the easiest and work up to the hardest. From a fitness point of view, some prefer to tackle the easiest pass first as a warm-up for the harder ones later on. Others prefer to get the hardest pass out of the way first, from a psychological point of view. Sadly, there is no right or wrong answer to this subjective matter and you will have to make up your own mind.

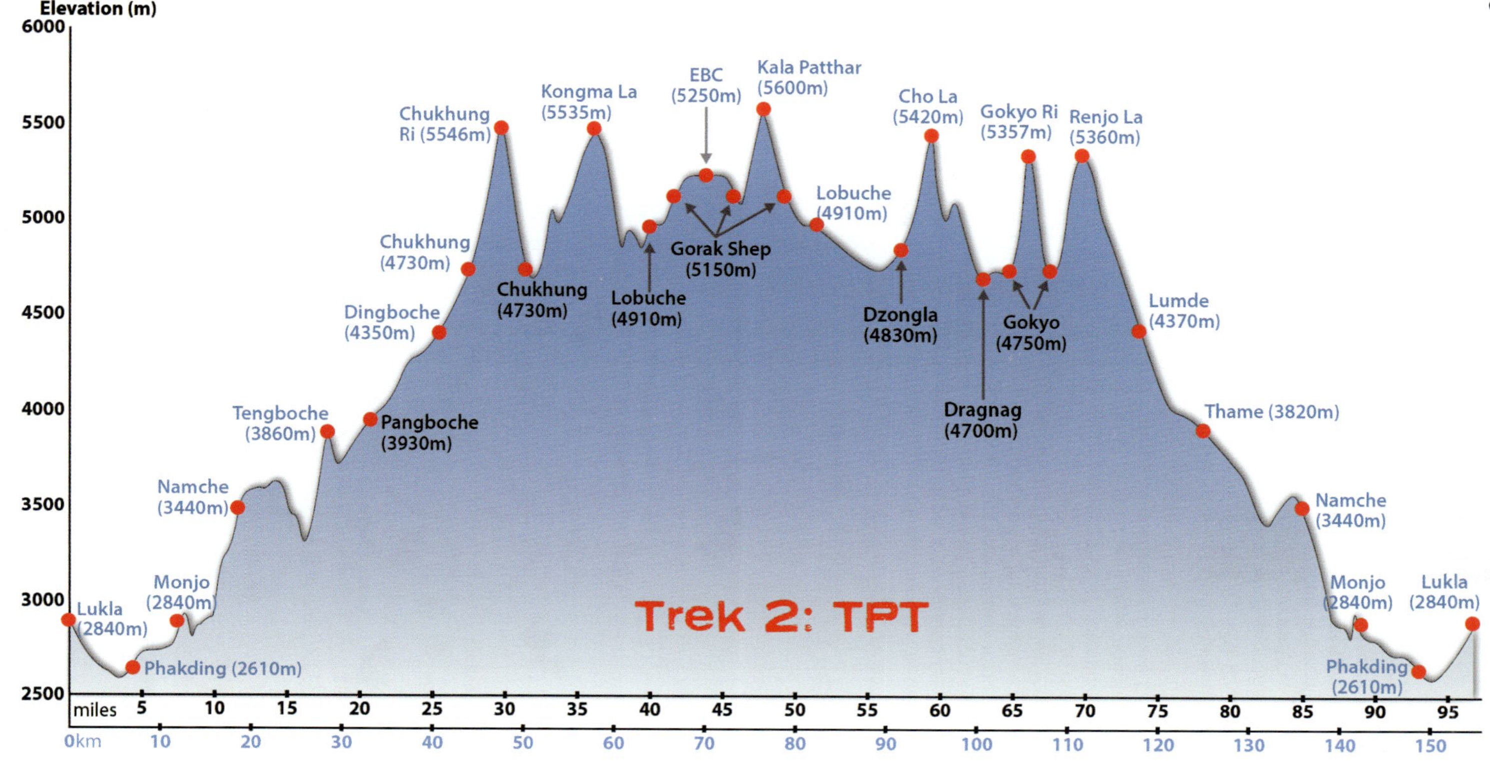

Trek 2: TPT
Elevation (m)
6000
5500
5000
4500
4000
3500
3000
2500
miles
5
10
15
20
25
30
35
40
45
50
55
60
65
70
75
80
85
90
95
0km
10
20
30
40
50
60
70
80
90
100
110
120
130
140
150
Lukla (2840m)
Phakding (2610m)
Monjo (2840m)
Namche (3440m)
Tengboche (3860m)
Pangboche (3930m)
Dingboche (4350m)
Chukhung (4730m)
Chukhung Ri (5546m)
Chukhung (4730m)
Kongma La (5535m)
Lobuche (4910m)
Gorak Shep (5150m)
EBC (5250m)
Kala Patthar (5600m)
Lobuche (4910m)
Dzongla (4830m)
Cho La (5420m)
Dragnag (4700m)
Gokyo (4750m)
Gokyo Ri (5357m)
Renjo La (5360m)
Lumde (4370m)
Thame (3820m)
Namche (3440m)
Monjo (2840m)
Phakding (2610m)
Lukla (2840m)

Trek 3: Gokyo Lakes Trek (GLT)

Stages: EBC1-2 » GL3-8 » EBC10h » EBC11

On its own, the spectacular area around Goyko would be a highlight of most people's hiking careers. The accessible viewpoints are some of the finest in the region, displaying the snowy summits of many of the world's highest mountains, longest glaciers and most exquisite lakes. In any other place, the trek up the Dudh Koshi valley to Gokyo would be the star attraction, however, as it does not lead directly to EBC, it is probably the least popular of the Khumbu's trekking itineraries. Because Gokyo has some of the region's best day-hikes, it is lovely to spend a few days there: Gokyo Ri is the most popular hike but the excursions to the lakes further N are awesome too.

Difficulty: Medium. The GLT is within the capabilities of most moderately fit people. It is the shortest and easiest of the Everest treks. In simple terms, it involves climbing from Lukla to Gokyo and then descending back to Lukla: of course, there are undulations along the way. Some of the climbs/descents are long and/or steep and the high altitude makes these more tiring. However, if you are following the recommended advice for altitude acclimatisation, then your itinerary will limit daily altitude gain and the distance that you will travel each day. In fact, the distance travelled and height gained each day will be less than on many lower altitude treks elsewhere in the world, and you should have plenty of downtime for rest and recovery. Generally, the paths are clear and straightforward to walk on although they tend to be rougher on the E side of the valley. Route-finding is largely straightforward although the less-trodden E side of the valley requires a little more concentration.

Direction: because there are high paths along both sides of the Dudh Koshi valley, it is possible to ascend to Gokyo along one side and descend back to Namche along the other. Along the way, the trail links the valley's settlements which are perched on the edge of the slopes. On the way up, you will need to proceed slowly to facilitate successful acclimatisation, however, on the way down, you can move more quickly (covering larger distances each day). With larger villages and more lodges, the W side has better facilities: consequently, our itinerary uses this side of the valley for the slower upwards journey and descends along the E side. Although more trekkers use the W side, the paths are rarely busy. The trails on the E side are probably the least frequented in the Khumbu and are extremely peaceful.

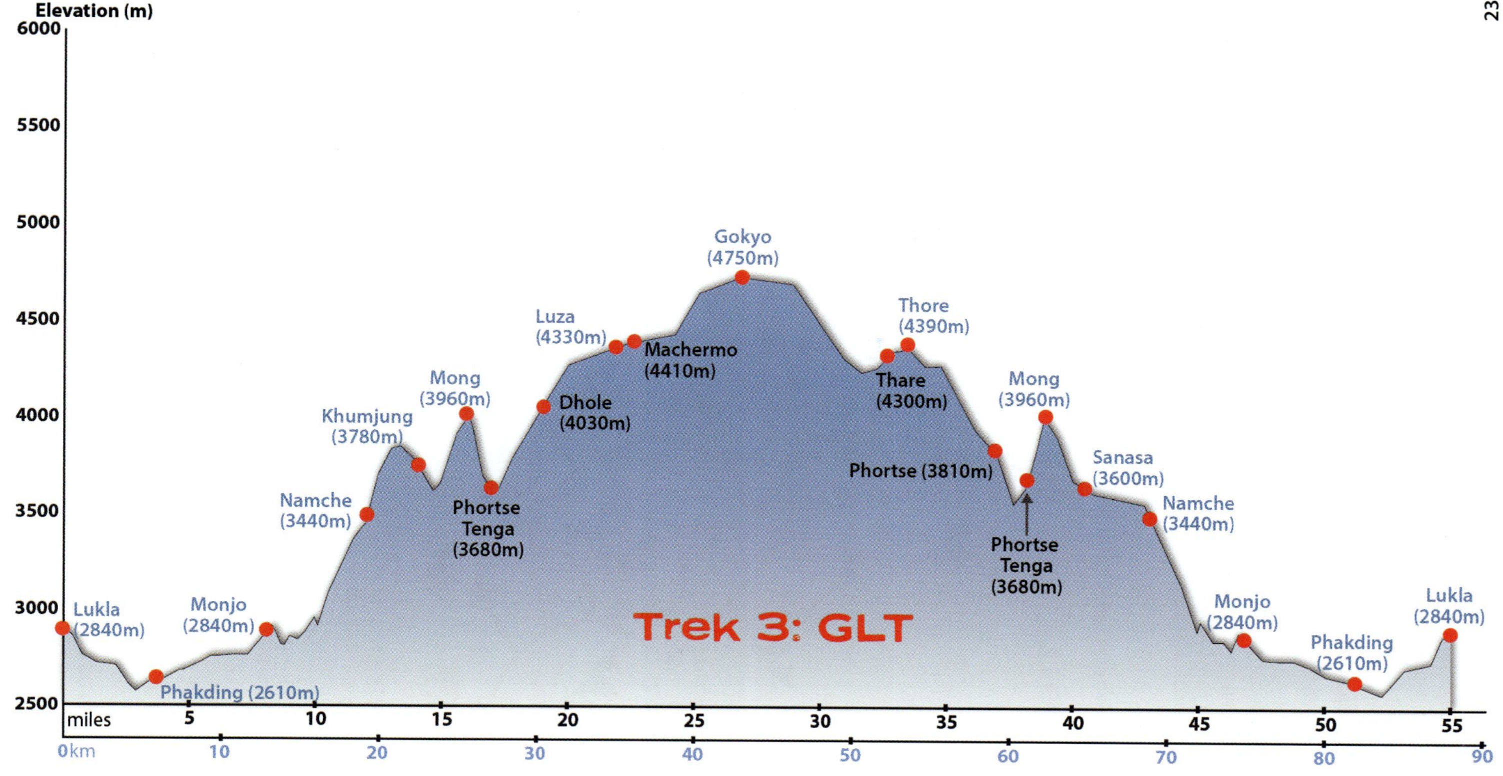
Elevation (m)
6000
5500
5000
4500
4000
3500
3000
2500
Lukla (2840m)
Phakding (2610m)
Monjo (2840m)
Namche (3440m)
Khumjung (3780m)
Mong (3960m)
Phortse Tenga (3680m)
Dhole (4030m)
Luza (4330m)
Machermo (4410m)
Gokyo (4750m)
Thare (4300m)
Thore (4390m)
Phortse (3810m)
Phortse Tenga (3680m)
Mong (3960m)
Sanasa (3600m)
Namche (3440m)
Monjo (2840m)
Phakding (2610m)
Lukla (2840m)
Trek 3: GLT
miles
5
10
15
20
25
30
35
40
45
50
55
0km
10
20
30
40
50
60
70
80
90

Trek 4: Gokyo Lakes and EBC (via Cho La)

ACW: EBC1-8 » EBC9a-9b » TP9c » TP10-11 » GL6-5 » GL4d » GL8b-8c » EBC10h » EBC11 (plus KP & Gokyo Ri)

CW: EBC1-2 » GL3-6 » TP11 » TP10 » TP9c » EBC7b » EBC8-11 (plus Gokyo Ri & KP)

This incredible route is the shortest way to visit both EBC and Gokyo, linking them using the Cho La pass. It can be considered to be the Khumbu's 'Greatest Hits' trek. It travels the entire CEBC between Lukla and EBC, crosses Cho La, visits Gokyo and travels one of the GLT's paths along the Dudh Koshi valley. A major advantage of this route is that it minimises back-tracking: CEBC trekkers use largely the same route for both the journey to EBC and the return trip.

Difficulty: Hard. Because of the Cho La crossing, this trek is a little harder than the CEBC and the GLT. However, it is still within the capabilities of most reasonably fit hikers. The paths shared with the CEBC are clear and well-maintained. Away from the CEBC, fewer people walk the paths and they are often narrower and rockier. In either direction, the climb to the pass (5420m) is long and challenging, however, you should be well acclimatised by then, having previously visited either EBC or Gokyo (depending upon direction of travel). The path on the W side of Cho La is exceptionally steep. Snow falls on the pass in winter making it inaccessible into early spring. Usually, it opens to hikers in the second half of March but in some years, access can be limited into April. In fact, because of the high altitude, snow can fall around the pass at any time of year and it is therefore wise to carry hiking crampons/spikes. The crossing of the Ngozumpa Glacier is also hard work.

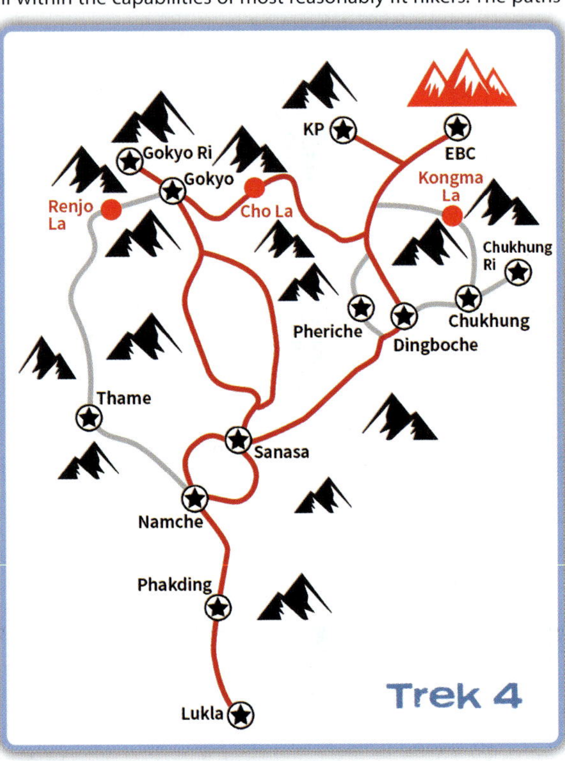

Cho La aside, navigation is generally simple (particularly, on the paths shared with the CEBC). However, route-finding on either side of Cho La can be tricky in snow or low visibility. Furthermore, on the E side of the pass, you will have to cross Cho La glacier: this is normally straightforward and the route is usually obvious but occasionally, it can be concealed by snow. We recommend that you take a guide.

Direction: from Namche, you can hike either CW or ACW and we provide an itinerary for both approaches. If EBC is your priority, then it can make sense to head there first (travelling ACW): having successfully ticked the EBC box, you can head to Gokyo and relax for a few days. On the other hand, if you travel CW, then any apprehension about Cho La and EBC can loom over you at Gokyo: that said, time spent at Gokyo followed by the crossing of Cho La should reduce your chances of altitude issues at EBC. However, if Gokyo and EBC are of equal priority

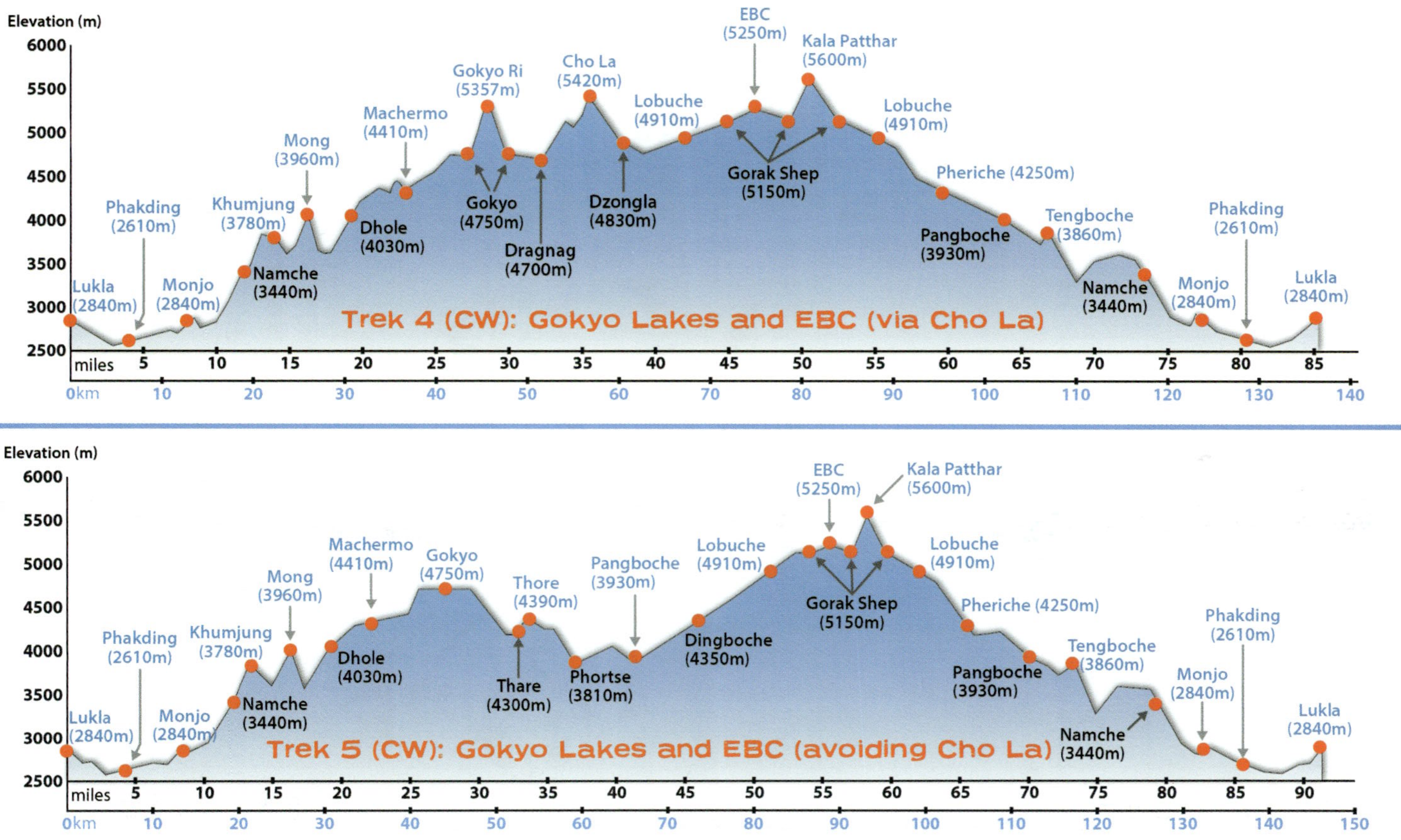
Elevation (m)
6000
5500
5000
4500
4000
3500
3000
2500
Lukla (2840m)
Phakding (2610m)
Monjo (2840m)
Namche (3440m)
Khumjung (3780m)
Mong (3960m)
Dhole (4030m)
Machermo (4410m)
Gokyo (4750m)
Gokyo Ri (5357m)
Dragnag (4700m)
Cho La (5420m)
Dzongla (4830m)
Lobuche (4910m)
Gorak Shep (5150m)
EBC (5250m)
Kala Patthar (5600m)
Lobuche (4910m)
Pheriche (4250m)
Pangboche (3930m)
Tengboche (3860m)
Namche (3440m)
Monjo (2840m)
Phakding (2610m)
Lukla (2840m)
Trek 4 (CW): Gokyo Lakes and EBC (via Cho La)
miles 5 10 15 20 25 30 35 40 45 50 55 60 65 70 75 80 85
0km 10 20 30 40 50 60 70 80 90 100 110 120 130 140
Elevation (m)
6000
5500
5000
4500
4000
3500
3000
2500
Lukla (2840m)
Phakding (2610m)
Monjo (2840m)
Namche (3440m)
Khumjung (3780m)
Mong (3960m)
Dhole (4030m)
Machermo (4410m)
Gokyo (4750m)
Thare (4300m)
Thore (4390m)
Phortse (3810m)
Pangboche (3930m)
Dingboche (4350m)
Lobuche (4910m)
Gorak Shep (5150m)
EBC (5250m)
Kala Patthar (5600m)
Lobuche (4910m)
Pheriche (4250m)
Pangboche (3930m)
Tengboche (3860m)
Namche (3440m)
Monjo (2840m)
Phakding (2610m)
Lukla (2840m)
Trek 5 (CW): Gokyo Lakes and EBC (avoiding Cho La)
miles 5 10 15 20 25 30 35 40 45 50 55 60 65 70 75 80 85 90
0km 10 20 30 40 50 60 70 80 90 100 110 120 130 140 150

to you then, in terms of acclimatisation, there is little to choose between the CW and ACW approaches: either way, you should be sufficiently acclimatised to cross Cho La.

Another consideration is how you will spend your acclimatisation time. You will have more spare time during your slow upwards journey than on the faster trip downwards. On the E side of the trek (between Namche and EBC), there is a wider variety of interesting sights and acclimatisation hikes than on the W side (between Namche and Gokyo). Consequently, we prefer to travel ACW, climbing slowly from Namche to EBC rather than rushing through that section on the way down.

Trek 5: Gokyo Lakes and EBC (avoiding Cho La)

CW: EBC1-2 » GL3-7 » AR2 » EBC5-11 (plus KP)

This route enables you to visit both EBC and Gokyo without having to cross Cho La (which may be too difficult or daunting for some). You can also use it as a bad weather alternative if Cho La is inaccessible due to snow. Our CW itinerary first travels almost the entire length of the GLT, heading up the W side of the Dudh Koshi to Gokyo and then returning down the E side of it. At Phortse, it leaves the GLT route and follows the high path to Pangboche (AR2). From Pangboche, the CEBC is followed to EBC and then from EBC back to Lukla.

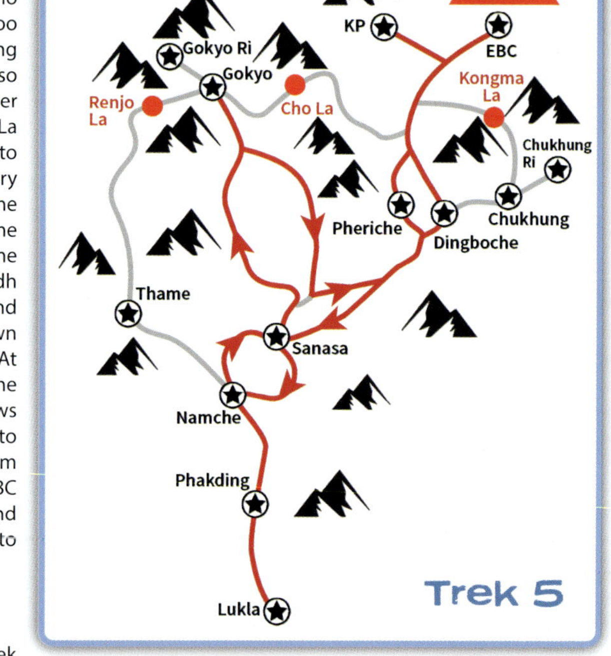

Difficulty: Medium-hard. Because this trek travels most of both the GLT and the CEBC (in each case in both directions), it is longer and harder than either the CEBC or the GLT. However, it is still within the capabilities of most reasonably fit hikers. For further information on difficulty, see Trek 1 and 3 above .

Direction: from Namche, you can hike either CW or ACW. Our itinerary heads CW, visiting Gokyo before EBC. Because the altitude at Gokyo is lower than that at Lobuche and Gorak Shep (where you will sleep in the days before EBC), a CW approach is probably marginally better for acclimatisation. Without the requirement to cross Cho La, there is less to worry about at Gokyo: you can simply relax, knowing that you have plenty of time at sensible altitudes to prepare for EBC.

Trek 6: Gokyo Lakes & Renjo La

Stages: ACW: EBC1-2 » GL3-6 » TP12-13 » EBC11

This fantastic trek along peaceful trails is perfect for those who prefer to avoid the crowds. After heading up the Dudh Koshi to Gokyo along the route of the GLT, you will follow the W part of the TPT. Although this trek does not visit EBC or KP, you will experience both Gokyo and Thame which are two of the most beautiful and enjoyable places in the Khumbu. It also incorporates a crossing of Renjo La, probably the most beautiful of the region's three famous high passes: from the E side of the pass, the views across Gokyo's lake towards Everest, Lhotse and Makalu are sublime.

Difficulty:

Medium-hard. Because of the Renjo La crossing, this trek is slightly harder than the CEBC. However, it is still within the capabilities of most reasonably fit hikers. Although Renjo La is probably the easiest of the three passes, the climb is still long and tough, particularly when tackled CW. Some sections are very steep and exposed. Snow falls on the pass in winter making it inaccessible into early spring. Usually, it opens to hikers in the second half of March but in some years, access can be limited into April. In fact, because of the high altitude, snow can fall around the pass at any time of year and it is therefore wise to carry hiking crampons/spikes.

Compared to the CEBC, fewer people walk the paths and they are sometimes narrower and rockier. The route is largely straightforward to follow, however, route-finding on either side of the pass would be more tricky in snow or low visibility.

Direction: from Namche, you can hike either CW or ACW. Our itinerary travels ACW (visiting Gokyo before crossing Renjo La) because this is the easier approach. ACW trekkers have an easier climb to Renjo La (5350m), tackling it from Gokyo (4750m): CW trekkers, on the other hand, climb to the pass from Lumde (4370m) which is much lower than Gokyo. Furthermore, an ACW approach is better for acclimatisation: ACW trekkers normally spend a few nights at Gokyo (4750m) before attempting Renjo La and many climb Gokyo Ri too, further aiding acclimatisation. CW trekkers, on the other hand, will not sleep higher than Lumde (4370m) before crossing the pass.

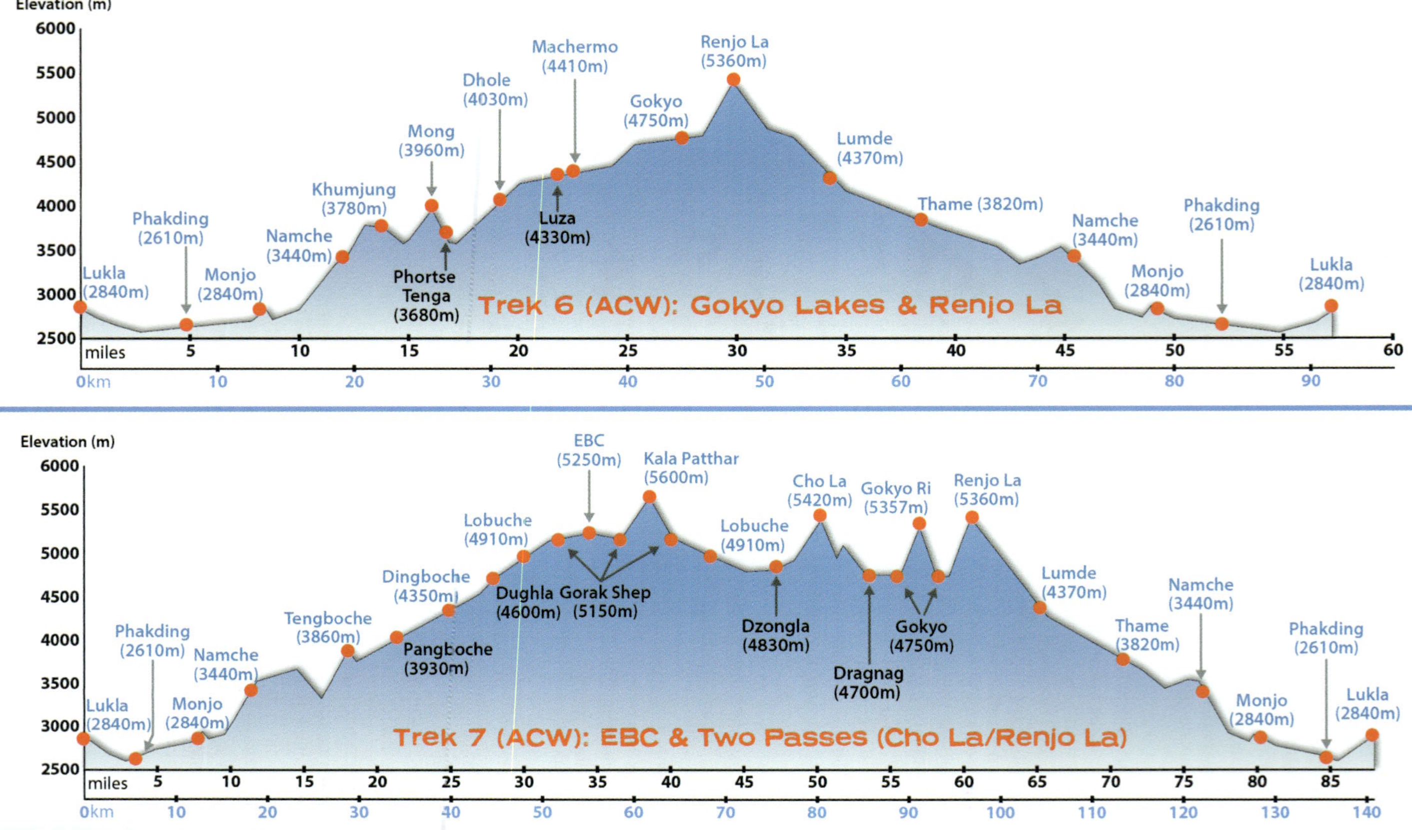
Elevation (m)
6000
5500
5000
4500
4000
3500
3000
2500
Lukla (2840m)
Phakding (2610m)
Monjo (2840m)
Namche (3440m)
Khumjung (3780m)
Mong (3960m)
Phortse Tenga (3680m)
Dhole (4030m)
Luza (4330m)
Machermo (4410m)
Gokyo (4750m)
Renjo La (5360m)
Lumde (4370m)
Thame (3820m)
Namche (3440m)
Monjo (2840m)
Phakding (2610m)
Lukla (2840m)
Trek 6 (ACW): Gokyo Lakes & Renjo La
miles 5 10 15 20 25 30 35 40 45 50 55 60
0km 10 20 30 40 50 60 70 80 90
Elevation (m)
6000
5500
5000
4500
4000
3500
3000
2500
Lukla (2840m)
Phakding (2610m)
Monjo (2840m)
Namche (3440m)
Tengboche (3860m)
Pangboche (3930m)
Dingboche (4350m)
Lobuche (4910m)
Dughla (4600m)
Gorak Shep (5150m)
EBC (5250m)
Kala Patthar (5600m)
Lobuche (4910m)
Dzongla (4830m)
Cho La (5420m)
Dragnag (4700m)
Gokyo Ri (5357m)
Gokyo (4750m)
Renjo La (5360m)
Lumde (4370m)
Thame (3820m)
Namche (3440m)
Monjo (2840m)
Phakding (2610m)
Lukla (2840m)
Trek 7 (ACW): EBC & Two Passes (Cho La/Renjo La)
miles 5 10 15 20 25 30 35 40 45 50 55 60 65 70 75 80 85
0km 10 20 30 40 50 60 70 80 90 100 110 120 130 140

Trek 7: EBC & Two Passes (Cho La/Renjo La)

ACW: EBC1-8 » EBC9a-9b » TP9c » TP10-13 » EBC11 (plus KP & Gokyo Ri)

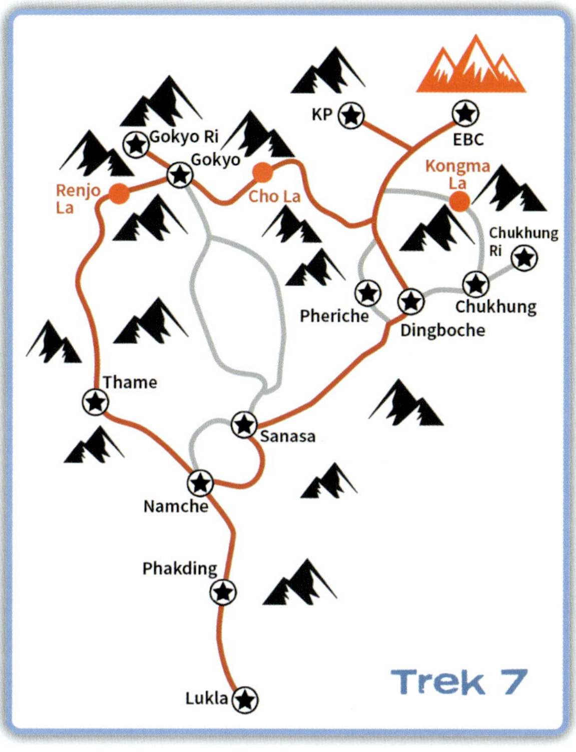

This itinerary is similar to the TPT except that it omits the visit to Chukhung and the crossing of Kongma La (the hardest of the three passes). Our ACW itinerary uses the CEBC all the way to EBC and then follows the TPT back to Namche. It is a great option for those who do not have sufficient time or stamina to attempt the full TPT.

Difficulty: Hard.

This trek is harder than the CEBC/GLT but is still within the capabilities of most fit hikers. With one less pass to cross, it is slightly easier than the TPT. The crossing of each of the two passes is long and challenging, requiring you to climb well above 5000m: you will need to be well-acclimatised before attempting the first pass. Snow falls on the passes in winter making them inaccessible into early spring. Usually, they open to hikers in the second half of March but in some years, access can be limited into April. In fact, because of the high altitude of the passes, snow can fall at any time of year and it is therefore wise to carry hiking crampons/spikes. The crossing of the Ngozumpa Glacier is also hard work.

The paths shared with the CEBC are clear and route-finding is largely straightforward. Away from the CEBC, fewer people walk the paths and they are often narrower and rockier. Although the route is generally straightforward to follow, some sections are tricky to navigate particularly when there is snow/ice on the ground. In particular, route-finding E of Cho La can be tricky in snow or low visibility. Furthermore, on the E side of Cho La, you will have to cross the Cho La glacier: this is normally straightforward and the route is usually obvious but occasionally, it can be concealed by snow. We recommend that you take a guide.

Direction: from Namche, you can hike either CW or ACW. Our itinerary travels ACW (visiting EBC before Gokyo) because this is probably the easier approach: Renjo La and Cho La are both harder CW. Furthermore, an ACW approach is better for acclimatisation purposes: ACW trekkers will have visited EBC (usually sleeping at Gorak Shep (5150m)) before crossing the first pass whereas CW trekkers will only have slept at 4370m (Lumde) before attempting their first pass. For a more detailed discussion of these matters, see Trek 2 (p19).

Trek 8: EBC & Two Passes (Cho La/Kongma La)

CW: EBC1-2 » GL3-6 » TP11 » TP10 » TP9c » EBC7b » EBC8 » EBC9a » TP7 » TP6 » EBC5c » EBC10-11 (plus Gokyo Ri, KP & Chukhung Ri)

This itinerary is similar to Trek 4 except that it adds a second pass (Kongma La) and a visit to Chukhung. It is a great option for those who do not have sufficient time or stamina to attempt the full TPT.

Difficulty: Hard.

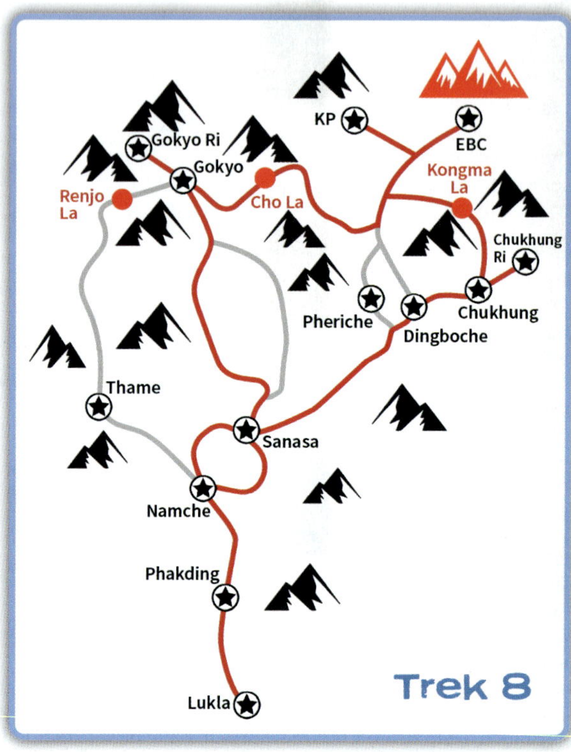

Although this trek is harder than the CEBC, it is within the capabilities of most fit hikers. With one less pass to cross, it is slightly easier than the TPT. However, it is slightly harder than Trek 7 (EBC & Two Passes (Cho La/Renjo La)) because it tackles Kongma La which is the hardest of the three passes. Snow falls on the passes in winter making them inaccessible into early spring. Usually, they open to hikers in the second half of March but in some years, access can be limited into April. In fact, because of the high altitude of the passes, snow can fall at any time of year and it is therefore wise to carry hiking crampons/spikes. The crossings of the Khumbu and Ngozumpa glaciers are also hard work.

The paths shared with the CEBC are clear and route-finding is largely straightforward. Away from the CEBC, fewer people walk the paths and they are often narrower and rockier. Although the route is generally straightforward to follow, some sections are tricky to navigate particularly when there is snow/ice on the ground. In particular, route-finding E of Cho La and Kongma La can be tricky in snow or low visibility. Furthermore, on the E side of Cho La, you will have to cross the Cho La Glacier: this is normally straightforward and the route is usually obvious but occasionally, it can be concealed by snow. We recommend that you take a guide.

Direction: from Namche, you can hike either CW or ACW. From the point of view of acclimatisation, there is little to choose between the two approaches: Renjo La is not included so the complications of a climb from relatively low Lumde are not an issue; in either direction, the sleeping altitude before the first pass is similar; in either direction, one pass must be crossed before heading to EBC; although Cho La has more altitude gain (on crossing day) for CW trekkers, Kongma La has less altitude gain (on crossing day) in that direction. If forced to choose, we would prefer to hike this trek CW, opting for a few ADs in Gokyo before the Ngozumpa Glacier, the first pass and EBC.

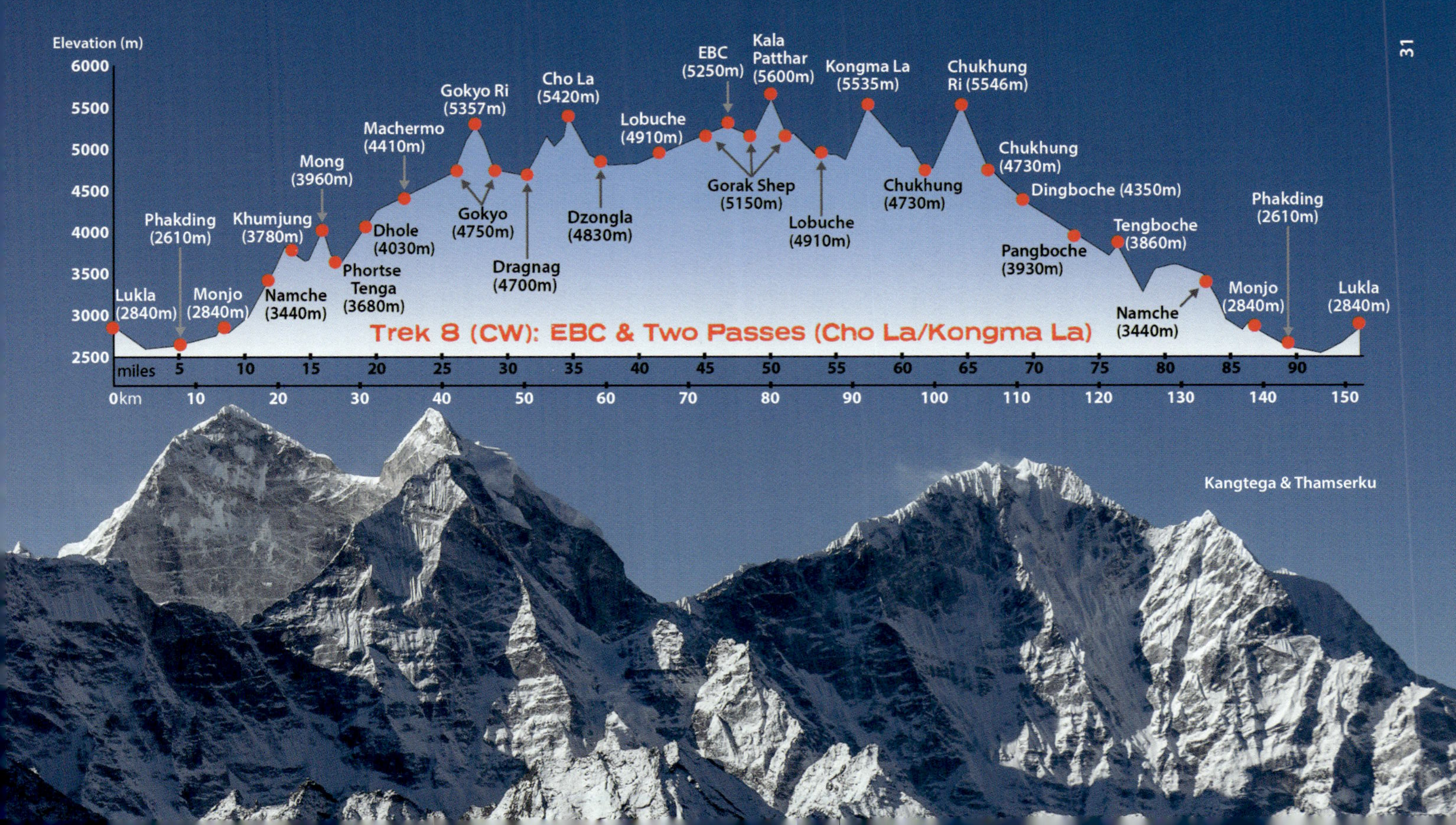

Kangtega & Thamserku

Hiking shorter sections of the treks

Although EBC and KP attract much of the attention, the scenery pretty much everywhere in the Khumbu is jaw-dropping and you do not need to hike all the way to EBC to reach incredible viewpoints. In fact, some of the finest panoramas are only a short walk from Namche and, because you can view Everest from the slopes above the village, some hikers are content simply to plan a few spectacular day walks using Namche as a base. Alternatively, you could continue further above Namche (along the route of one of the treks), spend a night or two in one of the higher villages, and then return to Namche: although doing so is a wonderful experience, you do not need to hike the treks in full.

However, because there are no roads in the Khumbu, even shorter treks normally start and finish with a hike between Lukla and Namche. And wherever you go from Namche, you will normally go on foot. The only way around this is to charter a helicopter to bring you to higher locations which you could use as a base for day-hikes. However, helicopters are very expensive and carry their own set of risks (see p61). Furthermore, a serious drawback to the use of a helicopter to ascend beyond Lukla is that, for most people, the climb is too rapid to enable the body to acclimatise to altitude, increasing the risk of AMS. Obviously, this problem does not apply when using a helicopter to descend from altitude.

Hiking into the Khumbu

These days, most hikers start their treks in Lukla, arriving there by plane or helicopter. However, prior to the construction of Lukla's airstrip, the only way to reach the isolated Khumbu was on foot and the early mountaineering expeditions pioneered a couple of fantastic access routes. You can still hike these routes today and, because few people take the time to do so, the pace of development in the villages along the way has been much slower than in the Khumbu: it really does feel like stepping back in time. Although there are few trekkers, there are still lodges in most of the villages: they are more basic than in the Khumbu but they are cheaper too. If you want to experience the life and culture of rural Nepal then this is the way to do it. Furthermore, walking into the Khumbu significantly improves acclimatisation because, by the time you get there, you will already have spent many days at 2000-3000m. Finally, these access routes provide a solution for travellers who prefer not to take the risk of flying into Lukla airstrip (which is often described as the world's most dangerous): one of the authors falls into this category.

Trek 9: Bhandar to Cheplung/Lukla

Probably the best-known of these access routes is the trail which travels E to Lukla from Jiri, through the fertile middle hills of the Solu region. These days, the route is slightly less difficult because the construction of new rural roads enables trekkers to start at Bhandar (which is a day's walk closer to Lukla). However, it is still a tough undertaking involving significant climbing/descent each day. It normally takes 5-6 days to reach Lukla or the nearby Cheplung.

It is a beautifully varied trek: winding paths lead along fertile terraced slopes, through colourful rhododendron forest and past isolated hill villages which have been barely touched by the modern age. Buddhist culture is at its most eye-catching: white-washed stupas (decorated with flamboyant prayer flags) perch precariously on high trails far above the green valleys; and strikingly painted monasteries, many of which were rebuilt after the 2015 earthquake, enliven the settlements. The people that you meet are welcoming and 'chang' (locally made barley wine) is available if you are brave enough to try it!

Difficulty: Hard. Significant daily distance and altitude gain/loss make this is a challenging route. However, because of the Solu's lower altitude (relative to the Khumbu), there is little risk of AMS: except for a few short excursions above 3000m, you will generally remain between 2000 and 3000m. The lower altitude also makes the climate warmer and more humid than in the Khumbu: between late spring and early autumn, hiking is a sweaty business. Paths are less trodden than in the Khumbu and can be muddy when wet. Route finding can be tricky because there are few signs.

Direction: because walking into the Khumbu assists with altitude acclimatisation, most people trek in that direction (W-E) and that is the approach described in this book. However, it would be perfectly possible to use the route to walk out of the Khumbu instead.

Getting to/from Bhandar: you will have to endure a long and uncomfortable journey by road from Kathmandu in a private vehicle or one of Nepal's crowded jeeps. See p61.

Trek 10: Phaplu to Cheplung/Lukla

Although Phaplu is further from Kathmandu than Bhandar, it is closer to Lukla. Accordingly, it is quicker to walk to Lukla/Cheplung from Phaplu (3 days) than it is from Bhandar (5-6 days). From Phaplu, it is a 3-4hr hike N to Ringmu where you join Trek 9 (Bhandar-Cheplung/Lukla) at the start of Stage W3b: you then follow Trek 9 all the way to Cheplung/Lukla.

Difficulty: Medium-hard. From Phaplu to Ringmu, the route follows a rough rural road which is easy to walk upon. After Ringmu, you follow the same paths as the E half of Trek 9 (see p32).

Direction: because walking into the Khumbu assists with altitude acclimatisation, most people trek in that direction (S-N) and that is the approach described in this book. However, it would be perfectly possible to use the route to walk out of the Khumbu instead.

Getting to/from Phaplu: jeep from Kathmandu (see p61) or plane/helicopter from Kathmandu to Phaplu airport. It may be possible to hire a jeep to drive you from Phaplu/Salleri to Ringmu (along the rural road).

Trekking Peaks

Although climbing one of the highest peaks (such as Everest or Lhotse) is a serious mountaineering challenge that is beyond the scope of this book, there are three summits over 6000m in the Khumbu that can be accessed by trekkers (with limited climbing experience). They have been officially classified as 'trekking peaks' by the Nepalese authorities and you must pay extra to climb them. Although this is harder than normal trekking activity, it is much less demanding than the true mountaineering peaks. It is possible to incorporate one or more trekking peaks into your Everest trekking itinerary.

The most popular of all the Nepalese trekking peaks is Island Peak (Imja Tse; 6165m) which is to the E of the Khumbu. Island Peak BC is easily accessible from Chukhung using Stage SR3 (see p182) and this would be an exciting side-trip for TPT trekkers. From BC, you climb to the summit and back in one long day. Ice axes and crampons are required and the summit ridge will give vertigo sufferers butterflies, but otherwise, it is not a very technical climb.

The other two trekking peaks in the Khumbu are less popular: Lobuche East (6090m) includes a tricky ridge walk; Mera Peak (6476m) is much higher and is the most challenging of the three.

To climb any trekking peak, you require a permit from the Nepal Mountaineering Association (NMA; **www.nepalmountineering.org**). Because this is a bureaucratic process, most people need the help of a trekking agency in Kathmandu to obtain one: they can normally do it in one day. Permits cost US$70-250 (depending on the season). Because you will need a trekking company to organise the permit anyway, it makes sense to get them to organise the whole climb: permits, guides and equipment. In theory, you could organise the guide and equipment separately but this would be a hassle: some lodges in Chukhung rent mountaineering gear but there is no guarantee that it will fit or that it will be in good working order. You could arrange to meet a guide for Island Peak at Chukhung.

How to organise a trek

There are a number of different ways to organise a trek in the Khumbu. These days, most trekkers book an organised tour with a trekking agency or tour company: this could be a private tour for just you and your companion(s) or you could book spaces on a larger group. Alternatively, you can trek independently (not part of a fully organised tour): you can do this either with or without a guide. The decision is a personal one and depends upon your own particular circumstances and requirements. We discuss all the options below.

Trekking independently

The main advantage to independent trekking is that costs are much lower: two people trekking with a guide and porter should budget for US$110-130/day between them (see p67); without a guide, you can get by on US$25-35/day per person. Furthermore, organised tours tend to have fixed itineraries whereas independent trekkers can easily change plans. And some people simply dislike trekking with groups of people and prefer the sense of freedom and adventure that independent trekking provides. If you have not done it before, the decision to organise the trek yourself, and to walk independently, can be almost life-changing, opening the door for other challenges in the future. Organising the trip yourself is extremely satisfying and the sense of achievement on completion is to be savoured.

Trekking independently in the Everest region is quite easy to arrange. Apart from sorting transport to/from the trail-head and hiring a guide/porter (which are optional), there is little that you need to pre-book: accommodation is usually sourced daily during the trek unless you plan to stay in one of the few luxury hotels/lodges in the Khumbu (which should be booked well in advance). However, although making the arrangements yourself is not logistically difficult, it does involve a certain amount of hassle and haggling (which some prefer to avoid). For information on arranging guides and porters, see p36 and p37.

Organised trekking groups

On an organised tour, you usually walk in a group on a fixed itinerary which you have selected in advance. The tour company typically organises food, accommodation and flights to Lukla. It also provides guides and porters so that you do not have to navigate on the trail or carry your own equipment (other than a day-pack). The guide makes all the decisions, enabling the trekker to concentrate on the hiking. The trekker does not really have to think about anything except booking an international flight to Kathmandu and, in fact, many overseas companies will do that as well.

Many tour companies offer different levels of accommodation at different prices. On the most expensive tours, you can stay in some of the few luxury hotels/lodges in the Khumbu. However, most organised groups will stay in the same trekking lodges as the independent trekkers, eating the same food and following the same trail. That said, some of the larger companies may have relationships with certain of the best lodges, ensuring that your accommodation is above average.

People choose an organised tour for many different reasons. It is a great solution for inexperienced trekkers and those who do not have the time or inclination to make their own arrangements. Others are attracted by the peace of mind that comes with having a trekking agency make all the arrangements on their behalf. And those travelling alone frequently prefer the comfort and companionship of an organised trek.

However, selecting a tour company can be a daunting prospect because there are hundreds to choose from, some located in Nepal and others based overseas. By using a well-established and respected international trekking company, you can usually be confident that your tour will run smoothly and be of reasonable quality. Normally, the tour will be operated on the ground by a tried and tested Nepalese trekking agency which is trusted by the international company. However, some of the best international companies also provide a western tour leader who will work alongside the local team. The downside is that trips organised by international companies can be expensive.

These days, with a quick internet search, you will find numerous Nepal-based tour companies offering a variety of itineraries. The prices are cheaper than those of the international companies but it can be difficult to be sure that the companies are trustworthy. Although there are many professional Nepalese trekking companies that have efficient back-office support staff and experienced guides and porters, other operators are not so reliable. Common complaints include inexperienced guides, overly fast itineraries with insufficient acclimatisation time and hidden extras. Before choosing, read online reviews, talk to company staff over the phone and thoroughly check the terms and conditions on the company website. Before setting out on the trek, visit the trekking company office in Kathmandu and meet the staff and, if possible, your guide.

In Kathmandu, there are countless trekking agencies and many of them are located in the Thamel area. Outside of the autumn peak season, you can usually walk into one of the offices, book then and there and set out on a trek a few days later. However, in peak season, guides, porters and flights to Lukla can be in short supply, making last minute bookings more difficult.

Visiting the agency office and chatting to the staff can give you a reasonable feel for the quality of the agency and it is a good opportunity to clarify exactly what your trip will include.

Good questions to ask:

- Are food (breakfast, lunch and dinner) and accommodation included?
- Who covers the food and accommodation of the guide and porter?
- Do the guide and porters have suitable insurance, clothing and footwear?
- Does the trek include transport (air or other means) to the trail-head?
- How much baggage will your porter carry?
- How should baggage for a porter be packed and in what kind of bag?
- Does the trek schedule allow sufficient time to acclimatise?
- Do guides have first aid training (sadly this is quite rare)?
- What kind of refund policy does the company have in case of changes of plan (get this in writing)?

With so many trekking agencies in Nepal, it can be difficult to select a good one. Never book with a 'guide' who you have found on the streets of Kathmandu or has been recommended by a taxi driver.

Local agencies with good reputations:

- **Third Rock Adventures** (www.thirdrockadventures.com): the agency that we use.
- **Kamzang Journeys** (www.kamzang.com).
- **She Nature Nepal** (www.shenaturenepal.com): female-run trekking company which has some female guides.
- **Snow Cat Travel** (Rural Heritage; www.snowcattravel.com).
- **Three Sisters Adventure Trekking** (www.3sistersadventuretrek.com): female-run trekking company which has some female guides.
- **Trekking Team Group** (www.trekkingteamgroup.com).

Guides

In 2023, the Nepalese government announced that it would become compulsory for all trekkers in Nepal, without exception, to use an official trekking guide. The reasons it cited were safety (every year, a few trekkers without guides have problems) and to generate jobs in a country where unemployment is high. However, the trekking industry in the Khumbu protested strongly, arguing that the new rules would harm business. The government relented and agreed that the new provisions would not apply to the Khumbu. Consequently, fully independent trekking (without a guide) continues to be allowed in the Everest region, even though it is forbidden everywhere else in Nepal.

In many respects, experienced trekkers do not necessarily need a guide: the trails are largely simple to follow (particularly, on the CEBC) and the large number of trekking lodges means that obtaining accommodation and food is rarely difficult (except in peak season). Nevertheless, there are some compelling reasons for hiring a guide, even for experienced trekkers:

- **Knowledge:** guides will usually know a lot about the region and can enrich your experience. Furthermore, Nepalese culture is very different to what most people will be used to: a guide will help you understand it and ensure that you know how to behave appropriately. They can also help you to identify summits and landmarks that you see along the way.
- **Communication:** not all locals speak good English and the guide will act as your translator. In many every day situations, this makes life much easier. For example, your guide will often take responsibility for ordering your food at lodges and, during busy periods, will make sure that you get a bed for the night: they can normally phone ahead to secure accommodation prior to arrival. Without a guide, choosing accommodation on a daily basis can be a burden.
- **Altitude issues:** the Everest treks take you to very high altitude and AMS is a real concern. Most experienced guides will be familiar with the symptoms of AMS and will know what to do if you develop any: quick action can be the difference between life and death and guides can enlist the help of colleagues to get you downhill fast. Without a guide, your group would have to manage the situation itself if someone fell ill. And significantly, guides will know how to prevent you from getting symptoms in the first place: trekking at altitude requires you to move slowly and steadily and they will help you pace yourself properly.
- **Safety:** although most trails are easy to follow, there are some stages where the presence of a guide can help enormously. In particular, the crossings of the TPT's three high passes are long, hard and potentially dangerous and the trail is often less obvious. Snow and ice are a real concern, particularly in early spring; crossing Cho La even requires you to walk along a glacier with crevasses that you must avoid. Furthermore, storms can arrive quickly and without much warning. Crossing these passes alone, especially outside of high season, can be risky. If you get lost, or sick from altitude, while crossing a pass without a guide then there might be nobody else to help you and that could cost you your life. During our research for this book, an independent trekker (without a guide) died attempting Kongma La an hour or so after we crossed with a guide. On the TPT, you will also cross the Ngozumpa and Khumbu Glaciers and the route occasionally changes (as the ice shifts): getting lost on the glaciers would be serious and a guide will help you find your way.
- **Social Responsibility:** employing a guide via a reputable trekking company gives a much-needed job to a local person.

Without a guide, you will be responsible for all daily decisions such as pacing, altitude management, which way to go at junctions, when to stock up with food and water, and choice of route in bad weather. For some, this will be too great a burden on top of the physical effort required simply to walk the route. However, for others, the cost of hiring a guide may be the determining factor. In the end, the decision as to whether to bring a guide will be a personal one, depending upon your own particular circumstances and requirements. A lot of people still trek independently (particularly on the CEBC) and problems are relatively few. However, most people who cross one or more of the TPT's high passes hire a guide.

If you book your whole trek with a trekking agency then they will organise the guide. If you are trekking independently then the easiest way to hire one is to get a trekking agency in Kathmandu to do it. Alternatively, the trekking lodges in Lukla or Namche can usually arrange for a guide to meet you at Lukla Airport: it is best to contact them in advance by email. Lastly, there are sometimes guides hanging around near Lukla airport, looking for work, but you could not be sure that they were reliable.

Guides are paid about US$35-45/day and you should tip (at least) the equivalent of one extra day worked for every week spent out on the trail: see also p84.

Porters

Porters have been vital to the Himalayan economy ever since the villages were first established in the high mountains: they ensured a connection with neighbouring regions by carrying goods up from the plains of India and over the high passes on the border with Tibet. In many parts of the Himalaya, porters continue to fulfil this original function but they are also the backbone of the trekking industry, hauling the baggage of foreign hikers and mountaineers along the trails. Without them, trekking in the Khumbu would be a much harder proposition and, for many people, would be impossible. A porter carries the bulk of your baggage, leaving you with only a small day-pack to carry on the trail. Not everybody needs a porter to carry their gear: some trekkers are accustomed to carrying heavy packs at home and are perfectly capable of doing so in Nepal even at the high altitudes of the Khumbu. However, the warm weather gear required at altitude is heavy and employing a porter will certainly make your trek easier and more enjoyable. You will also be giving a valuable job to a local person.

The maximum weight limit for porters is a grey area and can depend on the trekking company hiring the porters and the willingness of the porters themselves. Typically, the suggested maximum weight is 30kg, enabling one porter to carry the gear of two trekkers (15kg each). However, this is still a heavy load and some of the more responsible trekking companies impose a lower weight restriction of 20-25kg. In fact, on the trail, you will routinely see porters carrying far more than this.

If you book your whole trek with a trekking agency then they will organise any porters. If you are trekking independently then the easiest way to hire a porter is to get a trekking agency in Kathmandu to do it. Alternatively, the trekking lodges in Lukla or Namche can usually arrange for a porter to meet you at Lukla Airport: it is best to contact them in advance by email. Lastly, often there are also porters hanging around near Lukla airport, looking for work.

Any reputable trekking agency should ensure that porters have sufficient clothing and suitable footwear, however, you should check this when booking. If you are trekking independently and hiring your own porter, then this becomes your responsibility: you can buy gear cheaply or there are porter clothing banks in both Kathmandu and Lukla where you can rent gear. A responsible trekking agency should also pay for insurance for their porters, however, if you hire one independently then you will be responsible for their health, well-being and any rescue that might be needed if things go wrong: it is unlikely that an independently hired porter will insist on you arranging insurance for them but if they do need rescuing then they will insist on you paying for it.

Independent trekkers should also ensure that their porters have a bed each night: most lodges have a room where guides and porters sleep but occasionally, porters are forced to sleep out in the cold. See also 'Responsible Trekking' on page 78.

Porters are paid about US$25/day and you should tip (at least) the equivalent of one extra day worked for every week spent out on the trail: see also p84.

Itinerary Planner

Choose your Everest itinerary carefully, giving plenty of consideration to altitude acclimatisation and rate of ascent. The internet is awash with tour companies selling itineraries that are too fast to enable trekkers to properly acclimatise (increasing the risk of AMS). If you develop symptoms of AMS then, at best, you will probably have to descend without reaching your destination: at worst, you might become seriously ill or die. Do not assume that an itinerary is sensible just because a tour company is selling it. Before signing up, make sure that you understand the generally accepted rules for altitude acclimatisation (p11) and ensure that your itinerary complies with them. Even an extra day or two can make a massive difference. You will be spending a lot of time, money and effort to get to the Khumbu and it therefore makes sense to select an itinerary that is likely to help you to succeed, rather than an itinerary that, according to science, has a fair chance of leading you to failure (or worse). If you do not have enough time to trek safely then we would suggest that you wait until you do. To help you plan sensible itineraries, at the end of this book, we have included ascent profile charts for each of the three main valleys that are used to climb into the Khumbu: Imja Khola Valley for the CEBC and TPT (ACW); Dudh Koshi for the GLT; Bhote Koshi for the TPT (CW).

Climbing from Lobuche to Kongma La (TP7)

Stages: Trek 1 (CEBC)

Stage	Start	Finish	Finish SA		SA Increase		Time (hr)	Distance		Ascent		Descent		Max Alt	
			m	ft	m	ft		km	miles	m	ft	m	ft	m	ft
EBC1a	Lukla	Cheplung	2660	8727	-180	-591	0:50	2.4	1.5	20	66	200	656	2840	9318
EBC1b	Cheplung	Phakding	2610	8563	-50	-164	1:50	5.6	3.5	161	528	211	692	2680	8793
EBC2a	Phakding	Monjo	2840	9318	+230	+755	2:20	5.3	3.3	358	1175	128	420	2840	9318
EBC2b	Monjo	Namche	3440	11287	+600	+1969	3:45	6.0	3.7	728	2389	128	420	3440	11287
EBC3a	Namche	Sanasa	3600	11812	+160	+525	1:55	4.5	2.8	230	755	70	230	3600	11812
EBC3b	Sanasa	Phunki Tenga	3250	10663	-350	-1148	0:40	2.6	1.6	10	33	360	1181	3600	11812
EBC3c	Phunki Tenga	Tengboche	3860	12665	+610	+2001	2:15	3.0	1.9	610	2001	0	0	3860	12665
EBC4a	Tengboche	Deboche	3750	12304	-110	-361	0:15	0.8	0.5	0	0	110	361	3860	12665
EBC4b	Deboche	Pangboche	3930	12894	+180	+591	1:45	3.4	2.1	240	787	60	197	3930	12894
EBC5a	Pangboche	Shomare	4080	13386	+150	+492	1:00	2.0	1.2	175	574	25	82	4080	13386
EBC5b	Shomare	Orsho Junction	4180	13715	+100	+328	0:40	1.6	1.0	100	328	0	0	4180	13715
EBC5c	Orsho Junction	Dingboche	4350	14272	+170	+558	1:10	2.6	1.6	210	689	40	131	4350	14272
EBC6	Dingboche	Dughla (Thukla)	4600	15093	+250	+820	2:30	5.3	3.3	295	968	45	148	4600	15093
EBC7a	Dughla (Thukla)	Junction (4850m)					1:30	1.7	1.1	270	886	20	66	4850	15913
EBC7b	Junction (4850m)	Lobuche	4910	16110	+310	+1017	0:45	1.3	0.8	60	197	0	0	4910	16110
EBC8a	Lobuche	Gorak Shep	5150	16897	+240	+787	3:00	4.9	3.0	324	1063	84	276	5150	16897
EBC8b	Gorak Shep	EBC Rock					2:15	3.2	2.0	187	614	87	285	5260	17258
EBC8c	EBC Rock	Gorak Shep					1:45	3.2	2.0	87	285	187	614	5260	17258
EBC9a	Gorak Shep	Lobuche	4910	16110	-240	-787	2:00	4.9	3.0	84	276	324	1063	5150	16897
EBC9b	Lobuche	Junction (4850m)					0:20	1.3	0.8	0	0	60	197	4910	16110
EBC9c	Junction (4850m)	Dughla (Thukla)	4600	15093	-310	-1017	0:30	1.7	1.1	20	66	270	886	4850	15913
EBC9d	Dughla (Thukla)	Pheriche	4250	13944	-350	-1148	1:40	4.2	2.6	20	66	370	1214	4600	15093
EBC10a	Pheriche	Orsho Junction	4180	13715	-70	-230	0:40	2.1	1.3	69	226	139	456	4250	13944
EBC10b	Orsho Junction	Shomare	4080	13386	-100	-328	0:25	1.6	1.0	0	0	100	328	4180	13715
EBC10c	Shomare	Pangboche	3930	12894	-150	-492	0:40	2.0	1.2	25	82	175	574	4080	13386
EBC10d	Pangboche	Deboche	3750	12304	-180	-591	1:15	3.4	2.1	60	197	240	787	3930	12894
EBC10e	Deboche	Tengboche	3860	12665	+110	+361	0:40	0.8	0.5	110	361	0	0	3860	12665
EBC10f	Tengboche	Phunki Tenga	3250	10663	-610	-2001	0:45	3.0	1.9	0	0	610	2001	3860	12665
EBC10g	Phunki Tenga	Sanasa	3600	11812	+350	+1148	1:40	2.6	1.6	360	1181	10	33	3600	11812
EBC10h	Sanasa	Namche	3440	11287	-160	-525	1:30	4.5	2.8	70	230	230	755	3600	11812
EBC11a	Namche	Monjo	2840	9318	-600	-1969	2:15	6.0	3.7	128	420	728	2389	3440	11287
EBC11b	Monjo	Phakding	2610	8563	-230	-755	2:00	5.3	3.3	128	420	358	1175	2840	9318
EBC11c	Phakding	Cheplung	2660	8727	+50	+164	2:00	5.6	3.5	211	692	161	528	2660	8727
EBC11d	Cheplung	Lukla	2840	9318	+180	+591	1:15	2.4	1.5	200	656	20	66	2840	9318

Trek 1: CEBC

Our fastest CEBC itinerary takes 11 days: unless you are already acclimatised, we cannot recommend itineraries that climb more quickly than that. Although some tour companies offer faster itineraries, they inevitably incorporate fewer ADs and increase the risk of AMS.

In each of our CEBC itineraries, you visit EBC on the same day as hiking from Lobuche to Gorak Shep. After spending the night at Gorak Shep, you climb KP and then descend back towards Lobuche that day. However, it is perfectly possible to reverse the order of attack, climbing KP on the day of arrival at Gorak Shep and heading to EBC the following morning. For further information, see p155.

11 Days (including 2 ADs): popular with tour companies because it enables trekkers to complete the EBC in around two weeks (including travel). However, with quite a fast pace and only two ADs, this itinerary carries more risk than the slower options: most people will have no serious altitude issues but may not feel great at EBC; others may develop signs of AMS and will have to descend. The section between Tengboche and Dingboche (EBC4/EBC5) and the section between Dingboche and Lobuche (EBC6/EBC7) are each completed in one day instead of two: this means that the rate of altitude increase is pushing the limits of what is reasonable. For a better chance of success, we recommend a slower schedule.

Day	Stages	Start	Finish	Time (hr)	Distance km	miles	Ascent m	ft	Descent m	ft	SA change m	ft
1	EBC1a, 1b	Lukla	Phakding	2:40	8.0	5.0	181	594	411	1348	-230	-755
2	EBC2a, 2b	Phakding	Namche	6:05	11.3	7.0	1086	3563	256	840	+830	2723
3	AD	Namche	Namche								0	0
4	EBC3a, 3b, 3c	Namche	Tengboche	4:50	10.1	6.3	850	2789	430	1411	+420	1378
5	EBC4a-5c	Tengboche	Dingboche	4:50	10.4	6.5	725	2379	235	771	+490	1608
6	AD	Dingboche	Dingboche								0	0
7	EBC6-7b	Dingboche	Lobuche	4:45	8.3	5.2	625	2051	65	213	+560	1837
8	EBC8a, 8b, 8c	Lobuche	Gorak Shep	7:00	11.3	7.0	598	1962	358	1175	+240	787
9	KP, EBC9a-9d	Gorak Shep	Pheriche	8:00	17.3	10.8	620	2034	1520	4987	-900	-2953
10	EBC10a-10h	Pheriche	Namche	7:35	20.0	12.4	694	2277	1504	4935	-810	-2658
11	EBC11a-11d	Namche	Lukla	7:30	19.3	12.0	667	2188	1267	4157	-600	-1969

12 Days Option A (including 2 ADs): similar to the 11-day itinerary except that the section between Tengboche and Dingboche (EBC4/EBC5) is split into two days (with an overnight stop in Pangboche). It is popular with tour companies. Although there are only two formal ADs, the overnight stop in Pangboche is effectively a third AD because Pangboche is only 70m higher than Tengboche (where you will have slept the previous night).

Day	Stages	Start	Finish	Time (hr)	Distance km	miles	Ascent m	ft	Descent m	ft	SA change m	ft
1	EBC1a, 1b	Lukla	Phakding	2:40	8.0	5.0	181	594	411	1348	-230	-755
2	EBC2a, 2b	Phakding	Namche	6:05	11.3	7.0	1086	3563	256	840	+830	2723
3	AD	Namche	Namche								0	0
4	EBC3a, 3b, 3c	Namche	Tengboche	4:50	10.1	6.3	850	2789	430	1411	+420	1378
5	EBC4a, 4b	Tengboche	Pangboche	2:00	4.2	2.6	240	787	170	558	+70	230
6	EBC5a, 5b, 5c	Pangboche	Dingboche	2:50	6.2	3.9	485	1591	65	213	+420	1378
7	AD	Dingboche	Dingboche								0	0
8	EBC6-7b	Dingboche	Lobuche	4:45	8.3	5.2	625	2051	65	213	+560	1837
9	EBC8a, 8b, 8c	Lobuche	Gorak Shep	7:00	11.3	7.0	598	1962	358	1175	+240	787
10	KP, EBC9a-9d	Gorak Shep	Pheriche	8:00	17.3	10.8	620	2034	1520	4987	-900	-2953
11	EBC10a-10h	Pheriche	Namche	7:35	20.0	12.4	694	2277	1504	4935	-810	-2658
12	EBC11a-11d	Namche	Lukla	7:30	19.3	12.0	667	2188	1267	4157	-600	-1969

12 Days Option B (including 2 ADs): similar to the 11-day itinerary except that the section between Dingboche and Lobuche (EBC6/EBC7) is split in two (with an overnight stop in Dughla). It is popular with tour companies. Although there are only two formal ADs, the slower ascent after Dingboche will greatly aid acclimatisation.

Day	Stages	Start	Finish	Time (hr)	Distance km	Distance miles	Ascent m	Ascent ft	Descent m	Descent ft	SA change m	SA change ft
1	EBC1a, 1b	Lukla	Phakding	2:40	8.0	5.0	181	594	411	1348	-230	-755
2	EBC2a, 2b	Phakding	Namche	6:05	11.3	7.0	1086	3563	256	840	+830	2723
3	AD	Namche	Namche								0	0
4	EBC3a, 3b, 3c	Namche	Tengboche	4:50	10.1	6.3	850	2789	430	1411	+420	1378
5	EBC4a-5c	Tengboche	Dingboche	4:50	10.4	6.5	725	2379	235	771	+490	1608
6	AD	Dingboche	Dingboche								0	0
7	EBC6	Dingboche	Dughla	2:30	5.3	3.3	295	968	45	148	+250	820
8	EBC7a, 7b	Dughla	Lobuche	2:15	3.0	1.9	330	1083	20	66	+310	1017
9	EBC8a, 8b, 8c	Lobuche	Gorak Shep	7:00	11.3	7.0	598	1962	358	1175	+240	787
10	KP, EBC9a-9d	Gorak Shep	Pheriche	8:00	17.3	10.8	620	2034	1520	4987	-900	-2953
11	EBC10a-10h	Pheriche	Namche	7:35	20.0	12.4	694	2277	1504	4935	-810	-2658
12	EBC11a-11d	Namche	Lukla	7:30	19.3	12.0	667	2188	1267	4157	-600	-1969

13 Days (including 2 ADs): similar to the 11-day itinerary except that the section between Tengboche and Dingboche (EBC4/EBC5) and the section between Dingboche and Lobuche (EBC6/EBC7) are each completed in two days instead of one. Although there are only two formal ADs, the overnight stop in Pangboche is effectively a third AD (see above). The slower ascent after Dingboche will also greatly aid acclimatisation.

Day	Stages	Start	Finish	Time (hr)	Distance km	Distance miles	Ascent m	Ascent ft	Descent m	Descent ft	SA change m	SA change ft
1	EBC1a, 1b	Lukla	Phakding	2:40	8.0	5.0	181	594	411	1348	-230	-755
2	EBC2a, 2b	Phakding	Namche	6:05	11.3	7.0	1086	3563	256	840	+830	2723
3	AD	Namche	Namche								0	0
4	EBC3a, 3b, 3c	Namche	Tengboche	4:50	10.1	6.3	850	2789	430	1411	+420	1378
5	EBC4a, 4b	Tengboche	Pangboche	2:00	4.2	2.6	240	787	170	558	+70	230
6	EBC5a, 5b, 5c	Pangboche	Dingboche	2:50	6.2	3.9	485	1591	65	213	+420	1378
7	AD	Dingboche	Dingboche								0	0
8	EBC6	Dingboche	Dughla	2:30	5.3	3.3	295	968	45	148	+250	820
9	EBC7a, 7b	Dughla	Lobuche	2:15	3.0	1.9	330	1083	20	66	+310	1017
10	EBC8a, 8b, 8c	Lobuche	Gorak Shep	7:00	11.3	7.0	598	1962	358	1175	+240	787
11	KP, EBC9a-9d	Gorak Shep	Pheriche	8:00	17.3	10.8	620	2034	1520	4987	-900	-2953
12	EBC10a-10h	Pheriche	Namche	7:35	20.0	12.4	694	2277	1504	4935	-810	-2658
13	EBC11a-11d	Namche	Lukla	7:30	19.3	12.0	667	2188	1267	4157	-600	-1969

A typical trekking lodge shop

14 Days (including 3 ADs): this is our preferred itinerary. It is a tried and tested approach which provides an extremely good chance of success. It is identical to the 13-day itinerary except that there is an additional AD in Pangboche (which you could use to hike to Ama Dablam BC; SR1; p129). As an alternative, the rest day in Pangboche could be substituted with a second rest day in Namche.

Day	Stages	Start	Finish	Time (hr)	Distance		Ascent		Descent		SA change	
					km	miles	m	ft	m	ft	m	ft
1	EBC1a, 1b	Lukla	Phakding	2:40	8.0	5.0	181	594	411	1348	-230	-755
2	EBC2a, 2b	Phakding	Namche	6:05	11.3	7.0	1086	3563	256	840	+830	2723
3	AD	Namche	Namche								0	0
4	EBC3a, 3b, 3c	Namche	Tengboche	4:50	10.1	6.3	850	2789	430	1411	+420	1378
5	EBC4a, 4b	Tengboche	Pangboche	2:00	4.2	2.6	240	787	170	558	+70	230
6	AD	Pangboche	Pangboche								0	0
7	EBC5a, 5b, 5c	Pangboche	Dingboche	2:50	6.2	3.9	485	1591	65	213	+420	1378
8	AD	Dingboche	Dingboche								0	0
9	EBC6	Dingboche	Dughla	2:30	5.3	3.3	295	968	45	148	+250	820
10	EBC7a, 7b	Dughla	Lobuche	2:15	3.0	1.9	330	1083	20	66	+310	1017
11	EBC8a, 8b, 8c	Lobuche	Gorak Shep	7:00	11.3	7.0	598	1962	358	1175	+240	787
12	KP, EBC9a-9d	Gorak Shep	Pheriche	8:00	17.3	10.8	620	2034	1520	4987	-900	-2953
13	EBC10a-10h	Pheriche	Namche	7:35	20.0	12.4	694	2277	1504	4935	-810	-2658
14	EBC11a-11d	Namche	Lukla	7:30	19.3	12.0	667	2188	1267	4157	-600	-1969

15 Days (including 4 ADs): this cautious plan is similar to the 14-day itinerary except that there is an extra AD in Namche. Most people will be content to spend a further day there because there is so much to do.

Day	Stages	Start	Finish	Time (hr)	Distance		Ascent		Descent		SA change	
					km	miles	m	ft	m	ft	m	ft
1	EBC1a,1b	Lukla	Phakding	2:40	8.0	5.0	181	594	411	1348	-230	-755
2	EBC2a, 2b	Phakding	Namche	6:05	11.3	7.0	1086	3563	256	840	+830	2723
3	AD	Namche	Namche								0	0
4	AD	Namche	Namche								0	0
5	EBC3a, 3b, 3c	Namche	Tengboche	4:50	10.1	6.3	850	2789	430	1411	+420	1378
6	EBC4a, 4b	Tengboche	Pangboche	2:00	4.2	2.6	240	787	170	558	+70	230
7	AD	Pangboche	Pangboche								0	0
8	EBC5a, 5b, 5c	Pangboche	Dingboche	2:50	6.2	3.9	485	1591	65	213	+420	1378
9	AD	Dingboche	Dingboche								0	0
10	EBC6	Dingboche	Dughla (Thukla)	2:30	5.3	3.3	295	968	45	148	+250	820
11	EBC7a, 7b	Dughla (Thukla)	Lobuche	2:15	3.0	1.9	330	1083	20	66	+310	1017
12	EBC8a, 8b, 8c	Lobuche	Gorak Shep	7:00	11.3	7.0	598	1962	358	1175	+240	787
13	KP, EBC9a-9d	Gorak Shep	Pheriche	8:00	17.3	10.8	620	2034	1520	4987	-900	-2953
14	EBC10a-10h	Pheriche	Namche	7:35	20.0	12.4	694	2277	1504	4935	-810	-2658
15	EBC11a-11d	Namche	Lukla	7:30	19.3	12.0	667	2188	1267	4157	-600	-1969

Mani stones

CEBC: alternative descent itineraries

After visiting EBC, spending a night at Gorak Shep and climbing KP, most trekkers will be feeling the effects of altitude and will wish to descend rapidly. Accordingly, each of our CEBC itineraries (above) incorporates a rapid 3-day descent to Lukla. However, some hikers might find these three days to be overly long and may prefer to take their time. Accordingly, we have designed five slower descent itineraries.

4 Days Option A

Day	Stages	Start	Finish	Time (hr)	Distance km	Distance miles	Ascent m	Ascent ft	Descent m	Descent ft	SA change m	SA change ft
1	KP, EBC9a	Gorak Shep	Lobuche	5:30	10.1	6.3	580	1903	820	2690	-240	-787
2	EBC9b-10c	Lobuche	Pangboche	4:15	12.9	8.0	134	440	1114	3655	-980	-3215
3	EBC10d-10h	Pangboche	Namche	5:50	14.3	8.9	600	1969	1090	3576	-490	-1608
4	EBC11a-11d	Namche	Lukla	7:30	19.3	12.0	667	2188	1267	4157	-600	-1969

4 Days Option B

Day	Stages	Start	Finish	Time (hr)	Distance km	Distance miles	Ascent m	Ascent ft	Descent m	Descent ft	SA change m	SA change ft
1	KP, EBC9a-9d	Gorak Shep	Pheriche	8:00	17.3	10.8	620	2034	1520	4987	-900	-2953
2	EBC10a-10e	Pheriche	Tengboche	3:40	9.9	6.2	264	866	654	2146	-390	-1280
3	EBC10f-10h	Tengboche	Namche	3:55	10.1	6.3	430	1411	850	2789	-420	-1378
4	EBC11a-11d	Namche	Lukla	7:30	19.3	12.0	667	2188	1267	4157	-600	-1969

4 Days Option C (via Phortse)

Day	Stages	Start	Finish	Time (hr)	Distance km	Distance miles	Ascent m	Ascent ft	Descent m	Descent ft	SA change m	SA change ft
1	KP, EBC9a-9d	Gorak Shep	Pheriche	8:00	17.3	10.8	620	2034	1520	4987	-900	-2953
2	EBC10a-10c, AR2	Pheriche	Phortse	4:15	11.5	7.1	405	1329	845	2772	-440	-1444
3	GL8a-8c, EBC10h	Phortse	Namche	4:10	10.2	6.3	500	1641	870	2854	-370	-1214
4	EBC11a-11d	Namche	Lukla	7:30	19.3	12.0	667	2188	1267	4157	-600	-1969

5 Days

Day	Stages	Start	Finish	Time (hr)	Distance km	Distance miles	Ascent m	Ascent ft	Descent m	Descent ft	SA change m	SA change ft
1	KP, EBC9a	Gorak Shep	Lobuche	5:30	10.1	6.3	580	1903	820	2690	-240	-787
2	EBC9b-9d	Lobuche	Pheriche	2:30	7.2	4.5	40	131	700	2297	-660	-2165
3	EBC10a-10e	Pheriche	Tengboche	3:40	9.9	6.2	264	866	654	2146	-390	-1280
4	EBC10f-10h	Tengboche	Namche	3:55	10.1	6.3	430	1411	850	2789	-420	-1378
5	EBC11a-11d	Namche	Lukla	7:30	19.3	12.0	667	2188	1267	4157	-600	-1969

6 Days

Day	Stages	Start	Finish	Time (hr)	Distance km	Distance miles	Ascent m	Ascent ft	Descent m	Descent ft	SA change m	SA change ft
1	KP, EBC9a	Gorak Shep	Lobuche	5:30	10.1	6.3	580	1903	820	2690	-240	-787
2	EBC9b-9d	Lobuche	Pheriche	2:30	7.2	4.5	40	131	700	2297	-660	-2165
3	EBC10a-10e	Pheriche	Tengboche	3:40	9.9	6.2	264	866	654	2146	-390	-1280
4	EBC10f-10h	Tengboche	Namche	3:55	10.1	6.3	430	1411	850	2789	-420	-1378
5	EBC11a-11b	Namche	Phakding	4:15	11.3	7.0	256	840	1086	3563	-830	-2723
6	EBC11c-11d	Phakding	Lukla	3:15	8.0	5.0	411	1348	181	594	230	755

Other CEBC options

Our itineraries are not the only possibilities for the CEBC. In fact, there is a daunting array of things that you can alter in any itinerary. Here are a few more suggestions:

Namche: whatever your itinerary, consider taking a second AD in Namche. This greatly reduces the risk of AMS later on. There is so much to see in Namche that this is hardly an imposition.

Tengboche vs Deboche vs Pangboche: because of its lovely monastery and its strategic location along the CEBC, Tengboche's lodges are often full and it can become quite crowded in the afternoon/evening. Accordingly, some people prefer to stay at Deboche (15min further along the CEBC). They are both at similar altitudes so there is little to split the two in terms of acclimatisation. Tengboche is probably the nicer place but Dingboche is more peaceful. Alternatively, if you are in good shape, you could hike all the way from Namche to Pangboche in one day. If you do this, then we recommend two nights in Pangboche to assist with acclimatisation.

Pangboche: many people hike from Tengboche to Dingboche without spending the night in Pangboche. However, if you do spend the night in Pangboche, then the day of travel from Tengboche to Pangboche can be considered to be an extra AD because Pangboche is only 70m higher than Tengboche. Pangboche is also the staging point for the hike to Ama Dablam BC (one of the CEBC's finest side routes; SR1; p134) which can greatly assist with acclimatisation. If you are feeling good, you could do Ama Dablam BC either on the day of arrival in Pangboche or the following morning before leaving for Dingboche: however, it is more enjoyable to spend two nights in Pangboche, allowing a full day for Ama Dablam BC.

Dingboche vs Pheriche: in every itinerary, Dingboche and Pheriche are interchangeable because they are only a short distance apart and are both at similar altitudes. Most CEBC trekkers visit one on the way to EBC and the other on the way back. It does not really matter which way round you do it, although we prefer to ascend via Dingboche because there is more to do there and it is slightly higher (making it marginally better for acclimatisation).

Dughla (Thukla): many people combine Sections EBC6 and EBC7 (Dingboche to Lobuche) to avoid staying at Dughla which has limited accommodation. However, at Lobuche, you will be sleeping 560m higher than the previous night (at Dingboche) which is slightly outside the recommended limits. Most people will be fine with this provided that they have taken 2-3 ADs further down, however, for others this ascent will be too fast. The jump is even greater from Pheriche (which is about 100m lower than Dingboche).

Chukhung: instead of stopping overnight at Dughla, consider staying at Chukhung (which is the nicer place). After an AD at Dingboche, you could hike to Chukhung to spend the night: if you were feeling good, you could also climb Chukhung Ri that day (p186). The following day, you would return to Dingboche and then climb all the way to Lobuche (passing Dughla).

Phortse: on the return from EBC, consider taking the exquisite high path from Pangboche to Phortse (AR2; p126). From there, head to Namche via Mong (GL8; p238).

Blue Everest by Floyd Elzinga: on display at Sagarmatha Next (p112)

Stages: Trek 2 (Three Passes Trek ACW)

Stage	Start	Finish	Finish SA		SA Increase		Time	Distance		Ascent		Descent		Max Alt	
			m	ft	m	ft	(hr)	km	miles	m	ft	m	ft	m	ft
EBC1a	Lukla	Cheplung	2660	8727	-180	-591	0:50	2.4	1.5	20	66	200	656	2840	9318
EBC1b	Cheplung	Phakding	2610	8563	-50	-164	1:50	5.6	3.5	161	528	211	692	2680	8793
EBC2a	Phakding	Monjo	2840	9318	+230	+755	2:20	5.3	3.3	358	1175	128	420	2840	9318
EBC2b	Monjo	Namche	3440	11287	+600	+1969	3:45	6.0	3.7	728	2389	128	420	3440	11287
EBC3a	Namche	Sanasa	3600	11812	+160	+525	1:55	4.5	2.8	230	755	70	230	3600	11812
EBC3b	Sanasa	Phunki Tenga	3250	10663	-350	-1148	0:40	2.6	1.6	10	33	360	1181	3600	11812
EBC3c	Phunki Tenga	Tengboche	3860	12665	+610	+2001	2:15	3.0	1.9	610	2001	0	0	3860	12665
EBC4a	Tengboche	Deboche	3750	12304	-110	-361	0:15	0.8	0.5	0	0	110	361	3860	12665
EBC4b	Deboche	Pangboche	3930	12894	+180	+591	1:45	3.4	2.1	240	787	60	197	3930	12894
EBC5a	Pangboche	Shomare	4080	13386	+150	+492	1:00	2.0	1.2	175	574	25	82	4080	13386
EBC5b	Shomare	Orsho Junction	4180	13715	+100	+328	0:40	1.6	1.0	100	328	0	0	4180	13715
EBC5c	Orsho Junction	Dingboche	4350	14272	+170	+558	1:10	2.6	1.6	210	689	40	131	4350	14272
TP6	Dingboche	Chukhung	4730	15519	+380	+1247	2:30	5.0	3.1	410	1345	30	98	4730	15519
TP7	Chukhung	Lobuche	4910	16110	+180	+591	8:00	10.9	6.8	1020	3347	840	2756	5535	18160
EBC8a	Lobuche	Gorak Shep	5150	16897	+240	+787	3:00	4.9	3.0	324	1063	84	276	5150	16897
EBC8b	Gorak Shep	EBC Rock					2:15	3.2	2.0	187	614	87	285	5260	17258
EBC8c	EBC Rock	Gorak Shep					1:45	3.2	2.0	87	285	187	614	5260	17258
EBC9a	Gorak Shep	Lobuche	4910	16110	-240	-787	2:00	4.9	3.0	84	276	324	1063	5150	16897
EBC9b	Lobuche	Junction (4850m)					0:20	1.3	0.8	0	0	60	197	4910	16110
TP9c	Junction (4850m)	Dzongla	4830	15847	-80	-262	2:30	5.3	3.3	253	830	273	896	4863	15956
TP10	Dzongla	Dragnag	4700	15421	-130	-427	6:30	9.9	6.2	730	2395	860	2822	5420	17783
TP11	Dragnag	Gokyo	4750	15585	+50	+164	2:00	3.9	2.4	301	988	251	824	4836	15867
TP12	Gokyo	Lumde	4370	14338	-380	-1247	6:15	11.0	6.8	635	2083	1015	3330	5360	17586
TP13a	Lumde	Thame	3820	12533	-550	-1805	3:30	9.4	5.8	45	148	595	1952	4370	14338
TP13b	Thame	Namche	3440	11287	-380	-1247	3:30	8.4	5.2	276	906	656	2152	3820	12533
EBC11a	Namche	Monjo	2840	9318	-600	-1969	2:15	6.0	3.7	128	420	728	2389	3440	11287
EBC11b	Monjo	Phakding	2610	8563	-230	-755	2:00	5.3	3.3	128	420	358	1175	2840	9318
EBC11c	Phakding	Cheplung	2660	8727	+50	+164	2:00	5.6	3.5	211	692	161	528	2660	8727
EBC11d	Cheplung	Lukla	2840	9318	+180	+591	1:15	2.4	1.5	200	656	20	66	2840	9318

Trek 2: Three Passes Trek

Anti-clockwise

Most TPT trekkers travel ACW. All our ACW itineraries climb Chukhung Ri (SR4; p186): the two faster itineraries do it on the day of arrival at Chukhung (from Dingboche); the two slower itineraries do it on an AD taken at Chukhung.

All the ACW itineraries also incorporate a spare day in Gokyo because most trekkers will want to do at least one of the village's fabulous day-hikes. We refer to this as a free day rather than an AD because most ACW trekkers will be well acclimatised by this time. Each ACW itinerary also assumes that you will climb Gokyo Ri (SR5; p204) on the day of arrival in Gokyo: this is because the hike from Dragnag to Gokyo across the Ngozumpa Glacier is relatively short, enabling you to reach Gokyo early in the day. If you do that, you have time to hike to the lakes N of Gokyo on the free day. However, although the route across the glacier is short, it should not be underestimated: it is relentlessly undulating with steep and unstable slopes. Some hikers may therefore prefer to rest on arrival in Gokyo and then climb Gokyo Ri on the free day.

16 Days ACW (including 2 ADs and 1 free day): this itinerary is popular with tour companies because it enables trekkers to complete the TPT in under three weeks (including travel). However, with a relatively fast pace and only two ADs, the AMS risk is higher than with slower itineraries: most people will have no serious altitude issues but may not feel great in the first half of the trek; others may develop signs of AMS and will have to descend. The section between Tengboche and Dingboche (EBC4/EBC5) is completed in one day: this means that the rate of altitude increase in the early stages of the trek is quite fast. For a better chance of success, we recommend a slower schedule.

Day	Stages	Start	Finish	Time (hr)	Distance km	Distance miles	Ascent m	Ascent ft	Descent m	Descent ft	SA change m	SA change ft
1	EBC1a, 1b	Lukla	Phakding	2:40	8.0	5.0	181	594	411	1348	-230	-755
2	EBC2a, 2b	Phakding	Namche	6:05	11.3	7.0	1086	3563	256	840	+830	2723
3	**AD**	Namche	Namche								0	0
4	EBC3a, 3b, 3c	Namche	Tengboche	4:50	10.1	6.3	850	2789	430	1411	+420	1378
5	EBC4a-5c	Tengboche	Dingboche	4:50	10.4	6.5	725	2379	235	771	+490	1608
6	**AD**	Dingboche	Dingboche								0	0
7	TP6, Chukhung Ri	Dingboche	Chukhung	7:30	12.2	7.6	1260	4134	880	2887	+380	1247
8	TP7	Chukhung	Lobuche	8:00	10.9	6.8	1020	3347	840	2756	+180	591
9	EBC8a, 8b, 8c	Lobuche	Gorak Shep	7:00	11.3	7.0	598	1962	358	1175	+240	787
10	KP, EBC9a-9b, TP9c	Gorak Shep	Dzongla	8:20	16.7	10.4	833	2733	1153	3783	-320	-1050
11	TP10	Dzongla	Dragnag	6:30	9.9	6.2	730	2395	860	2822	-130	-427
12	TP11, Gokyo Ri	Dragnag	Gokyo	5:30	7.1	4.4	911	2989	861	2825	+50	164
13	**Free Day**	Gokyo	Gokyo								0	0
14	TP12	Gokyo	Lumde	6:15	11.0	6.8	635	2083	1015	3330	-380	-1247
15	TP13a, 13b	Lumde	Namche	7:00	17.8	11.1	321	1053	1251	4105	-930	-3051
16	EBC11a-11d	Namche	Lukla	7:30	19.3	12.0	667	2188	1267	4157	-600	-1969

The view W from Cho La (TP10)

17 Days ACW (including 3 ADs and 1 free day): this itinerary enables you to build into your schedule the hike to Ama Dablam BC (one of the region's finest side routes; SR1; p134). It is similar to the 16-day itinerary except that the schedule between Namche and Dingboche is altered. On day 4, you hike all the way from Namche to Pangboche (with no overnight stop at Tengboche): Pangboche is only 70m higher than Tengboche. Although this is a long day early in the trek, that is mitigated with an additional AD at Pangboche (which you can use to hike to Ama Dablam BC). Two nights at Pangboche will greatly aid acclimatisation before heading up to Dingboche.

Day	Stages	Start	Finish	Time (hr)	Distance		Ascent		Descent		SA change	
					km	miles	m	ft	m	ft	m	ft
1	EBC1a, 1b	Lukla	Phakding	2:40	8.0	5.0	181	594	411	1348	-230	-755
2	EBC2a, 2b	Phakding	Namche	6:05	11.3	7.0	1086	3563	256	840	+830	2723
3	AD	Namche	Namche								0	0
4	EBC3a-4b	Namche	Pangboche	6:50	14.3	8.9	1090	3576	600	1969	+490	1608
5	AD	Pangboche	Pangboche								0	0
6	EBC5a, 5b, 5c	Pangboche	Dingboche	2:50	6.2	3.9	485	1591	65	213	+420	1378
7	AD	Dingboche	Dingboche								0	0
8	TP6, Chukhung Ri	Dingboche	Chukhung	7:30	12.2	7.6	1260	4134	880	2887	+380	1247
9	TP7	Chukhung	Lobuche	8:00	10.9	6.8	1020	3347	840	2756	+180	591
10	EBC8a, 8b, 8c	Lobuche	Gorak Shep	7:00	11.3	7.0	598	1962	358	1175	+240	787
11	KP, EBC9a-9b, TP9c	Gorak Shep	Dzongla	8:20	16.7	10.4	833	2733	1153	3783	-320	-1050
12	TP10	Dzongla	Dragnag	6:30	9.9	6.2	730	2395	860	2822	-130	-427
13	TP11, Gokyo Ri	Dragnag	Gokyo	5:30	7.1	4.4	911	2989	861	2825	+50	164
14	Free Day	Gokyo	Gokyo								0	0
15	TP12	Gokyo	Lumde	6:15	11.0	6.8	635	2083	1015	3330	-380	-1247
16	TP13a, 13b	Lumde	Namche	7:00	17.8	11.1	321	1053	1251	4105	-930	-3051
17	EBC11a-11d	Namche	Lukla	7:30	19.3	12.0	667	2188	1267	4157	-600	-1969

18 Days ACW (including 4 ADs and 1 free day): the same as the 17-day itinerary except that an additional AD is taken at Chukhung. This allows you to complete two acclimatisation hikes: Chukhung Ri (SR4; p186) and Island Peak BC (SR3; p182). You could do one on the day of arrival at Chukhung and another on the following day. However, in our itinerary, you rest upon arrival at Chukhung and do Chukhung Ri on the AD.

Day	Stages	Start	Finish	Time (hr)	Distance		Ascent		Descent		SA change	
					km	miles	m	ft	m	ft	m	ft
1	EBC1a, 1b	Lukla	Phakding	2:40	8.0	5.0	181	594	411	1348	-230	-755
2	EBC2a, 2b	Phakding	Namche	6:05	11.3	7.0	1086	3563	256	840	+830	2723
3	AD	Namche	Namche								0	0
4	EBC3a-4b	Namche	Pangboche	6:50	14.3	8.9	1090	3576	600	1969	+490	1608
5	AD	Pangboche	Pangboche								0	0
6	EBC5a, 5b, 5c	Pangboche	Dingboche	2:50	6.2	3.9	485	1591	65	213	+420	1378
7	AD	Dingboche	Dingboche								0	0
8	TP6	Dingboche	Chukhung	2:30	5.0	3.1	410	1345	30	98	+380	1247
9	AD: Chukhung Ri	Chukhung	Chukhung	5:00	7.2	4.5	850	2789	850	2789	0	0
10	TP7	Chukhung	Lobuche	8:00	10.9	6.8	1020	3347	840	2756	+180	591
11	EBC8a, 8b, 8c	Lobuche	Gorak Shep	7:00	11.3	7.0	598	1962	358	1175	+240	787
12	KP, EBC9a-9b, TP9c	Gorak Shep	Dzongla	8:20	16.7	10.4	833	2733	1153	3783	-320	-1050
13	TP10	Dzongla	Dragnag	6:30	9.9	6.2	730	2395	860	2822	-130	-427
14	TP11, Gokyo Ri	Dragnag	Gokyo	5:30	7.1	4.4	911	2989	861	2825	+50	164
15	Free Day	Gokyo	Gokyo	0:00	0.0	0.0	0	0	0	0	0	0
16	TP12	Gokyo	Lumde	6:15	11.0	6.8	635	2083	1015	3330	-380	-1247
17	TP13a, 13b	Lumde	Namche	7:00	17.8	11.1	321	1053	1251	4105	-930	-3051
18	EBC11a-11d	Namche	Lukla	7:30	19.3	12.0	667	2188	1267	4157	-600	-1969

19 Days ACW (including 4 ADs and 1 free day): similar to the 18-day itinerary except that the section between Namche and Pangboche is split into two days (with an overnight stop in Tengboche). The slower ascent enables you to enjoy all the sights on offer and improves your chances of success.

Day	Stages	Start	Finish	Time (hr)	Distance km	Distance miles	Ascent m	Ascent ft	Descent m	Descent ft	SA change m	SA change ft
1	EBC1a, 1b	Lukla	Phakding	2:40	8.0	5.0	181	594	411	1348	-230	-755
2	EBC2a, 2b	Phakding	Namche	6:05	11.3	7.0	1086	3563	256	840	+830	2723
3	**AD**	Namche	Namche								0	0
4	EBC3a, 3b, 3c	Namche	Tengboche	4:50	10.1	6.3	850	2789	430	1411	+420	1378
5	EBC4a, 4b	Tengboche	Pangboche	2:00	4.2	2.6	240	787	170	558	+70	230
6	**AD**	Pangboche	Pangboche								0	0
7	EBC5a, 5b, 5c	Pangboche	Dingboche	2:50	6.2	3.9	485	1591	65	213	+420	1378
8	**AD**	Dingboche	Dingboche								0	0
9	TP6	Dingboche	Chukhung	2:30	5.0	3.1	410	1345	30	98	+380	1247
10	**AD: Chukhung Ri**	Chukhung	Chukhung	5:00	7.2	4.5	850	2789	850	2789	0	0
11	TP7	Chukhung	Lobuche	8:00	10.9	6.8	1020	3347	840	2756	+180	591
12	EBC8a, 8b, 8c	Lobuche	Gorak Shep	7:00	11.3	7.0	598	1962	358	1175	+240	787
13	KP, EBC9a-9b, TP9c	Gorak Shep	Dzongla	8:20	16.7	10.4	833	2733	1153	3783	-320	-1050
14	TP10	Dzongla	Dragnag	6:30	9.9	6.2	730	2395	860	2822	-130	-427
15	TP11, Gokyo Ri	Dragnag	Gokyo	5:30	7.1	4.4	911	2989	861	2825	+50	164
16	**Free Day**	Gokyo	Gokyo	0:00	0.0	0.0	0	0	0	0	0	0
17	TP12	Gokyo	Lumde	6:15	11.0	6.8	635	2083	1015	3330	-380	-1247
18	TP13a, 13b	Lumde	Namche	7:00	17.8	11.1	321	1053	1251	4105	-930	-3051
19	EBC11a-11d	Namche	Lukla	7:30	19.3	12.0	667	2188	1267	4157	-600	-1969

Ama Dablam, Kangtega & Thamserku (TP7)

Clockwise

Fewer trekkers travel CW because it is less favourable for altitude acclimatisation (see p20). The key to hiking CW is patience: even though Lumde is only a few days' walk from Namche, it is wise to take an AD there. Anecdotally, many Khumbu locals claim that a significant number of CW trekkers who do not take an AD at Lumde fail to complete the trek. For this reason, we recommend the 18-day and 19-day CW itineraries over our faster schedules.

All our CW itineraries incorporate an AD in Gokyo which you could use to hike N to the lakes. All the itineraries climb Gokyo Ri on the same day as the hike from Gokyo to Dragnag (TP11) across the Ngozumpa Glacier. However, although the route across the glacier is relatively short, do not underestimate it: it undulates relentlessly, with steep and unstable slopes. Some hikers may therefore prefer to climb Gokyo Ri on the AD so that the onward journey to Dragnag (on the following day) is more relaxed. All our CW itineraries also climb Chukhung Ri (on the same day as the short hike between Chukhung and Dingboche): the previous day from Lobuche to Chukhung is so hard that climbing Chukhung Ri that day is not feasible.

Stages: Trek 2 (Three Passes Trek CW)

Stage	Start	Finish	Finish SA		SA Increase		Time (hr)	Distance		Ascent		Descent		Max Alt	
			m	ft	m	ft		km	miles	m	ft	m	ft	m	ft
EBC1a	Lukla	Cheplung	2660	8727	-180	-591	0:50	2.4	1.5	20	66	200	656	2840	9318
EBC1b	Cheplung	Phakding	2610	8563	-50	-164	1:50	5.6	3.5	161	528	211	692	2680	8793
EBC2a	Phakding	Monjo	2840	9318	+230	755	2:20	5.3	3.3	358	1175	128	420	2840	9318
EBC2b	Monjo	Namche	3440	11287	+600	1969	3:45	6	3.7	728	2389	128	420	3440	11287
TP13b	Namche	Thame	3820	12533	+380	1247	4:15	8.4	5.2	656	2152	276	906	3820	12533
TP13a	Thame	Lumde	4370	14338	+550	1805	5:00	9.4	5.8	595	1952	45	148	4370	14338
TP12	Lumde	Gokyo	4750	15585	+380	1247	7:30	11.0	6.8	1015	3330	635	2083	5360	17586
TP11	Gokyo	Dragnag	4700	15421	-50	-164	2:00	3.9	2.4	251	824	301	988	4836	15867
TP10	Dragnag	Dzongla	4830	15847	+130	427	7:00	9.9	6.2	860	2822	730	2395	5420	17783
TP9c	Dzongla	Junction (4850m)					2:30	5.3	3.3	273	896	253	830	4863	15956
EBC7b	Junction (4850m)	Lobuche	4910	16110	+80	262	0:45	1.3	0.8	60	197	0	0	4910	16110
EBC8a	Lobuche	Gorak Shep	5150	16897	+240	787	3:00	4.9	3.0	324	1063	84	276	5150	16897
EBC8b	Gorak Shep	Everest Base Camp					2:15	3.2	2.0	187	614	87	285	5260	17258
EBC8c	Everest Base Camp	Gorak Shep					1:45	3.2	2.0	87	285	187	614	5260	17258
EBC9a	Gorak Shep	Lobuche	4910	16110	-240	-787	2:00	4.9	3.0	84	276	324	1063	5150	16897
TP7	Lobuche	Chukhung	4730	15519	-180	-591	7:30	10.9	6.8	840	2756	1020	3347	5535	18160
TP6	Chukhung	Dingboche	4350	14272	-380	-1247	2:00	5.0	3.1	30	98	410	1345	4730	15519
EBC5c	Dingboche	Orsho Junction	4180	13715	-170	-558	0:45	2.6	1.6	40	131	210	689	4350	14272
EBC10b	Orsho Junction	Shomare	4080	13386	-100	-328	0:25	1.6	1.0	0	0	100	328	4180	13715
EBC10c	Shomare	Pangboche	3930	12894	-150	-492	0:40	2	1.2	25	82	175	574	4080	13386
EBC10d	Pangboche	Deboche	3750	12304	-180	-591	1:15	3.4	2.1	60	197	240	787	3930	12894
EBC10e	Deboche	Tengboche	3860	12665	+110	361	0:40	0.8	0.5	110	361	0	0	3860	12665
EBC10f	Tengboche	Phunki Tenga	3250	10663	-610	-2001	0:45	3	1.9	0	0	610	2001	3860	12665
EBC10g	Phunki Tenga	Sanasa	3600	11812	+350	1148	1:40	2.6	1.6	360	1181	10	33	3600	11812
EBC10h	Sanasa	Namche	3440	11287	-160	-525	1:30	4.5	2.8	70	230	230	755	3600	11812
EBC11a	Namche	Monjo	2840	9318	-600	-1969	2:15	6	3.7	128	420	728	2389	3440	11287
EBC11b	Monjo	Phakding	2610	8563	-230	-755	2:00	5.3	3.3	128	420	358	1175	2840	9318
EBC11c	Phakding	Cheplung	2660	8727	+50	164	2:00	5.6	3.5	211	692	161	528	2660	8727
EBC11d	Cheplung	Lukla	2840	9318	+180	591	1:15	2.4	1.5	200	656	20	66	2840	9318

16 Days CW (including 2 ADs): we include this itinerary because it is popular with tour companies: it enables trekkers to complete the TPT in under three weeks, including travel. However, with a fast pace and only two ADs, the risk of AMS is much greater. Furthermore, there are no ADs between Namche and the first pass (Renjo La) which we believe to be risky. Accordingly, we would not recommend this approach: you will have a better chance of success if you choose a slower schedule.

Day	Stages	Start	Finish	Time (hr)	Distance km	Distance miles	Ascent m	Ascent ft	Descent m	Descent ft	SA change m	SA change ft
1	EBC1a, 1b	Lukla	Phakding	2:40	8.0	5.0	181	594	411	1348	-230	-755
2	EBC2a, 2b	Phakding	Namche	6:05	11.3	7.0	1086	3563	256	840	+830	2723
3	AD	Namche	Namche								0	0
4	TP13b	Namche	Thame	4:15	8.4	5.2	656	2152	276	906	+380	1247
5	TP13a	Thame	Lumde	5:00	9.4	5.8	595	1952	45	148	+550	1805
6	TP12	Lumde	Gokyo	7:30	11.0	6.8	1015	3330	635	2083	+380	1247
7	AD	Gokyo	Gokyo								0	0
8	Gokyo Ri, TP11	Gokyo	Dragnag	5:30	7.1	4.4	861	2825	911	2989	-50	-164
9	TP10	Dragnag	Dzongla	7:00	9.9	6.2	860	2822	730	2395	+130	427
10	TP9c, EBC7b	Dzongla	Lobuche	3:15	6.6	4.1	333	1093	253	830	+80	262
11	EBC8a, 8b, 8c	Lobuche	Gorak Shep	7:00	11.3	7.0	598	1962	358	1175	+240	787
12	KP, EBC9a	Gorak Shep	Lobuche	5:30	10.1	6.3	580	1903	820	2690	-240	-787
13	TP7	Lobuche	Chukhung	7:30	10.9	6.8	840	2756	1020	3347	-180	-591
14	Chukhung Ri, TP6	Chukhung	Dingboche	7:00	12.2	7.6	880	2887	1260	4134	-380	-1247
15	EBC5c, EBC10b-10h	Dingboche	Namche	7:40	20.5	12.7	665	2182	1575	5168	-910	-2986
16	EBC11a-11d	Namche	Lukla	7:30	19.3	12.0	667	2188	1267	4157	-600	-1969

17 Days CW (including 3 ADs): identical to the 16-day itinerary except that there is an additional AD in Thame on day 5. This extra day should greatly help your acclimatisation before tacking the first pass. Thame, with its interesting monastery, is a spectacular place to spend some time. However, there is no AD at Lumde and accordingly, this is not our favoured approach: you will have a better chance of success if you choose a slower schedule. You could take an AD in Lumde instead of Thame but climbing the 930m between Namche and Lumde in two days is an extremely fast ascent.

Day	Stages	Start	Finish	Time (hr)	Distance km	Distance miles	Ascent m	Ascent ft	Descent m	Descent ft	SA change m	SA change ft
1	EBC1a, 1b	Lukla	Phakding	2:40	8.0	5.0	181	594	411	1348	-230	-755
2	EBC2a, 2b	Phakding	Namche	6:05	11.3	7.0	1086	3563	256	840	+830	2723
3	AD	Namche	Namche								0	0
4	TP13b	Namche	Thame	4:15	8.4	5.2	656	2152	276	906	+380	1247
5	AD	Thame	Thame								0	0
6	TP13a	Thame	Lumde	5:00	9.4	5.8	595	1952	45	148	+550	1805
7	TP12	Lumde	Gokyo	7:30	11.0	6.8	1015	3330	635	2083	+380	1247
8	AD	Gokyo	Gokyo								0	0
9	Gokyo Ri, TP11	Gokyo	Dragnag	5:30	7.1	4.4	861	2825	911	2989	-50	-164
10	TP10	Dragnag	Dzongla	7:00	9.9	6.2	860	2822	730	2395	+130	427
11	TP9c, EBC7b	Dzongla	Lobuche	3:15	6.6	4.1	333	1093	253	830	+80	262
12	EBC8a, 8b, 8c	Lobuche	Gorak Shep	7:00	11.3	7.0	598	1962	358	1175	+240	787
13	KP, EBC9a	Gorak Shep	Lobuche	5:30	10.1	6.3	580	1903	820	2690	-240	-787
14	TP7	Lobuche	Chukhung	7:30	10.9	6.8	840	2756	1020	3347	-180	-591
15	Chukhung Ri, TP6	Chukhung	Dingboche	7:00	12.2	7.6	880	2887	1260	4134	-380	-1247
16	EBC5c, EBC10b-10h	Dingboche	Namche	7:40	20.5	12.7	665	2182	1575	5168	-910	-2986
17	EBC11a-11d	Namche	Lukla	7:30	19.3	12.0	667	2188	1267	4157	-600	-1969

18 Days CW (including 4 ADs): similar to the 17-day itinerary except that there is an additional AD in Lumde on day 7. Three ADs are scheduled before the ascent of Renjo La and this greatly increases your chance of success. On your spare day at Lumde, you could undertake an acclimatisation hike up the Bhote Koshi valley (Stage SR11; see p214).

Day	Stages	Start	Finish	Time (hr)	Distance		Ascent		Descent		SA change	
					km	miles	m	ft	m	ft	m	ft
1	EBC1a, 1b	Lukla	Phakding	2:40	8.0	5.0	181	594	411	1348	-230	-755
2	EBC2a, 2b	Phakding	Namche	6:05	11.3	7.0	1086	3563	256	840	+830	2723
3	**AD**	Namche	Namche								0	0
4	TP13b	Namche	Thame	4:15	8.4	5.2	656	2152	276	906	+380	1247
5	**AD**	Thame	Thame								0	0
6	TP13a	Thame	Lumde	5:00	9.4	5.8	595	1952	45	148	+550	1805
7	**AD**	Lumde	Lumde								0	0
8	TP12	Lumde	Gokyo	7:30	11.0	6.8	1015	3330	635	2083	+380	1247
9	**AD**	Gokyo	Gokyo								0	0
10	Gokyo Ri, TP11	Gokyo	Dragnag	5:30	7.1	4.4	861	2825	911	2989	-50	-164
11	TP10	Dragnag	Dzongla	7:00	9.9	6.2	860	2822	730	2395	+130	427
12	TP9c, EBC7b	Dzongla	Lobuche	3:15	6.6	4.1	333	1093	253	830	+80	262
13	EBC8a, 8b, 8c	Lobuche	Gorak Shep	7:00	11.3	7.0	598	1962	358	1175	+240	787
14	KP, EBC9a	Gorak Shep	Lobuche	5:30	10.1	6.3	580	1903	820	2690	-240	-787
15	TP7	Lobuche	Chukhung	7:30	10.9	6.8	840	2756	1020	3347	-180	-591
16	Chukhung Ri, TP6	Chukhung	Dingboche	7:00	12.2	7.6	880	2887	1260	4134	-380	-1247
17	EBC5c, EBC10b-10h	Dingboche	Namche	7:40	20.5	12.7	665	2182	1575	5168	-910	-2986
18	EBC11a-11d	Namche	Lukla	7:30	19.3	12.0	667	2188	1267	4157	-600	-1969

19 Days CW (including 4 ADs): the same as the 18-day itinerary except that the descent from Dingboche to Namche is split in two (with an overnight stop in Tengboche). This slower descent enables you to enjoy all the sights on offer at your leisure.

Day	Stages	Start	Finish	Time (hr)	Distance		Ascent		Descent		SA change	
					km	miles	m	ft	m	ft	m	ft
1	EBC1a, 1b	Lukla	Phakding	2:40	8.0	5.0	181	594	411	1348	-230	-755
2	EBC2a, 2b	Phakding	Namche	6:05	11.3	7.0	1086	3563	256	840	+830	2723
3	**AD**	Namche	Namche								0	0
4	TP13b	Namche	Thame	4:15	8.4	5.2	656	2152	276	906	+380	1247
5	**AD**	Thame	Thame								0	0
6	TP13a	Thame	Lumde	5:00	9.4	5.8	595	1952	45	148	+550	1805
7	**AD**	Lumde	Lumde								0	0
8	TP12	Lumde	Gokyo	7:30	11.0	6.8	1015	3330	635	2083	+380	1247
9	**AD**	Gokyo	Gokyo								0	0
10	Gokyo Ri, TP11	Gokyo	Dragnag	5:30	7.1	4.4	861	2825	911	2989	-50	-164
11	TP10	Dragnag	Dzongla	7:00	9.9	6.2	860	2822	730	2395	+130	427
12	TP9c, EBC7b	Dzongla	Lobuche	3:15	6.6	4.1	333	1093	253	830	+80	262
13	EBC8a, 8b, 8c	Lobuche	Gorak Shep	7:00	11.3	7.0	598	1962	358	1175	+240	787
14	KP, EBC9a	Gorak Shep	Lobuche	5:30	10.1	6.3	580	1903	820	2690	-240	-787
15	TP7	Lobuche	Chukhung	7:30	10.9	6.8	840	2756	1020	3347	-180	-591
16	Chukhung Ri, TP6	Chukhung	Dingboche	7:00	12.2	7.6	880	2887	1260	4134	-380	-1247
17	EBC5c, EBC10b-10e	Dingboche	Tengboche	3:45	10.4	6.5	235	771	725	2379	-490	-1608
18	EBC10f-10h	Tengboche	Namche	3:55	10.1	6.3	430	1411	850	2789	-420	-1378
19	EBC11a-11d	Namche	Lukla	7:30	19.3	12.0	667	2188	1267	4157	-600	-1969

Stages: Trek 3 (Gokyo Lakes Trek CW)

Stage	Start	Finish	Finish SA		SA Increase		Time (hr)	Distance		Ascent		Descent		Max Alt	
			m	ft	m	ft		km	miles	m	ft	m	ft	m	ft
EBC1a	Lukla	Cheplung	2660	8727	-180	-591	0:50	2.4	1.5	20	66	200	656	2840	9318
EBC1b	Cheplung	Phakding	2610	8563	-50	-164	1:50	5.6	3.5	161	528	211	692	2680	8793
EBC2a	Phakding	Monjo	2840	9318	+230	+755	2:20	5.3	3.3	358	1175	128	420	2840	9318
EBC2b	Monjo	Namche	3440	11287	+600	+1969	3:45	6.0	3.7	728	2389	128	420	3440	11287
GL3	Namche	Khumjung	3780	12402	+340	+1116	2:10	3.4	2.1	425	1394	85	279	3840	12599
GL4a	Khumjung	Sanasa	3600	11812	-180	-591	0:20	1.2	0.7	0	0	180	591	3780	12402
GL4b	Sanasa	Mong	3960	12993	+360	+1181	1:45	2.3	1.4	400	1312	40	131	3960	12993
GL4c	Mong	Phortse Tenga	3680	12074	-280	-919	0:30	1.5	0.9	25	82	305	1001	3960	12993
GL4d	Phortse Tenga	Dhole	4030	13222	+350	+1148	2:20	3.3	2.1	444	1457	94	308	4030	13222
GL5a	Dhole	Luza	4330	14207	+300	+984	2:20	4.1	2.5	340	1116	40	131	4330	14207
GL5b	Luza	Machermo	4410	14469	+80	+262	0:45	1.2	0.7	125	410	45	148	4430	14535
GL6	Machermo	Gokyo	4750	15585	+340	+1116	3:20	7.6	4.7	443	1453	103	338	4750	15585
GL7a	Gokyo	Thare	4300	14108	-450	-1476	2:45	8.3	5.2	140	459	590	1936	4750	15585
GL7b	Thare	Thore	4390	14404	+90	+295	0:45	1.2	0.7	120	394	30	98	4390	14404
GL7c	Thore	Phortse	3810	12501	-580	-1903	2:15	5.6	3.5	107	351	687	2254	4390	14404
GL8a	Phortse	Phortse Tenga	3680	12074	-130	-427	0:40	1.9	1.2	85	279	215	705	3680	12074
GL8b	Phortse Tenga	Mong	3960	12993	+280	+919	1:20	1.5	0.9	305	1001	25	82	3960	12993
GL8c	Mong	Sanasa	3600	11812	-360	-1181	0:40	2.3	1.4	40	131	400	1312	3960	12993
EBC10h	Sanasa	Namche	3440	11287	-160	-525	1:30	4.5	2.8	70	230	230	755	3600	11812
EBC11a	Namche	Monjo	2840	9318	-600	-1969	2:15	6.0	3.7	128	420	728	2389	3440	11287
EBC11b	Monjo	Phakding	2610	8563	-230	-755	2:00	5.3	3.3	128	420	358	1175	2840	9318
EBC11c	Phakding	Cheplung	2660	8727	+50	+164	2:00	5.6	3.5	211	692	161	528	2660	8727
EBC11d	Cheplung	Lukla	2840	9318	+180	+591	1:15	2.4	1.5	200	656	20	66	2840	9318

Trek 3: Gokyo Lakes Trek

12 Days CW (including 2 ADs and 1 free day): this is the easiest way to hike to Gokyo. The route climbs the W side of the Dudh Koshi valley and descends along the E side. In addition to two ADs, our 12-day itinerary incorporates a free day in Gokyo and a slow descent to Namche (with an overnight stop in Phortse). Trekkers who are feeling the effects of altitude may wish to descend more rapidly: it is possible to hike from Gokyo to Namche in one go but it makes for a very long day.

Day	Stages	Start	Finish	Time (hr)	Distance km	Distance miles	Ascent m	Ascent ft	Descent m	Descent ft	SA change m	SA change ft
1	EBC1a, 1b	Lukla	Phakding	2:40	8.0	5.0	181	594	411	1348	-230	-755
2	EBC2a, 2b	Phakding	Namche	6:05	11.3	7.0	1086	3563	256	840	+830	2723
3	**AD**	Namche	Namche								0	0
4	GL3	Namche	Khumjung	2:10	3.4	2.1	425	1394	85	279	+400	1312
5	GL4a-4d	Khumjung	Dhole	4:55	8.3	5.2	869	2851	619	2031	+190	623
6	GL5a, GL5b	Dhole	Machermo	3:05	5.3	3.3	465	1526	85	279	+380	1247
7	**AD**	Machermo	Machermo								0	0
8	GL6	Machermo	Gokyo	3:20	7.6	4.7	443	1453	103	338	+340	1116
9	**Free Day**	Gokyo	Gokyo								0	0
10	GL7a, 7b, 7c	Gokyo	Phortse	5:45	15.1	9.4	367	1204	1307	4288	-940	-3084
11	GL8a-8c, EBC10h	Phortse	Namche	4:10	10.2	6.3	500	1641	870	2854	-370	-1214
12	EBC11a-11d	Namche	Lukla	7:30	19.3	12.0	667	2188	1267	4157	-600	-1969

Trek 4: Gokyo Lakes and EBC (via Cho La) ACW

15 Days ACW (including 2 ADs): follow the EBC to Gorak Shep (using our CEBC 12-day Option A itinerary). From there, visit EBC and climb KP. Then head W across Cho La pass to Gokyo. Climb Gokyo Ri before descending the W side of the Dudh Koshi valley back to Namche. Although there are only two formal ADs, the overnight stop in Pangboche is effectively an extra AD because Pangboche is only 70m higher than Tengboche (where you slept the previous night). If you would prefer a slower or faster ascent to Gorak Shep then replace days 1 to 9 (CEBC 12-day Option A itinerary) with one of our other CEBC itineraries.

Day	Stages	Start	Finish	Time (hr)	Distance km	Distance miles	Ascent m	Ascent ft	Descent m	Descent ft	SA change m	SA change ft
1	EBC1a, 1b	Lukla	Phakding	2:40	8.0	5.0	181	594	411	1348	-230	-755
2	EBC2a, 2b	Phakding	Namche	6:05	11.3	7.0	1086	3563	256	840	+830	2723
3	**AD**	Namche	Namche								0	0
4	EBC3a, 3b, 3c	Namche	Tengboche	4:50	10.1	6.3	850	2789	430	1411	+420	1378
5	EBC4a, 4b	Tengboche	Pangboche	2:00	4.2	2.6	240	787	170	558	+70	230
6	EBC5a, 5b, 5c	Pangboche	Dingboche	2:50	6.2	3.9	485	1591	65	213	+420	1378
7	**AD**	Dingboche	Dingboche								0	0
8	EBC6, EBC7a-7b	Dingboche	Lobuche	4:45	8.3	5.2	625	2051	65	213	+560	1837
9	EBC8a, 8b, 8c	Lobuche	Gorak Shep	7:00	11.3	7.0	598	1962	358	1175	+240	787
10	KP, EBC9a-9b, TP9c	Gorak Shep	Dzongla	8:20	16.7	10.4	833	2733	1153	3783	-320	-1050
11	TP10	Dzongla	Dragnag	6:30	9.9	6.2	730	2395	860	2822	-130	-427
12	TP11	Dragnag	Gokyo	2:00	3.9	2.4	301	988	251	824	+50	164
13	Gokyo Ri, GL6	Gokyo	Machermo	6:50	10.8	6.7	713	2339	1053	3455	-340	-1116
14	GL5b, GL5a, GL4d, GL8b, GL8c, EBC10h	Machermo	Namche	6:00	16.9	10.5	594	1949	1564	5131	-970	-3183
15	EBC11a-11d	Namche	Lukla	7:30	19.3	12.0	667	2188	1267	4157	-600	-1969

CW

15 Days CW (including 2 ADs): the CW route climbs the W side of the Dudh Koshi valley to Gokyo, summits Gokyo Ri and then heads E across Cho La pass to EBC and KP. Afterwards, return to Namche via Pheriche. Although there are only two ADs (Namche and Machermo), the ascent to Gokyo is paced sensibly. That said, we would highly recommend adding a third AD at Gokyo.

Day	Stages	Start	Finish	Time (hr)	Distance km	Distance miles	Ascent m	Ascent ft	Descent m	Descent ft	SA change m	SA change ft
1	EBC1a, 1b	Lukla	Phakding	2:40	8.0	5.0	181	594	411	1348	-230	-755
2	EBC2a, 2b	Phakding	Namche	6:05	11.3	7.0	1086	3563	256	840	+830	2723
3	**AD**	Namche	Namche								0	0
4	GL3	Namche	Khumjung	2:10	3.4	2.1	425	1394	85	279	+400	1312
5	GL4a-4d	Khumjung	Dhole	4:55	8.3	5.2	869	2851	619	2031	+190	623
6	GL5a, GL5b	Dhole	Machermo	3:05	5.3	3.3	465	1526	85	279	+380	1247
7	**AD**	Machermo	Machermo								0	0
8	GL6	Machermo	Gokyo	3:20	7.6	4.7	443	1453	103	338	+340	1116
9	Gokyo Ri, TP11	Gokyo	Dragnag	5:30	7.1	4.4	861	2825	911	2989	-50	-164
10	TP10	Dragnag	Dzongla	7:00	9.9	6.2	860	2822	730	2395	+130	427
11	TP9c, EBC7b	Dzongla	Lobuche	3:15	6.6	4.1	333	1093	253	830	+80	262
12	EBC8a, 8b, 8c	Lobuche	Gorak Shep	7:00	11.3	7.0	598	1962	358	1175	+240	787
13	KP, EBC9a-9d	Gorak Shep	Pheriche	8:00	17.3	10.8	620	2034	1520	4987	-900	-2953
14	EBC10a-10h	Pheriche	Namche	7:35	20.0	12.4	694	2277	1504	4935	-810	-2658
15	EBC11a-11d	Namche	Lukla	7:30	19.3	12.0	667	2188	1267	4157	-600	-1969

Trek 5: Gokyo Lakes and EBC (avoiding Cho La)

16 Days CW (including 3 ADs): this clever CW itinerary visits both Gokyo and EBC without the need to cross Cho La pass. After ascending to Gokyo along the W side of the Dudh Koshi valley, you descend S back along the valley's E side to Phortse (instead of climbing E to Cho La). From Phortse, use a superb balcony path to hike to Pangboche where you join the main CEBC route: follow it to EBC, KP and then back to Namche.

Day	Stages	Start	Finish	Time (hr)	Distance km	Distance miles	Ascent m	Ascent ft	Descent m	Descent ft	SA change m	SA change ft
1	EBC1a, 1b	Lukla	Phakding	2:40	8.0	5.0	181	594	411	1348	-230	-755
2	EBC2a, 2b	Phakding	Namche	6:05	11.3	7.0	1086	3563	256	840	+830	2723
3	**AD**	Namche	Namche	0:00							0	0
4	GL3	Namche	Khumjung	2:10	3.4	2.1	425	1394	85	279	+400	1312
5	GL4a-4d	Khumjung	Dhole	4:55	8.3	5.2	869	2851	619	2031	+190	623
6	GL5a, GL5b	Dhole	Machermo	3:05	5.3	3.3	465	1526	85	279	+380	1247
7	**AD**	Machermo	Machermo								0	0
8	GL6	Machermo	Gokyo	3:20	7.6	4.7	443	1453	103	338	+340	1116
9	GL7a, 7b, 7c	Gokyo	Phortse	5:45	15.1	9.4	367	1204	1307	4288	-940	-3084
10	AR2, EBC5a-5c	Phortse	Dingboche	5:35	12.0	7.5	916	3005	376	1234	+540	1772
11	**AD**	Dingboche	Dingboche								0	0
12	EBC6, EBC7a-7b	Dingboche	Lobuche	4:45	8.3	5.2	625	2051	65	213	+560	1837
13	EBC8a, 8b, 8c	Lobuche	Gorak Shep	7:00	11.3	7.0	598	1962	358	1175	+240	787
14	KP, EBC9a-9d	Gorak Shep	Pheriche	8:00	17.3	10.8	620	2034	1520	4987	-900	-2953
15	EBC10a-10h	Pheriche	Namche	7:35	20.0	12.4	694	2277	1504	4935	-810	-2658
16	EBC11a-11d	Namche	Lukla	7:30	19.3	12.0	667	2188	1267	4157	-600	-1969

Trek 6: Gokyo Lakes & Renjo La

11 Days ACW (including 2 ADs): this ACW itinerary ascends the W side of the Dudh Koshi valley to Gokyo. Then it heads W across Renjo La pass. Descend to Namche via the villages of Lumde and Thame. Although there are only two ADs (Namche and Machermo), the ascent to Gokyo is paced sensibly. That said, we recommend adding a third AD at Gokyo: this will greatly aid acclimatisation before crossing Renjo La.

Day	Stages	Start	Finish	Time (hr)	Distance		Ascent		Descent		SA change	
					km	miles	m	ft	m	ft	m	ft
1	EBC1a, 1b	Lukla	Phakding	2:40	8.0	5.0	181	594	411	1348	-230	-755
2	EBC2a, 2b	Phakding	Namche	6:05	11.3	7.0	1086	3563	256	840	+830	2723
3	**AD**	Namche	Namche								0	0
4	GL3	Namche	Khumjung	2:10	3.4	2.1	425	1394	85	279	+400	1312
5	GL4a-4d	Khumjung	Dhole	4:55	8.3	5.2	869	2851	619	2031	+190	623
6	GL5a, 5b	Dhole	Machermo	3:05	5.3	3.3	465	1526	85	279	+380	1247
7	**AD**	Machermo	Machermo								0	0
8	GL6	Machermo	Gokyo	3:20	7.6	4.7	443	1453	103	338	+340	1116
9	TP12	Gokyo	Lumde	6:15	11.0	6.8	635	2083	1015	3330	-380	-1247
10	TP13a, 13b	Lumde	Namche	7:00	17.8	11.1	321	1053	1251	4105	-930	-3051
11	EBC11a-11d	Namche	Lukla	7:30	19.3	12.0	667	2188	1267	4157	-600	-1969

Trek 7: EBC & Two Passes (Cho La/Renjo La)

16 Days ACW (including 2 ADs and 1 free day): this ACW itinerary is similar to the TPT except that it skips Kongma La pass. It follows our CEBC 12-day Option A itinerary to Gorak Shep. From there, visit EBC and climb KP. Then head W across Cho La pass to Gokyo. Climb Gokyo Ri before heading W over Renjo La pass. Finally return to Namche via Lumde and Thame. Although there are only two formal ADs, the overnight stop in Pangboche is effectively an extra AD because Pangboche is only 70m higher than Tengboche (where you slept the previous night). If you would prefer a slower or faster ascent to Gorak Shep then replace days 1 to 9 (CEBC 12-day Option A itinerary) with one of our other CEBC itineraries. Although this is an ACW itinerary, you could also head CW: however, acclimatisation is more difficult for CW trekkers (see p20).

Day	Stages	Start	Finish	Time (hr)	Distance		Ascent		Descent		SA change	
					km	miles	m	ft	m	ft	m	ft
1	EBC1a, 1b	Lukla	Phakding	2:40	8.0	5.0	181	594	411	1348	-230	-755
2	EBC2a, 2b	Phakding	Namche	6:05	11.3	7.0	1086	3563	256	840	+830	2723
3	**AD**	Namche	Namche								0	0
4	EBC3a, 3b, 3c	Namche	Tengboche	4:50	10.1	6.3	850	2789	430	1411	+420	1378
5	EBC4a, 4b	Tengboche	Pangboche	2:00	4.2	2.6	240	787	170	558	+70	230
6	EBC5a, 5b, 5c	Pangboche	Dingboche	2:50	6.2	3.9	485	1591	65	213	+420	1378
7	**AD**	Dingboche	Dingboche								0	0
8	EBC6, EBC7a-7b	Dingboche	Lobuche	4:45	8.3	5.2	625	2051	65	213	+560	1837
9	EBC8a, 8b, 8c	Lobuche	Gorak Shep	7:00	11.3	7.0	598	1962	358	1175	+240	787
10	KP, EBC9a-9b, TP9c	Gorak Shep	Dzongla	8:20	16.7	10.4	833	2733	1153	3783	-320	-1050
11	TP10	Dzongla	Dragnag	6:30	9.9	6.2	730	2395	860	2822	-130	-427
12	TP11, Gokyo Ri	Dragnag	Gokyo	5:30	7.1	4.4	911	2989	861	2825	+50	164
13	**Free Day**	Gokyo	Gokyo								0	0
14	TP12	Gokyo	Lumde	6:15	11.0	6.8	635	2083	1015	3330	-380	-1247
15	TP13a, 13b	Lumde	Namche	7:00	17.8	11.1	321	1053	1251	4105	-930	-3051
16	EBC11a-11d	Namche	Lukla	7:30	19.3	12.0	667	2188	1267	4157	-600	-1969

Trek 8: EBC & Two Passes (Cho La/Kongma La)

17 Days CW (including 2 ADs): this CW itinerary is similar to the TPT except that it skips Renjo La pass. The route ascends the W side of the Dudh Koshi valley to Gokyo. Climb Gokyo Ri before heading E across Cho La pass. Visit EBC and climb KP. Then head SE across Kongma La pass to Chukhung. After climbing Chukhung Ri, descend to Dingboche where you will join the main CEBC route: follow it back to Namche. Although there are only two ADs (Namche and Machermo), the ascent to Gokyo is paced sensibly. That said, we would recommend adding a third AD at Gokyo. This is a CW itinerary but it could also be hiked ACW.

Day	Stages	Start	Finish	Time (hr)	Distance km	miles	Ascent m	ft	Descent m	ft	SA change m	ft
1	EBC1a, 1b	Lukla	Phakding	2:40	8.0	5.0	181	594	411	1348	-230	-755
2	EBC2a, 2b	Phakding	Namche	6:05	11.3	7.0	1086	3563	256	840	+830	2723
3	AD	Namche	Namche								0	0
4	GL3	Namche	Khumjung	2:10	3.4	2.1	425	1394	85	279	+400	1312
5	GL4a-4d	Khumjung	Dhole	4:55	8.3	5.2	869	2851	619	2031	+190	623
6	GL5a, 5b	Dhole	Machermo	3:05	5.3	3.3	465	1526	85	279	+380	1247
7	AD	Machermo	Machermo								0	0
8	GL6	Machermo	Gokyo	3:20	7.6	4.7	443	1453	103	338	+340	1116
9	Gokyo Ri, TP11	Gokyo	Dragnag	5:30	7.1	4.4	861	2825	911	2989	-50	-164
10	TP10	Dragnag	Dzongla	7:00	9.9	6.2	860	2822	730	2395	+130	427
11	TP9c, EBC7b	Dzongla	Lobuche	3:15	6.6	4.1	333	1093	253	830	+80	262
12	EBC8a, 8b, 8c	Lobuche	Gorak Shep	7:00	11.3	7.0	598	1962	358	1175	+240	787
13	KP, EBC9a	Gorak Shep	Lobuche	5:30	10.1	6.3	580	1903	820	2690	-240	-787
14	TP7	Lobuche	Chukhung	7:30	10.9	6.8	840	2756	1020	3347	-180	-591
15	Chukhung Ri, TP6	Chukhung	Dingboche	7:00	12.2	7.6	880	2887	1260	4134	-380	-1247
16	EBC5c, EBC10b-10h	Dingboche	Namche	7:40	20.5	12.7	665	2182	1575	5168	-910	-2986
17	EBC11a-11d	Namche	Lukla	7:30	19.3	12.0	667	2188	1267	4157	-600	-1969

Hiking into the Khumbu (Treks 9 & 10)

Trek 9: Bhandar to Cheplung (5 days)

Day	Stages	Start	Finish	Time (hr)	Distance km	miles	Ascent m	ft	Descent m	ft	SA change m	ft
1	W1a,1b	Bhandar	Sete	6:30	15.3	9.5	1112	3648	782	2566	+330	1083
2	W2a, 2b	Sete	Junbesi	6:45	15.5	9.6	1025	3363	925	3035	+100	328
3	W3a, 3b, 3c	Junbesi	Nunthala	6:45	17.9	11.1	1013	3324	1483	4866	-470	-1542
4	W4a, 4b, 4c	Nunthala	Bupsa	5:10	12.6	7.8	971	3186	831	2727	+140	459
5	W5a, 5b, 5c, 5d	Bupsa	Cheplung	7:45	19.2	11.9	1284	4213	1053	3455	+320	1050

Trek 9: Bhandar to Lukla (5 days)

Day	Stages	Start	Finish	Time (hr)	Distance km	miles	Ascent m	ft	Descent m	ft	SA change m	ft
1	W1a,1b	Bhandar	Sete	6:30	15.3	9.5	1112	3648	782	2566	+330	1083
2	W2a, 2b	Sete	Junbesi	6:45	15.5	9.6	1025	3363	925	3035	+100	328
3	W3a, 3b, 3c	Junbesi	Nunthala	6:45	17.9	11.1	1013	3324	1483	4866	-470	-1542
4	W4a, 4b, 4c	Nunthala	Bupsa	5:10	12.6	7.8	971	3186	831	2727	+140	459
5	W5a, 5b, 5c, AR3	Bupsa	Lukla	8:00	18.1	11.2	1472	4830	1061	3481	+500	1641

Trek 10: Phaplu to Cheplung (3 days)

Day	Stages	Start	Finish	Time (hr)	Distance km	Distance miles	Ascent m	Ascent ft	Descent m	Descent ft	SA change m	SA change ft
1	AR4, W3b-3c	Phaplu	Nunthala	6:00	19	11.8	853	2799	1113	3652	-260	-853
2	W4a-4c	Nunthala	Bupsa	5:10	12.6	7.8	971	3186	831	2727	140	459
3	W5a-5d	Bupsa	Cheplung	7:45	19.2	11.9	1284	4213	1053	3455	320	1050

Stages: Hiking into the Khumbu

Stage	Start	Finish	Finish SA m	Finish SA ft	SA Increase m	SA Increase ft	Time (hr)	Distance km	Distance miles	Ascent m	Ascent ft	Descent m	Descent ft	Max Alt m	Max Alt ft
W1a	Bhandar	Kinja	1610	5282	-630	-2067	3:00	10.4	6.5	152	499	782	2566	2240	7349
W1b	Kinja	Sete	2570	8432	960	3150	3:30	4.9	3.0	960	3150	0	0	2570	8432
W2a	Sete	Goyam	3200	10499	630	2067	2:45	3.8	2.4	630	2067	0	0	3200	10499
W2b	Goyam	Junbesi	2670	8760	-530	-1739	4:00	11.7	7.3	395	1296	925	3035	3530	11582
W3a	Junbesi	Ringmu	2740	8990	70	230	4:15	10.8	6.7	650	2133	580	1903	3020	9909
W3b	Ringmu	Taksindu	2930	9613	190	623	1:30	2.9	1.8	352	1155	162	532	3080	10105
W3c	Taksindu	Nunthala	2200	7218	-730	-2395	1:00	4.2	2.6	11	36	741	2431	2930	9613
W4a	Nunthala	Jubing	1660	5446	-540	-1772	1:40	5.4	3.4	190	623	730	2395	2200	7218
W4b	Jubing	Kharikhola	2050	6726	390	1280	1:30	3.2	2.0	390	1280	0	0	2050	6726
W4c	Kharikhola	Bupsa	2340	7678	290	951	2:00	4.0	2.5	391	1283	101	331	2340	7678
W5a	Bupsa	Puiya	2780	9121	440	1444	3:45	8.1	5.0	700	2297	349	1145	2900	9515
W5b	Puiya	Chheubas	2720	8924	-60	-197	1:00	2.7	1.7	85	279	145	476	2810	9220
W5c	Chheubas	Surke	2280	7481	-440	-1444	1:00	3.8	2.4	89	292	529	1736	2775	9105
W5d	Surke	Cheplung	2660	8727	380	1247	2:00	4.6	2.9	410	1345	30	98	2660	8727
AR3	Surke	Lukla	2840	9318	560	1837	2:15	3.5	2.2	598	1962	38	125	2840	9318
AR4	Phaplu	Ringmu	2740	8990	280	919	3:30	11.9	7.4	490	1608	210	689	2740	8990

Travelling to Bhandar by jeep

Travel to Nepal

Despite the construction of a new airport in Pokhara, all international flights continue to land at Tribhuvan International Airport in Kathmandu: it is small and chaotic but close to the city centre. Currently, there are no direct flights between Nepal and Europe, North America or Australia: travellers from those places usually fly to the Middle East or another Asian destination, before transferring to a flight heading for Kathmandu. The rise of the Middle Eastern airlines like Emirates, Fly Dubai, Qatar Airways and Turkish Airlines means that Dubai, Qatar and Istanbul are very useful hubs for Nepal. From SE Asia, there are also direct flights from Bangkok, Singapore and Kuala Lumpur. There are also plenty of connections via India (mainly Delhi), however, you will need a transit visa for India which makes this a more bureaucratic option. China is also well served with direct flights from several cities. Since Covid, flight prices to Kathmandu have risen and it pays to book well in advance. Those with tight schedules should be aware that, in winter, heavy morning mist (mixed with a lot of pollution) is common and flights scheduled to land early in the day can be delayed.

Visas

Almost everybody needs a visa to enter Nepal and tourist visas are available on arrival at Tribhuvan Airport: this is usually straightforward although you might have to queue. You can also obtain visas in advance from Nepalese embassies outside Nepal but few people do this. To apply for the 'on arrival' visa, there are three steps:

- **Online Tourist Visa Form (OTVF):** you will first need to fill in the OTVF at **www.immigration.gov.np**. It is best to do this online before leaving home, printing off the bar-coded submission receipt: the OTVF expires after 15 days. Alternatively, you can fill in the OTVF at the electronic kiosks at the airport but we do not recommend relying upon them.
- **Payment:** once you have filled in the OTVF, you need to pay for the visa at the payment desk (which is located off to the side of the immigration desks). Do not join the queue for immigration until you have done this: often people forget and get turned back at immigration, having already queued there for a long time. Bring cash to pay for the visa: US$ are best but £ Sterling and Euros should be fine too; if you forget to bring cash then there are ATMs at the airport but we would not recommend relying upon them. Currently, the fee for almost everyone is US$30/50/125 for 15/30/90 days; visas are free for children under 10 years, SAARC citizens and Chinese nationals. Make sure that you obtain a receipt because you will need to show it at the immigration desks.
- **Immigration:** after paying, join the queue for the immigration desks where you will obtain the visa. Afterwards, proceed to the baggage carousels to pick up your baggage.

To navigate this time-consuming process most efficiently, make sure that you know what you need to do before you get off the plane: do not forget to fill in the arrival card (separate from the OTVF) before disembarking the plane. If you have filled in the OTVF online, head immediately to the payment desk: many people will be milling around unsure of where to go and what to do.

Travel from Tribhuvan International Airport to Kathmandu City Centre

Tribhuvan International Airport is 5km E of the city centre: allow 1hr for the journey between them. Many hotels and tour companies offer a pre-arranged airport pick-up service: this is the least stressful option. There is also a booth for official pre-paid taxis by the airport exit: prices to different areas of the city are fixed. Ride sharing services are used in Nepal but, unless you already have a local SIM card, your cell-phone roaming charges are likely to make this an expensive option. Unofficial taxis are also available outside the airport and drivers will approach you as you step outside: although they may offer to take you to the city centre for a lower price than the official fixed fares, you are likely to find that additional fees will be added later or they will take you to the wrong hotel. The cheap local buses are less convenient: they depart from the intersection by the road leading up to the airport and then drop off at the City Bus Park. From there, you will need a taxi to bring you to your hotel so you might as well just take a taxi directly from the airport. Expect heavy traffic on the roads into the city and allow extra time on your return to the airport to catch your outbound flight.

Travel around Kathmandu

Officially Kathmandu is not a huge city, however, nearby towns such as Patan and Bhaktapur have now been consumed by Kathmandu's ever-expanding urban sprawl (which is increasingly drowning in pollution and dust). Traffic throughout Kathmandu and the wider Kathmandu Valley is invariably gridlocked: if, like many trekkers, you do not intend to wander further than the tourist district of Thamel and Kathmandu's old town then it is easiest to travel on foot. However, take care because Kathmandu is not very pedestrian-friendly: often there are no footpaths/side-walks and even in 'pedestrianised' areas, mopeds and taxis still race along the streets. To go further afield, you can take a taxi or an auto-rickshaw: agree the fare before departing (your hotel can help). Alternatively, you could use a ride sharing app: InDrive and Pathao are the most popular and both have apps that you can download onto your phone; Uber does not operate in Nepal.

Travel from Kathmandu to the trail-head

All the main Everest treks start/finish at Lukla: these days, most people take a scheduled aeroplane flight from Kathmandu to Lukla and a smaller number travel there by helicopter. However, 70 years ago, the only way to get to the Khumbu was to walk and a small number of adventurous trekkers still take the time to hike these old trekking routes to Lukla (see p32).

By plane

The airlines which fly to Lukla include Summit Air (**www.summitair.com.np**), Tara Air (**www.taraair.com**) and Sita Air (**www.sitaair.com.np**). The good news is that flights take less than an hour and the views are staggering. The bad news is that there is actually quite a lot of bad news! In fact, many would agree that actually getting to Lukla is the greatest deterrent to trekking in the Khumbu.

Firstly, flying is expensive: around US$170-200 one-way. Secondly, actually getting on the plane can be an ordeal. Because Kathmandu's Tribhuvan Airport is small and has only one runway, it has insufficient capacity to service both international and domestic flights at peak times. Accordingly, in 2022, the authorities announced that all flights to Lukla would instead depart from Ramechhap Airport. Although Ramechhap is only 130km SE of Kathmandu, the roads are poor and the journey to the airport takes 4-5hr: up to 8hr on the return to Kathmandu. This is a significant inconvenience and, because Ramechhap is a small town with few hotels, most trekkers have to travel there on the morning of their flight to Lukla: for weather reasons, all flights to Lukla leave very early in the morning (from 6am) and therefore you need to leave your Kathmandu hotel in the small hours of the morning to make a flight from Ramechhap. To get to Ramechhap, you can rent a private taxi or buy a seat in a tourist mini-bus: hotels/tour companies can arrange this.

Thirdly, a permanent veil of uncertainty shrouds all flights to Lukla. The small planes cannot fly when there is even a hint of bad weather at Lukla. Because the best chance of clear weather, with little wind, is in the early morning, the first flights leave at first light and a rapid cavalcade of planes then rushes to Lukla to land before any cloud arrives. However, cancellations and delays are frequent: if your flight is cancelled, then you can either hang around in Ramechhap until the following day (with little to do and probably nowhere to sleep) or return to Kathmandu and try again the next day.

Fourthly, add a little more confusion into the mix because, even though it has been officially declared that flights to Lukla will depart from Ramechhap, in fact, at certain times of year (normally winter), some flights still leave from Kathmandu airport. Make sure that you check with the airline or your tour company the day before your flight.

Whichever airport your plane is leaving from (or returning to at the end of the trek), it is wise to incorporate a few spare days into your itinerary, in case a flight is cancelled. This is especially important on the return to Kathmandu because you would not want to miss your international flight. One extra day is usually sufficient but, to be on the safe side, two or more are preferable: occasionally, if there is a run of bad weather, flights to/from Lukla can be cancelled for 3 or 4 days in a row. The cancellation of flights is problematic because the following day, you will be competing for a seat with those who are actually scheduled to fly on that day. As an alternative, it can pay to act quickly and try to snag a seat on a helicopter instead: this may cost a lot but that can be better than your plans being thrown into disarray.

Finally, there is one sobering reason why you might not want to travel to Lukla by plane: Lukla is frequently described as the 'world's most dangerous airport'. Whilst the veracity of this statement is debatable, it is fair to say that landing and taking off at Lukla can be sketchy. The runway is very short and sloped (12% incline): when landing, it rises and ends abruptly at the foot of a big cliff. The final approach to the airstrip is narrow too: planes have to squeeze between two mountain slopes and, once the pilot is committed to landing, there is no room to turn the plane around. Furthermore, the high altitude makes the air thin and the planes have less lift. Factor in the reportedly dubious safety and maintenance standards of Nepalese airlines (all of which are banned from EU airspace), and the temperamental weather, and you will quickly understand that nobody looks forward to flying to Lukla. And the return flight from Lukla to Kathmandu can be no less traumatic because the plane will basically free-wheel down the sloping runway before dropping off the end of a cliff! All that said, almost all planes land and take off safely: however, every few years, there is an incident and sometimes there are fatalities.

Baggage allowance: only 15kg of baggage is included within the ticket price for flights to Lukla. You will pay about US$1/kg for excess baggage. The 15kg allowance incorporates both cabin (5kg) and hold bags (10kg).

Lukla Airport

By helicopter

You can also travel to Lukla by helicopter: because helicopter flights still operate out of Kathmandu's Tribhuvan Airport, they can save a lot of time and hassle. Sometimes they can also fly in weather conditions that ground the planes. If your scheduled plane to Lukla is cancelled, then a helicopter may help you to avoid the carnage of the following days when many trekkers are competing to get seats on the planes: move quickly though and ask your trekking company to find you space on a helicopter before everyone else has the same idea!

Helicopter landings and take-offs at Lukla are arguably safer too than on a plane. Another advantage is that you can fly to/from locations other than Lukla (such as Namche or all the way to EBC). Many people end their trek at EBC/Gorak Shep and use helicopters to return downwards to Kathmandu: however, flying in the other direction (upwards towards destinations above Lukla) puts you at increased risk of AMS because you have insufficient time to acclimatise.

There are a few disadvantages to helicopter flights though. Firstly, a helicopter ticket costs considerably more than a plane ticket. The price of a seat varies and depends on demand: if planes are cancelled then the price of helicopter tickets tend to increase. Generally though, you can expect to pay US$300-600 or more per person one way. For the best deals, book in advance through your trekking company. Furthermore, flying in a helicopter also carries risk and occasionally, there are crashes (some of which are fatal). Whether helicopters are more dangerous than the planes of Nepalese airlines is anyone's guess but some say that the pilots who fly helicopters in Nepal tend to be better than those who fly the domestic planes: many of the helicopter pilots are seasonal workers and fly in North America and other places during the remainder of the year.

Helicopters in action at Gorak Shep

By overland transport

Currently, the only way to travel overland to Lukla is to walk there and most people who do that start from Bhandar or Phaplu (see p32). Travelling to those trail-heads can be an ordeal: you can either book a private vehicle or take public transport. Public transport is very cheap and takes the form of shared jeeps which are usually overloaded, uncomfortable and not very safe: even when you think that it would not be possible to squeeze anyone else inside, the driver will often stop and pick up more people. A few hours after leaving Kathmandu, the tarmac ends and you continue on dirt roads which get gradually rougher throughout the unpleasant journey. Journey times vary but plan to spend the whole day crammed into the crowded vehicle: our most recent trip from Kathmandu to Bhandar, for example, took 13hr. A much more pleasant way of making that journey is to hire a private vehicle: it is fairly expensive but makes sense if you are in a small group and can share the cost: the bumpy roads will not change but at least you will have a seat to yourself and the jeep will not make regular stops to pick up/drop off passengers. Most trekking agencies can arrange both public and private transport.

Accommodation

Kathmandu

There is a wide variety of accommodation, catering to all budgets. Before or after your trek, you can choose to crash in a budget hotel or hostel costing US$15-20/night or enjoy one of the city's up-market boutique hotels. In-between there are hundreds of comfortable mid-range hotels. Although quality varies, prices are usually cheaper than in most western cities. Many trekkers stay in the Thamel area (Kathmandu's tourist ghetto) where US$40-50 will snag you a reasonably good mid-range hotel. Most Kathmandu hotels offer hot water, WiFi and a restaurant. The better hotels will book up more quickly but you can usually get something without booking far ahead.

On the trail

Most of the accommodation is in basic trail-side lodges. Although the Everest region has probably the best selection of trekking accommodation in Nepal, there is little to differentiate one place from another. In the past, a trail-side lodge was known as a tea-house and some people still use this term: before the advent of trekking, tea-houses were used exclusively by herders and traders who could get a basic meal and space on the floor to sleep. Although tea-houses like these still exist in remote corners of the Nepalese mountains, you will not find them along the Everest trekking trails: here the trail-side accommodation is less basic and the properties are more accurately referred to as trekking lodges.

Although modern lodges are considerably more comfortable than the traditional tea-houses, they frequently have a similar layout. All life centres around the dining room because it is the warmest place: it is normally lined with tables and chairs and has a large samovar-like stove in the middle (around which people huddle for warmth). The dining rooms usually have large windows which enable the sun to heat the room during the day: unfortunately, however, they are single-glazed and the heat escapes rapidly again after the sun sets. The dining room is where you will buy food and drinks and it is often the only place where the WiFi will work and where you can charge your electronic equipment.

Bedrooms are normally small and wood-panelled with two single beds. There will be a bed sheet and sometimes blankets but most people chose to use their own sleeping bag. The rooms are poorly insulated and are very cold at night. The thin walls mean that you can almost hear whispers in the neighbouring room. There will usually be a shared toilet/bathroom in the corridor outside although occasionally, there are more expensive rooms with en-suite facilities. Bathrooms are normally cleaned regularly but they are cold and are not places to linger in. Increasingly, there are hot showers (solar or gas powered) although there is an

Typical lodge bedroom

additional charge for them (US$5-6). In the past, your bed was often free of charge if you ate all your meals in the lodge: these days, that is rarely the case and virtually every lodge charges around US$4-6/night for a bed. Except in Lukla and Namche, it is expected that you will eat breakfast and dinner in your lodge: in any case, few trekkers are inclined to eat elsewhere because it is so cold outside during the evening and early morning.

In Lukla and Namche, in addition to standard lodges, you can find some more upmarket accommodation offering electric blankets, power sockets in the room and en-suite facilities with hot water. Naturally, all this comes at a cost. There are also a small number of genuinely luxurious offerings costing upwards of US$100/night.

If you are trekking in an organised group, all accommodation will be taken care of by the guide and often it is booked in advance. However, independent trekkers do not normally book in advance and simply organise accommodation on arrival each day. Outside the peak periods, you will have little problem finding a lodge. However, at peak times, lodges can be full and it can be prudent to arrive earlier in the day (especially in places like Tengboche and Dughla where there is limited accommodation): this is where it pays to have a guide who can often call ahead to reserve a room at a lodge (often at their preferred place).

Typical lodge (Pangboche)

Food

Kathmandu

There are a wide variety of restaurants serving all types of local and international food. In fact, the city has arguably the best selection of food in Asia: Indian, Chinese, pizzas, steaks and burgers are all available cheaply. In particular, Thamel is stuffed full of restaurants and cafés catering to foreign tastes. Throughout the city, there are also numerous good Nepalese and Tibetan restaurants, as well as cheaper places catering to local workers. In fact, outside of Thamel and other tourist zones, the food quality can be better and prices lower.

On the trail

Food choice on the trail is more limited and more expensive, which is not surprising when you consider that all ingredients have to be carried up to altitude on the backs of animals or porters. That said, the Khumbu probably has a wider variety of food than any other Himalayan mountain region. You will find the broadest choice in Lukla and Namche which have dozens of restaurants serving international dishes. Above Namche, however, menus become more limited and are almost identical: usually there is a mix of local and western dishes. Prices also rise the higher you climb but everything is still reasonably priced by western standards. However, do not expect authentic western food with imported ingredients: normally you will be presented with a Nepalese approximation of the dish, cooked using whatever ingredients were available. As long as you are not too exacting, and have a sense of humour, everything is normally perfectly edible! Hygiene standards have improved greatly over recent years and stomach upsets, although still common, are less frequent than before.

Egg Noodles

Breakfast: eggs, porridge, cereals, toast and pancakes are common. Sometimes you will also find a few tasty Tibetan dishes such as tsampa: this porridge-like dish, made from barley and Tibetan tea, is delicious with honey and warm Tibetan bread. Tea and coffee (normally instant) are always available. It is a good idea to order your breakfast the night before to avoid a long wait the following morning.

Momos

Lunch: you will normally eat lunch at a trail-side lodge. Menus everywhere are similar but the closer to EBC you climb, the higher the prices. Lunch menus are exactly the same as dinner menus (see below). At lunchtime, bear in mind that some things take longer to prepare than others: order something quick if you are eager to get back on the trail. Simple dishes like noodles, rice or soup are usually served quickly. Anything else can take a lot longer to cook. Even dhal bhat (which is Nepal's national dish of rice, lentils and curried vegetables) can take a surprisingly long time in trekkers' restaurants.

Dinner: Lukla and Namche aside, you are expected to eat dinner in the lodge at which you are staying. However, this is no imposition as

Dhal bhat

menus are similar everywhere with similar prices. In the evening, with more time to spare, there is no issue with choosing something that takes longer to prepare. You will find a variety of dishes with rice, noodles or potatoes. Pizzas, curries, burgers, chicken and yak steaks are available too. And, there is always dhal bhat, spring rolls and momos (delicious Tibetan-style dumplings which are either steamed or fried). You might also find thukpa which is a hearty Tibetan stew. To avoid a long wait at dinner time, order your food when you arrive in the afternoon.

Egg fried rice

Drinks: because it is cold and most people do not drink alcohol at altitude, hot drinks are a big thing when trekking in the Khumbu. Coffee and a variety of different teas (black, green, mint, ginger, lemon & masala) are available everywhere. Ginger tea is said to help altitude acclimatisation. Bottled water is also sold everywhere but trekkers are increasingly discouraged from buying it due to the difficulty in disposing of the plastic bottle afterwards: in any case, you can save a lot of money by treating your own water instead of buying bottles (see p69). Beer and stronger alcoholic drinks are available but above Namche, they are expensive and (for reasons of acclimatisation) are best avoided. Teas are cheap but drinks in a can/bottle are expensive because they are heavy and have to be carried up to the lodges.

Vegetarians: it is easy to be vegetarian in Nepal. For religious reasons, the concept of being a vegetarian is well understood and many Nepali dishes contain no meat (though unexpected pieces of meat do sometimes appear!). That said, if you are hoping to survive on crisp, fresh salads and soya then you are out of luck. The climate around Everest means that the range of fruit and vegetables grown is limited: there are plenty of potatoes but, more often than not, they find themselves in an unhealthy frying pan. Vegans will have a harder time finding appropriate food.

A porter near EBC

A Typical Trekking Day

Island Peak BC hike (SR3)

The average day on the trail starts early with most people shivering their way out of their sleeping bags around 6-6:30am. Breakfast will be served in the communal dining room where you will find trekkers huddling around the stove. You will probably hit the trail by 7-7:30am and, depending upon your itinerary, you will reach your destination somewhere between lunchtime and late afternoon. Although it is quite a long day, high altitude means that you will travel more slowly than usual and distances tend to be shorter than on low altitude treks. If you have a guide, your altitude acclimatisation will be one of his key concerns and he will seek to ensure that you do not travel too quickly. Furthermore, there will be numerous breaks for snacks, photos, pausing to chat with locals and fellow trekkers, and simply taking in the magnificent views. Normally, you will also stop at a lodge along the way for a tea break and/or lunch.

Be aware that any gear carried by porters will not be accessible during the day until you get to the overnight stop: in your day-pack, you should carry extra warm clothing, waterproofs and anything else you might need during the hike.

On reaching the overnight stop, most people head straight to the dining room for a hot drink and perhaps a slice of apple pie. Meanwhile, the porters will normally carry your bags to your room. Often you will have plenty of time to relax in the afternoon before dinner. Some try to find a seat in the sun somewhere but others like to climb a little further to a nearby viewpoint: the latter option can help greatly with altitude acclimatisation.

As the sun drops, temperatures fall dramatically: you will probably need to put on your warmest gear and huddle around the heater again. Dinner is served early (5-6pm) and your guide will be keen to get this finished because he will not get to relax until after you are safely in bed. Most people are in their sleeping bags before 9pm, desperately trying to keep warm.

On the Trail

Taboche, Everest, Nuptse, Lhotse & Ama Dablam

Costs & budgeting

For most western travellers, Nepal will not seem overly expensive. Food, accommodation and transport are generally good value. In Kathmandu, basic hotel rooms start at around US$15-20 per night, however, US$40-50 will buy more comfort. Food is cheap everywhere with the Nepalese classic dhal bhat normally costing only a few US$ outside of mountain areas. Western dishes (such as pizza or steak) will cost more, however, even in the Kathmandu tourist ghetto of Thamel, you will rarely pay more than US$10-15 for a meal with a beer. Public transport is very cheap everywhere, except for flights within Nepal which are fairly expensive (US$170-200 one-way to Lukla).

Costs along the trail are usually low too, even though the Khumbu is probably the most expensive mountain region in Nepal. Simple lodge accommodation costs US$4-8/night per person. A meal of dhal bhat, noodles, rice or momos costs US$5-10: if you order simple dishes like these, you are unlikely to spend more than US$20/day on food (and many survive on less). However, if you order treats like apple pie, yak steaks, burgers and pizzas (which can be hard to resist after a long day on the trail), your costs will increase. As for drinks, tea is cheap but anything canned/bottled is expensive (as it needs to be carried up). In fact, as you climb towards EBC, all costs tend to rise with you because the lodges' cost of resupply increases.

	Approximate Cost (Kathmandu)	Approximate Cost (Khumbu)
Mid-range hotel/ upmarket trekking lodge (Double/twin room)	US$40-50/room	US$50-100/room
Trekking lodge/budget hotel (Double/twin room)	US$15-30/room	US$4-8/person
Breakfast meal	US$4-7	US$4-7
Meal at lunch/dinner	US$3-12	US$5-10
Apple pie	US$4-6	US$3-6
Beer (0.5L)	US$3-4	US$6-10
Coke	US$1-5	US$4-7
Boiled water (1 litre)	N/A	US$4-7
Shower	Free	US$5-6
WiFi (24hr)	Free	US$4-7
Guide (excluding tips)	N/A	US$35-45/day
Porter (excluding tips)	N/A	US$25/day

At the date of press, US$1 was worth around NPR133

Weather

Although the monsoon instils a certain amount of predictability into the Khumbu's climate, you should never forget that it is a mountainous region at very high altitude. At any time of year, high winds, snow, heavy rain, low cloud and poor visibility are possible: winds can be ferocious, especially near the TPT's high passes. Poor visibility can make some paths hard to follow and snow can completely obscure the trail. Conditions can change very quickly and temperatures can drop very low. Nepal's trekking disaster of October 2014 is a cautionary tale: at least 20 trekkers died in the Annapurna region during a snowstorm in which 1.8m of snow fell in 12 hours.

This information is not intended to discourage you but to make you aware of the conditions that you might face and to ensure that you carry gear which can cope with them. If you can, obtain a weather forecast on your smartphone before setting out each day. The website of the Nepalese Government's Meteorological Forecasting Division provides daily forecasts, although their format is not very user-friendly (**www.mfd.gov.np**). Many other internet sites and apps also provide forecasts, with a varying degree of reliability. The information at **www.mountain-forecast.com** is often well-regarded: it has forecasts for many summits including KP and Gokyo Ri. If you are concerned about a forecast or you are unable to obtain one on your smartphone, then it is sensible to discuss the conditions with your guide and/or staff at the lodges: their understanding of local weather conditions is often invaluable and you should follow their advice if they tell you it is not safe to hike.

Park fees, permits & entry requirements

Currently, you require two permits to trek in the Everest region. The SNP Entry Permit and the Khumbu Pasang Lhamu Rural Municipality Entry Permit (KPLP). If you are using a trekking company, then they will organise these for you: check with them in advance what paperwork they will require from you. However, if you are trekking independently then you will have to organise it yourself (although a guide will usually assist).

SNP Entry Permit: costs around NPR3000 (NPR1500 for SAARC citizens). You can buy it at the Nepal Tourist Board in Kathmandu (Pradarshani Marg, 44617) or at the SNP entrance in Monjo.

KPLP: replacing the TIMS (Trekker Information Management System) card for the Everest region, the KPLP is issued by the local authorities in the Khumbu region and costs around NPR2000. You can buy this along the trail at the checkpoints in Lukla or Monjo: arrive at the checkpoints early in the day to avoid queues.

Those walking between Bhandar/Phaplu and Cheplung/Lukla will also need a third permit: the Gaurishankar Conservation Area Permit covers the protected area S of Lukla. It costs around NPR2000-3000 and can also be obtained at the Nepal Tourist Board in Kathmandu.

To obtain any of these permits, you need to present your passport with a valid Nepal visa. You may also be asked for one or two passport-sized photos for each permit: in recent years, we have not needed these but it is better to have them just in case. Alternatively, you may be asked for a digital passport-sized photo: take a selfie (against a neutral background) on your smartphone in advance. If obtaining permits in Kathmandu, allow at least half a day to complete the process. Be aware that rules and regulations change frequently.

Maps

In this book, there are 1:40,000 scale maps for every stage of the treks. Because we were unable to find commercially available maps which fulfilled our requirements, we commissioned our own maps: we believe that these are the finest maps available for the Everest treks (with the largest scale of any map available for the Khumbu). They are perfect for navigation on the trail. However, we also recommend obtaining our 1:40,000 scale sheet map for the region: '**Trekking Map: Everest Base Camp (ISBN 9781912933532)**'; it makes it easier to plan the trek, identify peaks/features along the trail and navigate in poor conditions. It covers the entire

Khumbu region and can be used seamlessly with this book. It is best to buy this map before leaving home because it is not available in Nepal. It is available from **www.knifeedgeoutdoor.com**, online retailers and many shops.

Alternatively, in shops in Kathmandu, Lukla and Namche, you will find a confusing array of locally produced maps for the Khumbu. Those made by Map House and Nepal Map Publisher are the most common: although they come in a variety of different shapes, scales and sizes, the information displayed on each seems to be similar. They are fine for planning but, in our opinion, they are of limited use for navigation: accordingly, since most trekkers do most of their planning before arriving in Nepal, it is probably better to buy a map before leaving your home country. In any case, the largest scale of the locally available maps is 1:50,000 which is less favourable than the 1:40,000 scale map produced by Knife Edge Outdoor Guidebooks. Furthermore, you should exercise caution when using some locally produced maps: trekkers frequently complain that some paths shown are not in fact suitable for trekking or do not even exist. You could also consider the Everest Base Camp map by National Geographic (1:50,000; 2019): however, it does not cover the whole W side of the Khumbu and is therefore not suitable for some of the treks (including the TPT).

Paths and Waymarking

Typically, paths are clear, well-defined and straightforward to walk upon. However, occasionally, there are rocky sections which are more challenging. The terrain undulates regularly and gradients can be steep: sometimes drops are sheer and occasionally, ropes/chains have been fixed to the rocks for safety. Some paths can be muddy and slippery after rain. In general, the CEBC's paths are extremely well-trodden, well maintained and simple to navigate. However, away from the CEBC, the trails are sometimes rougher, steeper and more exposed.

Route-finding along the CEBC is usually straightforward even though there are few signs or waymarks. Even away from the CEBC, route-finding is largely straightforward in good conditions, however, there are a few sections where paths are less easy to follow and navigation is more difficult: for example, where the trail crosses rocky zones and around the TPT's high passes (where snow can remain). Furthermore, because fewer people walk the trails away from the CEBC, snow covering paths gets tracked by others less quickly, making progress and navigation more difficult. Always be wary of following someone else's footprints: although there is a good chance that they are on the correct path, it is obviously possible that they may have strayed from the trail.

Water

For a number of reasons, the body's rate of loss of fluids is greater at altitude, making dehydration more likely than normal. Firstly, because there is less oxygen in the air you breathe, your body compensates by breathing more rapidly while it is undergoing the process of altitude acclimatisation. Your body expels moisture in exhaled air so the faster you breathe, the more fluid you lose: this is exacerbated by the inherent dryness of mountain air. Furthermore, the process of acclimatisation requires your body to expel bicarbonate and it does this by increased urination which results in additional fluid loss. To replace lost fluids, you will have to drink much more than usual while your body is acclimatising. Consequently, drinking water will be one of your primary considerations each day and it can be a challenge to force yourself to consume the often recommended 4-5 litres/day.

Generally, it is not advisable to drink untreated tap water in Nepal. Furthermore, we do not recommend drinking water from a river, stream or lake, without first dealing with possible contaminants including visible particulates, bacteria, viruses, protozoa (for example, giardia) and parasites. Even though most of the water sources in the Khumbu are thought to be safe, why risk consuming a pathogen that could make you sick and spoil your trip when there are many different ways of ensuring that your water is clean?

The most obvious solution is to buy bottled water which is widely available in the countless lodges and shops along the trails. However, these days, the use of disposable plastic bottles is discouraged for environmental reasons: to remove plastic waste from mountain areas, it has to be carried out by porters (which is difficult) or flown out in helicopters (which is expensive); as a result, some of it reportedly gets burnt or buried locally instead. Furthermore, stories abound of plastic bottles being refilled locally with tap water and then resealed. As an alternative to bottled water, lodges also sell boiled water but this is expensive and you have no guarantee that it has been properly boiled. If you are relying on bottled or boiled water, then filling up is simply a matter of stopping at a lodge or shop along the route.

However, the cheapest and most environmentally friendly solution is to purify tap or stream water yourself by using the correct equipment or chemicals. There are a variety of possible ways to treat water yourself:

- **Boiling** is the traditional method, however, it is not a realistic option for treks in the Khumbu because few trekkers will want to carry a stove and source fuel. A rolling boil of 1min should kill everything in the water. However, it does not remove visible particulates so the boiled water will remain the same colour as when you found it, which can be off-putting.
- **Filtering** usually removes visible particulates, working miracles by turning coloured water clear. It also normally removes around 99.9% of bacteria, protozoa and parasites. Filters are often cheap and light. It is the quickest method of treatment so it is useful for long-distance routes. However, most filters cannot remove viruses (unlikely but still possible in the Khumbu): if you are concerned about viruses then you will need to invest in one of the more expensive filters that remove them or combine filtering with another method (boiling, UV or chemical treatment).
- **Chemical treatment** can remove bacteria, protozoa, viruses and parasites: each product is different so read the labels carefully. However, there are many disadvantages to chemicals: they do not remove visible particulates so the water will remain the same colour as when you found it; water treated with chemicals often has a taste (although you can usually buy different chemicals to deal with that); the water usually cannot be drunk immediately as chemicals take time to kill pathogens; and from a health perspective, consuming chemicals may not be good for you.
- **UV treatment** kills bacteria, protozoa, viruses and parasites. However, it does not remove visible particulates so the water will remain the same colour as when you found it: coloured water can be off-putting and the UV treatment is less effective if the water is not completely clear. That said, coloured water is not usually a problem on these treks. The most common products are Steripens which are very light. The main disadvantage is that they require batteries which will need to be recharged/replaced periodically: furthermore, batteries can fail in the Khumbu's low temperatures.

Perhaps the most practical single method for this trek is filtering: many hikers drink water which has only been filtered with a standard filter, running a small risk of virus contamination. However, we prefer to be more cautious and use a filter which removes viruses (such as the MSR Guardian Purifier).

The actual effectiveness of individual products varies and is beyond the scope of this book so do your research beforehand. However, it is worth noting that many products claim to be only 99.9% effective indicating that drinking water from wild sources can never be said to be 100% risk free. You will have to weigh up the risks and make up your own mind. You drink the water at your own risk!

	Visible Particulates	Bacteria	Virus	Protozoa	Parasites
Boiling	✗	✓	✓	✓	✓
Filter	✓	✓	Only top of the range filters remove viruses	✓	✓
Chemical Treatment	✗	✓	✓	✓	✓
UV Treatment (such as Steripen)	✗	✓	✓	✓	✓

If, like many, you do decide to drink from natural sources then, as well as treating the water, there are a few rules that you should follow to reduce further any risk:

- Avoid water where there is evidence nearby of animals: carcasses (of dead animals) or faeces can cause contamination
- Do not collect water downstream from buildings or grazing areas
- Preferably drink from moving water. The faster the better
- The bigger the river/stream the better
- Generally the higher the altitude the better

It is good practice to start the day with around 1.5 litres of water: that should last most people until they reach the next fill-up point (whether a lodge, shop or stream). Plan carefully so that you know where the next fill-up point is: always check your water levels when you pass one.

Storing Bags

If you wish to spend some time in Kathmandu (or elsewhere) after the trek, then you will probably have additional baggage which you need to store while trekking. Because most flights to Lukla depart in the morning, trekkers usually spend at least one night in Kathmandu before the trek. Normally, hotels in Kathmandu will store your bags until your return: some may charge extra for this so check when booking. Alternatively, if you did not want to return to Kathmandu after your trek, you could leave surplus luggage at a lodge in Lukla: however, remember that the baggage allowance on internal flights is usually 15kg and you will have to pay a small additional charge for extra luggage (see p60). Wherever you store your bags, ensure that they are locked and do not leave valuables inside.

Outdoor shops

Usually, it is best to source all your equipment in your home country so that you arrive in Nepal with all the necessary gear. However, it is possible to buy almost anything you will need in Kathmandu and, to a lesser extent, Lukla and Namche: in particular, Kathmandu's Thamel area is packed with outdoor stores. However, be aware that most of the clothes and equipment purporting to be manufactured by big-name outdoor brands are in fact fakes made cheaply in Nepal. They may look pretty good but they will be made with cheaper, less technical materials and their seams may soon split. That said, they are very cheap (especially if you haggle) and, if you only need them to last for one trek, then they will probably do fine. In recent years, a few shops have opened in Kathmandu which do sell genuine branded gear but, with so many knock-offs kicking around elsewhere, it is difficult to be certain that the gear is, in fact, real.

Some outdoor shops in Kathmandu (and sometimes Lukla and Namche) also rent gear such as sleeping bags and down jackets. However, you normally have to leave a large deposit and therefore it can be better simply to buy them outright. Many outdoor shops also sell gas canisters: if you are flying to Lukla, buy them there because you are not permitted to carry them on internal flights.

Drones

The use of drones is not permitted in the SNP or the SNP buffer zone between Lukla and Monjo (unless you buy an expensive commercial licence). This means that you cannot fly drones anywhere N of Lukla and it is not therefore worth bothering to bring one.

Charging electronic equipment

In Kathmandu, most hotels have power sockets in the bedrooms. However, high up in the Khumbu, electricity is at a premium because power comes largely from solar panels. Although there are charging facilities at most trekking lodges, there are rarely electrical sockets in bedrooms: there are usually communal sockets in the dining area but there is an additional charge to use them (and it can be expensive); furthermore, you may have to queue. Consequently, many trekkers prefer to bring their own portable battery packs: depending upon how many devices you need to charge, 10,000-20,000 mAh should be sufficient to last the entire CEBC with only a couple of top-ups. Portable solar panels are useful too but they can be quite heavy to carry.

Most hotels/trekking lodges catering to foreigners have sockets for the two-pin Type-C plug used in Europe. However, Nepal also uses Type-D and Type-M which are both 3-pin plugs. You can usually get by with Type-C in the Khumbu: however, those hiking into the Khumbu might stay in older lodges which only have Type-D/M sockets. You can buy adapters cheaply online.

The Khumbu Glacier near EBC

Equipment

Lhotse at sunrise

If you are carrying your own pack then the more it weighs, the harder the trek will be. Lugging a heavy pack can make you very tired (possibly hampering altitude acclimatisation) and can lead to exhaustion, injury and/or abandonment: give equipment choice careful consideration as it will be crucial to your enjoyment of the trek and the likelihood of success.

However, most trekkers carry only a light day-pack on the trail, using a porter to transport the bulk of their gear to their nightly stop. But that does not mean that there are no limits on how much gear you can bring because the more your bag weighs, the harder your porter's trek will be. Officially, porters are not permitted to carry more than 30kg but because bags are rarely weighed, they sometimes end up carrying more than that. Often porters carry the duffel bags of two trekkers (as well as their own gear) and accordingly, most responsible trekking companies restrict clients to 10-12kg of porter-carried equipment: this does not, in fact, allow you to bring much surplus kit.

Accordingly, whether you are carrying your own gear or employing a porter, you should be aiming to keep your pack as light as possible. However, it can be tricky to put this into practice when there are so many things that you 'need' in daily life. Many trekkers bring equipment which is unnecessary or simply too heavy. With experience, it becomes easier to sift between essentials and luxuries but, if you have not previously undertaken a multi-day trek, this can be an unfathomable dilemma. However, if you follow the advice here, and limit yourself to the items on our checklist, then you should not go far wrong.

When it comes to hiking clothing and equipment, weights can vary enormously. An investment in some modern lightweight gear can help reduce your pack weight greatly. Many people are quick to tell you that the lighter the gear, the greater the price but that is not always the case. While it is true that lightweight gear can be expensive, there are also some excellent lightweight products which are great value. Sleeping bags and backpacks are the two heaviest items you will use and so they offer the biggest opportunities for weight-saving. However, do not ignore the smaller items either as the weight can quickly add up. Be ruthless as every ounce counts.

Recommended basic kit

When undertaking any long-distance route, you should be properly equipped for the worst terrain and the worst weather conditions which you could encounter. Although the Khumbu is normally dry during the main trekking seasons, rain or snow is always a possibility and you should bring clothing to deal with it: getting wet will make you cold and, at high altitude, that can be dangerous. Even in dry weather, the climate is cold (particularly in the evenings) so warm clothing is a priority. Furthermore, the sun is fierce at altitude and you will need gear to protect against sun exposure too.

Layering of clothing is the key to managing body temperature. In cool weather, layers can be added: warm air becomes trapped between the layers, acting as insulation. In warmer weather, you simply remove layers and carry them in your day-pack. For base-layers and mid-layers, merino wool or man-made materials are preferable: they are lightweight and warm and they wick moisture away from the skin. Do not wear cotton: it is heavy and it does not dry quickly (making you cold). For insulated jackets, duck or goose down is the warmest and lightest filling (see 'Sleeping bags' on p77).

Boots/Shoes	Good quality, properly fitting and worn in. Robust soles (such as Vibram) are advisable. Some use trail-running shoes but many prefer boots with ankle support. Shoes/boots with a waterproof membrane (such as Gore-Tex) are good, particularly if there is snow on the ground.
Socks	2-3 pairs of good quality, quick-drying walking socks. A mix of medium and heavy-weight socks is a good idea: keep the warmest pair for EBC and KP. Light-weight socks will not be warm enough for most trekkers.
Waterproof jacket	Although it is usually dry in the main hiking seasons, rain or snow is always a possibility. Even if it does not rain, a waterproof jacket will also protect you from wind: you can layer a waterproof over the top of a down jacket. Breathable fabrics are best. Few trekkers bring waterproof trousers.
Down jacket	An insulated jacket is light and extremely warm. More than any other item of clothing, this will keep you cosy, especially in the evening and early morning. Jackets filled with goose/duck down are best (see 'Sleeping bags' on p77). Choose a jacket with a higher fill-weight (i.e. more down): the lighter jackets will not be warm enough.
Base-layers: Top	2-3 T-shirts/long-sleeved tops: man-made fabrics or merino wool, which wick moisture away from your body. Keep the warmest one for EBC/KP.
Base-layers: Bottom	2-3 pairs of underwear: man-made fabrics or merino wool. 1 pair of merino long-johns: can be used under trousers during the day (for extra warmth) or as pyjamas at night.
Fleeces	2 fleeces: one thick and one thin. Man-made fabrics. We like hoodies with full-length zips because they are best for managing body temperature.
Trousers	2 pairs of walking trousers. Standard walking trousers are normally fine: at higher altitudes, you can wear your long-johns underneath. However, we like to bring 1 pair of standard trousers (for the lower altitudes and warmer days) and 1 pair of windproof soft-shell trousers for higher altitudes. Few people wear shorts at altitude, however, convertible trousers may be useful if you are walking to Lukla through the middle hills: you have the option to remove the legs on warm days. Skimpy shorts are not culturally appropriate in Nepal: furthermore, those who prefer to trek in skirts should also wear leggings.

Warm gloves, hat and buff	As you get higher, you will increasingly depend on these items to keep your hands, head and neck warm.
Sunglasses, sun hat, sunscreen and lip salve	The sun at high altitude is strong and can quickly cause sun-burn: do not set out without these items. Sunglasses should be of good quality to protect your eyes from the strong UV rays: polarising lenses are an excellent choice. Good sunglasses cannot be replaced on a trek so keep them in a hard case to avoid breakage.
Duffel bag	Most trekkers use a duffel bag to hold gear to be carried by a porter: 60-80 litres should be sufficient. Many tour companies provide them or you can buy your own (either at home or in Kathmandu). Make sure you use an internal pack-liner: see below.
Backpack	If you are using a porter, a day-pack of 25-35 litres should be sufficient to hold the items that you will require during the day (waterproof jacket, down jacket, snacks, camera, etc.). If you are carrying all your own gear, 55-75 litres should be adequate. If you need a pack bigger than these then you are most likely carrying too much. The difference in the weights of various backpacks can be surprisingly large: some are quite heavy so check before buying. Look for well-padded shoulder straps and waist band. Much of the weight of the pack should sit on your hips rather than your shoulders.
Waterproof pack-liners	Most backpacks and duffel bags are not completely waterproof. Internal liners will keep your gear dry if it rains. Many trekkers use external pack covers but we do not find them to be very useful: they flap in the wind and, in heavy rain, water still leaks into the pack around the straps (so you need an internal liner anyway).
Sleeping bag	To ensure that you are warm at night, you should bring a sleeping bag: see p77. Pillows are supplied but you might want to bring a pillow case.
Water purification equipment/ chemicals	Unless you are planning to buy bottled/boiled water, you will need to bring a filter, steripen or chemicals to purify water for drinking: see p69.
Water bottle	1 to 1.5 litres should be sufficient.
Head-light with spare batteries	If you are planning to climb KP for sunrise then you will start hiking in the dark and will need a head-light. It is also useful in lodges for finding the bathrooms at night.
Whistle	For emergencies. Many rucksacks have one incorporated into the sternum strap.
First-aid kit	See p76.
Map, compass & GPS device	If you do not have a guide, a map and compass are essential. For maps, see p68. A GPS unit or smart-phone mapping app is a useful addition but they are no substitute for a map/compass: after all, batteries can die and electronics can fail (especially, in the Khumbu's low temperatures).
Phone and charging cable	A smartphone is a very useful tool on a trek. It allows you to keep in touch with people at home and can be used for emergencies. Furthermore, apps for weather, mapping and hotel booking are invaluable. It can also serve as your camera, saving weight.
Nepal plug adapter	For charging electronic equipment, see p72
Portable battery pack	Many people carry their own battery packs: see p72. Anker make good ones.

Ziplock plastic bag	A lightweight way of keeping money and passports dry.
Emergency food	Carry some emergency food over and above your planned daily rations. Energy bars, nuts and dried fruit are all good.
Toilet paper and trowel	Bring a backpacking trowel in case nature calls on the trail: bury toilet waste and carry out used toilet paper. Do not burn used toilet paper: this can cause bush-fires.
Hand Sanitiser	Sanitising hands before eating can help you to avoid stomach problems.
Toiletries	If you wish to take showers, a small hotel-size bottle of shower gel should be enough to last the trek, saving weight. An almost empty toothpaste tube will also save weight. Leave that make-up behind!
Pee bottle	When acclimatising, you will need to pee a lot more than usual. This can involve many long (and very cold) trips to the communal bathrooms in the lodges at night. It might sound unpleasant but using a pee bottle will get you back in your sleeping bag faster: you can empty it the following morning.
Towel	You will need a towel to take showers. Lightweight trekking towels are best.
Cash	Nepal is a cash economy: see p83
Insurance details	Carry details of your rescue and medical insurance in your day-pack in case you need it on the trail: see p83.
Hiking poles	These transfer weight from your legs onto your arms, keeping you fresher. They also save your knees (particularly on descents) and can reduce the likelihood of falling or twisting an ankle. Poles are invaluable in snowy conditions.
Hiking crampons/ micro-spikes	Useful for those trekking in snowy conditions, particularly in early spring. Most CEBC/GLT trekkers will not need them but they are recommended if you are crossing any of the three high passes of the TPT.
Small padlock	Many lodge bedrooms do not have locks. Some trekkers carry a small padlock for piece of mind although frequently, the flimsy doors would be simple to breach even if locked.

First-aid kit

Above Namche, medication is hard to find and it is a good idea to carry a first-aid kit. It is best to buy everything you might need before arriving in Nepal although, these days, most items are available in Kathmandu, Lukla and Namche. Recommended items include:

- Plasters, bandages, dressings, antiseptic (wipes or liquid).
- Blister plasters, moleskin padding and/or tape (such as Leukotape): useful to prevent or combat blisters.
- Painkillers: Paracetamol (Acetaminophen/Tylenol) and/or an anti-inflammatory such as Ibuprofen (Advil).
- Acetazolamide (Diamox): see p12.
- Throat lozenges: can help with the Khumbu Cough (see p82).
- Electrolytes: help to prevent or treat dehydration.

Sleeping bags

Lodges do not always provide blankets or duvets so you will need a sleeping bag (unless you are staying in one of the region's few luxury lodges). And because the Khumbu is so cold at night, you will need a warm one: the lower levels of oxygen in the air you breathe makes sleeping at high altitude uncomfortable enough and you will not want to make things worse by having to shiver your way through the night.

Choosing a sleeping bag can be surprisingly difficult. Every sleeping bag has a 'comfort rating': this is the lowest temperature at which the standard woman should enjoy a comfortable night's sleep. There is also a 'lower comfort limit' which is for men. That may sound simple but it is not. Although all reputable sleeping bag manufacturers use the same independent standard, the bags are not tested in the same place so there is a lack of consistency amongst ratings. Also, the ratings are designed with an average man and woman in mind, however, every person is different: some people get colder than others and need a warmer bag. The ratings should therefore be used as a guide only and it is wise to choose a bag with a comfort rating which is at least 5°C lower than the night temperatures that you are likely to encounter.

If in doubt, be cautious and over-spec: if you are slightly too warm, it is easy to unzip the bag for ventilation but if you are too cold, then you will just have to grin and bear it. Warmer bags are heavier but this will be less of an issue for those using a porter. However, if you are carrying all your own gear then you will need to give weight more consideration: although you want to be warm at night, you do not want to bring a bag that is much too warm as that would add unnecessary weight to your pack.

The season may also play a part in your decision-making: winter, for example, is colder than late spring. On balance, we recommend a comfort rating of between -15°C and -30°C, depending on whether you sleep hot or cold. We use a -30°C bag in the Khumbu in all trekking seasons and have never regretted that decision.

Unfortunately, with sleeping bags, price tends to be inversely proportional to weight. This is largely because the lightest bags are filled with goose/duck down which is expensive. Synthetic bags are also available but they are much heavier so down is a better choice for trekking. The disadvantage of down bags is that they can lose their warmth if they get wet but that is not likely if you have a good pack-liner. Our advice is first to decide what comfort rating you will require. Then choose the lightest bag (with that rating) which you can afford.

Pangboche

Responsible Trekking

Pumori seen from the route to Ama Dablam BC (SR1)

Trekkers in the Khumbu should obey all the usual rules for hiking: leave no trace; remove all rubbish; avoid damaging plants or disturbing wildlife; carry out 'bathroom activities' well away from watercourses. In addition, there are some other trekking rules which you should follow that are specific to Nepal.

Porters: although they are an essential part of the trekking industry in Nepal, porters are at the bottom of the hierarchy pyramid and are sometimes badly treated or placed in dangerous situations. Some studies have found that porters have been involved in four times as many accidents as trekkers. Often they carry too much and walk in unsuitable footwear/clothing. On occasion, they have been left behind in difficult weather conditions after falling ill. Before starting your trek, ensure that your group has enough porters for the amount of equipment. It is generally accepted that one porter can carry the gear of two trekkers provided that each trekker has no more than 15kg of gear (packed into a single duffel bag). In fact, many trekking companies request that a trekker's gear weighs no more than 10-12kg. Guides should ensure that porters are not overloaded, however, porters rarely complain so this is often overlooked. If you think your porter is overloaded then speak to your guide about it.

If you are trekking independently, also check that the porters and guides have sufficient clothing and suitable footwear: no matter what anyone says, a pair of sandals is not suitable for crossing the TPT's high passes! When you arrive at your destination each day, make sure that there is a bed for the guide and porters: most lodges have a room where guides and porters sleep but occasionally, porters are forced to sleep out in the cold.

Litter & waste: litter is a growing problem on Nepal's trails. Sometimes the culprits are guides, porters and locals rather than trekkers but you should make sure nobody in your party drops any litter. The disposal of waste is also an issue in the Khumbu: refuse plastic bags in shops and avoid buying bottled water.

Firewood: over the years, many of the Khumbu's forests were cut down to feed and heat trekkers and eventually, trekkers were asked to avoid lodges that still burned wood. Fortunately, this is largely a thing of the past and lodges in the Khumbu almost all burn bottled gas for cooking and yak dung in heating stoves. If other trekkers tell you that they stayed in a lodge that burned wood then you should avoid staying there.

Safety

Generally, Nepal is a safe country to visit and people are polite, friendly and helpful. However, there are a few country-specific matters to be aware of which can affect safety:

Transport: all modes of transport in Nepal suffer from poor safety standards. On the roads, accidents are very common: roads are narrow and winding; road surfaces are poor; vehicles are frequently overloaded; and the driving can be hair-raising. Air travel within Nepal also carries risk and is not for the faint-hearted: see p59.

Protests: strikes and protests are frequent in Nepal. Although they are mainly peaceful, shops close and transport is disrupted. However, occasionally strikes and protests get out of hand and result in riots. Although foreigners are not the target, you should avoid any areas where protests are taking place.

Crime: pickpockets work the tourist areas of Kathmandu (such as Thamel and Durbar Square). Violent crime, muggings and rape are rare but they do occur from time to time. In Kathmandu, watch your pockets, avoid poorly lit side-streets at night and do not carry valuables around. In the Khumbu, crime is very rare although it would not be wise to leave valuable objects unattended: lodge bedrooms often do not have locks on the doors so some trekkers bring a small padlock.

Earthquakes: Nepal sits in one of the world's most seismically active regions and has a long history of earthquakes, many of which have caused significant destruction and loss of life. One of its worst disasters occurred on 25 April 2015 when there was an earthquake measuring 7.8 on the Richter scale. Its epicentre was Gorkha which is only 85km from Kathmandu and it caused catastrophic damage in the capital city. Many historic sites were destroyed or badly damaged and at least 8857 people were killed. The earthquake also caused significant damage in the Solukhumbu (most of which has now been repaired). It is unlikely that you will be caught up in a serious earthquake or its aftermath but it could happen: check whether your travel insurance covers earthquakes. According to the US Geological Survey, between 1900 and 2021, Nepal had 76 earthquakes with a magnitude of 6.0 or greater. However, it is hoped that the 2015 quakes have dissipated a lot of the pent-up energy, reducing the risk of a very major quake for the time being.

Trekking safety

On a calm, clear day the Khumbu is paradise. However, a sudden weather shift or an injury can alter your circumstances dramatically so treat the mountains with respect and be conscious of your experience levels and physical capabilities. The following is a non-exhaustive list of recommendations:

- Unless you are already acclimatised to altitude, do not ascend faster than prescribed by the generally accepted rules of altitude acclimatisation. Take your time, listen to your body and, if in doubt, descend: this could save your life. For acclimatisation, see p9.
- The fitter you are at the start of your trip, the more you will enjoy the hiking.
- Start early to avoid ascending during the hottest part of the day and to allow more surplus time in case something goes wrong.
- Do not stray from the waymarked paths so as to avoid getting lost and to help prevent erosion of the landscape.
- Before you set out each day, study the route and make plans based upon the abilities of the weakest member of your party.
- Obtain a weather forecast (daily if possible) and reassess your plans in light of it. Avoid exposed routes if the weather is uncertain.
- Never be too proud to turn back or descend if you find the going too tough, the weather deteriorates or you feel unwell.

- If you do not have a guide, bring a map and compass and know how to use them. GPS devices are useful too.
- Carry surplus food and clothing for emergencies.
- Avoid exposed high ground in a thunderstorm. If you get caught out in one then drop your walking poles and stay away from trees, overhanging rocks, metal structures and caves. Generally accepted advice is to squat on your pack and keep as low as possible.
- In snowy conditions, take extra care not to leave the route. Be wary of following someone else's footprints: there is always a chance that they have strayed from the trail.
- In the event of an accident, move an injured person into a safe place and administer any necessary first-aid. Keep the victim warm. Send someone to the nearest lodge or settlement for help.
- When pack animals are passing, remain on the safer inside of the trail: do not stand on the exposed outside of the path because trekkers are sometimes knocked off the edge by the animals.

Passing yaks on Stage EBC3a

Health

Everest, Nuptse & Lhotse

Altitude acclimatisation

See p9.

Vaccinations

There are no compulsory vaccinations required for entering Nepal. However, generally recommended vaccinations include Diphtheria, Hepatitis A, Tetanus and Typhoid. For up to date advice, always consult a medical professional at least six weeks before you travel to Nepal.

Stomach upsets

Hygiene standards in Nepal are not very high and visitors commonly develop stomach upsets, particularly in Kathmandu: usually they are caused by eating or drinking something contaminated with a pathogen that your stomach does not like; normally, they last about 24hr and involve nothing worse than a few rushed toilet trips. That said, hygiene in the Khumbu has improved greatly in recent years as lodges have become accustomed to catering to foreigners. Nevertheless, it is sensible to be a little cautious about what you eat and drink. The following recommendations may help:

- Do not drink untreated water.
- Avoid drinks with ice (which could be contaminated).
- Avoid raw produce and other food that may have been washed with untreated water: for example, salads and unpeeled fruit.
- Avoid eating meat (which is thought to be the cause of many stomach upsets): in the Khumbu, meat is slowly carried up on the backs of porters/pack-animals and freshness is a concern.

- Some people claim that it is better to stick to local dishes (on the basis that the Nepalese understand better how to cook these properly) rather than the Nepali approximations of western dishes.
- Before eating, clean your hands with sanitiser. If possible, avoid touching the food with your hands.
- You are more likely to become sick in Kathmandu so spend as little time there as possible before your trek.
- If you develop a stomach upset, drink plenty of water to keep hydrated. Avoid rich foods. Rehydration salts and drinks with electrolytes may help.

Kathmandu pollution

The Kathmandu Valley suffers from chronic air pollution and Kathmandu is one of the worst cities in the world for air quality. Many local people wear face-masks on the streets to limit the dangers of breathing in this toxic haze: visitors with sensitive chests may also want to do so. We would also advise you to spend as little time in Kathmandu as possible before your trek to avoid developing a cough before you start hiking.

Khumbu Cough

Most people who spend time at altitude will develop a cough caused (at least partly) by breathing the cold, dry mountain air which dries out the throat and windpipe. It is nicknamed the 'Khumbu cough' but it can occur at high altitude in any part of the world. Although the cough is annoying, it is not (on its own) very serious: however, it can make you more susceptible to bronchial infections. There is little you can do to prevent it but breathing through a scarf or buff (worn over your mouth and nose) does seem to help by moistening the air you inhale: however, a scarf restricts your airflow and can leave you gasping for breath on ascents. Throat lozenges can help with symptoms.

Hypothermia/frostbite

It can be very cold in the Khumbu, particularly at night when temperatures in winter can drop to -30°C. The higher you are, the colder it gets. Getting caught out in such low temperatures would place you at risk of hypothermia or even frostbite. Fortunately, because there are lodges regularly spaced along most trails, the chances of being caught out are reduced, especially if you have a guide and porter who can run to the nearest lodge for help if something goes wrong. However, when crossing the TPT's high passes, you traverse remote terrain far from the nearest lodges: if a storm appears unexpectedly, and snow falls, then it can quickly become cold and seeking help is difficult. Hands and feet can quickly become numb and hypothermia or frostbite are real possibilities. Accordingly, always carry surplus warm clothing in your day-pack. Also, check weather forecasts before setting out each day and be prepared to turn back if the weather closes in.

The most obvious symptoms of hypothermia are low body temperature and shivering. Other symptoms (which are confusingly similar to AMS) include fatigue, loss of coordination and slurred speech. If someone in your party shows signs of hypothermia, ensure that they put on more warm clothes and, if possible, make them eat something. If they cannot walk then put them in a sleeping bag and, if necessary, get into the bag with them.

Frostbite is caused by freezing of the skin and underlying tissue. It usually affects fingers, toes, nose and ears (which all lose heat quickly), particularly if they are exposed to the elements. Symptoms include numbness, tingling, pain and patches of discoloured skin. Trail-side treatment for frostbite is similar to that for hypothermia. Make sure that the affected areas are covered with warm, dry clothing. Once you are out of the cold (but not before), re-warm the frostbitten areas by immersing them in warm water for at least 30min (37-39°C is recommended): if you start re-warming and the affected areas subsequently become exposed to cold again, then this can cause irreversible damage. After re-warming, clean the affected area and wrap it in clean bandages.

General Information

Language: Nepali is the official language in Nepal but English is also widely spoken. Tibetan and Sherpa are also spoken in the Khumbu.

Money: Nepal is a cash-based economy and the currency is the Nepalese Rupee (NPR). In the Khumbu, you will pay for almost everything in cash: because there are ATMs only in Lukla and Namche (which could be out of order or empty of cash), it is better to source in Kathmandu all the cash that you will need for the trek. There are numerous ATMs in Kathmandu that accept foreign debit/credit cards. Often there is a maximum withdrawal amount of NPR10,000-20,000 per transaction but you can make several consecutive withdrawals (paying a withdrawal fee each time of course!). In Kathmandu, hotels, airlines and tour companies usually accept credit/debit cards. These days, few banks accept travellers cheques, however, most will exchange cash: US$/GBP£/€ are most widely accepted. There are also money exchange offices in Kathmandu but rates may not be optimal.

Visas: see p58.

Cell-phones: cell coverage is good in most towns and lower villages. In the high mountains, reception is more unreliable, however, this seems to be improving: usually, there is network in Lukla, Phakding, Namche and Tengboche; sometimes, you can also get network at Gorak Shep and EBC. When network is available, it is often (but not always) a 4G service, enabling access to the internet from smart-phones. Your cell-phone provider may permit roaming, allowing you to access Nepali networks but this is likely to be expensive. It is much cheaper to buy a Nepali SIM card: you can find them in shops in Kathmandu Airport, Kathmandu city, Lukla and Namche. They normally include call time, text messages and internet data. Many people say that Ncell is the best provider for coverage in the Khumbu but that could change. You will need your passport when buying a SIM. The disadvantage of using a local SIM is that you have to remove your own SIM from the phone before installing the new one (unless you have two phones or your phone has slots for two SIMs). As an alternative, you could buy an eSIM from an international provider such as Airalo: they are more expensive than Nepalese SIMs and are slightly complicated to install but at least you can leave your existing SIM in your phone.

International dialling codes: the international dialling code for Nepal is +977.

WiFi: almost all hotels and restaurants in Kathmandu provide WiFi (normally free of charge) and speeds are generally reasonable. In the Khumbu, almost all trekking lodges offer WiFi (for a fee) and speeds are surprisingly good for such remote locations. Normally, you have to buy a prepaid WiFi card from the lodge owner which has a code allowing access for a specified period: at the time of writing, it was US$4-7 for 24hr of WiFi. Many of the lodges use the same networks so often a WiFi card bought at one lodge will work at some other lodges: network providers seem to change from year to year but currently Nepal Air Link is popular.

Emergencies & rescue: there are hospitals in Lukla and Khunde (near Namche) and smaller medical facilities in Zamphuti, Namche, Pheriche, Gokyo and Thame: staff normally have experience with altitude related issues. However, in the Khumbu, there is no official mountain rescue service. If you have a minor problem then the staff at lodges might be able to help. For more serious medical issues, the lodge staff or your guide should be able to call a helicopter which can transfer you to a hospital in Kathmandu: the main hospital in Kathmandu has a heli-pad on the roof. You will be responsible for the exorbitant cost of a helicopter evacuation so make sure that you have rescue insurance which covers trekking in Nepal. Rescue insurance is not the same as medical insurance and normal travel insurance policies do not usually cover rescue. Accordingly, you will need to buy specialist travel insurance which includes rescue or a separate rescue insurance policy. If you are looking for a separate rescue insurance policy, then joining the British section of the Austrian Alpine Club (which is open to everyone and not just British trekkers) is a good option. Membership costs £62 and includes worldwide rescue insurance: see **www.alpenverein.at/britannia**. Be aware that some insurance companies refuse to cover trips to Nepal because of the proliferation of insurance scams involving fake helicopter rescues: other insurers charge a hefty excess for helicopter rescues in Nepal. Always carry insurance papers in your day-pack while on the trail because you may need proof of insurance to arrange helicopter evacuation.

Medical insurance: medical treatment for foreigners in Nepal is expensive, as is international repatriation. Accordingly, you should buy good travel insurance. However, because EBC is well above 5000m and most standard travel insurance policies do not cover trekking at this altitude, you will need a specialist policy that covers high altitude trekking in Nepal.

Tipping: tips are not generally expected in restaurants or hotels but we think that you should leave them anyway. However, guides, porters and drivers will expect a tip because their basic wages are incredibly low. The general rule of thumb is to pay your guide/porter an extra day's wages for each week that you use him. However, in our opinion, good guides and porters deserve more than that. Give tips directly to the guides/porters rather than to the trekking company.

Time: Nepal is 5.75hr ahead of GMT.

Tourist information: the main Nepal Tourism Board office is in Kathmandu at Pradarshani Marg, 44617 (+977 1 4256909; **www.ntb.gov.np**). You can buy trekking permits there but otherwise, the offices of tour/trekking companies are probably more useful for tourist information.

The exquisite summit of Ama Dablam

Wildlife

Himalayan griffon soaring near Kangtega

Phakding, the lowest point on the treks, sits at 2610m in a fertile zone of temperate forest. On the other hand, KP (the highest point of the treks) is at 5600m and sits within a barren landscape of rock, snow and ice. In-between, there are almost three vertical km and you will find many different types of terrain including oak and rhododendron forest, high-altitude pasture, agricultural fields, huge glaciers and alpine scree. Within these landscapes, there is an impressive variety of wildlife (although it is often well hidden).

Mammals

One of the most commonly spotted large mammals is the **Himalayan tahr (Jharal)**, a member of the goat family which has a brown coat, dark face and curved horns: you may see them on grassy cliffs around Phortse, Pangboche or Dragnag. There are also **blue sheep (bharal)** although they are, in fact, more grey than blue and are more closely related to goats than sheep: they tend to congregate in groups on the rock/scree of steep mountain slopes, high above the tree-line.

Himalayan black bears are present but few people ever see them. In the forests between Lukla and Namche, there are **red pandas** (which are related to raccoons, weasels and skunks): these rare creatures have a chestnut coat and ringed tail. In the lower stages of the trek, you might see **musk deer** or grey **langur monkeys** in the forests.

The apex predator is the **snow leopard** which everyone wants to spot but very few ever do. They live at high altitude and usually prey on the blue sheep, however, they will also eat the Sherpas' livestock given half the chance. Because they are highly intelligent and have expert camouflage skills, your chances of seeing one are only slightly greater than your chances of spotting a yeti (see p95). But just because you cannot see them, does not mean that they are not watching you!

Marmots are smaller and more easily seen: everyone loves these fat rodents which graze relentlessly in summer to put on layers of fat to last the long winter hibernation. They live in colonies in grassy parts of the mountains, often standing upright on their hind legs like a meerkat. They whistle as you approach to warn their colony of an intruder. There are also **pika** which are much smaller: these hardy creatures can live as high as 6,000m and are related to rabbits but look more like large mice. There are also **wolves, jackals, foxes, civets, martens, weasels, hares** and **shrews**, however, they are all elusive.

You should see plenty of domestic **yaks** though: from the same family as cows, they are used as pack animals throughout the Khumbu. They have thick, shaggy coats; their horns curve backwards; and they are biologically suited to living at altitude. In fact, only males are referred to as 'yaks': females are known as 'naks'. There are also a lot of yak-cow hybrids hauling goods along the trails: the males are known as 'dzopkios' and the females are 'dzums'; they tend to have a better temperament and the females produce more milk than naks; they have forward-curving horns.

A yak (we think!)

Birds

There is plenty of bird-life too (118 species). In the forests, look out for several kinds of **pheasants**: the most eye-catching is the **Himalayan monal** (impeyan pheasant; national bird of Nepal) which has a glittery plumage of blue, green, red and orange. You might also glimpse a **blood pheasant**: the red marks on its chest look like blood.

In the alpine zone, there are alpine and red-billed **choughs**: large black birds with bright yellow or red beaks. You can often spot **Tibetan snowcocks** at altitude too: they are well camouflaged amongst the rocks.

Tibetan snowcock

There are also birds of prey: **golden eagles** are present but hard to spot; **kestrels** are more common. Above the tree line, you have a good chance of spotting vultures (**Himalayan griffon** and **bearded vultures**) which circle in the thermals as they search for food. There are also **pigeons, doves, cuckoos, crows** and **woodpeckers**.

A yak on the high path from Phortse to Pangboche (AR2)

Plants & Flowers

Rhododendron

The Khumbu has four distinct floral zones:

Temperate forest (2000-3000m): this is the most fertile zone with plenty of rain and mist. The climate is mild in summer and cool in winter. The area around Lukla lies within this zone and those walking from Bhandar to Lukla will also spend plenty of time within it. Species of trees include oak, chestnut, walnut, maple, magnolia, alder and rhododendron. The rhododendrons flower in March/April, painting the slopes red, pink and white: this is a highlight of the spring trekking season. There are around 500 species of rhododendron in the Himalaya and a good number of them are found in the Khumbu.

Sub-alpine zone (3000-4000m): colder than temperate forest. Mist is common. Snowfall is heavy in winter. Trees and shrubs grow slowly. Common trees include silver fir, birch and rhododendron (see above). 4000m is usually the upper limit for the growth of trees. Above 3700m, rhododendron and juniper shrub become common: juniper is often burnt in Buddhist temples.

Alpine zone (4000-5000m): this is the zone between the top of the tree-line and the edges of permanent snow. It is very cold with long winters. Dwarf rhododendron and juniper shrub are common. There is plenty of grassland too where wild-flowers grow (such as primulas and gentians).

Nival zone (5000m+): the high mountain zone where rock, snow, ice and a brutally cold climate largely prevent plant growth. Only lichens, fungi and a few small flowering plants (such as sandwort) can survive.

Sagarmatha National Park (SNP)

Established in 1976 to protect 1148km^2 of the Khumbu, the SNP was Nepal's first national park. In 1979, it was declared a UNESCO World Heritage Site. It stretches from Monjo in the S to the Tibetan border in the N and from the Bhote Koshi catchment area in the W to the Imja Khola catchment area in the E. As part of the Great Himalayan Range, it is a magnificent region of snowy peaks, glaciers, deep valleys and alpine lakes.

The SNP is home to Mount Everest, the world's highest mountain, and two other 8000ers (Lhotse and Cho Oyu). In total, it possesses eight peaks greater than 7,000m. There are also more than 20 villages within the SNP's borders which are home to 6,000 Sherpas. It is estimated that 57,000 tourists visited the SNP in 2022.

Yak train near EBC

Mount Everest

Discovery

The layering of the summits along the Himalayan chain is such that, when viewed from far away, it can be difficult to determine exactly which mountains are the very highest. For this reason, the tallest mountain in the world was not identified as such until 1852 when the Great Trigonometrical Survey of India triangulated 'Peak XV', the mountain that (in the western world) we now know as 'Mount Everest'. At that time, the height of Everest was calculated as 8840m above sea level which was astonishingly accurate given that current GPS calculations have it as 8848m. It was named after Sir George Everest, the head of the Survey in the early 19th century who completed the measurement of the great meridional arc of India: at the time, this was a stunning achievement upon which all mapping in the Indian sub-continent was eventually based. Although most people know the mountain as 'Everest', its local Tibetan and Sherpa name is 'Chomolungma' which means 'Goddess Mother of the Earth'. And to confuse matters further, the official Nepali name is 'Sagarmatha' meaning 'Goddess of the Sky': this was adopted in 1956 because Nepal's Hindi rulers thought that a Tibetan name was unacceptable. Interestingly, George Everest apparently did not want a mountain named after him, believing that the local name should be used: however, because nobody could find out the local name at that time, they were stuck with Everest! George Everest never actually saw Mount Everest.

Reconnaissance

Although Everest had been identified, few foreigners were able to approach it (never mind climb it) because both Nepal and Tibet were closed to foreigners and mountaineering was still in its infancy. However, in the second half of the 19th century, British Army officers and naturalists began to explore the Himalayan valleys and, towards the end of the century, started to climb some fairly high peaks. In 1921, the Dalai Lama gave permission for a reconnaissance expedition which took a month to travel to the region from Darjeeling in India (through Tibet). The expedition mapped approach routes, however, at this stage, nobody knew if it was even physiologically possible to climb to the summit. Among the members of the 1921 expedition was the 34 year-old George Mallory who was an experienced mountaineer. Together with Guy Bullock, he scouted a route to Everest's summit, reaching the 7000m North Col on 23 September 1921. From there, the summit appeared to be attainably close, however, it was not feasible to climb higher that year because the expedition was overextended and the winter was rapidly approaching. Instead, Mallory hatched plans for the following spring.

Mallory's first attempt (1922)

Mallory returned to the mountain in spring 1922 on an expedition designed not merely for reconnaissance but to make an attempt on the summit. To get there, the expedition had to cross the bleak Tibetan plateau again, a trek that could not be undertaken until the end of winter. For that reason, they arrived a month later in the season than modern expeditions and had to rush their climb because the monsoon was rapidly approaching. They made two attempts, one with supplementary oxygen and one without. Although they failed to reach the summit, two members of the expedition climbed higher than anyone had ever been before (8323m) and, if circumstances had been slightly different, they might have reached the top. Furthermore, the expedition proved that supplementary oxygen was a key that could unlock the summit. However, it also exposed the dark side of Everest: seven porters were killed in an avalanche on Mallory's second climb.

Mallory's second attempt (1924)

Mallory returned once again in 1924. This expedition also arrived late in the season and was plagued by brutal weather. Again, they made two unsuccessful attempts. On the first, Edward Norton reached 8575m without supplementary oxygen, a record that was not beaten until 1978. However, it is the second attempt, involving Mallory and Sandy Irvine (the youngest member of the team), that has gone down in history: on 8 June 1924, they were spotted climbing into clouds and were never seen alive again. Mallory's body was finally found and identified in 1999 by an American research expedition: it was almost perfectly preserved and showed that he had broken his right leg in a fall. Nobody knows whether they reached the summit.

Further attempts (1925-1952)

For political reasons, the next official attempt on Everest was not until 1933. Neither this expedition, nor any of the other three expeditions in the 1930s, managed to climb higher than Norton's 1924 record (8575m). Tenzing Norgay (who would later become one of the first two people to successfully summit Everest) was employed on the 1935 expedition as a personal servant to one of the climbers. In 1939, the outbreak of WW2 put a hold on further expeditions. After the war ended in 1945, the dismantling of the British Empire began: with the independence of India in 1947, Britain's influence over the Indian Sub-continent collapsed. Then, in 1950, China occupied Tibet making access to the N side of Everest much more difficult. However, Nepal was now allowing foreigners to visit and, in 1950, Maurice Herzog's famous French expedition upped the ante by reaching the summit of Annapurna: this was the first successful ascent of an 8000er. Meanwhile, an Anglo-American party (involving the famous explorer and mountaineer, Bill Tilman) was exploring the valleys of the Solukhumbu (which was still virtually untouched by the outside world).

In 1951, Eric Shipton, who had been involved in all of the expeditions in the 1930s, led a more organised reconnaissance of the Solukhumbu which involved a number of New Zealanders, including Edmund Hillary (who is now probably the most famous mountaineer of them all). They got high enough to plan what looked like a realistic route via the South Col and climbed almost all the way over the Khumbu Ice-fall, proving that crossing it was dangerous but possible: they laid the foundations for all later attempts from Nepal. When the London Times published a special supplement on the 1951 expedition, the race to the summit accelerated, with the Swiss, French and British all planning expeditions.

In 1952, a Swiss expedition almost reached the top but they were let down by poor teamwork and faulty oxygen equipment. They were the first to cross the crevasse at the top of the Khumbu Ice-fall, enter the Western Cwm (which is enclosed by the terrifying walls of Everest, Lhotse and Nuptse) and establish a camp on the South Col (7909m). Eventually, the summit team reached 8597m before they were forced to turn back: one of the members of the summit team was Tenzing Norgay who was, by then, probably the most experienced Sherpa alive.

The first successful ascent (1953)

The British expedition of 1953 was led by John Hunt and involved several New Zealanders including Hillary. Tenzing Norgay was employed as both sirdar (leader of the Sherpa team) and a member of the climbing team. They arrived at the mountain in spring, with plenty of time to spare. On 26 May, Tom Bourdillon and Charles Evans climbed from their camp at the South Col to 8751m (on the S Summit of Everest) before turning back: they found that it was too far to climb from the South Col to the main summit and back on the same day. On 28 May, Tenzing and Hillary started their summit attempt. Learning from the unsuccessful attempt a few days earlier, they made camp at 8504m (far above the South Col), with Hillary carefully calculating that they had sufficient remaining oxygen to do so: Evans had left partially used bottles near the South Summit. At 9am on 29 May, they crossed the South Summit. An hour later, they reached the foot of the 17m cliff that would become known as the 'Hillary Step'. Finally, at 11:30am, they reached the summit of Everest, unfurled the flags of Britain, Nepal and India and took the photographs that would become famous all over the world.

Breaking of records (1954-1980)

The successful conquest of Everest set in motion a flurry of mountaineering activity in the Himalaya: in a little over five years, another ten 8000ers were summited for the first time. Because Annapurna had already been climbed in 1950, that left only two 8000ers and they were climbed in 1960 and 1964 respectively. The experienced mountaineers then turned their attentions to the more difficult routes and faces of the highest peaks. In 1963, Americans Tom Hornbein and Willi Unsoeld reached the summit of Everest via the W Ridge, a route that had not even been previously scouted. In 1965, Nawang Gombu became the first person to summit Everest twice.

By the start of 1970, only 23 people had stood on Everest's summit. However, from 1973 onwards, the rate of successful climbs increased exponentially. In 1975, Chinese climbers successfully summited from the N: this is believed to be the first successful ascent of Everest from Tibet, although there is also an unverified Chinese claim to a previous ascent (in 1960). Later in 1975, Dougal Haston and Doug Scott became the first to summit via the terrifyingly difficult SW Face: they were also the first Britons to reach Everest's summit. Junko Tabei also reached the summit in 1975, becoming the first woman to do so. In 1978, Reinhold Messner and Peter Habeler were the first to reach the summit without using supplementary oxygen. In 1980, Messner also became the first person to climb the mountain solo (this time from the Tibet side). The first winter ascent was in 1980 too (Krzysztof Jerzy Wielicki and Leszek Cichy).

The commercial era

Since the first expeditions, the people attempting Everest had almost all been elite mountaineers. However, in 1985, that changed when David Breashears (an experienced young climber) led to the summit a wealthy Texan called Dick Bass (whose climbing experience was relatively limited). Victory on Everest made Bass the first person to successfully climb the Seven Summits (the highest mountain on each of the seven continents) and consequently, his success attracted plenty of positive media attention. Many people, who had previously thought that high altitude mountaineering was 'above their pay-grade', suddenly believed that they could emulate Bass's achievement. The floodgates had been opened and interest in climbing Everest soared. By the 1996 season, there were no less than two dozen different expeditions camped on the mountain's slopes and many of these were commercial groups (organised by private businesses) to guide paying clients to the summit: as is always the case, private enterprise had stepped in to meet demand. Dramatic increases, by the Nepalese Government, in the price of climbing permits did not dampen the demand.

In May 1996, tragedy struck when eight climbers on guided expeditions died in a blizzard while attempting to reach the summit. This was the highest death toll on Everest in a single weather event and it attracted significant media attention. Although it raised questions about the safety of the commercial expeditions, they continue to this day. So many climbers now attempt Everest that there are queues at the bottlenecks along the route. Most commercial summit attempts use the South Col (Hillary/Tenzing's route) or the route via the North Col. In 2019, 891 people summited Everest even though guiding companies charge US$40,000-100,000/person.

Everest's Conquerors

Edmund Hillary

Sir Edmund Hillary was born in Auckland, New Zealand in 1919. He became interested in mountaineering at the age of 16 on a school trip to Mount Ruapehu and honed his skills in New Zealand's Southern Alps. During WW2, he served as a navigator in the Royal New Zealand Air Force. He was a member of Eric Shipton's 1951 reconnaissance expedition to Everest and also an unsuccessful 1952 British expedition to climb Cho Oyu. Because of his strength and determination, he was chosen for the British/New Zealand Everest expedition of 1953. He quickly developed a strong climbing partnership with Tenzing Norgay Sherpa (see below). On 29 May 1953, Hillary and Tenzing became the first two people to reach the summit of the world's highest mountain.

The news of their historic achievement reached Britain just in time for the Coronation of Queen Elizabeth II on 2 June 1953. It captured the imagination of people everywhere and Hillary became one of the most famous people on earth. He was knighted on 6 June 1953. In later years, he climbed 10 other Himalayan peaks and reached the South Pole overland. However, Hillary's legacy extends far beyond his mountaineering exploits. Recognizing the contribution that the Sherpa people had made to his success, in 1960, he founded the Himalayan Trust, a charitable organization aimed at providing essential services and infrastructure to remote mountain villages in Nepal.

Through the trust, Hillary built schools, hospitals, health clinics, air-strips and bridges; he restored monasteries and helped establish clean water sources and sustainable agricultural practices. His efforts helped to alleviate poverty, improve healthcare, and promote education in the Khumbu. On 11 January 2008, he died of heart failure in Auckland. He is still revered by the Sherpa people.

Tenzing Norgay

Tenzing Norgay was born in 1914 but his place of birth is uncertain: he originally claimed to be from the Khumbu but in more recent accounts said that he was born in Tibet and raised in the Khumbu village of Thame. As a yak herder, he spent much time in the high pastures surrounding Everest. In his teens, he ran away from home and soon settled in Darjeeling in India. In 1935, he was selected as a porter on Eric Shipton's 1935 Everest reconnaissance expedition. He performed well and was chosen for three consecutive British expeditions to climb Everest, receiving a Tiger medal (see p94). In 1947, he became a sirdar for the first time, on a Swiss expedition in the Garhwal Himalaya: a sirdar manages all the other Sherpas on a climbing expedition. On this expedition, he bagged his first Himalayan summit (Kedarnath; 6940m) and developed a close relationship with the Swiss mountaineers. This led to his selection for the 1952 Swiss Everest expedition as a full climbing member. He developed a close relationship with Raymond Lambert and they reached 8600m, a new height record.

By 1953, Tenzing had been on six Everest expeditions and was clearly one of the most experienced members of the 1953 British/New Zealand Everest expedition. He quickly developed a strong climbing partnership with Edmund Hillary and on 29 May 1953, they became the first two people to reach the summit of Everest. Tenzing instantly became a household name. However, although Hillary was knighted for the achievement, Tenzing only received the George Medal (a British decoration awarded for gallantry): some suggest that the Indian Prime Minister refused to allow him to be knighted.

In the years that followed his Everest ascent, Tenzing became an advocate for the Sherpa community, working tirelessly to improve living conditions, healthcare, and education in the remote villages of Nepal. In 1954, he became Director of Field Training of the Himalayan Mountaineering Institute in Darjeeling, set up to train future generations of climbers and promote responsible mountaineering practices. He died of a brain haemorrhage in 1986. Time magazine has named him as one of the 100 most influential people of the 20th century.

The 8000ers

There are only 14 mountains in the world which are higher than 8,000m above sea level. They are known as the 8000ers.

	Mountain	Altitude	Countries	Range
1	**Everest**	8848	Nepal/China (Tibet)	Nepal Himalaya
2	**K2**	8611	Pakistan/China	Karakorum
3	**Kangchenjunga**	8586	Nepal/India	Sikkim Himalaya
4	**Lhotse**	8516	Nepal/China (Tibet)	Nepal Himalaya
5	**Makalu**	8485	Nepal/China (Tibet)	Nepal Himalaya
6	**Cho Oyu**	8188	Nepal/China (Tibet)	Nepal Himalaya
7	**Dhaulagiri I**	8167	Nepal	Nepal Himalaya
8	**Manaslu**	8163	Nepal	Nepal Himalaya
9	**Nanga Parbat**	8125	Pakistan	Kashmir Himalaya
10	**Annapurna I**	8091	Nepal	Nepal Himalaya
11	**Gasherbrum I**	8080	Pakistan/China	Karakorum
12	**Broad Peak**	8051	Pakistan/China	Karakorum
13	**Gasherbrum II**	8034	Pakistan/China	Karakorum
14	**Shisha Pangma**	8027	China (Tibet)	Nepal Himalaya

Makalu with Island Peak in the foreground (SR4)

The Sherpa People

Sherpa is the largest ethnic group in the Khumbu: today, there are approximately 6000 Sherpas living in about 20 villages. The word 'sherpa' means 'east people' in Tibetan: their ancestors originally reached the Khumbu 500-600 years ago, migrating across the Himalaya from eastern Tibet. Before the arrival of the mountaineers, Sherpas lived semi-nomadic lives, controlled by a Buddhist theocracy. Their language, which is also called 'Sherpa', is a dialect of Tibetan. In the Khumbu, they grazed yaks and grew barley and potatoes. Some used the remote mountain passes to carry trade goods (often salt) between Tibet and Nepal. It was a harsh existence in an unforgiving environment. The Khumbu is not the only place where Sherpas live: groups also established in other areas of eastern Nepal, Darjeeling in India and Tingri in Bhutan. In total, Sherpas represent about 1% of Nepal's population.

Back then, Sherpas did not climb the huge peaks that surrounded them because they believed that divine beings lived there. Even today, it is forbidden to climb a few of the Khumbu's most sacred summits (such as Khumbila near Namche). Nevertheless, living at the Khumbu's high altitudes made them physiologically well-suited to mountaineering, with strength and endurance at altitude that surpassed most other people's. For this reason, Sherpas were used on the first Everest reconnaissance expedition in 1921 and a tradition was born that continues to this day. The work was hard but better-paid, and more glamorous, than the meagre rural existence that they were used to. Early expeditions started from Darjeeling so many Khumbu Sherpas moved there to seek work. As the years passed, the experience of the Sherpas involved in the expeditions grew and many developed personal mountaineering ambitions. Quite early on, the tradition of 'Tigers of the Snow' began: Sherpas who made outstanding contributions to expeditions were awarded 'Tiger' status, and were paid more than their colleagues. In 1939, the Himalayan Club in Darjeeling began awarding official Tiger medals: this tradition continues today and it is a great honour to become a Tiger.

High performers on the most noteworthy expeditions became prosperous and famous. Ang Tharkay from Khunde, for example, was revered by western mountaineers: his ability at high altitude was unmatched and he was a skilled organiser. He worked on many of the most famous expeditions including Herzog's successful ascent of Annapurna I. He was awarded the French Légion d'Honneur and was the first Sherpa ever to travel to Europe. However, the most famous Sherpa of all is undoubtedly Tenzing Norgay who (together with Edmund Hillary) was the first to reach the summit of Everest (see p92). So great was the Sherpas' impact on Himalayan mountaineering, that the word 'sherpa' is often used as a generic term to refer to a climbing guide employed on any mountaineering expedition, irrespective of ethnicity.

Nepal's middle hills: above Junbesi (W3a)

Yetis

Even harder to spot than a snow leopard is the fabled yeti, and budding yeti hunters will be pleased to learn that the Everest region has a rich history of abominable snowman sightings. For centuries, tales have circulated of ape-like creatures roaming the remote corners of the Himalaya and depictions of them have been recorded in murals on monastery walls. Nobody is sure how the myth of the yeti came about but, 10,000 years ago, orangutans lived in the forests of the eastern Himalaya and it is possible that the 'yetis' sighted were in fact these hairy orange primates. However, most researchers believe that yeti sightings were actually encounters with bears.

Although few people in the western world today believe in yetis, residents of some remote Himalayan communities are convinced that they exist: living creatures with flesh, blood, and supernatural powers allowing them to vanish at will. So established is this belief in eastern Bhutan, for example, that Bhutan's government has established the Sakteng Wildlife Sanctuary in order to protect the yetis said to live there.

There have been many alleged yeti sightings in the Khumbu. The most famous include the following:

- **17th century:** Tibetan Buddhist master Lama Sange Dorje befriended a yeti while meditating in caves above Pangboche (see p130).
- **1923:** the first recorded yeti sighting in the Everest area by a foreigner. British mountaineer, Alan Cameron, spotted a hominid-like creature walking along a ridge near Everest.
- **1951:** the famous mountaineer, Eric Shipton, found yeti prints during a reconnaissance trip to the Khumbu.
- **1974:** a woman from the Khumbu claims to have been attacked by a yeti near Machermo.
- **1984:** strange footprints were discovered near the summit of Everest by Tim McCartney-Snape and Greg Mortimer.

Furthermore, in the gompas at Khumjung and Pangboche, you can view relics that are claimed to be authentic yeti body parts: see p114 and p130.

A variety of different opinions have emerged as to what you should do to escape a yeti. Some experts claim that their feet are the wrong way around so as to confuse pursuers: accordingly, if you spot yeti footprints, they advise you to walk in the direction its footprints appear to be travelling (in order to escape it). Others maintain that the escape strategy should depend upon the sex of the yeti: apparently, because a male yeti has an enormous penis, you should run uphill through scrub if chased by one so that its penis will become entangled in the foliage, causing it to stop; female yetis, on the other hand, have massive breasts apparently, and therefore you should run down a steep hill so that she will fall over (destabilised by the weight of her breasts). Unfortunately, nobody seems to elaborate on the course of action if you are chased by both a male and female yeti at the same time. Sadly, we cannot endorse any of this advice.

The approach to Kongma La (TP7)

Culture & Etiquette

Kani near Pangboche (EBC4)

In Nepal, Indian Hinduism and Tibetan Buddhism coalesce and learning about the rich and varied culture is a highlight of a trekking trip to this colourful country. More than 90 different languages are spoken in Nepal (each one representing a distinct culture) and, in addition to Hinduism and Buddhism, a variety of other religions are practised. All of the different ethnic and religious groups seem to co-exist in a relative harmony. This is best epitomised by the Kathmandu Valley's Newar people who can be described as a cultural fusion of all Nepal's people: although technically Hindu, they incorporate many aspects of Buddhism into their lives; they happily celebrate both Buddhist and Hindu festivals; and they are not averse to praying in the temples of both religions.

In the Himalaya, Nepal's northern strip, the culture is predominately Tibetan Buddhist. However, in the southern strip of the country (the Tarai), which feels and looks very much like northern India, the people are almost entirely Hindu. Between these two zones, you will find Nepal's middle hills where there is a broad tapestry of different cultures and religions. If you walk N through the middle hills between Bhandar and Lukla (Treks 9 & 10), you will observe Hindu culture gradually giving way to Tibetan Buddhism (which dominates in the Khumbu).

Although the Nepalese are generally welcoming, tolerant and forgiving, you should respect the local culture and follow a few simple rules:

- Avoid public shows of affection.
- Dress conservatively: in particular, women should cover their legs and shoulders.
- Do not point the soles of your feet at anyone.
- Remove footwear when you enter a monastery.
- Walk CW (to the left) around stupas and other Buddhist monuments.
- Do not take selfies in front of temple deities.
- When eating with hands, place food in your mouth only with your right hand.
- If sharing another person's water bottle, ensure that your lips do not touch the bottle.
- Ask permission before taking a person's photo: usually they will happily agree.
- Do not give pens or sweets to children in the villages. If you want to help, make a financial contribution to a respected charity.
- Do not buy Shahtoosh shawls which are made from the wool of the endangered Tibetan antelope (chiru).

Buddhism (in a nutshell)

Stupa near Ringmu (W3b)

Buddhism is a complicated religion about which countless books have been written over the centuries. Accordingly, any attempt to comprehensively explain it in a few paragraphs of a trekking guidebook is doomed to failure. Please forgive us therefore if the following few paragraphs pose more questions than they answer.

The Buddha (whose real name was Siddhartha Gautama) was born a prince in southern Nepal in the 5th or 6th Century BCE. Although he grew up in an affluent environment, he renounced his wealth and became a wanderer, searching for an end to all suffering. His search eventually led him to the famous Bodhi tree where he reached the awakening of Buddhahood. He spent the rest of his life teaching others about the path away from suffering towards spiritual fulfilment.

His teachings were based on Hinduism's ascetic practices, however, they rejected the concept of the caste system and the belief in a creator God. The teachings revolve around the Four Noble Truths: existence is suffering; suffering is caused by desire; the taming of desire ends suffering; and desire can be tamed by following the Eightfold Path. Buddhist belief is that if greed, hatred and desire can be defeated then a state of Nirvana can be achieved.

Today there are three main schools of Buddhism: Theravada, Mahayana and Vajrayana. Tibetan Buddhism is of the Vajrayana school and it can be further divided into four main sects including the Red Hats and Yellow Hats. One of the key elements of Tibetan Buddhism is its large (and often very confusing) pantheon of Bodhisattva's (enlightened ones who fill a role similar to saints in Catholicism). Perhaps the most important of these figures is Padmasambhava, or Guru Rinpoche, a 9th Century tantric master who did much to spread Buddhism across Tibet and the Himalaya. In order to navigate the complicated world of Tibetan Buddhism, close contact with a lama (or spiritual guide) is required. The most important lamas are believed to be reincarnations of earlier lamas. The most important contemporary figure in Tibetan Buddhism is, of course, the Dalai Lama.

Gompas, Stupas and other Buddhist Monuments

Stupa near Dingboche

Because Nepal is a highly religious country, temples, shrines and monasteries dot the landscape. Although those who walk to Lukla from Bhandar (Trek 9), will see evidence of Hinduism, in the Khumbu itself, the religious monuments are Buddhist. Although the backdrop of the world's highest mountains will dominate much of your attention, the colourful gompas and stupas in the foreground create wonderful atmosphere and context which can be a highlight of the region.

Gompa: a monastery which is a spiritual centre where Buddhist ideas and beliefs are taught. Larger gompas are like small universities and the complex usually contains accommodation for the monks, nuns and novices (trainee monks). Famous monasteries along the Everest trails include Tengboche Gompa (p123), Pangboche Gompa (p130) and Khumjung Gompa (p114).

Gompa

Stupa (chorten in Tibetan): structures which contain relics or remains of a holy person or artefacts associated with them. They are often hemispherical in shape (see above) and painted white. There is usually a spire at the top which is painted gold. You will see many stupas on prominent viewpoints around the Khumbu. Some stupas have a pair of eyes painted on each of the four sides: these symbolise the Buddha's all-seeing eyes.

Stupa

Mani stone: large stones engraved or painted with Tibetan Buddhist mantras (frequently, 'om mani padme hum' which means 'hail to the jewel in the lotus' and is a reference to the Buddha). You will find individual painted boulders, long walls of hundreds of individual mani stones and everything in between.

Mani stones

Prayer wheel: a metal or wooden cylinder mounted on a spindle that allows it to be spun by someone passing by. A mantra is usually written or embossed on the outside of the cylinder: the most common mantra is 'Om mani padme hum' (see p98). Spinning the wheel is supposed to have the same effect as reciting the mantra orally. Prayer wheels come in many sizes: the biggest ones are usually found inside monasteries and they sometimes need a team of people to turn them. There are also water-powered prayer wheels in some of the streams.

Prayer wheels

Prayer flags: these bright and colourful flags are a familiar feature of Nepalese mountain regions. Long strings of flags decorate mountain passes, summits, monastery courtyards, stupas, village houses, bridges and countless other structures. They are strung out in five different colours: blue (symbolising the sky and space), white (air and wind), red (fire), green (water) and yellow (earth). Often the centre of each flag has a drawing of a horse (a Lung ta) with three flaming jewels on its back. The horse is a symbol of speed and the transformation of bad fortune to good. The jewels symbolise the Buddha, the Dharma (Buddhist teachings) and the Sangha (Buddhist community). The writing around the Lung ta will be one of about 400 Buddhist mantras.

Prayer flags

It is believed that they promote peace, compassion, strength, and wisdom: when the wind blows the flags, the blessings, good will and compassion embodied in the prayers and mantras are spread across the land; when the prints fade, the prayers become a permanent part of the universe. Contrary to popular belief they do not carry mantras to the gods.

Kani

Kani: brightly painted gateways at village entrances. Inside, they depict scenes from the lives of the Buddhas and other enlightened teachers.

The inside of a kani

CEBC Stages (also used by the TPT)

Taboche (6495m)

Nuptse I (7864m)

Everest (8848m)

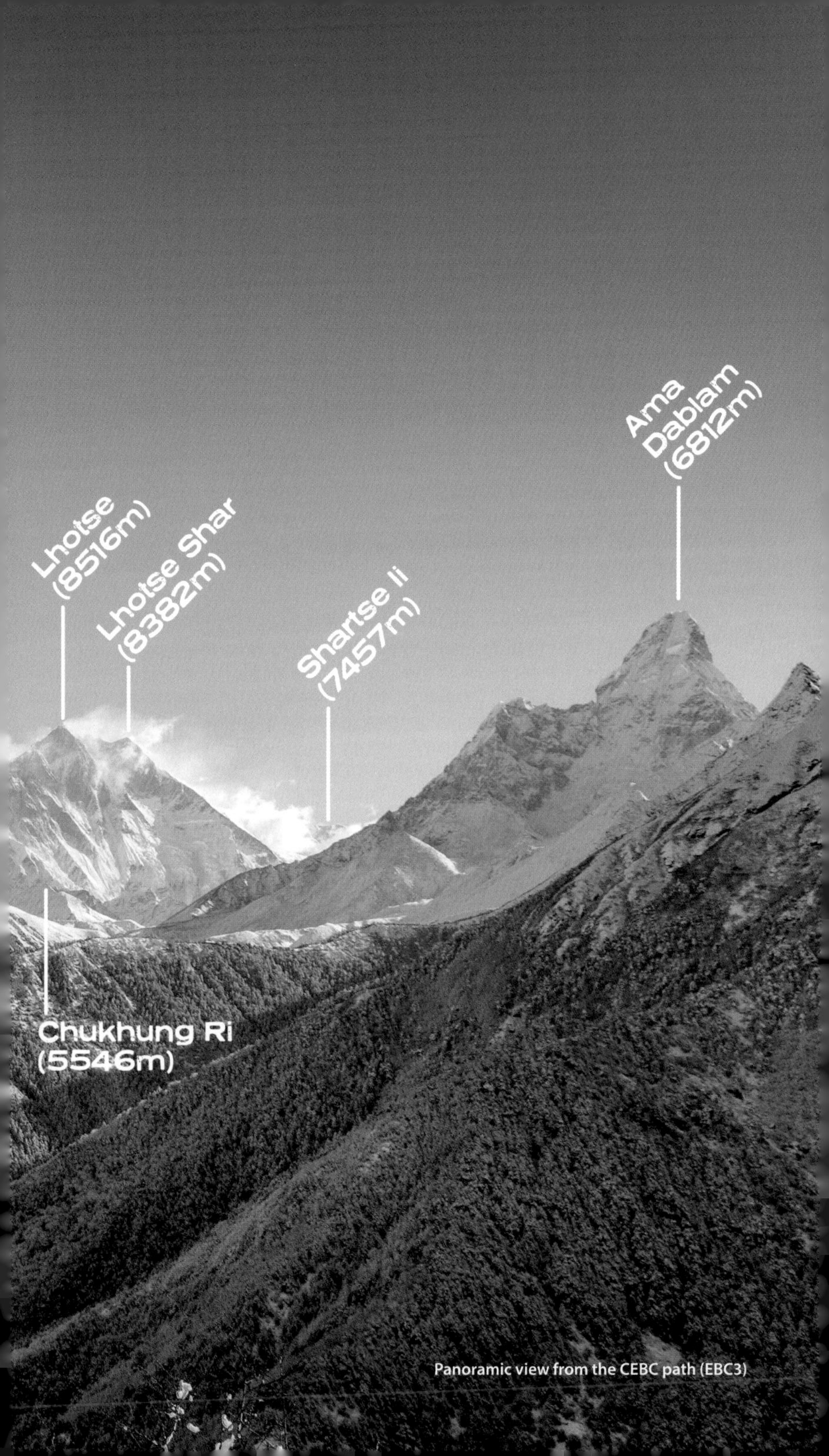

Lhotse (8516m)

Lhotse Shar (8382m)

Shartse II (7457m)

Ama Dablam (6812m)

Chukhung Ri (5546m)

Panoramic view from the CEBC path (EBC3)

EBC1 Lukla to Phakding

For most people, the excitement begins with an exhilarating landing on the airstrip in Lukla (the main staging point for the Everest treks). The streets of this busy little town are flanked with restaurants and numerous shops selling food and trekking gear. There is a decent range of lodges and normally, there are plenty of rooms: however, they can fill up quickly if flights back to Kathmandu have been cancelled for a few days in a row. For medical issues, you will find a pharmacy and a hospital. And if you need cash, the ATMs are fairly reliable.

After arriving in Lukla, most people grab breakfast in a café, pick up any last-minute supplies and then head straight out onto the trail. A clear path heads N up the E side of the Dudh Koshi valley but you will not see much of the river until the village of Cheplung (which also has lodges and restaurants). After Cheplung, you drift closer to the base of the valley and finally, cross the river at Phakding. Although the highest summits do not show themselves yet, there are still plenty of peaks on display above the beautiful forested slopes of the valley. However, the real joy of this section is the sudden immersion in Sherpa culture. Almost instantly, the influence of Buddhism is apparent: seemingly everywhere, you will spot Buddhist monuments and symbols. The starkly whitewashed stupas adorned with golden spires, the brightly painted boulders and mani walls, and the colourful prayer flags, are a feast for the eye. And even the most agnostic trekkers will delight in spinning the numerous prayer wheels: a practice that can easily become an addiction over subsequent days!

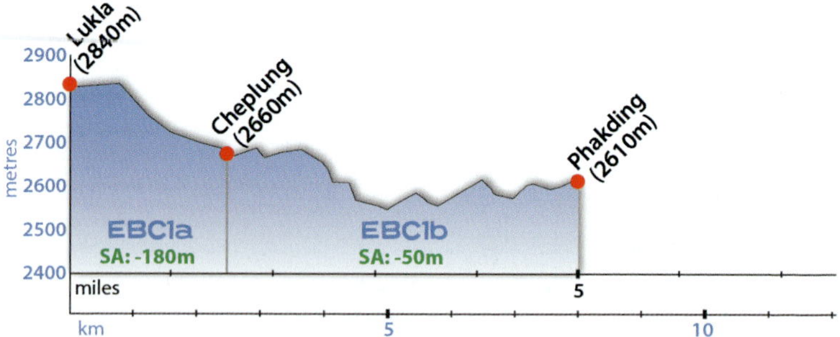

		Time	Distance	Ascent	Descent	SA Increase	Max Alt
EBC1a	Lukla to Cheplung	0:50	2.4km 1.5miles	20m 66ft	200m 656ft	-180m -591ft	2840m 9318ft
EBC1b	Cheplung to Phakding	1:50	5.6km 3.5miles	161m 528ft	211m 692ft	-50m -164ft	2680m 8793ft

Prayer wheels

The activity along the trail is fascinating too, especially for those who have not previously trekked in Nepal. In many other parts of the world, mountain trails are the sole domain of hikers. However, in the Khumbu, you share the path with the many porters who make trekking in the region possible. Because helicopter flights are so expensive, most supplies for the Khumbu's lodges and shops are carried up by human porters or pack-animals. The closer to Lukla, the more porters there are on the trail: consequently, on this part of the trek, you will see a great many of them, shouldering the ubiquitous multi-coloured duffel bags filled with trekkers' belongings and a staggering variety of other goods in all shapes and sizes. Their job is a difficult one so give them the right of way.

Phakding is a lovely settlement with blue-roofed buildings on both sides of the Dudh Koshi: to connect the two parts, there is an exciting suspension bridge which is busy throughout the day with both trekkers and porters. It is the first overnight stop for many trekkers: at 2610m, it is a good place to acclimatise before ascending to Namche (especially, if you have just flown in from Kathmandu) and there is plenty of accommodation. However, because Section EBC1 is quite short and Phakding can be busy, some trekkers prefer to continue along Section EBC2a to spend the first night at Monjo instead. This approach has a few advantages. Firstly, at 2840m, Monjo is a little higher than Phakding, making it a slightly better acclimatisation stop for many: few people will feel ill at that altitude. Secondly, if you overnight near Monjo, you should reach Monjo's SNP checkpoint the following morning before large queues start to form (see p107).

Lodges (with accommodation, restaurant, & shop)	**Lukla** (0km) » **Cheplung** (2.4km) » **Thado Kosi** (4.7km) » **Ghat/Nurning** (5.6km) » **Phakding** (8.0km) Lukla has plenty of lodges and shops selling food and equipment. Between Lukla and Phakding, there are many lodges and shops along the route.
Terrain/ Navigation	Wide paths which are easy to follow.
Difficulty	**Easy**
Medical Assistance	**Lukla Hospital** (0km) **Zamphuti** (4; 0.7km N of Phakding): Himalayan Sherpa Foundation health post; basic treatment for locals and tourists.
Points of Interest	**Lukla**: main staging point for Everest treks. **Buddhist monuments**: numerous monasteries, stupas, mani walls and prayer wheels.

EBC2a
EBC11b
Toc Toc (2710m)
4 Zamphuti (2700m)
Gumela
3 Phakding (2610m)
Sano Gumela
Dudh Koshi
Chhuthawa
Nurning
EBC1b
EBC11c
Ghat
2
Thado Koshi Khola
Thado Kosi
Nachipan
Dudh Koshi
Senma
Cheplung (2660m)
1
EBC1a
EBC11d
Chaurikharka
W5d
Tate
Lukla (2840m)
S F

Stage EBC1a: Lukla to Cheplung

S From the airport, head N along **Lukla's main street**. As you exit the town, pass a **kani** (whitewashed archway topped with a stupa) and a **checkpoint**: you must buy a Khumbu Pasang Lhamu Rural Municipality Entrance Permit and list your valuables. Shortly afterwards, pass through the **Pasang Lhamu Memorial Gate** which is a memorial to the first Nepali woman to climb Everest: descend steeply past a **stupa**. 10min before **Cheplung**, ignore a path on the left which leads to **Chaurikharka**.

1 0:50: TR at a junction at the village of **Cheplung (2660m)**: the path on the left leads to **Surke (Stage W5d)**. There is a monastery set into the cliffs above Cheplung.

Stage EBC1b: Cheplung to Phakding

1 Continue N through **Cheplung**.

2 0:40: Cross the bridge at **Thado Kosi** and then climb. 10-15min later, pass through the villages of **Ghat** and **Nurning**: Ghat has a small monastery. There are plenty of prayer wheels, stupas, mani walls and painted boulders. Shortly afterwards, pass the small village of **Chhuthawa**.

3 1:50: Arrive in **Phakding (2610m)**.

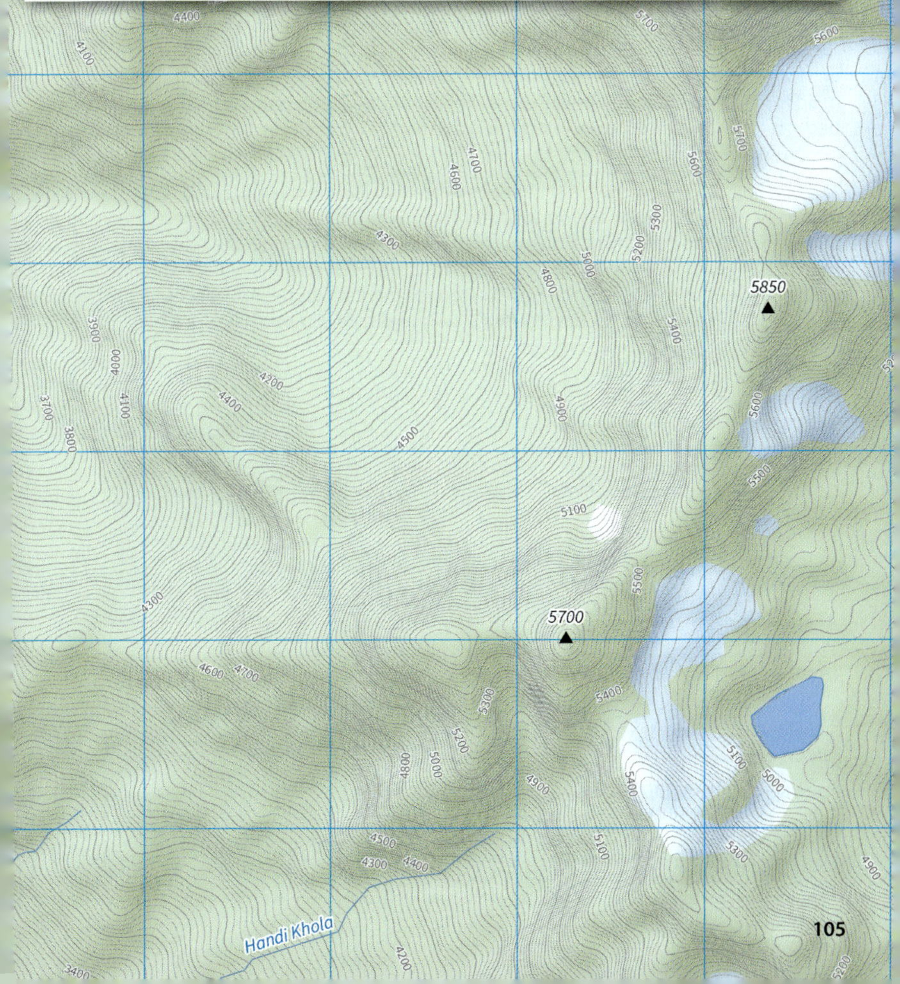

EBC2 Phakding to Namche

Hillary Suspension Bridge

The journey up the Dudh Koshi valley continues and the views become increasingly impressive as you gain height. Five suspension bridges add drama to proceedings: the final one (the Hillary Suspension Bridge) is an exhilarating delight, at least for those with a head for heights. However, once across the last bridge, excitement is replaced by suspense because, if the weather gods are kind, you might (for the first time) see Everest and its famous neighbours, Lhotse and Nuptse.

The first half of Section EBC2 is similar to the previous stage: the route undulates constantly, gradually gaining height as you proceed from village to village; and there are countless places to grab food or drinks. However, N of Jorsale, things change: the real climb of the day begins and you head steeply upwards through forest towards the village of Namche; there are no lodges on this part of the trail so stop for food at Jorsale. Approaching 3000m, high altitude starts to impose itself so ascend slowly and take plenty of breaks.

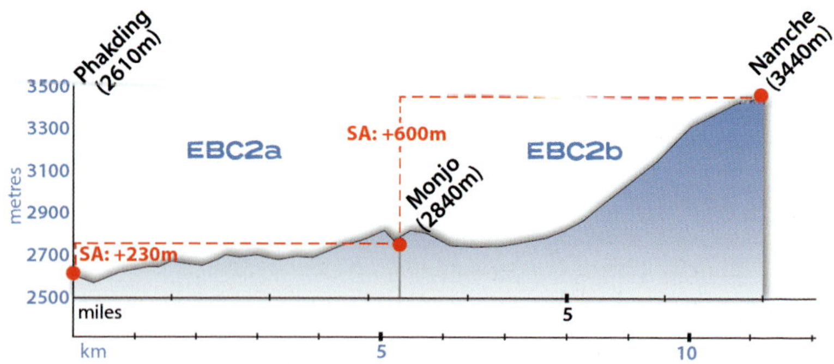

		Time	Distance	Ascent	Descent	SA Increase	Max Alt
EBC2a	Phakding to Monjo	2:20	5.3km 3.3miles	358m 1175ft	128m 420ft	+230m +755ft	2840m 9318ft
EBC2b	Monjo to Namche	3:45	6.0km 3.7miles	728m 2389ft	128m 420ft	+600m +1969ft	3440m 11287ft

At Monjo, there is a checkpoint where you must show your passport and buy a permit to enter the SNP (p68). Because most people sleep at Phakding, large numbers of trekkers start arriving in Monjo around mid-morning and queues develop at the checkpoint: in peak season, it can take an hour to pass through and it therefore makes sense to aim to pass the checkpoint earlier in the day. The best way to achieve this is to overnight at Monjo instead of Phakding, enabling you to reach the checkpoint immediately after breakfast. Trekkers who have walked from Bhandar/Phaplu (without passing Lukla) will also have to buy the Khumbu Pasang Lhamu Rural Municipality Entrance Permit here (p68). In any case, because Monjo is a little closer to 3000m than Phakding, many people find it marginally better for acclimatisation at this stage of the trek.

The generally accepted rules for altitude acclimatisation (see p11) dictate that (1) above 2500m, you should sleep no more than 500m above the previous night's altitude, and (2) if you have to break rule 1 and sleep more than 500m higher, then you should take an enforced AD to give your body time to catch up. At 3440m, Namche is 830m higher than Phakding (where most people overnight) and 600m higher than Monjo (the highest place where you can sleep before Namche): this means that you cannot comply with rule 1 and you should take an AD in Namche. Most trekkers are happy to spend extra time in Namche anyway because it is a highlight of a trek in the Khumbu.

Namche is the unofficial capital of the Khumbu and is often known as Namche Bazaar because of its vibrant and lively market (every Saturday). It is spectacularly situated in a bowl, high above the Dudh Koshi and Bhote Koshi valleys: the colourful buildings are perched precariously on tiers, built into the slopes of the bowl. On all sides, there are mountains. Heaps of them! However, it is not just the natural environment that makes Namche such a special place because the man-made attractions are fantastic too, particularly the monastery and the museums: see p108.

Namche has plenty of accommodation: standard trekking lodges and some upmarket options offering electric blankets, power sockets in the rooms and en-suite bathrooms with hot water. The town is stuffed with restaurants, bars and coffee shops, offering a much wider variety of food and drink than anywhere higher up: most trekkers seize the opportunity to eat their fill before heading higher. There are plenty of shops too and it is wise to pick up last minute supplies before you go higher (where choice is more limited). For medical issues, there are a few pharmacies and you will find a hospital in Khunde (2.7km to the N). If you need cash, the ATMs are fairly reliable.

Lodges (with accommodation, restaurant, & shop)	**Phakding** (0km) » **Zamphuti** (1.3km) » **Toc Toc** (2km) » **Benkar** (3.6km) » **Chumoa** (4.5km) » **Monjo** (5.3km) » **Jorsale** (6.5km) » **Namche** (11.3km) Before Jorsale, there are plenty of lodges and shops. No facilities between Jorsale and Namche (except shop at checkpoint above 8).
Terrain/ Navigation	Undulating paths which are well-maintained but occasionally steep. S of Jorsale, the undulating route gradually gains height. However, after Jorsale, the path climbs more steeply. Route-finding is mostly straightforward. However, navigate carefully between Phakding and Toc Toc: if in doubt, keep N, alongside the river.
Difficulty	**Medium**. Most trekkers start to feel the effects of altitude above Jorsale. The suspension bridges are straightforward for most but will be more challenging for those with a fear of heights.
Medical Assistance	**Lukla Hospital**; **Zamphuti health post** (4; 1.3km; see p103); **Khunde Hospital** (2.7km N of Namche).
Points of Interest	Five suspension bridges The first Everest viewpoints of the trek: 8 The town of Namche: 9

Things to do in Namche

Namche Gompa: this colourful monastery has a prominent position on the W slopes of the town (along the route to Thame). It is about 100 years old and the outside is lined with prayer wheels. Inside, you will find a large statue of Guru Rinpoche. Nauche Gonda Visitor Centre, located in the monastery's courtyard, contains interesting objects and displays on Sherpa traditions and history.

Sherpa Culture Museum (www.sherpa-culture.com.np): this excellent museum is located on the hill to the E of town (see p116 for directions). It has three sections, all of which are fascinating. Firstly, there is a reconstruction of a traditional sherpa house (stuffed with exhibits) which you can fully explore. Secondly, there is a suite of rooms full of photographs and newspaper cuttings, documenting the Khumbu's mountaineering history. Thirdly, there is a new building filled with exhibits on every part of Sherpa culture and life in the Khumbu.

Sagarmatha National Park Visitor Centre: located near the Sherpa Culture Museum (see p116 for directions). It has a superb Everest viewpoint, a famous statue of Tenzing Norgay and a simple museum on the people, culture, natural history and geology of the Khumbu.

Sagarmatha Next: see p112.

Acclimatisation hike to Khumjung village: three different routes climb N from Namche to Khumjung: SR9 (p112), SR10 (p118) and GL3 (p224). You can use one route on the outbound journey and a different one on the return. We like to use SR9 to climb to Khumjung and then SR10 to descend back to Namche (via the village of Khunde): the scenery is exquisite and you pass Namche Gompa on the return. Save plenty of time for a coffee at Hotel Everest View on the way up.

Surprise snowfall at Namche with Kongde Ri in the background

GL8c
Khumjung (3780m)
Khunde (3840m)
Sanasa (3600m)
GL4a
Kyāñajumā (3600
SR10
GL3
Hotel Everest View
Phurte
Syangboche
SR9
EBC3a
EBC10h
Sagarmatha Next
Tenzing Norgay Memorial Stupa
Sherpa Culture Museum
Sagarmatha National Park Headquarters
Namche Bazar (3440m)
Dudh Koshi
Everest Viewpoint (3120m)
Bhote Koshi
Hillary Suspension Bridge (2930m)
EBC2b
EBC11a
Jorsale (2820m)
Monjo (2840m)
Chumoa (2760m)
Benkar (2715m)
N
W
E
S
Tengi Ragi Tau
Taboche
Nuptse I
Everest
Lhotse
Kongde Ri
Kusum Kangguru
360

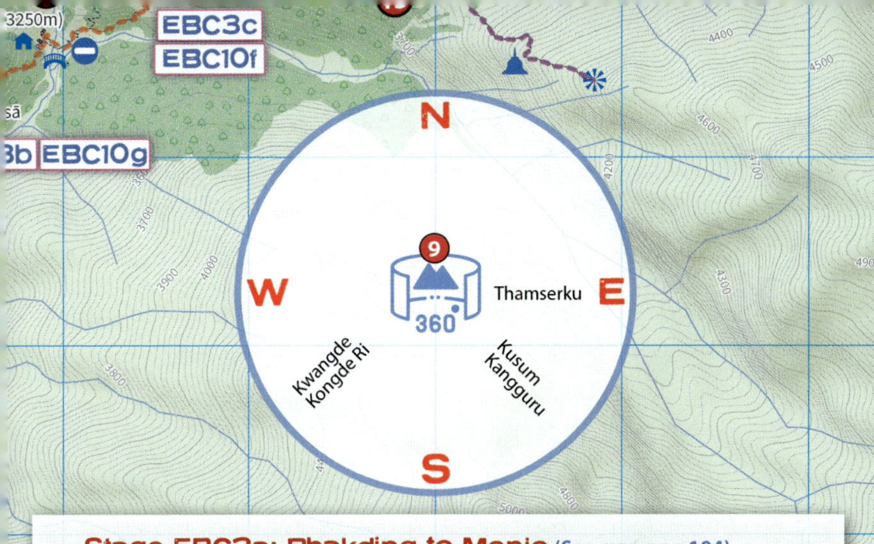

Stage EBC2a: Phakding to Monjo (See map on p104)

3 From the **E side of Phakding**, cross to the W bank of the Dudh Koshi using the **suspension bridge**. Pass between the lodges on the **W side of Phakding**. Then TR behind the lodges and follow a path upstream. 5min later, TR at a fork.

4 0:25: 10min later, pass through the village of **Zamphuti (2700m)**. 5min later, pass a police **checkpoint** where you may have to show your passport. Then pass through the village of **Toc Toc (2710m)** and continue up the valley. Pass a little waterfall and soon climb to a viewpoint: to the NE, you can see Thamserku.

5 1:25: **(See map on p110)**. Soon after another waterfall, pass through the village of **Benkar (2715m)**. The path descends before continuing upstream. Shortly after Benkar, cross to the E bank of the Dudh Koshi using a **suspension bridge**. Then head N again. Pass the village of **Chumoa (2760m)**.

6 2:20: Arrive in **Monjo (2840m)**.

Stage EBC2b: Monjo to Namche (See map on p110)

6 At the **N edge of Monjo**, reach a **SNP checkpoint**: after buying a permit, go through the archway to enter the SNP and continue N up the valley. 20min later, cross a suspension bridge over the Dudh Koshi. Shortly afterwards, pass through **Jorsale** (2820m; last accommodation before Namche). Shortly, after Jorsale, TR and cross another **suspension bridge** over the river. Just afterwards, reach a junction: most trekkers TL, following the path closest to the river; however, you can also use the higher path on the right which is slightly more difficult; both paths converge about 1km further N.

7 1:40: After a steep climb, cross the new **Hillary Suspension Bridge (2930m)**: you can see the old bridge below. This is the highest and most exhilarating bridge of the day. Afterwards, climb steeply through the trees. Pass a **viewpoint** from which you can see Everest in the distance to the NE.

8 2:30: Reach the **Everest Viewpoint (3120m)** where you can view Everest, Lhotse, Nuptse and Taboche. It is often claimed to be the first place from which to spot Everest (heading N from Lukla) but you may have already seen it at the earlier (lower) viewpoint. There is a toilet at the viewpoint. Continue climbing through the trees. After a while, pass a **checkpoint** where you need to show your permits: there are toilets and a shop.

9 3:45: Reach the entrance of **Namche (3440m)**.

Side Route: Namche to Khumjung (via Hotel Everest View)

This spectacular route climbs the hillside N of Namche to some incredible vantage points. It is one of the most popular acclimatisation hikes for those spending time in Namche. There are great views of Everest and a host of other peaks including Thamserku and Kongde Ri which dominate so much of your attention in the Namche area. At the top of the hill, you will reach Hotel Everest View which is the most famous hotel in the Khumbu and is a great place for lunch: see p116.

You will also pass Sagarmatha Next, a visitor centre with an art gallery and café. This beautiful complex promotes sustainable trekking and raises awareness of the waste disposal issues that the tourist industry causes in the Khumbu. The art gallery displays beautiful art, created by local and resident artists using some of the Khumbu's waste materials: you can buy artwork and have it shipped to your home. All profits generated are reinvested in improving waste management in the Khumbu region.

The lovely, green-roofed village of Khumjung is more peaceful than busy Namche. With plenty to do, it is one of the most enjoyable villages in the region and is a fabulous place to stay if you have time. The monastery (with its 'yeti scalp') is located to the N of the village

		Time	Distance	Ascent	Descent	SA Increase	Max Alt
SR9 S-N	Namche to Khumjung	2:10	3.5km 2.2miles	450m 1476ft	110m 361ft	+340m +1116ft	3890m 12763ft
SR9 N-S	Khumjung to Namche	1:30	3.5km 2.2miles	110m 361ft	450m 1476ft	-340m -1116ft	3890m 12763ft

Everest, Lhotse & Nuptse from Hotel Everest View

(see p114). The Edmund Hillary School lies to the S of the village: it was built by Hillary in 1961, making it the first school in the Khumbu. Nearby, you will find the region's longest mani wall.

You can return to Namche by retracing your steps but it is nicer to make a circuit by combining SR9 with either SR10 (p118) or GL3 (p224). Alternatively, rather than hiking SR9 as a side-route during a Namche AD, you can actually incorporate it into the main part of your trek by using it to travel between Namche and Sanasa (as an alternative to EBC3a): after using SR9 to travel from Namche to Khumjung, follow GL4a to Sanasa (see p121).

Lodges (with accommodation, restaurant, & shop)	**Namche** (0km) » **Sherpa Panorama Hotel** (1.6km) » **Hotel Everest View** (2.7km) » **Khumjung** (3.5km) Also, there is a café at **Sagarmatha Next** (1.2km)
Terrain/ Navigation	The rocky paths are uneven at times but straightforward to follow. The route between Namche and Sagarmatha Next is very steep.
Difficulty	**Medium**. The route is short but most trekkers will be feeling the effects of altitude.
Medical Assistance	**Khunde Hospital** (1km W of Khumjung)
Points of Interest	**Sagarmatha Next** **Hotel Everest View** **Khumjung:** monastery with 'yeti scalp' (p114); Edmund Hillary School; longest mani wall in the Khumbu

Khumjung Monastery & the Yeti Scalp

Khumjung's gompa (Samten Choling Gompa) is thought to be the second oldest in the Khumbu (after Pangboche). It was badly damaged in the 2015 earthquake but has now been restored. Visitors are welcome to visit and to view the purported yeti scalp on display. The scalp has been kept at the monastery for more than 200 years. In 1960, Edmund Hillary returned to Nepal to investigate the existence of yetis. With the permission of village elders, Hillary took the scalp out of Nepal for examination. After scientists concluded that the scalp was in fact made from the hide of a serow goat, it was returned to Khumjung. Curiously, a duplicate made by a villager was also removed by Hillary and it now resides in the Explorers Club in New York.

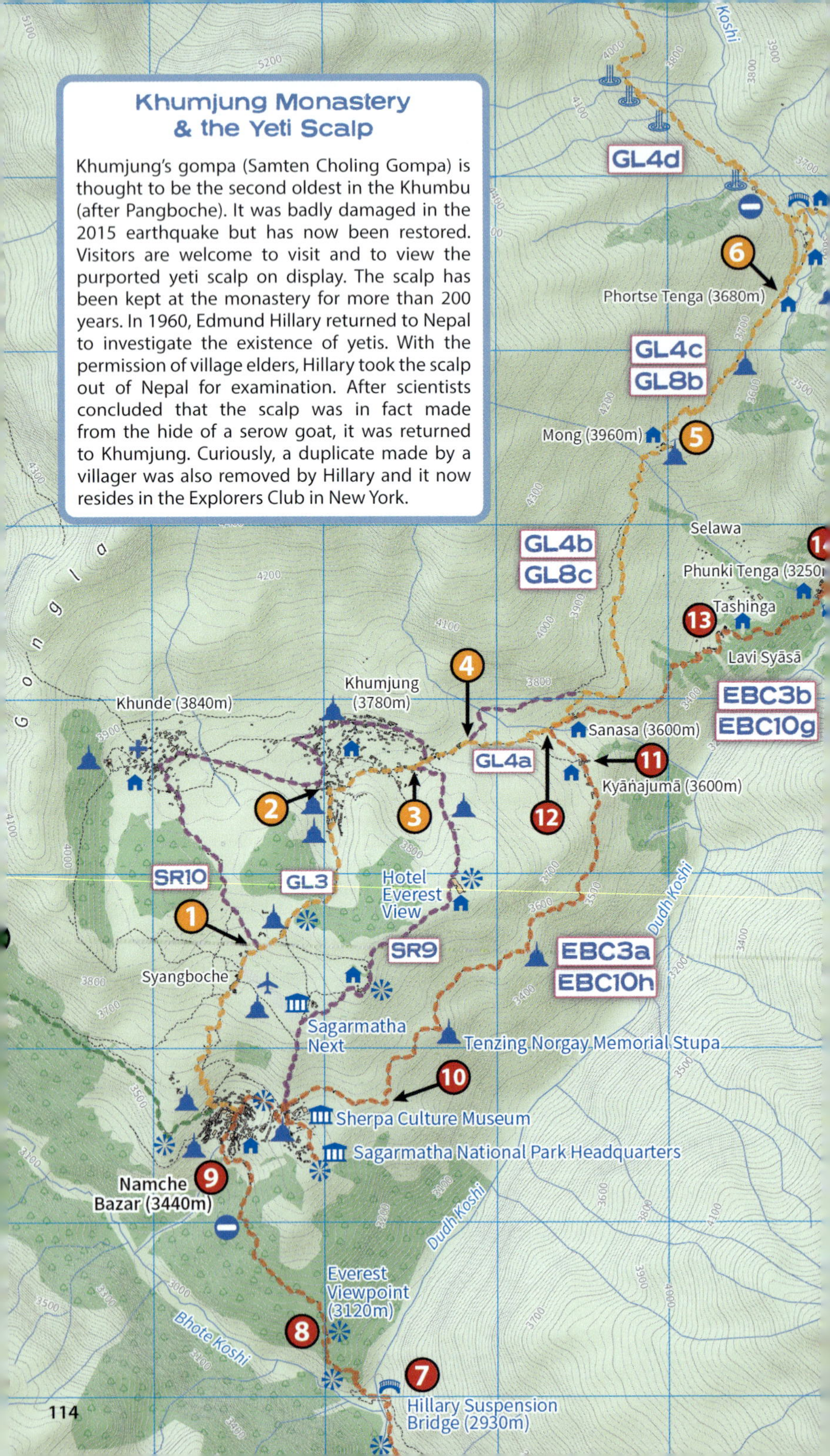

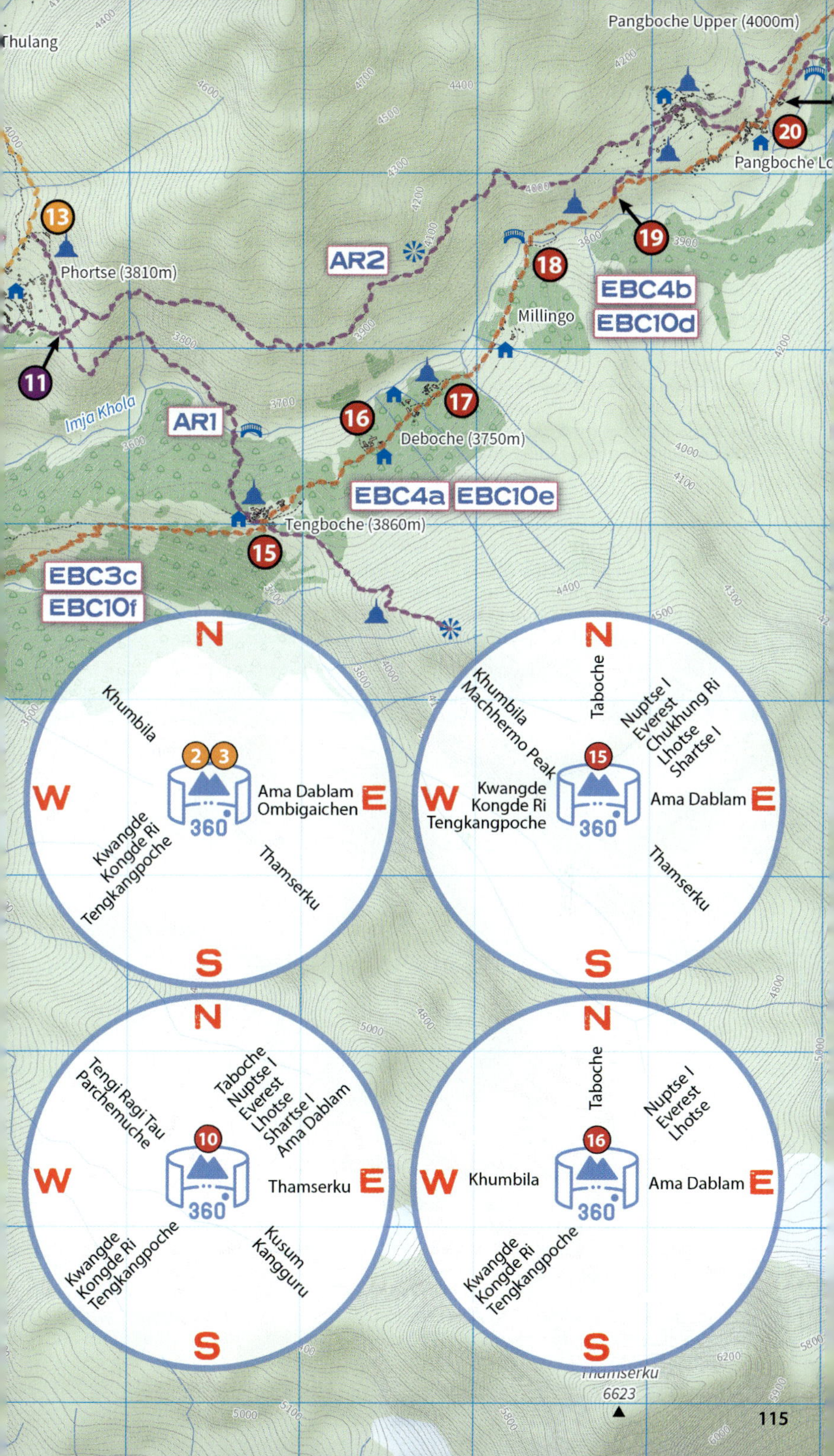

Thulang
Pangboche Upper (4000m)
Pangboche Lo
Phortse (3810m)
AR2
Millingo
EBC4b
EBC10d
Imja Khola
AR1
Deboche (3750m)
EBC4a
EBC10e
Tengboche (3860m)
EBC3c
EBC10f
N
W
E
S
Khumbila
Ama Dablam
Ombigaichen
Kwangde
Kongde Ri
Tengkangpoche
Thamserku
360
N
W
E
S
Taboche
Khumbila
Machhermo Peak
Nuptse I
Everest
Chukhung Ri
Lhotse
Shartse I
Kwangde
Kongde Ri
Tengkangpoche
Ama Dablam
Thamserku
360
N
W
E
S
Tengi Ragi Tau
Parchemuche
Taboche
Nuptse I
Everest
Lhotse
Shartse I
Ama Dablam
Thamserku
Kwangde
Kongde Ri
Tengkangpoche
Kusum
Kangguru
360
N
W
E
S
Taboche
Nuptse I
Everest
Lhotse
Khumbila
Ama Dablam
Kwangde
Kongde Ri
Tengkangpoche
360
Thamserku
6623

SR9: Namche/Khumjung (via Hotel Everest View)

(See map on p114)

S-N

9 Climb Namche's main cobbled street. At the top of the town, the path bends right past the **Moonlight Lodge** and climbs SE. Shortly after **Mountain Lodge**, TL at a junction beside a **prayer wheel**: alternatively, TR for the **Sherpa Culture Museum/SNP Visitor Centre** (p108). Soon pass to the left of a huge **mani stone**: after it, keep SH at a junction beside **Mustang Guest House**. Now the path zigzags steeply up to the N.

At about **3700m**, keep SH (N) at a junction: ignore the path on the left (which heads NW to meet GL3). Shortly afterwards, reach **Sagarmatha Next** (p112). From there, climb NE and soon pass to the right of **Sherpa Panorama Hotel**. Continue N: 15-20mins later, reach **Hotel Everest View** (terrace with superb views; see below). Bear left and head around the W side of the hotel on a path. 10-15min later, pass a **stupa**. 10min later, reach a junction at the E side of Khumjung (3): TL to enter the village of **Khumjung (3780m)**; alternatively, TR for Sanasa (GL4a).

N-S

From **Mount Everest Bakery Café** in **Khumjung**, head E. Shortly afterwards, TR at a junction at the E side of the village (3): head S on a path. 10min later, pass a **stupa**. 20-30min later, head around the W side of **Hotel Everest View** (terrace with superb views; see below). From the front of the hotel, descend S on a path. 15min later, pass to the left of **Sherpa Panorama Hotel**. From there, descend SW and soon reach **Sagarmatha Next** (p112). Head S on a path which descends in steep zigzags.

Eventually, keep SH at a junction (beside **Mustang Guest House**) and pass a huge **mani stone**. Shortly afterwards, TR at a junction (beside a **prayer wheel**): alternatively, TL for the **Sherpa Culture Museum/SNP Visitor Centre** (p108). Descend towards the buildings of Namche. Near **Moonlight Lodge**, the path bends left and descends steeply S through **Namche** on its main cobbled street 9.

Hotel Everest View

Hotel Everest View is located above Namche at an altitude of 3880m. When it opened in 1971, it claimed to be the highest hotel in the world. Each of the bedrooms has a view of Everest. With no road access, all materials for its construction were carried up by porters, pack-animals and helicopters. Initially, guests were flown in, directly from Kathmandu, to Syangboche Airstrip (a short distance SW of the hotel). However, many guests developed AMS and reportedly, some even died: incredibly, the hotel supplied oxygen tanks to guests to alleviate the symptoms of AMS! Eventually, the airstrip was shut down and guests then had to walk up from Lukla.

SR10: Namche/Khumjung (via Khunde) (See map on p114)

S-N

9 Head to **Namche Gompa**. From there, zigzag steeply up to the N: the path splits but the branches soon converge. After 1hr, keep SH at a junction: the path on the left goes to Thame. Shortly afterwards, cross **Syangboche Airstrip**. A few minutes later, TL at a junction (1; 'Khunde'): the path to the right heads directly to Khumjung (GL3). Cross the top of the ridge and descend into **Khunde (3840m)**. TR just before the **hospital** and descend ESE on a clear path. Reach the **S end of Khumjung** (2; 3780m).

N-S

2 From the **S end of Khumjung**, climb W on a clear path. After 20-30min, reach **Khunde (3840m)**. TL just after the hospital and head SE out of the village. Climb over a ridge and then descend SE. TR at a junction (1; 'Namche'). Shortly afterwards, cross **Syangboche Airstrip** and continue descending on a path. Shortly after that, keep SH at a junction: the path on the right goes to Thame. The path descends steeply in zigzags: it splits but the branches soon converge. Eventually, reach **Namche Gompa** (9).

Thamserku viewed from above Namche (SR9)

Thamserku (6623m)

Thamserku is far from the highest mountain in the Khumbu but its distinctive pyramid shape ensures that it is one of the most recognisable. It was first climbed in 1964 and since then, only a handful of people have successfully reached its difficult summit. In 2014, a Russian duo made the first ascent of the SW face.

SR10 Side Route: Namche to Khumjung (via Khunde)

Another spectacular hike which you can use to fill spare time in Namche. Like Stage SR9 (p112), this route climbs the hillside N of the village to some incredible vantage points. However, SR10 heads further W than SR9, visiting the village of Khunde as well as Khumjung. There are fabulous views of Thamserku and Kongde Ri.

Green-roofed Khumjung is a highlight of the Namche area: on arrival at (2), you can either follow GL3 east through the village (coloured orange on the map) or an alternative route (coloured purple on the map) which heads around the N of the village, passing the gompa (p114). For further information on Khumjung, see p112.

Khunde is also colourful but is more compact than Khumjung and attracts fewer visitors. Khunde is home to the region's main hospital which was built in 1966 by Sir Edmund Hillary.

		Time	Distance	Ascent	Descent	SA Increase	Max Alt
SR10 S-N	Namche to Khumjung	2:40	4.1km 2.5miles	400m 1312ft	60m 197ft	+340m +1116ft	3860m 12665ft
SR10 N-S	Khumjung to Namche	2:00	4.1km 2.5miles	60m 197ft	400m 1312ft	-340m -1116ft	3860m 12665ft

Khumjung

You can return to Namche by retracing your steps but it is nicer to make a circuit by combining SR10 with either SR9 (p112) or GL3 (p224). Alternatively, rather than hiking SR10 as a side-route during a Namche AD, you can actually incorporate it into the main part of your trek by using it to travel between Namche and Sanasa (as an alternative to EBC3a): after using SR10 to travel from Namche to Khumjung, follow GL4a to Sanasa (see p121).

For SR10 route description, see p117.

Lodges (with accommodation, restaurant, & shop)	**Namche** (0km) » **Khunde** (2.7km) » **Khumjung** (4.1km)
Terrain/ Navigation	The rocky paths are uneven at times but straightforward to follow. The route between Namche and Syangboche is very steep.
Difficulty	**Medium**. The route is short but most trekkers will be feeling the effects of altitude.
Medical Assistance	**Khunde Hospital** (1km W of Khumjung).
Points of Interest	**Syangboche Airstrip:** (see p116) **Khunde** **Khumjung:** monastery with 'yeti scalp' (p114); Edmund Hillary School; longest mani wall in the Khumbu

EBC3 Namche to Tengboche

EBC3a: Taboche (centre), Everest, Nuptse and Lhotse (behind to the right)

From Namche, an exquisite path heads NE, initially following the Dudh Koshi again. The main route starts at the top of the town, passing close to the Sherpa Culture Museum and the SNP Visitor Centre (p108): if you did not visit them during your AD, then now is the time to do it. In no time, you are out of the village: looking back towards it, you see Thamserku, towering above the colourful buildings. A short distance further along, heavenly scenes await if the weather is clear: after passing around a spur, you should spot the sublime Ama Dablam for the first time. Although it is not the highest mountain in the Khumbu, there is no doubt that Ama Dablam is one of its most spectacular. Lhotse and Nuptse soon appear too, with the dark triangular summit of Everest itself tucked in behind them. In the process of planning your trip, you will have spent many hours dreaming about these peaks and you will therefore be delighted to hear that they feature regularly throughout the day.

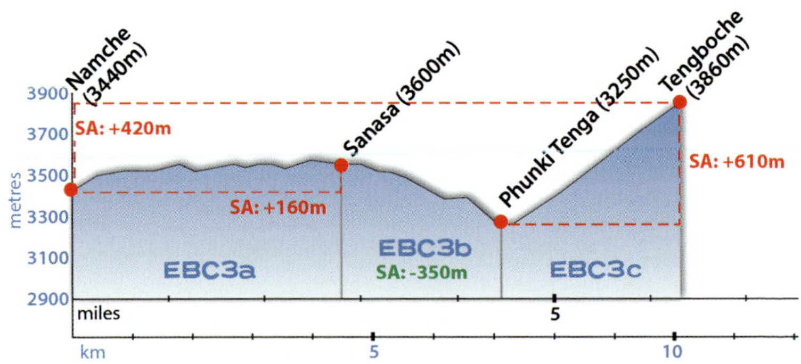

		Time	Distance	Ascent	Descent	SA Increase	Max Alt
EBC3a	Namche to Sanasa	1:55	4.5km 2.8miles	230m 755ft	70m 230ft	+160m +525ft	3600m 11812ft
EBC3b	Sanasa to Phunki Tenga	0:40	2.6km 1.6miles	10m 33ft	360m 1181ft	-350m -1148ft	3600m 11812ft
EBC3c	Phunki Tenga to Tengboche	2:15	3.0km 1.9miles	610m 2001ft	0m 0ft	+610m +2001ft	3860m 12665ft

Getting to Sanasa: 4.5km from Namche, you reach the important junction at Sanasa (3600m; 12): in fact, there are three other ways to get to this junction from Namche and they are all incredibly scenic:

- **Sanasa via Everest View Hotel** (SR9, GL4a; p112)
- **Sanasa via Khumjung** (GL3, GL4a; p224)
- **Sanasa via Khunde and Khumjung** (SR10, GL4a; p118)

All these routes are fully described in this book and marked on our maps. For CEBC trekkers, it makes sense to use different routes on the outbound and return journeys.

Moving up from Sanasa: from Sanasa, the main route heads directly to Tengboche (EBC3b/3c) and from there, continues directly to Pangboche (EBC4a/4b): **Sanasa » Tengboche » Deboche » Pangboche**. However, there are three alternative ways to travel from Sanasa to Pangboche:

- **Sanasa » Phortse » Tengboche » Deboche » Pangboche** (GL4b, GL4c, GL8a, AR1, EBC4a, EBC4b)
- **Sanasa » Tengboche » Phortse » Pangboche** (EBC3b, EBC3c, AR1, AR2)
- **Sanasa » Phortse » Pangboche** (GL4b, GL4c, GL8a, AR2)

Of these four routes to Pangboche, three visit Tengboche but one does not. They are all spectacular and are all described in this book. For CEBC trekkers, it makes sense to use different routes on the outbound and return journeys. The two routes which use AR2 (p126) are our favourites because this balcony path is quite simply divine: we like to break up the journey with an overnight stop at Khumjung or Phortse.

Because it is only 420m higher than Namche, Tengboche is an important overnight stop for CEBC trekkers. It is set on a ridge running from the summit of Kangtega (which is not actually visible from the village): however, Everest, Lhotse and Nuptse are on display, in all their glory. Even without such a great outlook, Tengboche would be a fabulous place to visit, having one of the region's finest monasteries (see p123). It can be busy in the afternoon (when trekkers arrive from Namche), however, it is quieter in the mornings. Because there are only a handful of lodges, beds can be hard to find. For alternative places to stay, see p122.

Lodges (with accommodation, restaurant, & shop)	**Namche** (0km) » **Kyanajuma** (4km) » **Sanasa** (4.5km) » **Tashinga** (6.2km) » **Phunki Tenga** (7.1km) » **Tengboche** (10.1km) Plenty of lodges and shops along the route; Tengboche Bakery has good cakes (NE of the monastery).
Terrain/ Navigation	Undulating paths which are generally well-maintained and easy to follow. Some steep and/or sustained climbs and descents. In particular, the descent from Sanasa to Phunki Tenga is a knee-jerker and the climb from Phunki Tenga to Tengboche is long and tiring. Route-finding is mostly straightforward. However, navigate carefully at the junctions at Sanasa where there is a variety of different options.
Difficulty	**Medium**. At 3860m, most trekkers will feel the altitude. The suspension bridge at 14 is straightforward (unless you have a fear of heights).
Medical Assistance	**Khunde Hospital** (1km W of Khumjung)
Points of Interest	Superb views of Everest, Lhotse, Nuptse and Ama Dablam Tenzing Norgay Memorial Stupa (near 10) Suspension Bridge at Phunki Tenga 14 Tengboche Gompa 15

Tengboche Overnight Alternatives

Deboche 16: 15min NE of Tengboche (along EBC4a/4b). At 3750m, Deboche is good for acclimatisation but its shady location among trees can make it a cold place.

Phunki Tenga 14: about 2hr before Tengboche (EBC3b/3c). It can be easier to find a room but the village is too close to Namche for most people. Furthermore, at 3250m, it is lower than Namche which is not optimal for acclimatisation purposes.

Phortse 11: 2hr N of Tengboche (along AR1; p124). At 3810m, it is a great place for acclimatisation.

Stage EBC3a: Namche to Sanasa (See map on p114)

9 Climb Namche's main cobbled street. At the top of the town, the path bends right past the **Moonlight Lodge** and climbs SE. Shortly after **Mountain Lodge**, TL at a junction (beside a **prayer wheel**): alternatively, TR for the **Sherpa Culture Museum/ SNP Visitor Centre**. Soon pass to the left of a huge **mani stone**: after it, TR and head E past **Mustang Guest House**. The beautiful path now contours around the slopes.

10 0:30: The path bends left to head NE up the **Dudh Koshi valley**. Soon, the 'big guns' come into view: Ama Dablam is closest (on the right); Lhotse is further back on the left; the pyramid summit of Everest appears to Lhotse's left. As you continue, Nuptse's ridge shows itself. 15min later, pass **Tenzing Norgay Memorial Stupa**. 20min later, pass another **stupa**.

11 1:45: Keep SH past the lodges and bakery at **Kyanajuma (3600m)**: the path heading W goes to Khumjung.

12 1:55: Reach a junction at **Sanasa (3600m)** where there are three options: head E for Phunki Tenga (EBC3b); N for Mong (GL4b; p227); W for Khumjung (GL4a; p227).

Stage EBC3b: Sanasa to Phunki Tenga (See map on p114)

12 From the junction, head E. Soon, the path descends through forest.

13 0:25: Pass the lodges at **Tashinga**. Then descend through trees.

14 0:40: Reach the lodges and restaurants at **Phunki Tenga (3250m)**.

Stage EBC3c: Phunki Tenga to Tengboche (See map on p114)

14 At the N side of **Phunki Tenga**, TL sharply to climb up to a suspension bridge over the **Dudh Koshi**. Cross the bridge and pass some restaurants on the other side. Shortly afterwards, pass a SNP checkpoint. Then climb steeply through trees, following the **Imja Khola** NE and leaving the Dudh Koshi behind (which heads N).

15 2:15: After a long climb, go through an arched gateway to reach **Tengboche (3860m)**.

Tengboche side-route (2-3hr return)

Those with surplus energy, could ascend the ridge to the SE of Tengboche to a superb viewpoint. This 500m climb can help with acclimatisation but most trekkers will be too tired to try it on the same day as hiking from Namche: as an alternative, you could do it the following morning, before proceeding to Deboche or Pangboche.

Tengboche Gompa

Tengboche Monastery (Dawa Choling Gompa) was built in 1916 by Lamu Gulu. The current building is the third structure to have served as the monastery here. The original building was destroyed by earthquake in 1934 but it was quickly rebuilt. In 1989, that building was destroyed by electrical fire (together with many precious scriptures and other relics): it was rebuilt by volunteers, supervised by the spiritual leader, Nawang Tenzing Jangpo (who is believed to be the reincarnation of Lamu Gulu). The monastery suffered damage in the 2015 earthquake but this has now been repaired.

Tengboche Gompa gained international interest after the successful 1953 expedition to Everest because Tenzing Norgay (p92) claimed that he spent time in Tengboche during his childhood: later accounts have cast doubt upon this. Today, Everest mountaineers still visit the monastery to seek blessing. Trekkers are welcome too and, at the date of writing, opening hours were 7-8 a.m./9-11 a.m./1-5 p.m. You can also attend the daily puja (prayers): twice daily (early morning and mid-afternoon); exact times change so ask on arrival. In the gompa, remove your shoes and sit cross-legged (away from the practising monks): do not take photos unless a sign states that this is permitted and do not wear shorts. Leave a donation to help with the upkeep of the monastery.

This lovely route traverses the Imja Khola valley between Phortse and Tengboche: a bridge facilitates the crossing of the river. Fewer trekkers use this route and it therefore provides a reasonable chance of spotting wildlife. The hillsides on either side of the valley are steep: the Tengboche side is forested but the slopes on the Phortse side are more open, with spectacular views.

Lodges (with accommodation, restaurant, & shop)	**Phortse** (0km) » **Tengboche** (2.6km)
Terrain/ Navigation	The climb and descent are long and steep. The undulating rocky paths are uneven at times. Route-finding is generally straightforward.
Difficulty	**Hard**. A steep climb in either direction.
Medical Assistance	**Khunde Hospital** (1km W of Khumjung) **Pheriche Aid Post**: run by the Himalayan Rescue Association; open for emergencies at any time; altitude presentation at 3pm daily; **www.himalayanrescue.org**
Points of Interest	**Phortse village:** 11 **Tengboche Gompa:** 15 (p123)

Nuptse, Everest, Lhotse & Ama Dablam from Tengboche

(See map on p114)

N-S

From (11) at the **SE edge of Phortse**, follow a path that initially descends S. Soon, the path bends right and climbs briefly. After that, descend again, contouring around the slopes. Cross a bridge over the **Imja Khola**. Then climb steeply S through forest to **Tengboche (3860m; (15))**.

S-N

From **Tengboche (15)**, descend N through forest. Cross a bridge over the **Imja Khola**. Then climb NW on a path which contours around the slopes. Arrive at (11) at the **SE edge of Phortse (3810m)**.

		Time	Distance	Ascent	Descent	SA Increase	Max Alt
AR1 N-S	Phortse to Tengboche	1:40	2.6km 1.6miles	358m 1175ft	308m 1011ft	+50m +164ft	3860m 12665ft
AR1 S-N	Tengboche to Phortse	1:40	2.6km 1.6miles	308m 1011ft	358m 1175ft	-50m -164ft	3860m 12665ft

AR2 Alternative Route: Phortse/Pangboche

On a fine day, this will be a highlight of your trip. The route between Phortse and Pangboche takes advantage of one of the finest balcony paths that you will walk in your lifetime: even by the lofty standards of the Khumbu, it is exceptional in either direction. Across the valley to the S, you can see Tengboche Monastery (perched on its ridge) and Thamserku is so close that you can almost touch it. To the NE, the views of Everest, Lhotse and Nuptse are wonderful. If you are lucky, the enormous Himalayan Griffons will be in flight, soaring level with your shoulders.

Lodges (with accommodation, restaurant, & shop)	**Phortse** (0km) » **Pangboche Upper & Lower** (5.8km)
Terrain/ Navigation	The climb and descent are steep in places. The undulating rocky paths are uneven. Route-finding is generally straightforward except that the labyrinth of paths near Pangboche Upper can be confusing.
Difficulty	**Hard**. The path undulates regularly and there is more ascent/descent than you might think from looking at the map. The altitude reaches 4085m and your body will feel it.
Medical Assistance	**Khunde Hospital** (1km W of Khumjung) **Pheriche Aid Post**: see p124
Points of Interest	Phortse village: 11 Exquisite viewpoint at 4085m Superb views of Everest, Lhotse and Nuptse Pangboche Upper/Lower & Pangboche Monastery (p130): 20

AR2 balcony path: Kongde Ri (6187m) with Khatang (6853m) behind

(See map on p114)

W-E

From the **SE edge of Phortse** (11), follow a path that climbs NE. Soon, TR on a path that contours E up the **Imja Khola** valley. The route undulates, gradually climbing to an extraordinary **viewpoint (4085m)** overlooking Thamserku: porters often rest here. Afterwards, the path continues contouring around the slopes, generally descending NE. Eventually, reach the outskirts of **Pangboche Upper**: work your way NE through the village to reach **Pangboche Monastery** (4000m; p130).

From the N side of the monastery, follow a path heading E. Shortly after a lodge, TR at a fork (easy to miss; signpost on tree) to head to Pangboche Lower: the path on the left heads directly to Shomare (without passing through Pangboche Lower). Shortly, bear left around a big pile of mani stones. Soon descend more steeply. 10-15min from the top, TL at **Himalayan Lodge** to enter **Pangboche Lower (3930m; 20)**.

E-W

From **Himalayan Lodge** in **Pangboche Lower (20)**, take a path climbing W. After a while, keep left around a big pile of mani stones. Shortly before a lodge, keep SH at a junction. Head W though **Pangboche Upper** to reach **Pangboche Monastery** (4000m; p130).

Work your way SW through the buildings and soon exit the village. The undulating path contours around the slopes, gradually climbing SW to an extraordinary **viewpoint (4085m)** which overlooks Thamserku: porters often rest here. Afterwards, the path continues contouring around the slopes, generally descending W. Eventually, reach (11) at the **SE edge of Phortse (3810m)**.

		Time	Distance	Ascent	Descent	SA Increase	Max Alt
AR2 W-E	Phortse to Pangboche	2:45	5.8km 3.6miles	431m 1414ft	311m 1020ft	+120m +394ft	4085m 13403ft
AR2 E-W	Pangboche to Phortse	2:30	5.8km 3.6miles	311m 1020ft	431m 1414ft	-120m -394ft	4085m 13403ft

EBC4 Tengboche to Pangboche

Stupa in front of Ama Dablam

Acclimatisation continues with a stunning route up the Imja Khola valley to Pangboche. From Tengboche, descend briefly to reach the village of Deboche which is closer to the valley floor. Then follow the river NE, past Deboche Nunnery and some interesting mani walls. Cross the river on a fabulous suspension bridge which faces Ama Dablam. Then climb to Pangboche on a magnificent balcony path: Ama Dablam is visible all the way up and Lhotse, Nuptse and Everest soon make an appearance too.

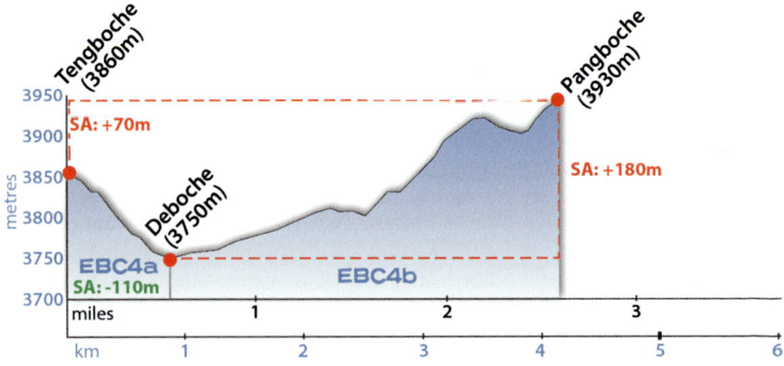

		Time	Distance	Ascent	Descent	SA Increase	Max Alt
EBC4a	Tengboche to Deboche	0:15	0.8km 0.5miles	0m 0ft	110m 361ft	-110m -361ft	3860m 12665ft
EBC4b	Deboche to Pangboche	1:45	3.4km 2.1miles	240m 787ft	60m 197ft	+180m +591ft	3930m 12894ft

There is also an alternative higher altitude route between Tengboche and Pangboche which travels via Phortse using AR1 (p124) and AR2 (p126). Although this is longer and more difficult than the main route, it is one of the finest hikes in the entire region.

Although the views from Pangboche are incredible, and it also has a fantastic gompa, it tends to play second fiddle to Tengboche. For many ascending CEBC trekkers, a night at Tengboche is deemed to be unmissable and this means that they simply pass through Pangboche the following day (on the way to Dingboche/Pheriche). As much as we love Tengboche, we think that Pangboche is the more relaxing place: it is well spread out and there are plenty of lodges. Furthermore, because Pangboche Lower and Tengboche are at similar altitudes, they are interchangeable from an acclimatisation point of view. In fact, we recommend spending a night at both places on the way to EBC: that way, you spend two nights at similar altitudes and the short day travelling from Tengboche to Pangboche is effectively an extra AD. If you have even more time, an extremely effective acclimatisation strategy is to spend one night in Tengboche plus two nights in Pangboche: you will reap the benefits as you climb higher towards EBC.

It is easy to keep yourself occupied in Pangboche by hiking between the upper and lower parts of the village and visiting the wonderful monastery (p130). With more energy, you can also hike from Pangboche Upper to the incredible 4085m viewpoint on the AR2 balcony path (2.75hr return; see p126).

Ama Dablam BC Hike: Pangboche is also the staging point for the exquisite acclimatisation hike to Ama Dablam BC (SR1; p134). With two nights in Pangboche, you can do it on your AD. However, even if you only have one night in Pangboche, if you are fit and acclimatising well, you could do Ama Dablam BC first thing in the morning (before hiking to Dingboche in the afternoon); or you could hike it in the afternoon, after walking from Tengboche to Pangboche earlier that day, and then spend the night at Pangboche.

Mid-section, Deboche is a good alternative if you cannot find accommodation in Tengboche. However, Deboche is situated closer to the valley floor and the views are inferior to those at Tengboche and Pangboche: this also means that the sun sets earlier and rises later in Deboche and it can be cold in the evenings and early mornings.

Lodges (with accommodation, restaurant, & shop)	**Tengboche** (0km) » **Deboche** (0.8km) » **Millingo** (1.9km) » **Pangboche Upper & Lower** (4.2km) **Top Tip:** the lodges in Pangboche Upper have superb views and are a great choice for lunch.
Terrain/ Navigation	Undulating paths which are generally well-maintained and easy to follow. Some steep and/or sustained climbs and descents. Route-finding is straightforward.
Difficulty	**Medium**. The altitude reaches 3930m and you will still be acclimatising. The suspension bridge at 18 is straightforward but will be more difficult for those with a fear of heights.
Medical Assistance	**Khunde Hospital:** 1km W of Khumjung **Pheriche Aid Post:** see p124
Points of Interest	Deboche village & Deboche Nunnery: 16 17 Views of Everest, Lhotse, Nuptse, Ama Dablam & Thamserku Suspension Bridge at 18 Beautifully situated stupas between 18 and 20 Pangboche Monastery in Pangboche (Upper): 20

Pangboche Gompa

Located in Pangboche Upper, Pangboche Gompa was founded in the 17th century by Lama Sanje Dorje who is also credited with bringing Tibetan Buddhism to the Khumbu region. It is believed to be the oldest Sherpa monastery in the Khumbu and houses some ancient artefacts and scripts. However, it is more famous for its non-religious treasures. Legend has it that Sanje Dorje frequently meditated in caves and a devoted yeti became his disciple, bringing him food and water. One day, the yeti was killed by falling rocks and, on his return to Pangboche, Sanje Dorje brought its scalp and hand to the monastery: they remained there, as sacred relics, until they were stolen in the 1990s. The hand and scalp currently on display in Pangboche are replicas which were made by a New Zealand film company and donated to the monastery in 2011.

Many locals swear that the relics were authentic yeti body parts but, in the absence of the originals, it is impossible to prove or disprove this theory conclusively. However, the story does not end there. In 2008, an item recorded as a 'yeti's finger' was found in the vaults of the Royal College of Surgeons Hunterian Museum in London: notes attached to it listed its origin as Pangboche Monastery and claimed that the item had been handed to the museum by a Peter Byrne. It turns out that Byrne was an explorer who discovered the hand in Pangboche Monastery in 1958, during an expedition to track down the Abominable Snowman in the Himalayas. Byrne claimed that he later returned to Nepal and persuaded the monastery to lend him one of the relic's fingers: apparently, he had brought with him an old human finger (the origin of which is uncertain!) which he attached to the relic so nobody would notice. Incredibly, he said that James Stewart (the Hollywood actor) smuggled the relic's finger out of Asia in his wife's lingerie case. However, at Heathrow airport in London, the lingerie case went missing and was not handed over by customs officials until a few days later. The finger was then given to primatologist Professor William Osman Hill for examination but nothing further was heard of it. In 2011, DNA tests by the Zoological Society of Scotland found that the finger was of human origin but they could not determine its racial origin conclusively. Unfortunately for science, the finger's chain of custody was broken too many times to make it reliable evidence and there are few people alive to corroborate Byrne's story. Accordingly, it seems likely that the mystery will remain unsolved.

You can visit the gompa (and view the replicas) daily between 8am and 5pm: please leave a donation.

Pangboche Gompa overlooks Kangtega & Thamserku

Stage EBC4a: Tengboche to Deboche (See map on p114)

15 From the **monastery**, descend NE and follow a path into rhododendron forest.

16 0:15: Reach the first lodges of **Deboche (3750m)**.

Stage EBC4b: Deboche to Pangboche (See map on p114)

16 Continue NE through **Deboche**.

17 0:10: Pass **Deboche Nunnery** (which you can usually visit). Shortly afterwards, pass some **mani walls**. For a while, the path stays in the trees, following the E bank of the **Imja Khola**.

18 0:50: Cross a **suspension bridge** over the Imja Khola. There are superb views of Ama Dablam. Afterwards, the path heads up the N bank of the river. Behind, you should spot Tengboche Monastery on its forested ridge. 20min later, pass a large **stupa**. Soon, go through an arched gate. There are more **stupas** and **mani stones**.

19 1:25: At a **fork**, TR for the lodges in Pangboche Lower. Alternatively, TL to climb to the lodges and monastery in Pangboche Upper: see below.

20 1:45: Arrive in **Pangboche Lower (3930m)**.

For Pangboche Upper (30-40min from 19): from the junction at 19, climb steeply NE. Soon continue climbing past a large stupa: the views back towards Tengboche are exquisite. Pass two more large stupas. Later, bear left around a large group of mani stones. Shortly afterwards, just after another stupa, reach a junction: TR for **Pangboche Upper**; alternatively, TL for **Phortse** (AR2; p126).

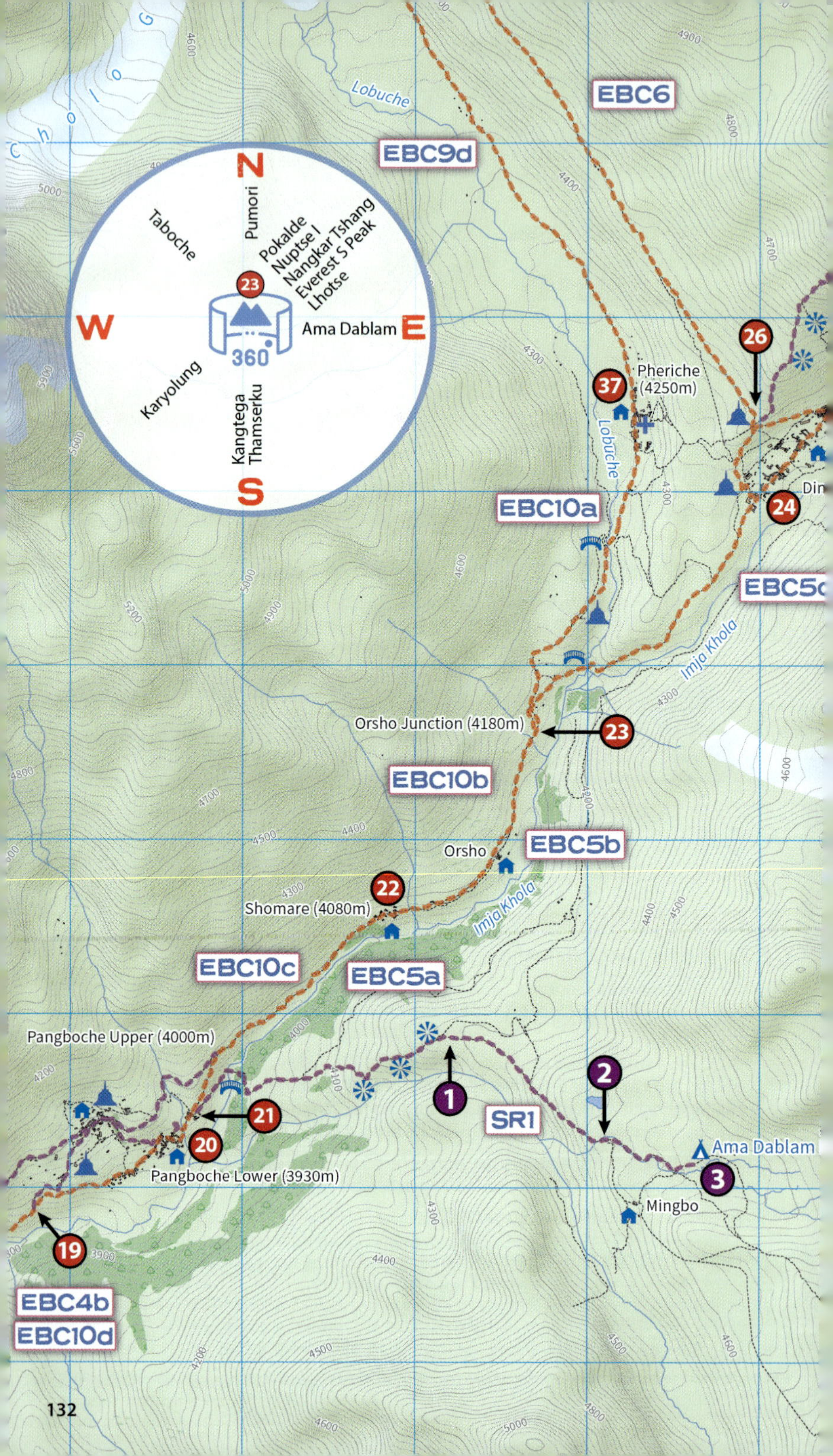

EBC6
EBC9d
Lobuche
N
Pumori
Taboche
Pokalde
Nuptse I
Nangkar Tshang
Everest S Peak
Lhotse
23
W
E
Ama Dablam
360
Karyolung
Kangtega
Thamserku
S
26
37
Pheriche (4250m)
Lobuche
EBC10a
24
Din
EBC5c
Imja Khola
Orsho Junction (4180m)
23
EBC10b
EBC5b
Orsho
22
Shomare (4080m)
Imja Khola
EBC10c
EBC5a
Pangboche Upper (4000m)
1
2
SR1
21
20
Ama Dablam
3
Pangboche Lower (3930m)
Mingbo
19
EBC4b
EBC10d

SR4
Chukhung (4730m)
TP6
Imja Khola
Dowo Tso
Duwo Glacier
Ama Dablam Glacier
Amphu Gyabjen
Ama Dablam
6812
N
Taboche
Nuptse I
Everest
Chukhung Ri
Lhotse
Shartse I
W
Ama Dablam
E
Karyolung
Khatang
Kongde Ri
Kangtega
Thamserku
S
360
N
Nuptse I
Everest S Peak
Lhotse
W
Ama Dablam
E
Kongde Ri
Khatang
Karyolung
Thamserku
S
360
N
Taboche
Khangri East
Pumori
Pokalde
Nuptse I
Chukhung Ri
Everest
Lhotse
W
Khumbila
Ama Dablam
E
Karyolung
Khatang
Numberchuli
Kongde Ri
Tengkangpoche
Thamserku
S
360
N
Taboche
Ngozumpa Kang
Hungchi
Gyachung Kang
LObuche W & E
W
Khumbila
Tengi Ragi Tau
Ama Dablam
E
Khatang
Kongde Ri
Tengkangpoche
Paniyo Tapa
Likhu Chuli
Kangtega
Malanphulan
S
360

SR1 Side Route: Ama Dablam Base Camp

View from 1: Pumori, Nuptse, Everest & Lhotse

Although it is overlooked by most trekkers in the rush towards EBC, the hike to Ama Dablam BC is one of the most spectacular hikes in the Khumbu. It is a highlight of any trek to EBC. For advice on how to incorporate the hike into your schedule, see p129.

Starting from Pangboche, cross the base of the Imja Khola valley and climb steeply up the other side. The views quickly open up and you pass a series of incredible vantage points to reach an exquisite plateau below Ama Dablam itself: at an altitude of 4300m, the 360°

		Time	Distance	Ascent	Descent	SA Increase	Max Alt
SR1	Pangboche to Ama Dablam BC (return)	4:30	8.5km 5.3miles	730m 2395ft	730m 2395ft	0m 0ft	4590m 15060ft

Ama Dablam (6812m)

Ama Dablam is widely considered to be the region's most aesthetically pleasing summit. Loosely translated, its name means 'mother's necklace': the ridges on either side of the summit look like the arms of a mother protecting her child and the summit's hanging glacier looks like a pendant.

It was first climbed in 1961 by a four-man team using the SW ridge. It is now one of the most popular Himalayan peaks for climbers and the SW ridge is still considered to be the safest route. In 2006, a huge serac broke away from the glacier and swept away Camp III, killing 6 people. Because of this, climbers nowadays only use two camps. In 2017, Valery Rozov (the famous Russian base jumper) was killed jumping from Ama Dablam's summit.

panorama is superior to any you have witnessed so far. From there, you can see Everest, Lhotse, Nuptse and a host of new peaks: in particular, Pumori (the stunning peak that will dominate on your final approach to EBC) looks wonderful from this angle.

The superb views continue all the way to Ama Dablam BC where, depending upon the season, you should find a variety of colourful tents which house climbers heading for the summit of Ama Dablam: most expeditions climb in spring and autumn. If you are adventurous and have plenty of energy, you can continue SE beyond Ama Dablam BC (along the path used by the climbers) to a fabulous viewpoint at around 4970m: 2.5-3hr return from Ama Dablam BC.

Lodges (with accommodation, restaurant, & shop)	**Pangboche Upper & Lower** (0km) » **lodge at Mingbo** (3.6km; not always open)
Terrain/ Navigation	Clear paths which are generally well-maintained but rocky in places. The climb/descent is steep and relentless. Route-finding is mostly straightforward.
Difficulty	**Hard**. The climb is long and sometimes steep. The altitude reaches 4590m and you will feel the altitude, making climbing more difficult.
Medical Assistance	**Khunde Hospital:** 1km W of Khumjung **Pheriche Aid Post:** see p124
Points of Interest	**Viewpoint at** (1)**:** see image above **Ama Dablam BC:** (3)

SR1: Ama Dablam Base Camp (See map on p132)

20 Head E through **Pangboche Lower**. Cross a bridge and climb.

21 0:10: TR at a junction beside a large mani rock and wall. Descend alongside a stone wall. Cross a metal bridge over the **Imja Khola**. Then start the long, steep climb.

1 1:45: Reach an incredible **plateau (4300m)** with some superb viewpoints (marked with cairns). From here, you can see Everest, Lhotse, Nuptse, Pumori and many other peaks.

2 2:35: TL at a fork: the path to the right heads to the lodge at **Mingbo**.

3 2:50: Arrive at **Ama Dablam BC (4590m)**. After admiring the views, retrace your steps.

20 4:30: Arrive back at **Pangboche Lower (3930m)**.

Ama Dablam BC: the world's best view from a toilet?!

EBC5 Pangboche to Dingboche

Ama Dablam (EBC5a)

This is a short stage for trekkers who have spent the night at Pangboche but there is plenty to fill time at Dingboche. For those hiking all the way from Tengboche to Dingboche (without an overnight stop at Pangboche), the day will be longer and harder with a lot of climbing. Ama Dablam is on display again, as eye-catching as ever: take the time to enjoy it with a tea break in the village of Shomare. N of Shomare, Nuptse steals the show: from the plateau at Orsho, you will gaze directly onto the S face of its jagged ridge. At Orsho, Pumori also makes its first brief appearance (at least for those who have not visited Ama Dablam BC), although you will need to be quick to spot it. In front of Nuptse, you should see two valleys separated by a ridge: on the right, is the valley of the Imja Khola; on the left, is the Lobuche valley; in-between, the ridge climbs to the top of Pokalde, with Nangkar Tshang Peak halfway up (SR2; p142).

A final steep climb brings you to the sprawling village of Dingboche which has a fabulous location at the base of the Imja Khola valley: looking up the valley, Lhotse looks wonderful, particularly at sunset, however, most of the Nuptse ridge is concealed; to the W, the views of Taboche are incredible.

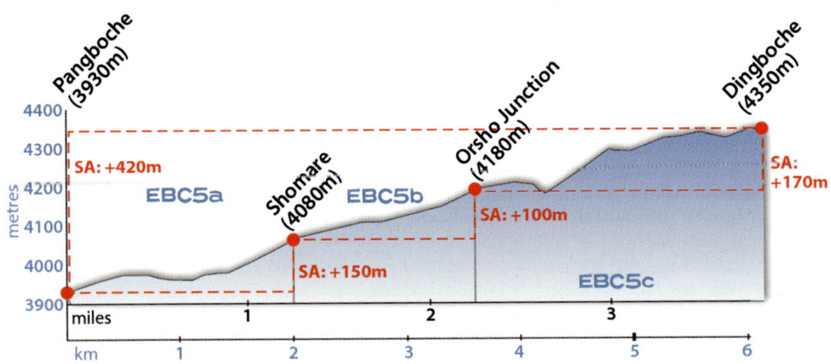

		Time	Distance	Ascent	Descent	SA Increase	Max Alt
EBC5a	Pangboche to Shomare	1:00	2.0km 1.2miles	175m 574ft	25m 82ft	+150m +492ft	4080m 13386ft
EBC5b	Shomare to Orsho Junction	0:40	1.6km 1.0miles	100m 328ft	0m 0ft	+100m +328ft	4180m 13715ft
EBC5c	Orsho Junction to Dingboche	1:10	2.6km 1.6miles	210m 689ft	40m 131ft	+170m +558ft	4350m 14272ft

Although the route is short, it is important to spend time at Dingboche rather than quickly pushing on to higher altitudes. Dingboche is almost 1000m higher than Namche and, according to the generally accepted rules of altitude acclimatisation (p11), it is time to take an AD: although the majority of trekkers do this in Dingboche (spending two nights there), you could instead do it in Pheriche (which is nearby, to the W, in the Lobuche valley). In days gone by, Pheriche was the more popular choice because, at 300-400m higher than Tengboche/Pangboche, it is perfect for acclimatisation. However, Dingboche has grown rapidly in recent years and is now the more popular choice because it is larger than Pheriche and has more lodges, making it easier to find accommodation. Dingboche is 100m higher than Pheriche though, making it 400-500m higher than Tengboche/Pangboche, which may be too much of an altitude jump for some. However, for most people, this jump is manageable provided that you take the recommended AD. If you are acclimatising well, then Dingboche makes more sense for three reasons: firstly, as a larger settlement, it has a wider variety of restaurants/cafés; secondly, the best acclimatisation hikes are more easily accessible from Dingboche; and thirdly, Dingboche keeps the sun longer in the evenings. CEBC trekkers who stay in Dingboche on the way up, can visit Pheriche on the return journey to Namche (or vice versa). For information on hiking from Pangboche to Pheriche, see p141.

Things to do in Dingboche: there is a lot to keep you occupied in Dingboche. Almost everyone does the short hike up to the stupas on the ridge just W of the village: the panorama is incredible (especially at sunrise and sunset); for the first time, you can see Makalu (the world's 5th highest mountain). From the ridge, there are two other options. Firstly, for even better views, you can continue up the ridge to Nangkar Tshang Peak: this side-trip is exquisite and, although you cannot see Everest from the top, it is arguably more dramatic than KP. Secondly, from the ridge, you can walk W down to Pheriche: Dingboche to Pheriche return takes 1.5hr. For directions onto the ridge and climbing Nangkar Tshang Peak, see SR2 (p142). Alternatively, you could use your AD to hike to Chukhung and back (Stage TP6; p178): the return journey from Dingboche takes about half a day.

Moving on from Dingboche: most trekkers head to Dughla or Lobuche after Dingboche using EBC6 (p144). However, instead of staying at Dughla (which is only a short distance from Dingboche and has limited accommodation), you could use Chukhung as your next overnight stop after Dingboche. Chukhung is a nicer place to stay than Dughla and, if you had time, you could even take another AD in Chukhung and use it to climb the exceptional Chukhung Ri (SR4; p186). After Chukhung, you would hike back down to Dingboche and then all the way up to Lobuche (via Dughla) on the main EBC trail: this is a long day but it avoids the need to overnight at Dughla.

Lodges (with accommodation, restaurant, & shop)	**Pangboche Upper & Lower** (0km) » **Shomare** (2km) » **Sunrise Lodge and Restaurant at Orsho** (2.8km) » **Dingboche** (6.2km) **Top Tip:** Café Himalaya (towards the N of Dingboche) has outdoor seats, a wonderful setting and fantastic coffee and cakes.
Terrain/ Navigation	The paths are generally well-maintained although there are rocky sections. Some steep and/or sustained climbs and descents. In particular, the climb from the Lobuche river to Dingboche is steep and tiring at the end of the day. Route-finding is straightforward.
Difficulty	**Medium.** The altitude reaches 4350m and your body will still be acclimatising: most trekkers will feel the altitude.
Medical Assistance	**Pheriche Aid Post**: see p124
Points of Interest	**Shomare village** 22 **Orsho plateau** 23: Nuptse's ridge looks wonderful; first sighting of Pumori (hard to spot) **Excellent views of Ama Dablam & Thamserku** **Dingboche village** 24

Stage EBC5a: Pangboche to Shomare (See map on p132)

20 Head E through **Pangboche Lower**. Cross a bridge and climb.

21 0:10: Keep SH at a junction beside a large mani rock and wall: the path to the right heads to Ama Dablam BC (SR1; p134). Initially, the path climbs NE: soon it undulates as it contours around the slopes (alongside the Imja Khola).

22 1:00: Reach the village of **Shomare (4080m)**, a super place for a tea break.

Stage EBC5b: Shomare to Orsho Junction (See map on p132)

22 Climb steeply through **Shomare**. Head E out of the village, contouring around the slopes. Pass the **Sunrise Lodge and Restaurant** at **Orsho**. Soon, the keen-eyed may spot the tip of **Pumori** to the N.

23 0:40: Reach a signpost at **Orsho Junction (4180m)**. TR for Dingboche (EBC5c) or TL for Pheriche (EBC10a; p141).

EBC5c: Orsho Junction to Dingboche (See map on p132)

23 TR at **Orsho Junction**: initially, the path to Dingboche runs parallel to the higher route to Pheriche. Soon, descend to a bridge at the confluence of the Imja Khola and Lobuche rivers. Cross a bridge over the Lobuche River. Then climb steeply NE alongside the **Imja Khola**.

24 1:10: Reach the village of **Dingboche (4350m)**.

One of the stupas on the ridge above Dingboche: in the background, Thamserku and Kangtega

Alternative: Orsho Junction to Pheriche (Stage EBC10a)

55min; 2.1km; +70m **(See map on p132)**

Because Pheriche is only a short distance W of Dingboche, and is at a similar altitude, it is also a good place to take an AD before heading up to Dughla. Pheriche is a pleasant village in the base of the barren Lobuche valley. It is fairly peaceful although sometimes battered by a cold wind blowing along the valley. There are lodges, restaurants and an aid post (p124). Pheriche is probably a more relaxing place to stay than Dingboche although the latter has better facilities. The main disadvantage to Pheriche is that the best day-hikes (to keep you occupied on your AD) are all closer to Dingboche (see p139): from Pheriche, there is a stiff hike up to Dingboche's ridge just to get to the start of the hikes and an extra walk back down to Pheriche at the end; in total, this adds about 1hr to your side-trip.

Terrain/Navigation: paths are generally well-maintained and simple to follow although there are rocky sections. Route-finding is straightforward.

Difficulty: medium.

(23) TL at **Orsho Junction (4180m)**. Initially, the path runs parallel to the lower route to Dingboche. Climb N to a little pass. Then descend N and cross a bridge over the Lobuche river. Afterwards, continue N up the valley. Arrive at **Pheriche ((37); 4250m)**.

SR2 Nangkar Tshang Peak

Andrew on Nangkar Tshang Peak

Because Dingboche is an important acclimatisation stop for ascending trekkers, most people have plenty of spare time there and hiking up Nangkar Tshang Peak is a perfect way to spend it. The 360° panorama from the summit is staggering: you can see Makalu (the 5th highest mountain on the planet) and a completely different perspective of Ama Dablam. However, in our opinion, the highlight is the view across the Lobuche valley towards Taboche and Cholatse: look into the valley and, far below, you should see CEBC trekkers heading towards Dughla and swarms of helicopters flying to EBC. In fact, the views all the way up the ridge are exceptional so you do not actually need to go all the way to the summit.

The route climbs Pokalde's ridge (which overlooks Dingboche) and returns the same way. There are a variety of ways to get onto the ridge: the route we describe climbs onto it from the NE end of Dingboche but, at the end of the hike, descends to the white stupa in the SW part of the village. This allows you to explore the village in full. However, you could just as easily hike this in reverse.

		Time	Distance	Ascent	Descent	SA Increase	Max Alt
SR2	Dingboche to Nangkar Tshang (return)	4:45	6.3km 3.9miles	740m 2428ft	740m 2428ft	0m 0ft	5073m 16645ft

24 **(See map on p147).** Head NE up Dingboche's main street.

25 0:10: At the **NE end of Dingboche**, TL at a junction and climb: the path to the right heads to Chukhung (TP6; p178). Just afterwards, TL again ('Lobuche'): the path now heads W across the face of the slope.

26 0:30: TR at a small **saddle with a stupa** and climb a path up the ridge; the path that descends N towards a plateau is EBC6 to Dughla (p144). The route climbs steeply and relentlessly all the way to the top.

5 3:00: Reach the summit of **Nangkar Tshang Peak (5073m)**. After admiring the view, retrace your steps.

26 4:30: From the small **saddle** passed earlier, bear left and drop off the crest of the ridge (using one of the paths heading S towards the higher of two white stupas). Immediately before the first stupa, TL and descend on a path towards the larger stupa below.

24 4:45: From the larger stupa, descend briefly to arrive in the **SW part of Dingboche**.

Lodges (with accommodation, restaurant, & shop)	**Dingboche** (0km)
Terrain/ Navigation	The path is occasionally faint but the route is not difficult to follow: if in doubt, stay close to the crest of the ridge. The gradient is very steep in places: towards the top, there are rocky sections.
Difficulty	**Very Hard**. The long, tough climb takes you above 5000m for the first time. Obviously, the hike is easier if you do not climb all the way to the top.
Medical Assistance	**Pheriche Aid Post**: see p124
Points of Interest	First sighting of Makalu Incredible view across the Lobuche valley towards Taboche and Cholatse Superbly situated stupas

EBC6 Dingboche to Dughla (Thukla)

This beautiful stage begins with a short climb to the stupa on the ridge which overlooks Dingboche. Most people will already have visited this viewpoint during their AD in Dingboche but a second visit is no imposition: you can see three 8000ers - Lhotse, Makalu and Cho Oyu, the 4th, 5th and 6th highest mountains on the planet. From the stupa, head NW across the barren plateau above Pheriche and the Lobuche valley, soon climbing steadily: the sublime Taboche and Cholatse keep you company to the W and, ahead to the N, the summit of Lobuche E draws the eye.

Although the stage is short, and you reach Dughla quite early in the day, an overnight stop there is a prudent choice. Although Dughla is only 250m higher than Dingboche, the village of Lobuche (the subsequent sleep stop above Dughla) is a further 310m higher: Dingboche to Lobuche in one day therefore involves an altitude increase of 560m which is a big jump.

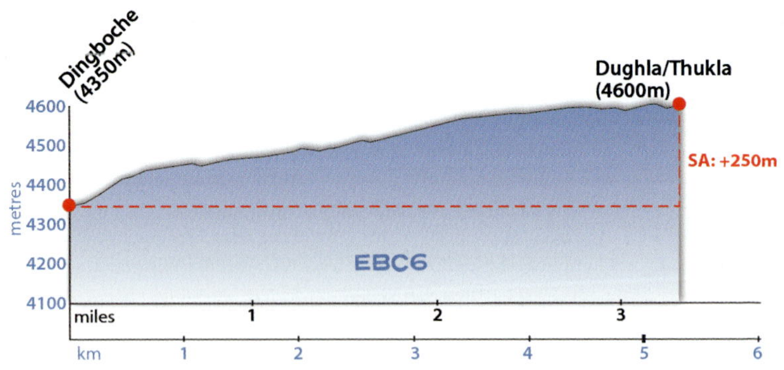

		Time	Distance	Ascent	Descent	SA Increase	Max Alt
EBC6	Dingboche to Dughla (Thukla)	2:30	5.3km 3.3miles	295m 968ft	45m 148ft	+250m +820ft	4600m 15093ft

Taboche & Cholatse (EBC6)

Nevertheless, a lot of trekkers (with limited time) do hike from Dingboche to Lobuche in a single day, combining Sections EBC6 and EBC7: most have no major problems (particularly, those who took an AD in Dingboche); however, for a few trekkers, such a big jump in altitude at this point in the trek can be too much, leading to discomfort over the subsequent days or even abandonment.

There is little in Dughla other than a few lodges and a café. For this reason, fit hikers might consider sleeping at Chukhung instead (see p139).

Pheriche to Dugla: trekkers who have taken an AD in Pheriche (instead of Dingboche), will use a different path (see p149): this route joins Stage EBC6 just S of Dughla.

Chola Tsho side-trip (1.5-2hr return): to fill time in Dughla, you could hike down to Chola Tsho (a glacial lake at 4500m; 1km W of Dughla). The path heads W and crosses a stream. Then it contours around the slopes before descending steeply S to the moraine of the Cholo Glacier. It then travels NW, briefly following the lake's N shore before climbing above it. You can walk as far as you wish along the path before retracing your steps back to Dughla: remember that you will have to climb back up the slope at the end though.

Lodges (with accommodation, restaurant, & shop)	**Dingboche** (0km) » **Dughla** (5.3km)
Terrain/ Navigation	Route-finding and terrain are straightforward and paths are generally easy to follow. If the bridge is out at Dughla, exercise caution fording the stream.
Difficulty	**Medium.** The terrain poses few difficulties but the altitude is high, reaching 4600m.
Medical Assistance	**Pheriche Aid Post**: see p124
Points of Interest	Stupa on Dingboche's ridge: 26 Excellent views of Taboche and Cholatse Dughla (Thukla): 28

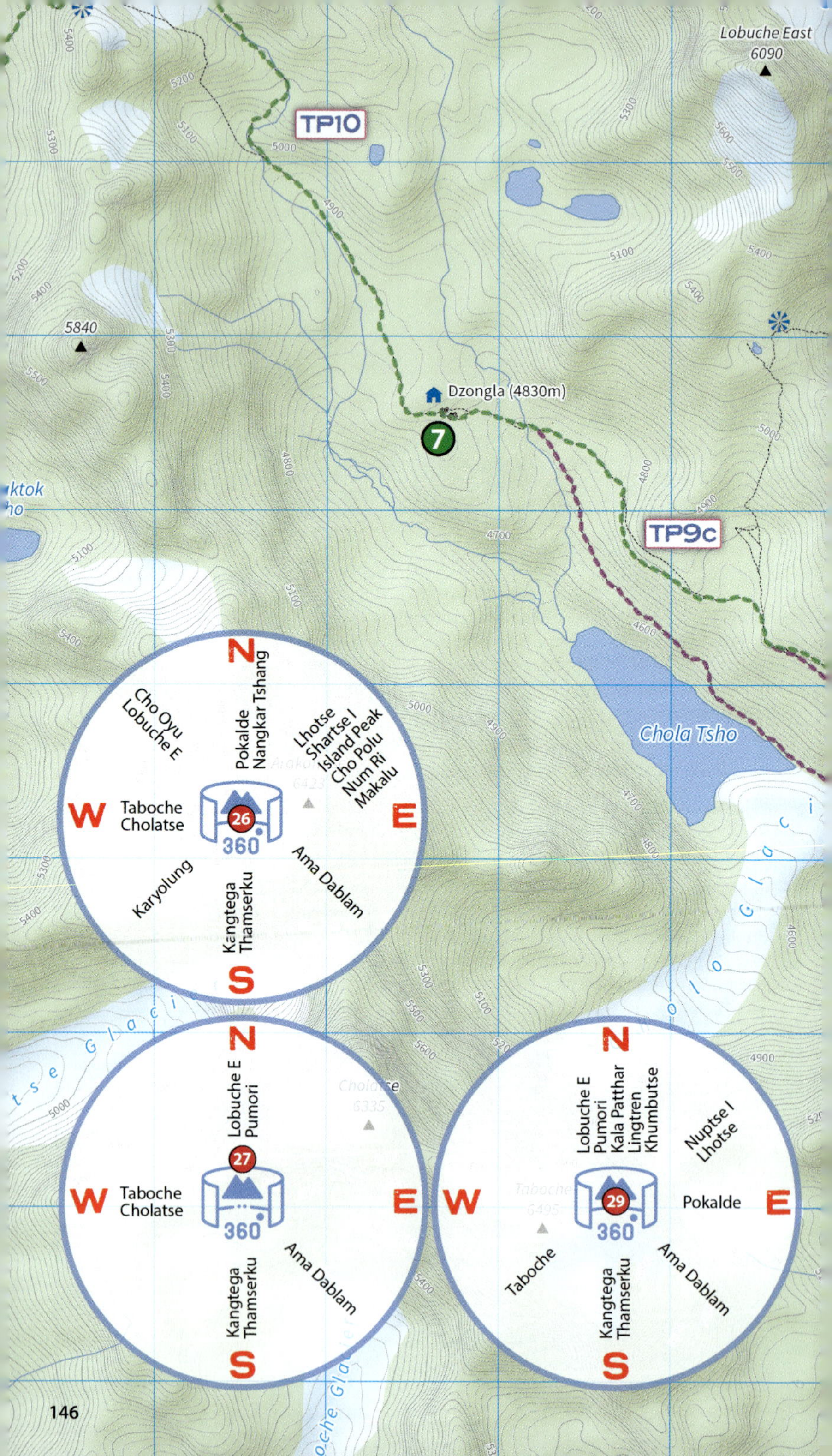

Lobuche East
6090
TP10
5840
Dzongla (4830m)
7
TP9c
Chola Tsho
N
Cho Oyu
Lobuche E
Pokalde
Nangkar Tshang
Lhotse
Shartse I
Island Peak
Cho Polu
Num Ri
Makalu
W
Taboche
Cholatse
26
360
E
Karyolung
Kangtega
Thamserku
Ama Dablam
S
N
Lobuche E
Pumori
27
W
Taboche
Cholatse
360
E
Kangtega
Thamserku
Ama Dablam
S
N
Lobuche E
Pumori
Kala Patthar
Lingtren
Khumbutse
Nuptse I
Lhotse
W
29
360
Pokalde
E
Taboche
Kangtega
Thamserku
Ama Dablam
S

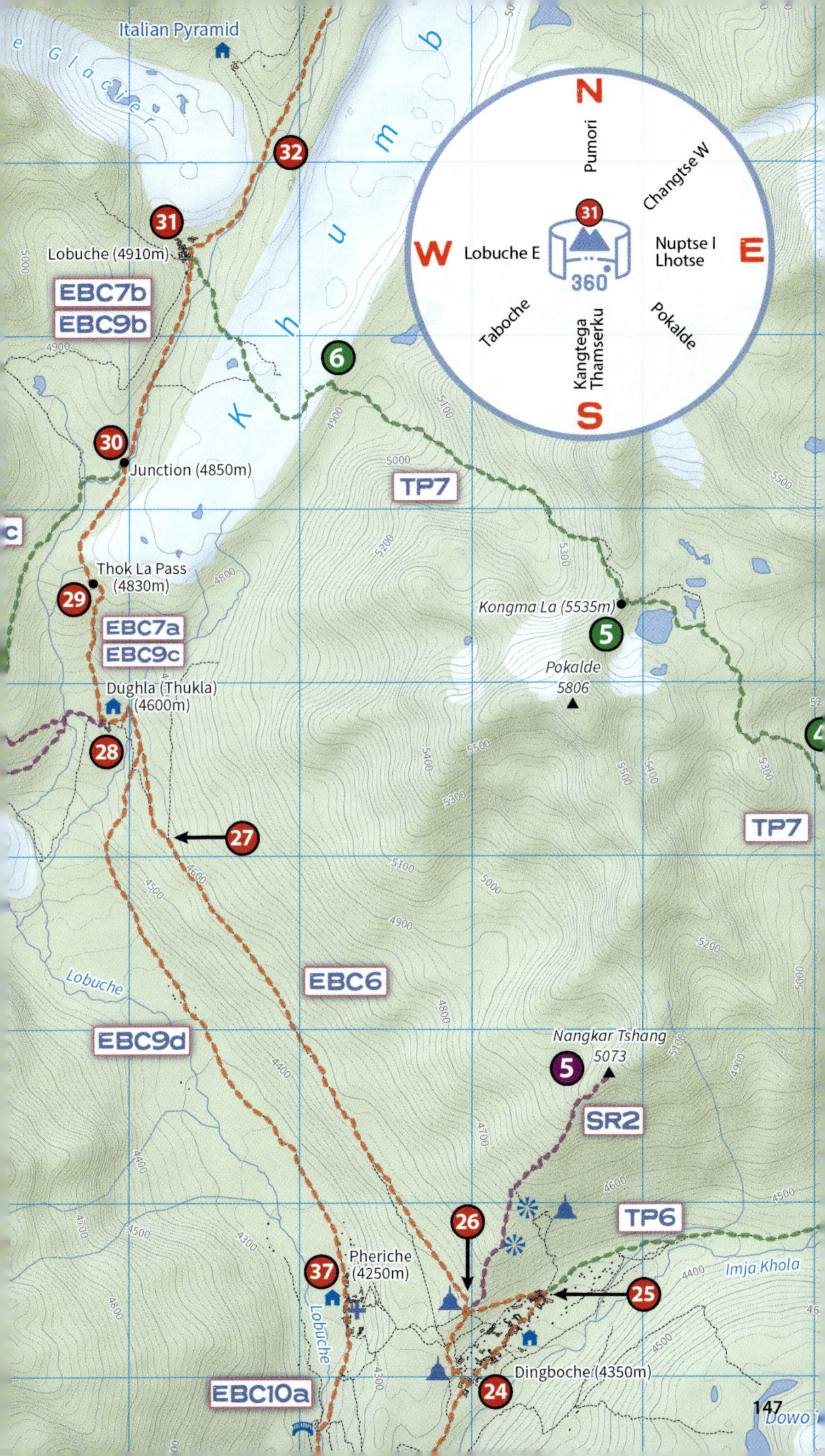

Italian Pyramid
Glacier
Khumbu
Lobuche (4910m)
EBC7b
EBC9b
Junction (4850m)
Thok La Pass (4830m)
EBC7a
EBC9c
Dughla (Thukla) (4600m)
TP7
Kongma La (5535m)
Pokalde 5806
EBC6
EBC9d
Lobuche
Nangkar Tshang 5073
SR2
TP6
Imja Khola
Pheriche (4250m)
Dingboche (4350m)
EBC10a
N
S
E
W
Pumori
Changtse W
Nuptse I
Lhotse
Pokalde
Kangtega
Thamserku
Taboche
Lobuche E
360

Stage EBC6: Dingboche to Dughla (Thukla) (See map on p147)

24 Head NE up Dingboche's main street.

25 0:10: At the **NE end of Dingboche**, TL at a junction and climb: the path to the right heads to Chukhung (TP6; p178). Just afterwards, TL again ('Lobuche'): the path now heads W across the face of the slope.

26 0:30: From a small **saddle with a stupa**, descend briefly N on a path to reach a plateau: head NW across it. The path soon starts to rise, heading towards the summit of Lobuche E.

27 2:10: TL at a fork. 10min later, the path from Pheriche joins from the left (see p149). 5min later, cross a bridge over a stream.

28 2:30: Shortly afterwards, reach **Dughla (4600m)**.

Cholatse (6335m) & Taboche (6495m)

Cholatse is renowned for its challenging climbing routes and its striking pyramid-shaped summit. It is connected to Taboche by a long ridge. The first successful ascent of Cholatse was made in 1982 via the SW Ridge. The N face was climbed in 1984.

Taboche's striking peak is connected to Cholatse by a long ridge. It was first climbed in the early 1970s by a French expedition.

Ama Dablam viewed from the summit of Nangkar Tshang Peak (SR2)

Alternative: Pheriche to Dughla (Stage EBC9d)

2.5hr; 4.2km; SA +350m (See map on p147)

This route is for those heading up towards EBC after taking an AD at Pheriche (instead of Dingboche). The beautiful views are similar to those seen on Stage EBC6 between Dingboche and Dughla (see p144), however, further down in the valley, the perspective is slightly different. On balance, the Dingboche route is marginally better because you stay higher for longer and are set back a little further from Cholatse and Taboche.

Terrain/Navigation: paths are generally well-maintained and simple to follow although there are rocky and steep sections. Route-finding is straightforward.

Difficulty: medium.

37 From **Pheriche**, the path heads NW up the valley (remaining on the E side of the **Lobuche river**). Later, the path bends right and climbs N (more steeply). Eventually, meet the path from Dingboche (which joins from the right): head N. 5min later, cross a bridge over a stream. Shortly afterwards, reach **Dughla (28; 4600m)**.

EBC7 Dughla (Thukla) to Lobuche

The journey upwards continues with a climb over Thok La pass which is home to a series of memorials to fallen climbers: these include Scott Fisher who died in the notorious Everest catastrophe of 1996. The views are extraordinary and the memorials are bedecked with colourful prayer flags, making it a particularly photogenic place. From the pass, you can fully appreciate the singular beauty of Pumori and you can spot KP (which most trekkers will climb from Gorak Shep; p162). Once you reach the pass, you have completed the bulk of the day's ascent: there is a little climbing on the onward route to Lobuche but the gradients are more gentle.

Lobuche is right beside the Khumbu Glacier (which forms below the summit of Everest). It is a cold place, especially in the evening (when the sun sets relatively early, behind the ridges to the W). There is palpable excitement in the air at Lobuche: the lodges are full of

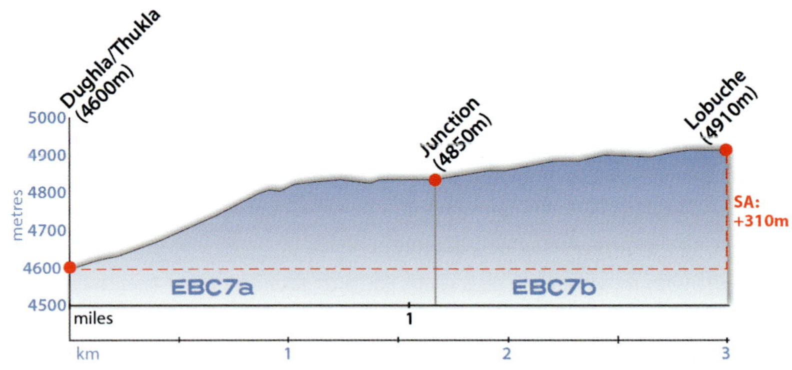

		Time	Distance	Ascent	Descent	SA Increase	Max Alt
EBC7a	Dughla to Junction (4850m)	1:30	1.7km 1.1miles	270m 886ft	20m 66ft	N/A (no lodges)	4850m 15913ft
EBC7b	Junction (4850m) to Lobuche	0:45	1.3km 0.8miles	60m 197ft	0m 0ft	+310m +1017ft	4910m 16110ft

Lobuche: in the background, Taboche & Cholatse

both nervous people aiming for EBC the next day and ecstatic trekkers who have just visited it. Almost every trekker spends the night at Lobuche on the way up, to acclimatise before the final push through the 5,000m barrier the following day. The next settlement further up, Gorak Shep, is the last one before EBC and it is located at the lofty altitude of 5150m: to move up from Dughla to Gorak Shep in one day would mean a sleeping altitude increase of 550m which is not advisable at these high altitudes. Accordingly, Lobuche's lodges are usually pretty busy and the shops tend to be expensive (even by the Khumbu's standards).

Lobuche Viewpoints: although most trekkers prefer to rest upon arrival at Lobuche, there are some great viewpoints to visit:

- **Khumbu Glacier moraine:** a few different paths climb onto the Khumbu Glacier moraine (to the E of Lobuche) where you will witness an immense 360° panorama. Nuptse and Pumori are the highlights and you can clearly see KP. The views are particularly good at sunset when Nuptse is lit up by the sun: wrap up warmly though.
- **Lobuche Glacier moraine:** there are also paths climbing steeply onto the Lobuche Glacier moraine (immediately behind Lobuche, to the N). From there, the view of the Lobuche Glacier is excellent.
- **Spur to the W:** you can also climb the spur immediately W of Lobuche. Initially, there are paths up the grassy slope. The greenery eventually gives way to rock (which is more difficult to negotiate) but you do not need to ascend far to enjoy spectacular views.

Lodges (with accommodation, restaurant, & shop)	**Dughla** (0km) » **Lobuche** (3.0km) **Top Tip:** World's Highest Bakery Café has great coffee and apple pie.
Terrain/ Navigation	The paths are rocky but well-maintained and simple to follow. The terrain poses few difficulties although the climb to the pass is steep.
Difficulty	**Medium**. The terrain is straightforward but the altitude is very high, making the climb hard work.
Medical Assistance	**Pheriche Aid Post** (see p124)
Points of Interest	Excellent views of Pumori, Taboche and Cholatse Climbers' memorials at Thok La pass: 29 Lobuche: 31

The Khumbu Glacier

The Khumbu Glacier is probably the world's most infamous glacier. It is also the world's highest, with elevations ranging from 7600m at its source all the way down to 4900m. Currently, it is around 17km long, flowing from the Western Cwm (between Everest and Lhotse) to its terminus near Lobuche. The glacier's huge ice-fall, known as the 'Khumbu Ice-fall', is a notorious obstacle for climbers attempting to summit Everest via the South Col: to reach the Western Cwm, they have to climb across the ice-fall, carefully navigating its unstable towers of ice and deep crevasses. Because the ice constantly shifts, it is extremely dangerous and many consider it to be the most perilous part of the summit climb. Between 1953 and 2016, at least 44 climbers and guides have lost their lives in the ice-fall: 16 of those were killed by an avalanche in 2014. Like many of the world's glaciers, climate change is causing the Khumbu Glacier to retreat.

Thok La pass: in the background, Kangtega

EBC7a: Dughla (Thukla) to Junction (4850m) (See map on p147)

28 From **Dughla**, climb steeply N: ignore the paths heading W.

29 1:15: Cross **Thok La pass (4830m)**: there are memorials to climbers who have died in the Khumbu.

30 1:30: Reach **Junction (4850m)**. Keep SH for Lobuche (EBC7b): the path to the left goes to Dzongla (TP9c; p192).

EBC7b: Junction (4850m) to Lobuche (See map on p147)

30 From the junction, climb N on a clear path beside the **Khumbu Glacier**.

31 0:45: Arrive at **Lobuche (4910m)**.

EBC8 Lobuche to EBC to Gorak Shep

Arrival at EBC's famous rock

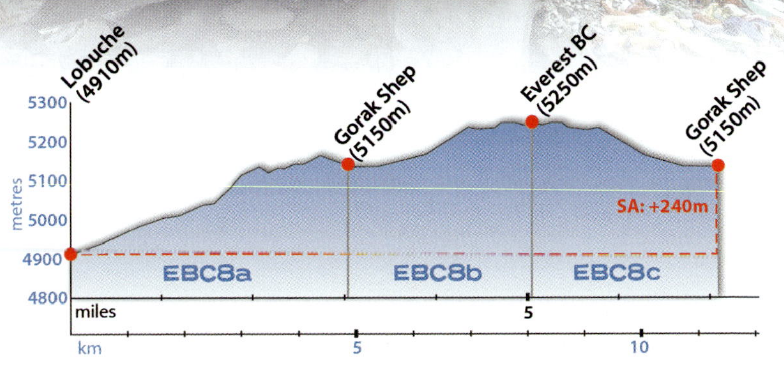

		Time	Distance	Ascent	Descent	SA Increase	Max Alt
EBC8a	Lobuche to Gorak Shep	3:00	4.9km 3.0miles	324m 1063ft	84m 276ft	+240m +787ft	5150m 16897ft
EBC8b	Gorak Shep to EBC	2:15	3.2km 2.0miles	187m 614ft	87m 285ft	N/A (no lodges at EBC)	5260m 17258ft
EBC8c	EBC to Gorak Shep	1:45	3.2km 2.0miles	87m 285ft	187m 614ft	+240m +787ft (Lobuche to Gorak Shep)	5260m 17258ft

Section EBC8 is the climax of the CEBC: you will trek to Gorak Shep and from there, visit EBC and/or KP. Most trekkers aspire to visit both viewpoints, however, in practice not everyone does so because the extremely high altitude takes its toll. Both are spectacular hikes offering incredible panoramas but each has its own specific attributes and merits. On a clear day, most would agree that KP delivers the better views: because it is so high, you get a much better look at Everest and the Khumbu Glacier; Lhotse is visible too, tucked in behind Nuptse; furthermore, KP is located on the S ridge of Pumori, the superlatively beautiful summit of which is jaw-droppingly close. From KP, you can also appreciate fully the challenging route the climbers use to reach Everest's summit.

However, that is not to say that the hike to EBC is inferior because, on the way to EBC, you witness exquisite scenery throughout and are fully immersed in Everest history and legend. You will finally lay eyes on EBC, a place where so much drama and tragedy has unfolded over the years. And, at EBC, you can really appreciate the scale and significance of the Khumbu Ice-fall where so many climbers have lost their lives (see p152). These days, most people consider that the N terminus of the CEBC is the famous rock (marked 'Everest Base Camp 5364m') which is the scene of countless Instagram images. Although some tents are usually pitched near the rock, the bulk of them are located further N along the glacier: you can continue further towards the centre of EBC but guides seem to discourage this and those attempting to summit Everest prefer not to be disturbed by trekkers. April/May is the best period to visit EBC because most summit attempts are made in May and the camp will be full of colourful tents. In late 2023, the EBC rock toppled over slightly. Bewilderingly, the authorities have since erected a pointless signboard in front of the much-loved rock: we hope that the sign will not be a permanent feature.

If you have to choose only one of the two viewpoints, then KP is the better choice if scenery is your priority and the weather is clear. However, if mountaineering history has a significant pull on you, or if the weather is not so clear, then EBC may be the better choice. That said, high altitude may well make this choice for you: the climb up KP (to 5600m) is tough at these lofty elevations and, for some, climbing much higher than Gorak Shep may be troublesome; the maximum altitude on the hike to EBC is much lower (5260m). If you are planning to hike only one of them, then it is possible to ascend from Lobuche to Gorak Shep, visit either KP or EBC, and then descend back to Lobuche, all on the same day: it is a long day but it avoids the need to spend a night at Gorak Shep where few people sleep well.

If, like most, you are planning to hike both, then opinion varies on the best order of play. At these altitudes, most people will find it too difficult to hike from Lobuche to Gorak Shep, visit EBC, climb KP and return to Lobuche, all on the same day. You could use Lobuche as a base for two nights, hiking from there to EBC (and back) on the first day and hiking from Lobuche to KP (and back) on the second day: however, that is time consuming, involves walking the same route twice (the return journey between Lobuche and Gorak Shep), and requires more climbing overall. Accordingly, most trekkers prefer to spend one night at Gorak Shep (5150m) which is the highest sleeping place on the CEBC (or indeed any of the other Everest treks). Few trekkers will want to spend more than one night at Gorak Shep though because the adverse effects of altitude frequently manifest themselves there. This means that most people plan to do one of EBC and KP on the day of their arrival at Gorak Shep, and then the other one the following morning (before descending back towards Lobuche that day). Because the air is frequently clearer first thing in the morning, a sunrise ascent of KP has become almost de rigeur and, these days, the orthodox approach is probably as follows:

- **Day 1:** hike from Lobuche to Gorak Shep; then hike to EBC; return to Gorak Shep and spend the night there.
- **Day 2:** hike from Gorak Shep to the summit of KP; then descend back to Lobuche (or further).

Because of its popularity, this is the approach incorporated into each of our CEBC itineraries. However, although many trekkers climb KP for sunrise, this is not necessarily the best time to do it. Later in the morning, fewer of the surrounding slopes will be in shadow and the views are spectacular (if there is no cloud cover). Furthermore, sunset on a clear day is sublime. Also bear in mind that it can be unpleasantly cold on KP at sunrise and it may be more enjoyable to climb later in the day. Accordingly, some prefer to do KP on the day that they arrive at Gorak Shep, leaving the EBC return journey for the following day (when they will also descend back to Lobuche or further).

Although both of these strategies involve two tough days, they have the significant advantage of ensuring that you descend back to lower altitudes without delay. However, if you are well acclimatised, then it is possible to spend two nights at Gorak Shep, allowing three days to travel from Lobuche to Gorak Shep, visit EBC, climb KP and then descend to Lobuche (or further).

With all the focus on the hikes to EBC and KP, it is easy to overlook the wonderful journey to reach their staging point at Gorak Shep. In fact, the scenery on the approach to Gorak Shep is so fine that, even if you did not continue any further, it would still constitute a world class hike: there are high summits everywhere and Pumori, in particular, looks exquisite. You also get a really good look at the ice of the Khumbu Glacier. The route from Gorak Shep to EBC is wonderful too with Everest periodically showing itself amongst the other spectacular snowy peaks.

Gorak Shep: it is fair to say that Gorak Shep often gets a bad rap. While it is true that it is situated in a barren plain alongside the Khumbu Glacier and that its lodges are busy, comparatively expensive and far from the most comfortable in the Khumbu, we think that some of the criticism is unwarranted these days. In recent years, newer buildings have been erected and conditions in many of the lodges have improved. Furthermore, the views of Pumori and other peaks are incredible. However, there is no getting away from the fact that it is a very cold place to spend the night in poorly insulated buildings: this is where warm sleeping bag investment really pays dividends. Nor can you escape the very high altitude which can make the night even more uncomfortable: few trekkers feel great at Gorak Shep. Despite the difficulties, in peak season, Gorak Shep is packed and beds can be difficult to find.

Lodges (with accommodation, restaurant, & shop)	**Lobuche** (0km) » **lodge at Italian Pyramid** (1.3km; OR) » **Gorak Shep** (4.9km)
Terrain/ Navigation	The paths are generally well-maintained and easy to follow. Some sections are steep and rocky. Route-finding is straightforward.
Difficulty	**Hard.** The terrain is straightforward but, above 5000m, the altitude really starts to bite.
Medical Assistance	**Pheriche Aid Post** (see p124)
Points of Interest	Broad Himalayan panoramas Incredible views of Pumori, a mountain that would rival Ama Dablam in a beauty contest Khumbu Glacier: see p152 Gorak Shep 34 Yak trains heading to EBC Everest Base Camp 36

A porter on the way to EBC

N
Chumbu
Khangri E
Pumori
Kala Patthar
Lingtren
Khumbutse
Changtse
34
W
Lobuche E
Nuptse I
E
360
Taboche
Cholatse
Pokalde
Kangtega
Thamserku
S
Everest Base Camp (5364m)
Dride Lake
6
Kala Patthar
5600
36
Rock marki
KP
35
EBC8b/8c
Gorak Shep (5150m)
34
33
EBC8a
EBC9a
N
Khangri E
Pumori
Kala Patthar
Lingtren
Khumbutse
Changtse
33
W
Lobuche E
Nuptse I
E
360
Taboche
Cholatse
Pokalde
Thamserku
S
Italian Pyramid
32
31
Lobuche (4910m)
3C7b
3C9b
6

EBC and the Khumbu Glacier

EBC8a: Lobuche to Gorak Shep (See maps on p158 and p160)

31 From **Lobuche**, head NE on a clear path along the W side of the **Khumbu Glacier**. To the N, Pumori looks exquisite. For a while, the trail rises gently.

32 0:25: Keep SH at a junction (information board); the path on the left heads to the **Italian Pyramid** (see below). Continue climbing N: the gradient is mostly gentle with a few steep sections thrown in.

33 1:40: After climbing steeply, reach a spectacular viewpoint (amazing views of Pumori). Afterwards, continue N on an undulating path. Soon, there are superb views of the **Khumbu Ice-fall**.

34 3:00: Reach the blue-roofed village of **Gorak Shep (5150m)**.

EBC8b/8c: Gorak Shep to EBC to Gorak Shep (p158 & p160)

34 Follow the broad path which heads NE along Gorak Shep's rocky plain. Soon, Everest peeks out from behind Nuptse's ridge on the right: spot it quickly because it soon disappears again. The path undulates, gradually creeping upwards: however, there are a few steep sections too. Later, Everest reappears.

35 1:30: At the top of a small ridge, there are excellent views of EBC's tents. After a while, the path descends and bends right, leading onto the **Khumbu Glacier**. Mostly, you will walk on rock (covering the ice): in places, the path skirts the edge of sheer drops.

36 2:15: Reach the famous **rock overlooking EBC (5364m)**. For most trekkers, this is the goal of the trek. After admiring the stupendous views, retrace your steps.

34 4:00: Arrive back in **Gorak Shep (5150m)**.

The Italian Pyramid

A short distance W of the EBC8a route, there is a curious rectangular stone building topped with a pyramid. It was built in 1990 with funding from the Italian and Nepalese Governments. Its official name is 'EV-K2-CNR', however, it is commonly known as the 'Italian Pyramid'. Initially, it was designed as part of a project to accurately determine (using the latest GPS technology) the heights of Everest and K2. After Everest was confirmed as the higher of the two summits, the mission of the project changed and the pyramid was used to conduct high altitude environmental research. In recent years, the pyramid's government funding has largely dried up and it has been converted into a comfortable trekking lodge which makes a fabulous alternative to a night in Lobuche.

Mount Lingtren
6714
Pumori
7138
Everest Base Camp (5364m)
Rock marking end of EBC trek (5250m)
Kala Patthar
5600
Dride Lake
KP
EBC8b/8c
Gorak Shep
(5150m)
Glacier
Nuptse li
N
Lingtren
Pumori
Khumbutse
Changtse
W Kala Patthar
Everest E
Taboche
Cholatse
Lobuche E
Pokalde
Kangtega
Thamserku
Nuptse li
S
360
N
Chumbu
Khangri W
Pumori
Lingtren
Khumbutse
Changtse
W Nirekha
Changri
Everest
Lhotse
Nuptse li E
Taboche
Cholatse
Lobuche E & W
Ombigaichen
Peak 41
Ama Dablam
Kyashar
Kangtega
Thamserku
S
360

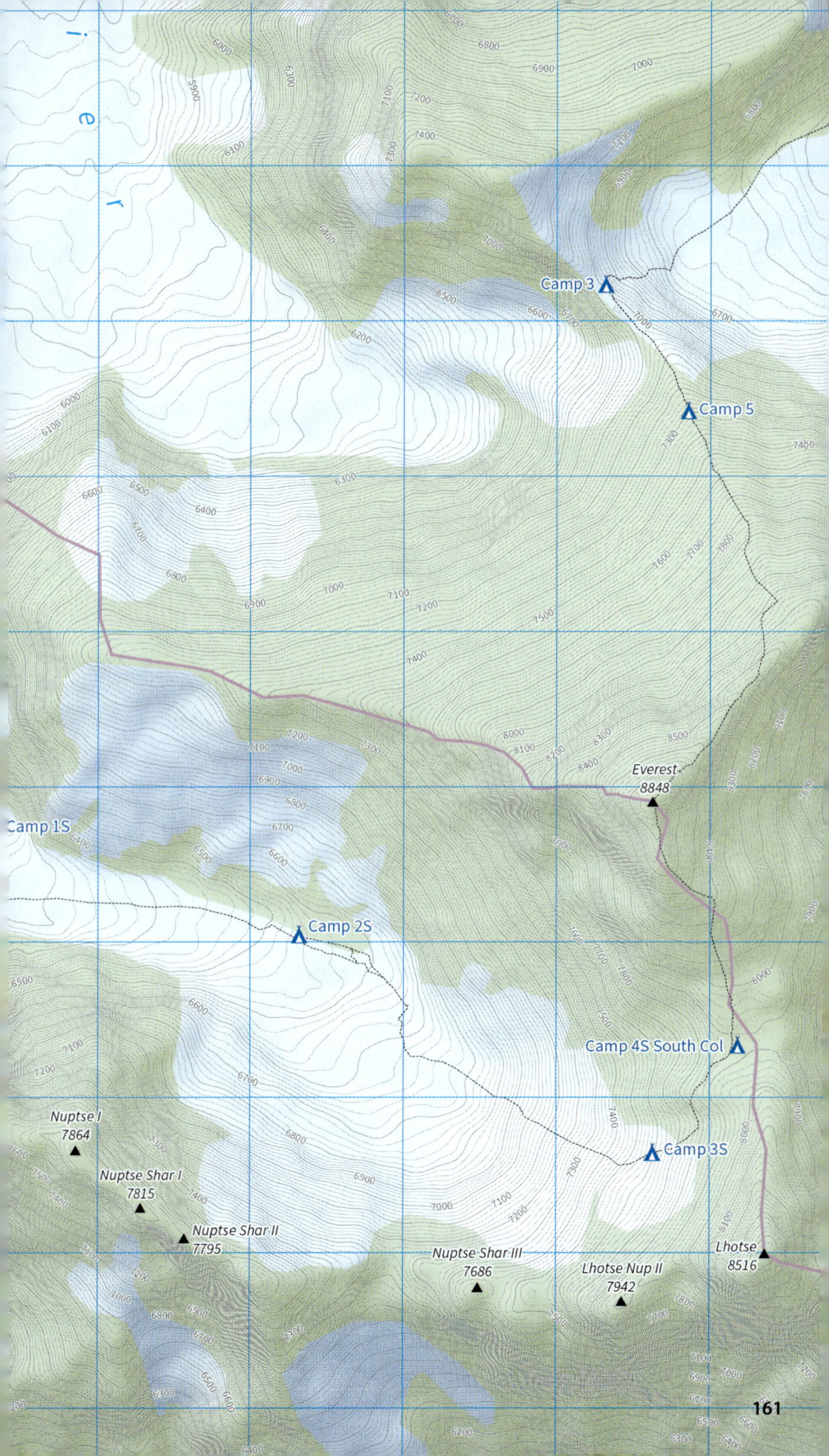
Camp 3
Camp 5
Everest
8848
Camp 1S
Camp 2S
Camp 4S South Col
Camp 3S
Nuptse I
7864
Nuptse Shar I
7815
Nuptse Shar II
7795
Nuptse Shar III
7686
Lhotse Nup II
7942
Lhotse
8516

KP Kala Patthar

Kala Patthar sunrise:
Everest (left) and Nuptse (right)

Kala Patthar is a minor outcrop on the S ridge of Pumori. Seen from afar, it is completely overshadowed by Pumori's exceptional elegance and does not appear to be particularly noteworthy. However, its significance becomes clearer on the approach to Gorak Shep (from Lobuche): if you follow the line of the conspicuous paths to its rocky top, you can quickly appreciate that this little hill faces directly onto the summit of Everest (which is only 9km away to the E). The view across the Khumbu Glacier is completely unimpeded and KP is the highest, the closest and (probably) the best Everest viewpoint that is easily accessible to trekkers: of course, there are higher viewpoints in this region of superlatives but getting to them requires technical skills.

The hike climbs the ridge, starting immediately to the N of Gorak Shep. There are two main paths: most people choose the right-hand one which heads directly to KP's main summit and this is the route described below. The left path climbs a slightly lower summit: the climb is shorter and the views are almost as good as those from the main summit; you might choose this option if you are tired or feeling the altitude. If you are keen, you could of course climb both summits: head up the left path to the lower summit; then descend to the saddle between the two summits; from there, climb the ridge to the higher summit; and finally descend back to Gorak Shep using the right-hand path.

		Time	Distance	Ascent	Descent	SA Increase	Max Alt
Kala Patthar	Gorak Shep to Gorak Shep	3:30	5.2km 3.2miles	496m 1627ft	496m 1627ft	0m 0ft	5600m 18374ft

The paths are clear and easy to follow, however, the high altitude makes the climb tough. It can be extremely cold at the top, especially at sunrise and sunset: bring plenty of warm layers. To reach the top before sunrise, you will have to get up very early: it is best to bring snacks on the climb, saving breakfast for your return to Gorak Shep; you will need a head-torch as it will be dark during the climb. For the best time to climb KP, see p155.

Gorak Shep: KP is the 'hill' in front of Pumori; you can see the paths to the summit

Lodges (with accommodation, restaurant, & shop)	**Gorak Shep** (0km)
Terrain/ Navigation	The gradient is very steep. Towards the top, there is a boulder field to cross: watch your step. If you wish to climb the final outcrop on the summit, you will need to use your hands to scramble up: take great care. Otherwise, the route is straightforward: the path is well-trodden and simple to follow.
Difficulty	**Hard.** The altitude reaches 5600m and the climb is long and tough.
Medical Assistance	**Pheriche Aid Post:** see p124
Points of Interest	Everest, Everest, Everest! The highest point on any of the Everest treks

Everest (left) and Nuptse (right)

Kala Patthar (See map on p158 & p160)

34 From **Gorak Shep**, cross the plain (heading N towards Pumori). Climb steeply using the more easterly of two visible paths which run up the ridge. The gradient eases when you reach a plateau but soon steepens again. The path zigzags up the slope. Continue N past the saddle between the higher and lower summits. Climb across a boulder field.

6 2:10: Reach the prayer flags at the higher summit of **Kala Patthar (5600m)**. If you are feeling adventurous, you can scramble up the rock outcrop on the summit to reach the very top. After admiring the incredible views, retrace your steps.

34 3:30: Arrive back in **Gorak Shep (5150m)**.

Gorak Shep to Pheriche

Our porter & guide taking a break at 33: Pumori in the background

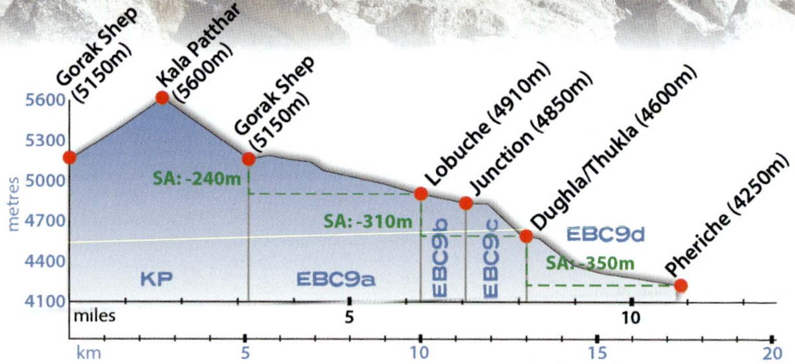

		Time	Distance	Ascent	Descent	SA Increase	Max Alt
EBC9a	Gorak Shep to Lobuche	2:00	4.9km 3.0miles	84m 276ft	324m 1063ft	-240m -787ft	5150m 16897ft
EBC9b	Lobuche to Junction (4850m)	0:20	1.3km 0.8miles	0m 0ft	60m 197ft	N/A (no lodges)	4910m 16110ft
EBC9c	Junction (4850m) to Dughla	0:30	1.7km 1.1miles	20m 66ft	270m 886ft	-310m -1017ft (Lobuche to Dughla)	4850m 15913ft
EBC9d	Dughla to Pheriche	1:40	4.2km 2.6miles	20m 66ft	370m 1214ft	-350m -1148ft	4600m 15093ft

Gorak Shep is the highest settlement on the CEBC and all trekkers must retrace their steps and descend to Lobuche. If the weather gods have been kind at EBC/KP, a strange mixture of elation, sorrow and relief will accompany you on departure from Gorak Shep: elation because of the incredible scenes you have witnessed; sorrow because you are leaving them behind; and relief at the prospect of returning to more comfortable altitudes. Fortunately, any sorrow will be short-lived because you will enter, once again, the spectacular landscapes explored a few days previously when ascending: heading S, the perspective is completely different, with Taboche & Cholatse dominating your attention; however, do not forget to look back longingly at your gorgeous friend, Pumori.

If short of time, you could consider taking a helicopter from EBC/Gorak Shep to Lukla (or even Kathmandu). This is a wonderful experience but it is expensive and not without risk: see p61. All trekkers descending on foot will first need to return to Lobuche: however, your route from there will depend upon which trek you have selected. Heading rapidly for lower elevations, most descending CEBC trekkers do not stop at Lobuche again and continue down to Pheriche/Dingboche to spend the night. However, if you were tired after climbing KP that morning, you could spend the night in Lobuche on the descent: then the following day, you should be able to reach Pangboche or even Tengboche.

Direct route from Lobuche to Namche (CEBC): all of our CEBC itineraries descend from Lobuche to Lukla, via Pheriche, over three days. You will first retrace your steps to Dughla. Heading S from Dughla, the path soon splits: most trekkers descend to Pheriche, having already visited Dingboche on the ascent. However, if you ascended via Pheriche, then it makes sense to return via Dingboche (see p169). If you have more time and would prefer a slower descent, see the five alternative descent itineraries on p43.

Lobuche to Dzongla via Cho La (TPT-ACW): retrace your steps from Lobuche to Junction (4850m; 30). Then TR and take the path to Dzongla (TP9c; p192) which contours around the slopes to the W. Most trekkers will need to overnight at Dzongla before tackling Cho La pass the following morning. Many trekkers climb KP and then walk from Gorak Shep to Dzongla on one long day. Others may prefer to spend the night at Lobuche and head for Dzongla the following morning: however, even then, most trekkers will need to spend a night in Dzongla before attempting the challenging Cho La.

Lobuche to Chukhung via Kongma La (TPT-CW): from Lobuche, head SE and cross the Khumbu Glacier (TP7; p188). Then climb across Kongma La and descend to Chukhung. Because Kongma La is so difficult, most trekkers spend the night at Lobuche (after descending from Gorak Shep) and leave for the pass the following morning.

Lodges (with accommodation, restaurant, & shop)	**Gorak Shep** (0km) » **Lobuche** (4.9km) » **Dughla** (7.9km) » **Pheriche** (12.1km)
Terrain/ Navigation	Paths are generally well-maintained and simple to follow although there are rocky and steep sections. Route-finding is straightforward. If the bridge is out at Dughla, exercise caution fording the stream.
Difficulty	**Medium.** The distance is fairly long but you will largely be heading downhill.
Medical Assistance	**Pheriche Aid Post** (see p124)
Points of Interest	**EBC9a (Gorak Shep to Lobuche):** see p156 **EBC9b/EBC9c (Lobuche to Dughla):** see p151 **EBC9d (Dughla to Pheriche):** excellent views of Taboche & Cholatse

EBC9a: Gorak Shep to Lobuche (See map on p158)

34 From **Gorak Shep**, head S on the undulating path travelled on Stage 8a.

33 0:50: At the spectacular viewpoint, do not forget to look back at Pumori. Then descend steeply. Soon the gradient eases: the path still undulates but generally descends.

32 1:40: Keep SH at a junction (information board): the path on the right heads to the **Italian Pyramid** (p159).

31 2:00: Arrive at **Lobuche (4910m)**.

EBC9b: Lobuche to Junction (4850m) (See map on p147)

31 From **Lobuche**, follow the clear path down to the S.

30 0:20: Reach **Junction (4850m)**. CEBC trekkers should TL for Dughla (EBC9c): TPT (ACW) trekkers should TR for Dzongla (TP9c; p192).

EBC9c: Junction (4850m) to Dughla (Thukla) (p147)

30 From **Junction (4850m)**, head S (ignoring the path to Dzongla on the right).

29 0:15: Cross **Thok La pass (4830m)**: there are memorials to climbers who have died in the Khumbu. Then descend S.

28 0:30: Arrive at **Dughla (4600m)**.

EBC9d: Dughla (Thukla) to Pheriche (See map on p147)

28 From **Dughla**, head E on a path. After a few minutes, cross a bridge over a stream. Then head S. 5min later, reach a junction: TR and descend to head to Pheriche; alternatively, TL for Dingboche (see p169). Initially, the gradient is steep but it eases further down. Follow the **Lobuche river** S.

37 1:40: Arrive at **Pheriche (4250m)**.

Alternative: Dughla to Dingboche (Stage EBC6)

1.75hr; 5.3km; SA -250m (See map on p147)

The views are beautiful and slightly better than those on Stage EBC9d between Dughla and Pheriche: you stay higher for longer and are set back a little further from Cholatse and Taboche.

Terrain/Navigation: paths are generally well-maintained and simple to follow although there are rocky sections. Route-finding is straightforward.

Difficulty: medium.

28 From **Dughla**, head E on a path. After a few minutes, cross a bridge over a stream. Then head S. 5min later, reach a junction: TL to head to Dingboche; alternatively, TR for Pheriche (EBC9d; p168). Soon, the path heads SE across a plateau.

26 1:30: Climb briefly to reach a small **saddle with a stupa** (overlooking Dingboche). Descend S, dropping off the crest of the ridge: use any one of the paths heading S; aim for the higher of two white stupas. Immediately before the first stupa, TL and descend on a path towards the larger stupa below.

24 1:45: From the larger stupa, descend briefly to arrive in the **SW part of Dingboche (4350m)**.

EBC9a: Khumbu Glacier (left), Thamserku (centre) & Taboche (right)

EBC10 Pheriche to Namche

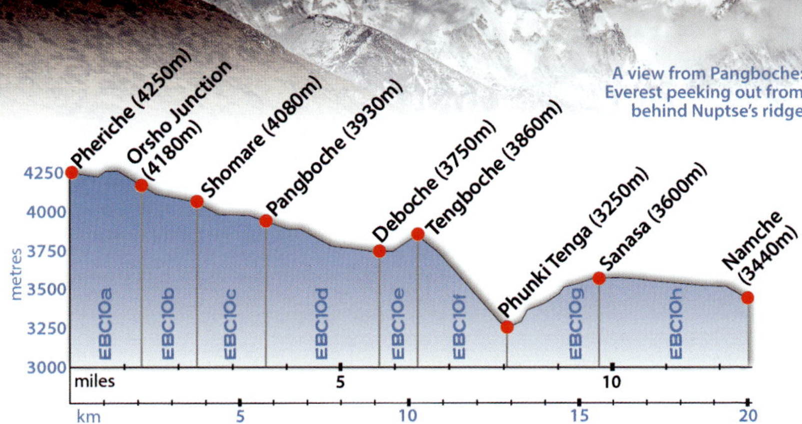

A view from Pangboche: Everest peeking out from behind Nuptse's ridge

Elevation profile, in metres, with markers for each waypoint:

- Pheriche (4250m)
- Orsho Junction (4180m)
- Shomare (4080m)
- Pangboche (3930m)
- Deboche (3750m)
- Tengboche (3860m)
- Phunki Tenga (3250m)
- Sanasa (3600m)
- Namche (3440m)

Segments: EBC10a, EBC10b, EBC10c, EBC10d, EBC10e, EBC10f, EBC10g, EBC10h

Vertical axis (metres): 3000, 3250, 3500, 3750, 4000, 4250. Horizontal axes: miles (5, 10) and km (5, 10, 15, 20).

		Time	Distance	Ascent	Descent	SA Increase	Max Alt
EBC10a	Pheriche to Orsho Junction	0:40	2.1km 1.3miles	69m 226ft	139m 456ft	-70m -230ft	4250m 13944ft
EBC10b	Orsho Junction to Shomare	0:25	1.6km 1.0miles	0m 0ft	100m 328ft	-100m -328ft	4180m 13715ft
EBC10c	Shomare to Pangboche	0:40	2.0km 1.2miles	25m 82ft	175m 574ft	-150m -492ft	4080m 13386ft
EBC10d	Pangboche to Deboche	1:15	3.4km 2.1miles	60m 197ft	240m 787ft	-180m -591ft	3930m 12894ft
EBC10e	Deboche to Tengboche	0:40	0.8km 0.5miles	110m 361ft	0m 0ft	+110m +361ft	3860m 12665ft
EBC10f	Tengboche to Phunki Tenga	0:45	3.0km 1.9miles	0m 0ft	610m 2001ft	-610m -2001ft	3860m 12665ft
EBC10g	Phunki Tenga to Sanasa	1:40	2.6km 1.6miles	360m 1181ft	10m 33ft	+350m +1148ft	3600m 11812ft
EBC10h	Sanasa to Namche	1:30	4.5km 2.8miles	70m 230ft	230m 755ft	-160m -525ft	3600m 11812ft

The descent continues and many trekkers walk back to Namche in one day (20km): although this is a long hike, it is largely downhill and you should, by now, be accustomed to the daily exertions; in fact, as the altitude drops, many people feel stronger. However, if 20km sounds too daunting, you can break it up with an overnight stop at one of the many settlements along the route: if you did not sleep at Tengboche on the ascent, then you may wish to do so now.

Pheriche to Pangboche: from Pheriche, head S down the Lobuche valley to reach Orsho Junction (which CEBC trekkers passed on the ascent). From there, retrace your steps to Pangboche. For Dingboche to Pangboche, see p173.

Pangboche to Sanasa: there are four ways to hike from Pangboche to Sanasa:

- **Main CEBC route: Pangboche » Deboche » Tengboche » Sanasa** (Stages EBC10d, EBC10e, EBC10f, EBC10g)
- **Pangboche » Deboche » Tengboche » Sanasa** (Stages EBC10d, EBC10e, AR1, GL8a, GL8b, GL8c)
- **Pangboche » Phortse » Tengboche » Sanasa** (AR2, AR1, EBC10f, EBC10g)
- **Pangboche » Phortse » Sanasa** (AR2, GL8a, GL8b, GL8c)

If you used the main CEBC route on the way to EBC, it makes sense to use a different route on the return. We prefer the two routes which incorporate AR2 (a divine balcony path which will be a trip highlight; p126): you can break up the journey with an overnight stop at Phortse or Khumjung.

Sanasa to Namche: there are four ways to hike from Sanasa to Namche:

- **Main CEBC route** (Stage EBC10h)
- **Namche via Everest View Hotel** (Stages GL4a, SR9): see p112
- **Namche via Khumjung** (GL4a, GL3): see p224
- **Namche via Khumjung and Khunde** (GL4a, SR10): see p118

They are all incredibly scenic and it makes sense to return using a different route from that used on the ascent.

Lodges (with accommodation, restaurant, & shop)	**Pheriche** (0km) » **Sunrise Lodge and Restaurant at Orsho** (2.9km) » **Shomare** (3.7km) » **Pangboche Upper & Lower** (5.7km) » **Millingo** (8.0km) » **Deboche** (9.1km) » **Tengboche** (9.9km) » **Phunki Tenga** (12.9km) » **Tashinga** (13.8km) » **Sanasa** (15.5km) » **Kyanajuma** (16.0km) » **Namche** (20km)
Terrain/ Navigation	Paths are generally well-maintained and easy to follow (although sometimes rocky). Some steep and/or sustained climbs and descents. In particular, the descent from Tengboche to Phunki Tenga is a knee-jerker and the climb from Phunki Tenga to Sanasa is long and tiring.
Difficulty	**Hard.** The distance is long and the route undulates delivering a few tough little climbs. However, you will largely be heading downhill and you should be acclimatised by now.
Medical Assistance	**Pheriche Aid Post:** see p124 **Khunde Hospital:** 1km W of Khumjung
Points of Interest	**Stage EBC10a-EBC10c (Pheriche to Pangboche):** see p139 **Stage EBC10d/EBC10e (Pangboche to Tengboche):** see p129 **Stage EBC10f/EBC10g/EBC10h (Tengboche to Namche):** see p121

Stage EBC10a: Pheriche to Orsho Junction (See map on p132)

37 From **Pheriche**, head S down the valley on a clear path. After 15min, cross a bridge over the **Lobuche river**. Then continue S on a path which climbs to a little pass. Afterwards, descend S.

23 0:40: Reach a signpost at **Orsho Junction (4180m)**. Keep SH for EBC10b. The path on the left heads to Dingboche (EBC5c).

Stage EBC10b: Orsho Junction to Shomare (See map on p132)

23 From the junction, head S. Pass **Sunrise Lodge and Restaurant** at **Orsho**. The path bends right, contouring around the slopes.

22 0:25: Reach the village of **Shomare (4080m)**.

Stage EBC10c: Shomare to Pangboche (See map on p132)

22 Descend steeply through **Shomare** and exit the village. Soon, the path undulates as it contours around the slopes, alongside the **Imja Khola**.

21 0:35: After descending S, keep SH at a junction beside a large mani rock and wall: the path on the left heads to Ama Dablam BC (SR1; p134)

20 0:40: Shortly after crossing a bridge, reach **Pangboche Lower (3930m)**: to climb to Pangboche Upper, see p127.

Stage EBC10d: Pangboche to Deboche (See map on p114)

20 Descend SW through **Pangboche Lower**. Exit the village and continue SW along the N flank of the valley.

19 0:20: Keep SH at a junction (ignoring the path on the right which climbs to Pangboche Upper; see p131). Pass some stupas and mani stones. Then go through an arched gate. Pass a large stupa and continue descending: ahead, you should spot Tengboche Monastery on its forested ridge.

18 0:35: Cross a **suspension bridge** over the **Imja Khola**. Then climb through forest. Later, pass some mani walls.

17 1:05: Pass **Deboche Nunnery** (which you can usually visit) and the lodges at the **E side of Deboche**.

16 1:15: Reach the **W end of Deboche (3750m)**.

Stage EBC10e: Deboche to Tengboche (See map on p114)

16 From **Deboche**, climb SW through rhododendron forest.

15 0:40: Arrive at the monastery in **Tengboche (3860m)**.

Stage EBC10f: Tengboche to Phunki Tenga (See map on p114)

15 To leave **Tengboche**, descend SE through an **arched gateway** (the start of a long, steep descent). As you approach the **Dudh Koshi**, pass a **national park checkpoint**. Shortly afterwards, pass some restaurants. Then cross a **suspension bridge** over the river.

14 0:45: At the other side of the bridge, reach **Phunki Tenga (3250m)**.

Stage EBC10g: Phunki Tenga to Sanasa (See map on p114)

14 Climb SW through trees.

13 0:40: Pass the lodges at **Tashinga** and continue climbing.

12 1:40: Reach a junction at **Sanasa (3600m)** where there are three options: for the main route to Namche, head S (EBC10h); for Khumjung, head W (GL4a; p227); for Mong/Gokyo, head N (GL4b; p227).

Stage EBC10h: Sanasa to Namche (See map on p114)

12 From the junction, follow the path heading S.

11 0:05: Keep SH past the tea houses and bakery at **Kyanajuma:** the path on the right heads to Khumjung. 25min later, pass a stupa. 20min after that, pass **Tenzing Norgay Memorial Stupa.**

10 1:05: 15min later, the path bends right to head W. Shortly after **Mustang Guest House,** TL and pass a huge mani stone. Shortly afterwards, TR at a junction (beside a prayer wheel): alternatively, TL for the **Sherpa Culture Museum/SNP Visitor Centre** (p108). Descend towards the buildings of Namche. Near **Moonlight Lodge,** the path bends left and descends steeply S through Namche on a cobbled street.

9 1:30: Reach the lower part of **Namche (3440m).**

Kangtega (EBC10d)

Alternative: Dingboche to Orsho Junction (Stage EBC5c)

45min; 2.6km; SA -170m (See map on p132)

Terrain/Navigation: paths are generally well-maintained and simple to follow although there are rocky and steep sections. Route-finding is straightforward.

Difficulty: medium.

24 From the **SW part of Dingboche**, head SW on a path. Soon, descend steeply SW alongside the **Imja Khola**. Cross a bridge over the **Lobuche river**. Then climb SW.

23 0:45: Reach a signpost at **Orsho Junction (4180m)**. Keep SH for EBC10b: the path on the right heads to Pheriche (EBC10a).

EBC11 Namche to Lukla

Cheplung: prayer wheels, mani stones & a stupa

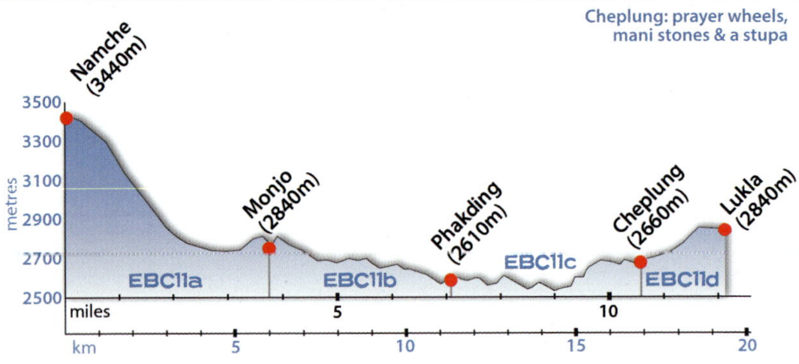

		Time	Distance	Ascent	Descent	SA Increase	Max Alt
EBC11a	Namche to Monjo	2:15	6.0km 3.7miles	128m 420ft	728m 2389ft	-600m -1969ft	3440m 11287ft
EBC11b	Monjo to Phakding	2:00	5.3km 3.3miles	128m 420ft	358m 1175ft	-230m -755ft	2840m 9318ft
EBC11c	Phakding to Cheplung	2:00	5.6km 3.5miles	211m 692ft	161m 528ft	+50m +164ft	2660m 8727ft
EBC11d	Cheplung to Lukla	1:15	2.4km 1.5miles	200m 656ft	20m 66ft	+180m +591ft	2840m 9318ft

The village of Jorsale, beside the Dudh Koshi river

Unless you are hiking out of the Khumbu (to Phaplu/Bhandar), all the Everest treks finish back at Lukla and almost everybody returns there on foot, along the same path used to ascend many days previously: most people hike from Namche to Lukla in one day. Because flights back to Kathmandu depart early in the day, most returning trekkers spend a night in Lukla before their flight the following morning: they get to know the town a little better by celebrating success in its bars and restaurants. However, if you are unlucky, and your flight is cancelled due to bad weather, then you might get to know Lukla a little too well!

If short of time, or flights are likely to be cancelled for a few days, you could consider taking a helicopter from Lukla (or higher up) to Kathmandu. This is a wonderful experience but it is expensive and not without risk: see p61.

On the other hand, if you are not in a rush, then we recommend leaving the Khumbu on foot on the trail to Phaplu or Bhandar (see p32). To access this trail from Lukla, follow AR3 to Surke (p252). However, it is quicker to skip Lukla, leaving the CEBC at Cheplung (1) and heading directly to Surke on W5d (p251).

For further information on Lukla, see p102.

Lodges (with accommodation, restaurant, & shop)	**Namche** (0km) » **Jorsale** (4.8km) » **Monjo** (6.0km) » **Chumoa** (6.8km) » **Benkar** (7.7km) » **Toc Toc** (9.3km) » **Zamphuti** (10.0km) » **Phakding** (11.3km) » **Ghat/Nurning** (13.7km) » **Thado Kosi** (14.6km) » **Cheplung** (16.9km) » **Lukla** (19.3km) No facilities between Namche and Jorsale. Plenty of tea houses and grocery stores along the route between Jorsale and Lukla.
Terrain/ Navigation	The undulating paths are clear and well maintained, although steep at times. Route-finding is generally straightforward: however, take care at junctions between Toc Toc and Phakding: if in doubt, keep S alongside the river.
Difficulty	**Medium.** The distance is long but the route is largely downhill.
Medical Assistance	**Zamphuti health post** (4): see p103 **Lukla Hospital**
Points of Interest	**EBC11a/EBC11b (Namche to Phakding):** see p107 **EBC11c/EBC11d (Phakding to Lukla):** see p103

Stage EBC11a: Namche to Monjo (See map on p110)

9 From the **arched gateway** to the S of **Namche**, head S. Soon, descend steeply through forest. Descend past the **SNP checkpoint**.

8 0:30: Descend past the **Everest Viewpoint**. Soon pass another viewpoint: the last chance to see Everest.

7 1:00: Cross the **Hillary Suspension Bridge (2930m)** and continue descending. Afterwards, TR at a junction to choose the path closest to the river (the fastest route). After a while, cross another suspension bridge over the Dudh Koshi. Shortly afterwards, pass through **Jorsale (2820m)**. Then cross a third suspension bridge over the river.

6 2:15: Go through an archway to reach the **SNP checkpoint** at **Monjo (2840m)**.

Stage EBC11b: Monjo to Phakding (See map on p110)

6 Descend through **Monjo** and continue S out of the village. Pass the village of **Chumoa (2760m)**. Cross to the W bank of the Dudh Koshi using a suspension bridge: then continue S.

5 0:50: Head through the village of **Benkar (2715m)**. Pass a waterfall, a viewpoint and then another waterfall. After the village of **Toc Toc (2710m)**, pass a police checkpoint.

4 1:35: (See map on p104). 5min later, go through the village of **Zamphuti (2700m)**: at junctions, remain on the main path (closest to the river). TL and walk between the lodges of the **W part of Phakding**. Cross a suspension bridge. Then head S.

3 2:00: Arrive in the **E part of Phakding (2610m)**.

Stage EBC11c: Phakding to Cheplung (See map on p104)

3 From **Phakding**, head S. Pass the villages of **Chhuthawa**, **Nurning** and **Ghat**.

2 1:15: Cross the bridge at **Thado Kosi**.

1 2:00: Reach a junction at the S side of the village of **Cheplung (2660m)**: bear left and stay on the main path for Lukla; alternatively, those hiking to Phaplu/Bhandar can TR at the junction to proceed directly to Surke (W5d; p251). There is a monastery in the cliffs above Cheplung.

Stage EBC11d: Cheplung to Lukla (See map on p104)

1 From the junction, head SE (ignoring the path on the right which heads to Surke). At any junctions, continue SE. Eventually, go through the **Pasang Lhamu Memorial Gate**. Shortly afterwards, pass the Pasang Lhamu Rural Municipality checkpoint and head S down Lukla's main street.

F 1:15: Arrive at the **airport** at the S side of **Lukla (2840m)**.

Mani stones at Cheplung

Three Passes Trek: non-CEBC sections

Descending from Kongma La to Lobuche: in the background, Lobuche E and W

TP6 Dingboche/Chukhung

From Dingboche, TPT (ACW) trekkers head E along the Imja Khola, leaving the CEBC for the first time. The path is blissfully peaceful because most trekkers head N, directly towards EBC. The early morning sun lights up the broad valley: to the S, Ama Dablam looks sublime; to the W, Taboche is perfectly positioned to catch the low morning light.

There are 8000ers to see too: as you leave Dingboche, you should spot Makalu to the E (peeking out from behind Num Ri). Although it disappears quickly, that hardly matters because today is mostly about Lhotse (the world's 4th highest peak): this spectacular mountain is gradually and tantalisingly revealed as you progress towards Chukhung (which is situated just beneath its terrifying S face).

Scenically, Chukhung is a fabulous place. It is located at the base of the Imja Khola valley, surrounded by high peaks: because the valley is broad, you have a wide field of vision. The village has some decent lodges and is a peaceful place, far removed from the bustle of the

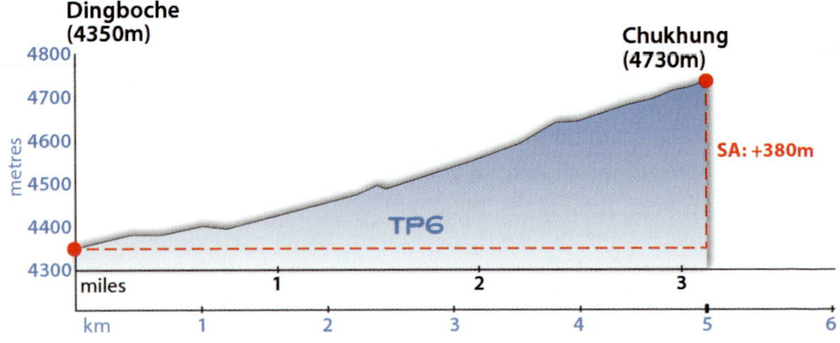

		Time	Distance	Ascent	Descent	SA Increase	Max Alt
TP6 (ACW)	Dingboche to Chukhung	2:30	5.0km 3.1miles	410m 1345ft	30m 98ft	+380m +1247ft	4730m 15519ft
TP6 (CW)	Chukhung to Dingboche	2:00	5.0km 3.1miles	30m 98ft	410m 1345ft	-380m -1247ft	4730m 15519ft

Lhotse's terrifying S face (TP6)

CEBC. However, Chukhung's real drawcard is that it is the staging point for two of the best day-hikes in the Khumbu (which can aid acclimatisation). The ascent of Chukhung Ri is the most popular hike (SR4; p186): the panorama from its summit rivals the more famous KP. However, the underused hike to Island Peak BC is also exceptional (SR3; p182). Fit ACW trekkers could do one of the hikes on the day of arrival from Dingboche and take an AD to complete the other one. CW trekkers will have little surplus energy on the day of arrival at Chukhung (after crossing Kongma La): however, they could do one of the day-hikes before departing for Dingboche the following day; to complete both, they would also need to take an extra day at Chukhung.

For ACW trekkers who have spent two nights at Dingboche, it is not essential (according to the generally accepted rules of altitude acclimatization) to spend two nights at Chukhung: however, because there is so much to do, we highly recommend doing so. You could spend one night in Dingboche followed by two nights in Chukhung but this breaks the rules and, if you have not had an AD since Namche, it can push you too high too quickly. However, two nights in each of Dingboche and Chukhung is an excellent choice if you have time: this approach should leave you extremely well acclimatised before the challenging crossing of Kongma La (TP7); furthermore, it enables you to complete all of Nangkar Tshang Peak (SR2; p142), Chukhung Ri and Island Peak BC, some of the best hikes you will do in your life.

Lodges (with accommodation, restaurant, & shop)	**Dingboche** (0km) » **Chukhung** (5km) Tea shop in yak herders' shelter: (1); opening times uncertain
Terrain/ Navigation	The path is rocky and sometimes faint, however, route-finding is straightforward. The gradient is rarely steep.
Difficulty	**Medium.** The distance is short and the climb is gradual but the altitude is high.
Medical Assistance	**Pheriche Aid Post:** see p124
Points of Interest	Kukuczka's Chorten (1) Lhotse's S face Village of Chukhung (2)

ACW

Stage TP6: Dingboche to Chukhung (See map on p147)

24 Head NE up **Dingboche's main street**.

25 0:10: At the NE end of the village, keep SH at a junction ('Chukhung'). Follow a path which climbs gently up the Imja Khola valley. Makalu appears (to the right of Num Ri); Island Peak is SH; Lhotse gradually reveals itself on the left.

1 2:00: (See map on p184). Continue E past a **yak herders' shelter (4630m)** which sometimes opens as a tea-shop. Just afterwards, pass **Kukuczka's Chorten** (see p181).

2 2:30: Arrive at **Chukhung (4730m)**.

CW

Stage TP6: Chukhung to Dingboche (See map on p184)

2 From **Chukhung**, descend W on a path.

1 Continue W past **Kukuczka's Chorten** (see p181). Just afterwards, pass a **yak herders' shelter (4630m)** which sometimes opens as a café.

25 1:50: (See map on p147). On the outskirts of Dingboche, TL at a junction and head SW along the main street.

24 2:00: Arrive at the **SW end of Dingboche (4730m)**.

Kukuczka's Chorten

On Stage TP6, 1.1km W of Chukhung, there is a memorial to three Polish climbers who died in separate incidents on Lhotse's S face: Rafal Cholda, Czeslaw Jakiel and Jerzy Kukuczka. The latter was the best-known so the memorial is named after him.

Jerzy Kukuczka is considered to be one of history's finest mountaineers. He was the second person (after Reinhold Messner) to climb all fourteen of the world's 8000ers. Furthermore, he did this 'alpine style' (unsupported with no fixed ropes or Sherpas) and used supplemental oxygen only on one of them: even today, this is an amazing feat but at the time, it was considered practically impossible. He also claimed many first ascents in the Himalaya and pioneered numerous new routes (some of which have never been repeated). His record of 10 new routes on the 8000ers still stands. He also specialized in winter ascents. He died in 1989, during an unsuccessful attempt to scale the S face of Lhotse (which had not yet been climbed). He fell from 8200m and his rope snapped: it had been bought second-hand from a market in Kathmandu. His body was never recovered. Lhotse's S face was successfully climbed the following year by a Soviet team: this feat has never been repeated.

Yak herder's cabin: in the background, Taboche

SR3 Side Route: Island Peak Base Camp

Views of Lhotse (SR3)

This exceptional day-hike is the equal of most other trekking routes in the Khumbu and it is inexplicably underrated. Most trekkers undertake only one acclimatisation hike from Chukhung and the majority opt for Chukhung Ri (SR4; p186) which is also amazing. However, if you do continue up the Imja Khola valley to Island Peak BC, you will not be disappointed. As you head along the moraine of the Lhotse Glacier, into a wonderland of ice and snowy peaks, the 360° panorama is astounding: Lhotse, Nuptse and Shartse to the N; Island Peak, Cho Polu, Num Ri and Baruntse to the E; Ama Dablam to the S; Taboche and Cholatse to the W. It is unforgettable. Depending upon the season, Island Peak BC will be packed with colourful tents to house climbers attempting Island Peak's summit: it is one of the most popular trekking peaks in the region (see p33).

		Time	Distance	Ascent	Descent	SA Increase	Max Alt
SR3	Chukhung to Island Peak BC (return)	5:15	13.2km 8.2miles	530m 1739ft	530m 1739ft	0m 0ft	5090m 16700ft

Imja Tsho

Imja Tsho lake started to form in the 1950s when melt water from the Imja and Lhotse Shar Glaciers began to accumulate. As the glaciers shrink, the lake fills and it is now the fastest growing glacial lake in the Himalaya. The water is only held in place by a terminal moraine: as the lake grows, it is feared that the moraine will rupture, causing a glacial outburst flood which could destroy settlements downstream. Because the 2015 earthquake may have destabilised the moraine, the Nepalese army constructed an outlet and partially drained the lake in 2016: the level of the lake was lowered by more than 3m.

Lodges (with accommodation, restaurant, & shop)	**Chukhung** (0km) No food/drinks at Island Peak BC
Terrain/ Navigation	The path is rocky but generally straightforward to negotiate. Gradients are rarely steep. Route-finding is generally simple but occasionally, paths are faint and harder to follow.
Difficulty	**Hard**. The altitude is very high, reaching 5090m.
Medical Assistance	**Pheriche Aid Post:** see p124
Points of Interest	Island Peak BC: 8 Imja Tsho lake

SR3: Island Peak Base Camp (See map on p184)

2 From the top (E) of **Chukhung**, pick up a path heading S. Shortly afterwards, cross a bridge and climb. Shortly, the path bends left and heads E along a narrow ridge (on the moraine of **Lhotse Glacier**): the panorama is excellent. At the end of the ridge, a clear rocky path continues E up the valley.

7 1:45: Keep SH at a junction: ignore the path on the right which descends towards the river. Afterwards, the path climbs NE. Eventually, bear right and head E along the N side of **Imja Tsho**: the lake is hidden behind moraine but there are plenty of snowy peaks to view.

8 3:00: Arrive at **Island Peak BC (5090m)**. If you have energy, climb the moraine to the S for a great view of **Imja Tsho**. To return to Chukhung, retrace your steps.

2 5:15: Arrive back at **Chukhung (4730m)**.

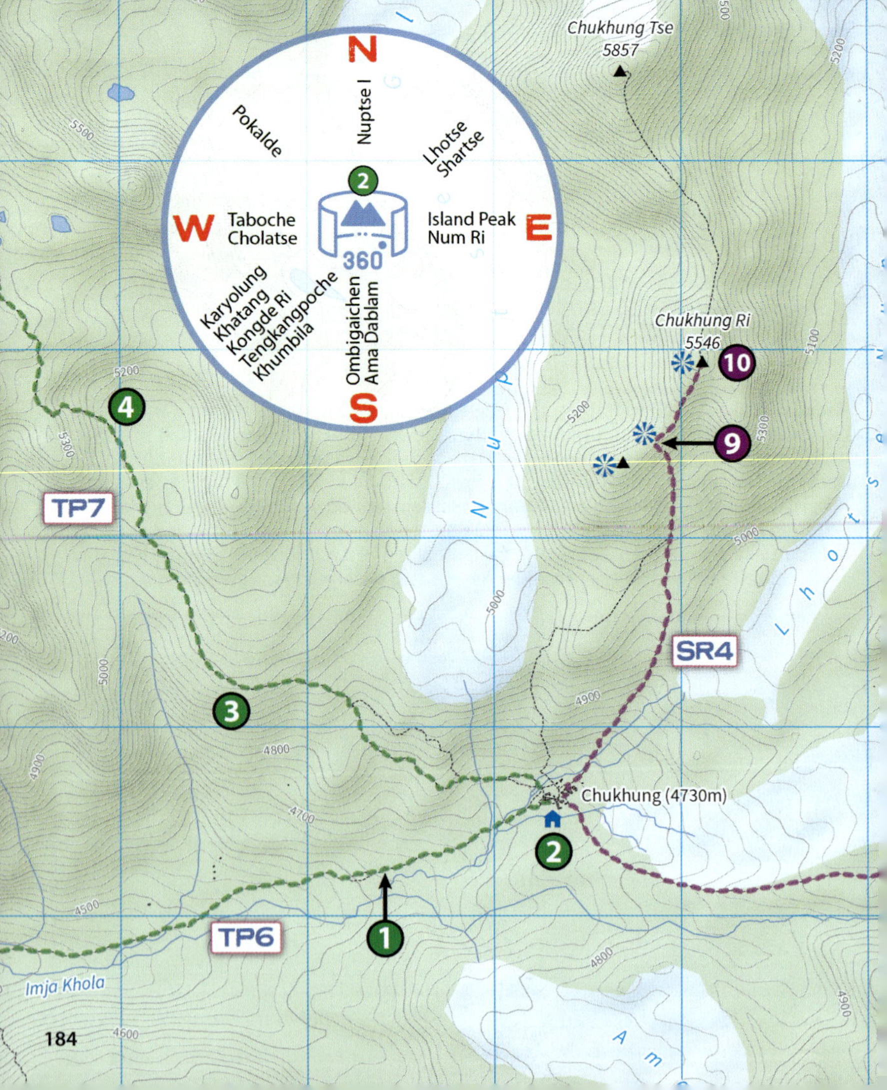

SR4: Chukhung Ri (See map on p184)

2 From the top (E) of **Chukhung**, pick up a path climbing NE. Cross a small bridge. Shortly afterwards, climb more steeply. After a while, the gradient eases as you cross a large plateau. Afterwards, climb steeply again, up a grassy slope. As you climb, **Makalu** appears to the E.

9 2:30: Reach a **saddle covered with cairns (5370m)**. From here, you have two options: TR and climb NE for the main summit; alternatively, TL and climb SW for the lower summit. The route to the lower summit involves a straightforward climb up the crest of the ridge (10-15min). However, the route to the main summit is more difficult: the path up the ridge becomes very steep and there are rocks to scramble over.

10 3:15: Reach the summit of **Chukhung Ri (5546m)**. After admiring the views, retrace your steps.

2 5:00: Arrive back at **Chukhung (4730m)**.

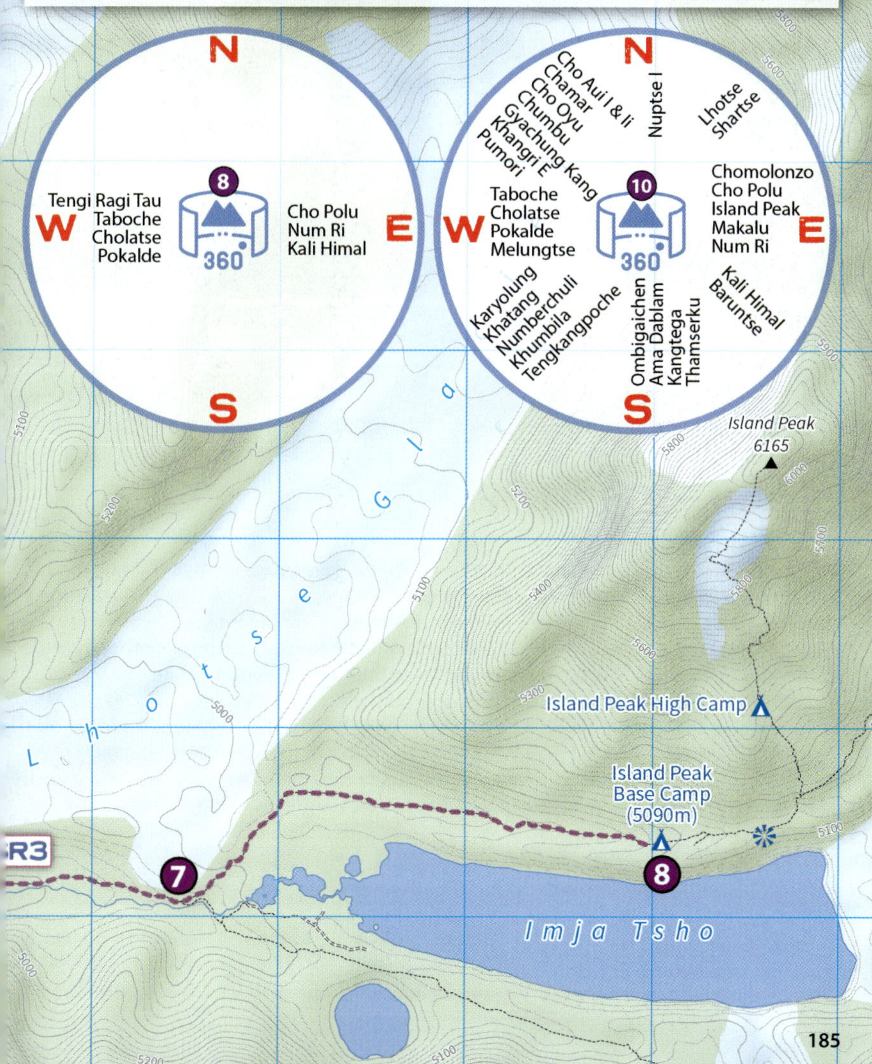

SR4 Side Route: Chukhung Ri

This side-route rivals the more popular KP (p162) and Gokyo Ri (p204). Chukhung Ri is only a minor peak which is located a short distance N of Chukhung. However, there is nothing 'minor' about the views from the top. Although you cannot see Everest, you get a good look at three 8000ers (the 4th, 5th and 6th highest mountains on the planet): early in the climb, Makalu appears and, by the time you reach the summit, you are breathtakingly close to Lhotse and the Nuptse ridge. But that is only part of the story because, on a clear day, the unforgettable 360° panorama allows you to view great swathes of the Khumbu and beyond. Peering all the way down the Imja Khola valley, you gain a much better understanding of the region's geography and how its peaks and glaciers fit together. Chukhung Ri is also a great place from which to view Imja Tsho (p183). **For the SR4 route description, see p185.**

		Time	Distance	Ascent	Descent	SA Increase	Max Alt
SR4	Chukhung to Chukhung Ri (return)	5:00	7.2km 4.5miles	850m 2789ft	850m 2789ft	0m 0ft	5546m 18196ft

Epic views from the summit of Chukhung Ri

Lodges (with accommodation, restaurant, & shop)	**Chukhung** (0km)
Terrain/ Navigation	Between Chukhung and the saddle at ❾, the path (although steep) poses no technical difficulties and is simple to follow. However, between ❾ and the summit, the route is very steep and you will need to use your hands to scramble over sections of rocks: if you lose the path, just continue up the ridge (across rocks).
Difficulty	**Very Hard.** The ascent is long, steep and relentless. Furthermore, the high altitude really bites. If the main summit is too difficult for you, climb the easier, lower summit instead: 10-15min SW of ❾.
Medical Assistance	**Pheriche Aid Post:** see p124
Points of Interest	Mind-blowing 360° panorama Imja Tsho lake

Chukhung/Lobuche

Crossing the Khumbu Glacier: Pumori in the background

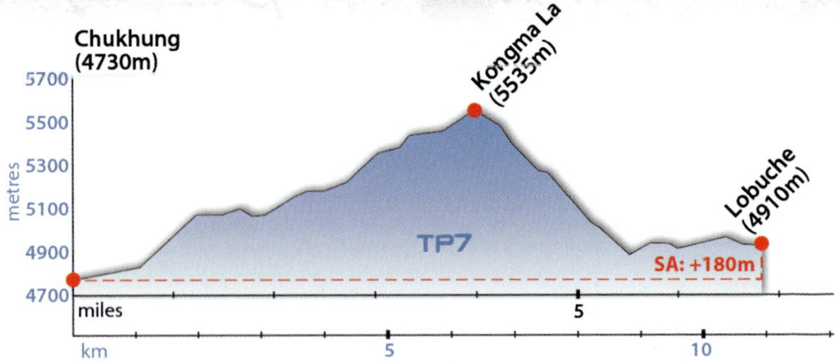

		Time	Distance	Ascent	Descent	SA Increase	Max Alt
TP7 (ACW)	Chukhung to Lobuche	8:00	10.9km 6.8miles	1020m 3347ft	840m 2756ft	+180m +591ft	5535m 18160ft
TP7 (CW)	Lobuche to Chukhung	7:30	10.9km 6.8miles	840m 2756ft	1020m 3347ft	-180m -591ft	5535m 18160ft

This is a world class hike: the landscape is remote, the altitude and exposure are exhilarating and the views throughout are superlative. From Kongma La, the highest pass on the TPT, a great many of the world's highest mountains and longest glaciers are on display. Although Everest is not visible, you should see three 8000ers: Lhotse, Makalu and Cho Oyu, the world's 4th, 5th and 6th highest peaks. Pray for a clear day!

However, there is a high price to pay for such beauty because TP7 is probably the hardest part of the TPT: the distance between settlements is long; the terrain is tougher than the CEBC's paths; the gradients are very steep; some sections are very exposed; and the altitude is very high. For ACW trekkers, Kongma La is the first and most challenging of the three passes. It is slightly easier for CW trekkers who face less metres of climbing in that direction and, having already crossed two passes, should be better acclimatised and more trail-hardened. Whichever the direction of travel, most trekkers need a full day for this hike so make sure that you set out early: carry plenty of food because there are no facilities along the way.

Snow lies around Kongma La until well into the spring and the high altitude means that fresh falls are always possible: it is sensible to carry spikes/crampons. Snow conceals paths, making walking more challenging and route-finding more difficult. Navigation is also difficult in low visibility. In such conditions, do not leave without a guide and, when deciding whether to set out, bear in mind that guides can get lost too. During our research for this book, it snowed heavily overnight at Chukhung. Having winter experience, the correct equipment and a guide, we decided to set out and successfully made it to Lobuche without incident. A trekker, who left the lodge in Chukhung shortly after us (alone and without a guide) was not so lucky: after an extensive search involving helicopters, he was found dead a few days later.

For information on Lobuche and Chukhung, see p150 and p178 respectively.

Lodges (with accommodation, restaurant, & shop)	**Chukhung** (0km) » **Lobuche** (10.9km)
Terrain/ Navigation	High altitude mountainous route with steep, rocky, challenging terrain: a guide is recommended. Some sections are very steep and exposed. Occasionally, you may need to scramble over boulders. The climb is long and tough with the high altitude really biting: snow on the ground will make it even harder. In icy conditions, the steep paths near the pass can be treacherous and spikes/crampons may be required. Sometimes, paths are faint, making navigation more difficult. Navigation in snowy conditions is challenging, particularly on the E side of Kongma La. Immediately SE of Lobuche, the route crosses the Khumbu Glacier: fortunately, the ice is almost entirely covered with rock so crampons are not usually required. Normally, the route across the rock can be tricky to follow (cairns/waymarks) and the going is tough: you may have to clamber over sections of boulders. Furthermore, shifting of the underlying ice can make the route unstable: watch your step and look out for falling rocks. Occasionally, the path is re-routed due to movements in the ice.
Difficulty	**Very hard**. The terrain is extremely tough and the altitude is very high. Kongma La is the toughest of the three passes.
Medical Assistance	**Pheriche Aid Post:** see p124
Points of Interest	Kongma La pass: 5 Khumbu Glacier: 6 Lobuche: 31

Stage TP7: Chukhung to Lobuche (See map on p184)

2 Cross a bridge at the NW side of **Chukhung.** Then head W on a path, passing below **Nuptse Glacier.** About 0.5km from the bridge, the path splits: both branches converge later but most people use the more southerly path. Climb a grassy ridge.

3 1:30: Cross the crest of the ridge. Then climb along the W side of it. Soon, head NW: the path drifts away from the ridge, climbing the W side of a valley.

4 2:30: **(See map on p147).** The path bends left and climbs steeply up the W side of the valley: watch your footing. At the top of the slope, bear right and climb more gently to the N: the views of Lhotse and Nuptse are fabulous. Soon the gradient increases again. Eventually, reach a plateau with some beautiful lakes: pass to the N of the largest lake. Then the path heads briefly N, steeply up the slope: after a few minutes, bear left and climb W across the face of the slope.

5 4:30: Cross **Kongma La (5535m)** with its incredible views and colourful prayer flags. Initially, descend N across the face of the rocky slope. Soon the path bends left, heading NW straight down the slope.

6 6:20: After a long knee-jerking descent, keep SH and climb the lateral moraine of the **Khumbu Glacier**. Then TL and walk SW along the moraine. Soon the path bends right and winds its way NW across the glacier. At the far side, climb the moraine. Then descend NW towards Lobuche which you will see below.

31 8:00: Arrive at **Lobuche (4910m).**

CW

Stage TP7: Lobuche to Chukhung (See map on p147)

31 From Lobuche, follow a path which heads SE (up the lateral moraine of the Khumbu Glacier). From the top of the moraine, the path winds SE across the glacier. At the far side of the glacier, bear left and head NE along the moraine.

6 1:30: Soon TR and head steeply down the moraine. Then follow a path climbing towards Kongma La (which you can clearly see to the SE). As you gain height, the gradient increases. At around 5300m, the path heads directly up the steep slope: soon it bends right and climbs S across the face of the slope.

5 4:15: Cross Kongma La (5535m) with its incredible views and colourful prayer flags. Initially, descend E across the face of the slope. Soon, TR and descend briefly S towards the largest of the lakes below. Shortly, TL and head E along the N side of the lake. Then descend SE. After a while, the path bends left and descends a steep, rocky slope: take care.

4 5:40: **(See map on p184)**. At the bottom of the slope, TR and head S down a valley.

3 6:25: Bear left and soon cross the crest of a ridge. Then descend SE off the ridge. Soon, the path splits: both paths converge later but most people use the more southerly path.

2 7:30: Cross a bridge to enter Chukhung (4730m).

Descending from Kongma La towards Lobuche

TP9c Junction (4850m) to Dzongla

Cholatse (TP9c)

This route features a magnificent and tranquil balcony path which faces directly onto the stunning summit of Cholatse. Although the trail undulates regularly, you stay high throughout and the constantly shifting views are never less than exquisite. Chola Tsho lake sits in the valley far below and, to the SE, Ama Dablam looks wonderful (as usual). You will not wish to rush this section.

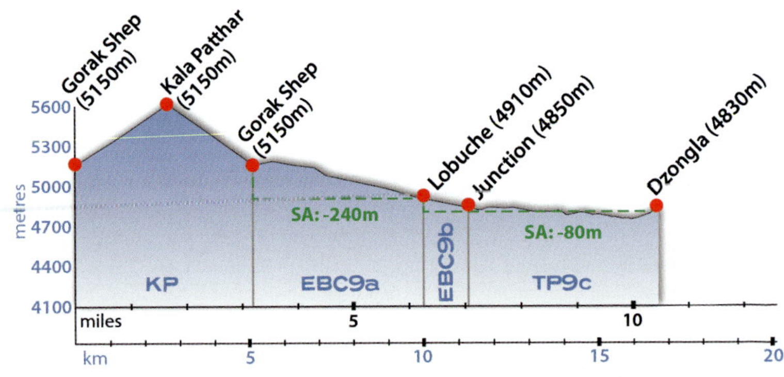

		Time	Distance	Ascent	Descent	SA Increase	Max Alt
TP9c (ACW)	Junction (4850m) to Dzongla	2:30	5.3km 3.3miles	253m 830ft	273m 896ft	-80m -262ft (Lobuche to Dzongla)	4863m 15956ft
TP9c (CW)	Dzongla to Junction (4850m)	2:30	5.3km 3.3miles	273m 896ft	253m 830ft	N/A (no lodges)	4863m 15956ft

ACW trekkers leave the CEBC behind and will not see it again before returning to Namche: consequently, the trails should be quieter. Many ACW trekkers climb KP and then hike all the way from Gorak Shep to Dzongla, all on the same day. Most spend the night at Dzongla because the following day (crossing Cho La) is so difficult. Furthermore, a night in Dzongla enables you to cross the pass earlier in the morning (when the weather is often better than later in the day). Very fit trekkers could hike all the way from Lobuche to Dragnag in one day but for most people, that would be too challenging at these high altitudes.

CW trekkers will meet the CEBC for the first time since leaving Namche: the higher number of hikers can be a shock after the more peaceful paths of the previous days.

Compared to the busier settlements along the CEBC, Dzongla is a small and peaceful place. Originally, a yak-herding settlement, it now benefits from a steady flow of TPT trekkers and there are a handful of lodges. The views are good but it is very cold at night.

Lodges (with accommodation, restaurant, & shop)	**Dzongla** (5.3km)
Terrain/ Navigation	Although the terrain poses no technical difficulties and there are no long climbs, the path undulates constantly and is quite tiring. Route-finding is fairly straightforward, however, the paths are not as clear as those on the CEBC, so pay attention.
Difficulty	**Medium**
Medical Assistance	**Pheriche Aid Post:** see p124
Points of Interest	Excellent views of Cholatse Chola Tsho lake (in the valley below) Village of Dzongla: 7

ACW

Stage TP9c: Junction (4850m) to Dzongla (See map on p195)

30 From **Junction (4850m)**, head W across a rocky plateau ('Cho La'): the path heading S goes to Dughla (EBC9c; p168). Aim for a large rock on the other side of the plateau: just after it, TL on a path climbing S. To the NW, **Lobuche E** towers above. After a magnificent traverse (S across the slopes), the path bends right, heading NW up the valley: the viewpoint as the path bends is sublime. Afterwards, **Cholatse** dominates (to the SW). After a long traverse, descend into the valley. Cross a bridge over a stream and climb steeply W: a tiring slog at the end of the day.

7 2:30: Reach the village of **Dzongla (4830m)**.

CW

Stage TP9c: Dzongla to Junction (4850m) (See map on p195)

7 From **Dzongla**, descend E. At the bottom of the slope, cross a bridge over a stream. Then climb SE. The narrow, undulating path continues SE above **Chola Tsho**: **Cholatse** dominates (to the SW). After a magnificent traverse SE, the path bends left, heading N towards the **Khumbu Glacier**: the viewpoint as the path bends is sublime. Eventually, TR and head E across a rocky plateau: to the NW, Lobuche E towers above.

30 2:30: At the E side of the plateau, reach **Junction (4850m)**; head N for Lobuche (EBC7b; p153); alternatively, head S for Dughla (EBC9c; p168).

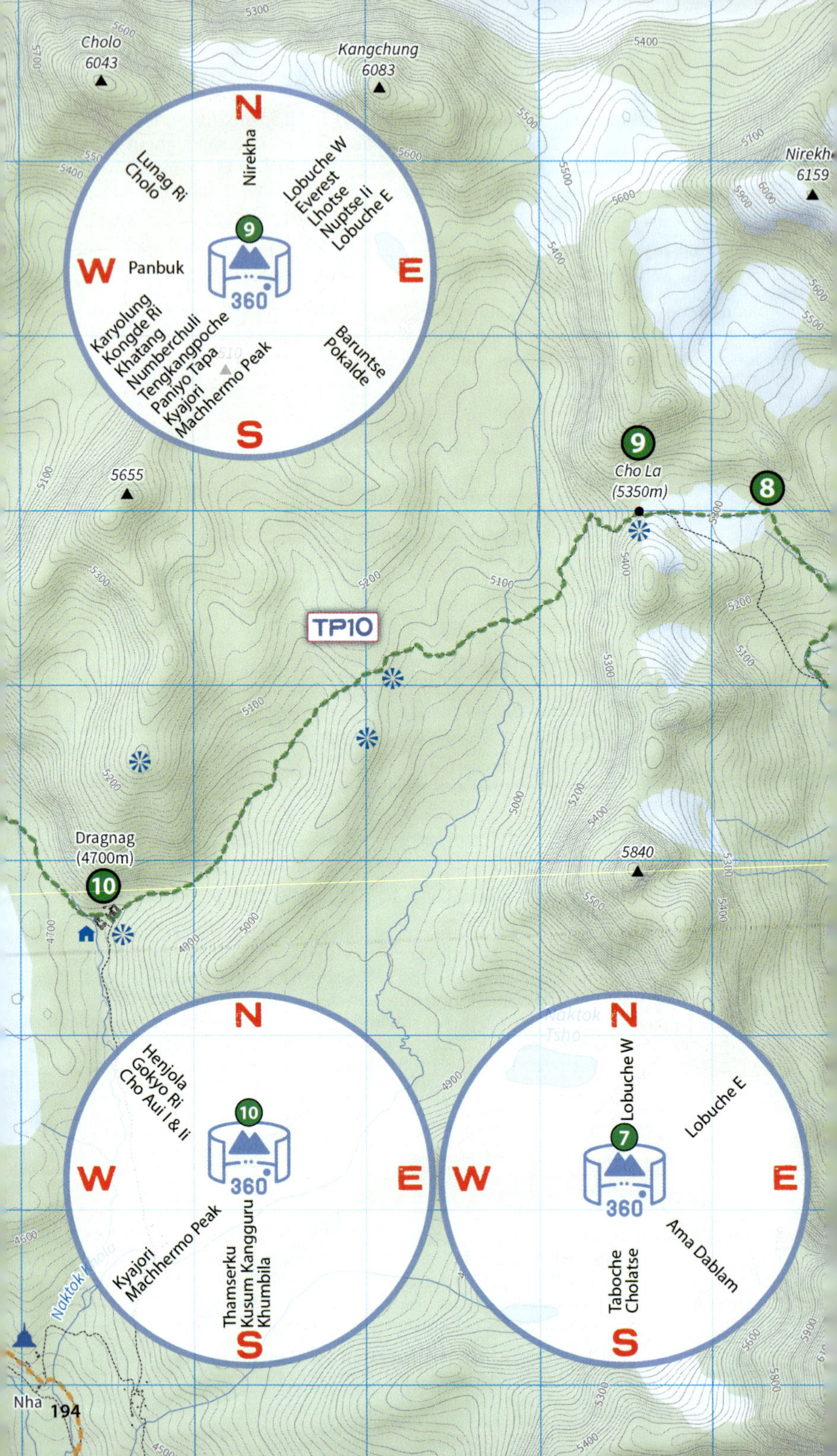

Cholo
6043
Kangchung
6083
Nirekha
6159
N
Nirekha
Lunag Ri
Cholo
Lobuche W
Everest
Lhotse
Nuptse Ii
Lobuche E
W
Panbuk
E
9
360
Karyolung
Kongde Ri
Khatang
Numberchuli
Tengkangpoche
Paniyo Tapa
Kyajori
Machhermo Peak
Baruntse
Pokalde
S
5655
9
Cho La
(5350m)
8
TP10
Dragnag
(4700m)
10
5840
Naktok
Tsho
N
Henjola
Gokyo Ri
Cho Aui I & Ii
10
W
360
E
Kyajori
Machhermo Peak
Thamserku
Kusum Kangguru
Khumbila
S
N
Lobuche W
Lobuche E
7
W
360
E
Ama Dablam
Taboche
Cholatse
S
Naktok Khola
Nha

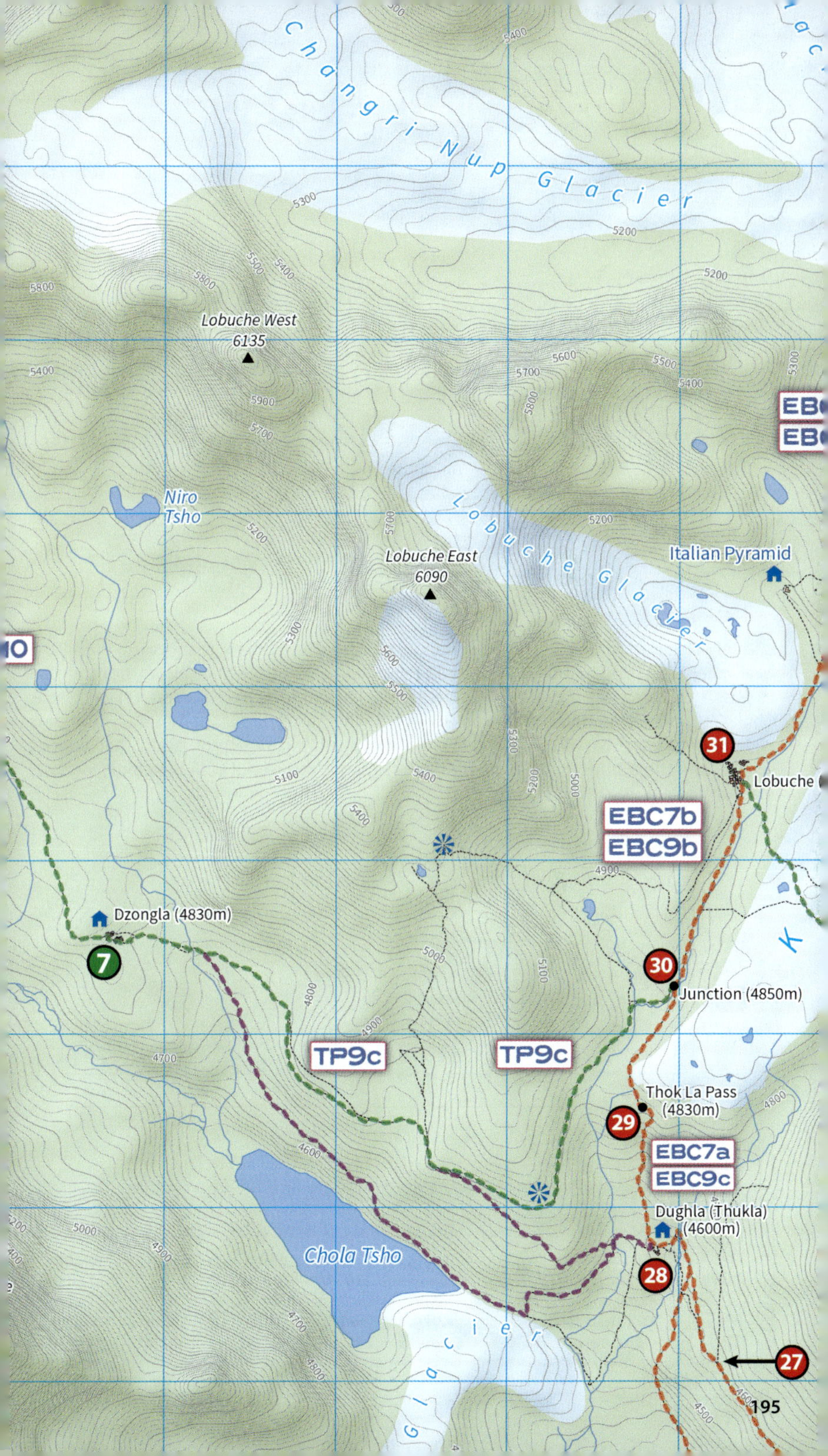

Changri Nup Glacier
Lobuche West
6135
Niro Tsho
Lobuche East
6090
Lobuche Glacier
Italian Pyramid
Lobuche
EBC7b
EBC9b
Dzongla (4830m)
7
31
30
Junction (4850m)
TP9c
TP9c
Thok La Pass
(4830m)
29
EBC7a
EBC9c
Dughla (Thukla)
(4600m)
28
27
Chola Tsho
Glacier

TP10 Dzongla/Dragnag

Cho La pass

Difficulties aside, Stage TP10 is a wonderful hike. The scenery is spectacular and the glacier crossing will be a once in a lifetime experience for many. Both sides of Cho La pass are completely different and crossing it is like entering a new world. On the E side, Cholatse dominates and Ama Dablam looks splendid (as always). The W side of the pass is equally spectacular with a broader panorama featuring plenty of peaks that are not visible from the E side. The final descent to Dragnag is wonderful with incredible views of Machermo Peak and Kyajori.

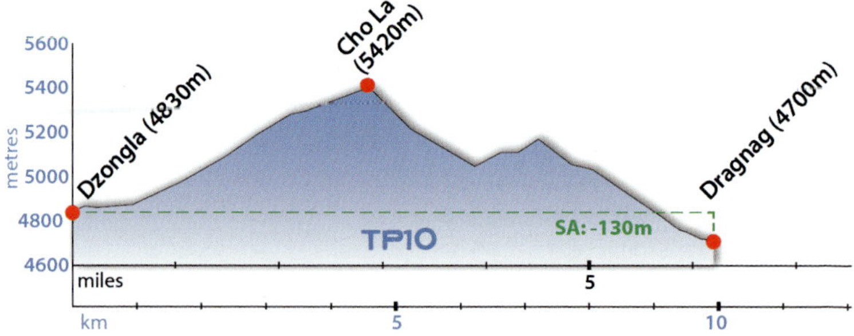

		Time	Distance	Ascent	Descent	SA Increase	Max Alt
TP10 (ACW)	Dzongla to Dragnag	6:30	9.9km 6.2miles	730m 2395ft	860m 2822ft	-130m -427ft	5420m 17783ft
TP10 (CW)	Dragnag to Dzongla	7:00	9.9km 6.2miles	860m 2822ft	730m 2395ft	+130m +427ft	5420m 17783ft

The crossing of Cho La pass is long and tough from either side: there are extremely steep and exposed slopes which can be treacherous when covered with snow/ice (particularly, on the W side of the pass). The pass is harder for CW trekkers who have more altitude gain and tackle the steepest section of the route (just W of the pass) in an uphill direction.

E of the pass, you must traverse Cho La Glacier which can be icy, especially early in the morning. Although this glacier crossing is not particularly difficult technically, and is normally straightforward, exercise caution and do not leave the path: a fall into a crevasse can be fatal. At the time of writing, the trail ran up the middle of the glacier (marked with metal poles) but the exact route changes, depending on the location of the crevasses. In clear weather, the route is usually obvious, tracked by the footprints of earlier hikers. However, early in the spring, if you are one of the first trekkers to cross, the route may not be apparent. Furthermore, at any time of year, low visibility can make the trail harder to spot in the snow and fresh snow can completely conceal the route: in such conditions, it can be prudent to turn back. More so than anywhere else on the TPT, we recommend employing a guide for the crossing (even if just for peace of mind).

Dragnag is located on the E edge of the Ngozumpa Glacier and is a great overnight stop for ACW trekkers. Although hemmed in by mountains to the E, the outlook W is far-reaching and the village keeps the sun quite late into the evening. There are several lodges where you can eat and sleep. However, if you are in good shape, you can continue to Gokyo the same day (along TP11; p200) and many trekkers do that: however, crossing the Ngozumpa Glacier immediately after Cho La is exhausting and will be too much for some. Likewise, some CW trekkers start the day from Lobuche, first crossing the Ngozumpa Glacier before tackling Cho La: however, because the Cho La crossing is so hard, we prefer to overnight at Dragnag so that we can start the climb first thing in the morning.

There are no facilities between Dragnag and Dzongla so carry food.

Lodges (with accommodation, restaurant, & shop)	**Dzongla** (0km) » **Dragnag** (9.9km)
Terrain/ Navigation	High altitude mountainous route with steep, rocky, challenging terrain: a guide is recommended. Some sections are very steep and exposed. Occasionally, you may need to scramble over boulders. The climb is long and tough with the high altitude really biting: snow on the ground will make it even harder. In snowy/icy conditions, the steep paths near the pass can be treacherous and spikes/crampons may be required. In particular, the route immediately W of the pass is very steep and exposed (with fixed cables for assistance): snow/ice here can be treacherous. The route crosses Cho La Glacier: see above. Sometimes, paths are faint, making navigation more difficult. Navigation in snowy conditions is challenging, particularly on the E side of the pass.
Difficulty	**Very hard.** The terrain is challenging and the altitude tops out at 5420m. In these difficult conditions, progress can be slow so start early.
Medical Assistance	**Pheriche Aid Post:** see p124 **Gokyo International Health Care Centre:** beside Namaste Lodge; the old rescue post in Gokyo (run by the International Porter Protection Group) closed in 2019
Points of Interest	Excellent views of Cholatse Cho La Glacier: 8 Cho La pass: 9 Village of Dragnag: 10

Crossing Cho La Glacier

ACW

Stage TP10: Dzongla to Dragnag (See map on p195)

7 From **Dzongla**, head W and contour around a ridge. Enter a huge mountain bowl and head N up it. Towards the head of the valley, climb more steeply. Eventually, the path bends right and climbs steeply NE, through a cleft in cliffs (cairns; rocky and icy). After a while, the gradient eases and the path bends left, heading NW up a gully.

8 2:45: Climb W across **Cho La Glacier**, following metal posts. At the top of the glacier, climb steeply through rocks.

9 3:45: Cross **Cho La (5420m)** and descend steeply W. If there is ice/snow, the route is very slippery and there are fixed cables to assist: crampons/spikes recommended. Eventually, the gradient eases and the path heads SW down the valley. Later, the path bends right, undulates across the valley and then climbs a ridge. Cross the ridge at a large boulder and descend SW through a narrow valley: Dragnag lies at the bottom of the valley. As you descend, there are superb views of Machermo Peak and Kyajori.

10 6:30: Arrive at **Dragnag (4700m)**.

CW

Stage TP10: Dragnag to Dzongla (See map on p195)

10 From **Dragnag**, follow the path NE up a narrow valley. After a long climb, cross a ridge and head NE across another valley. Initially, the path undulates and then climbs more steadily: the gradient increases as you gain height. The final section before the pass is very steep: if there is ice/snow, it is very slippery and there are fixed cables to assist (crampons/spikes are recommended).

9 4:15: Cross **Cho La (5420m)** and descend steeply E across rocks. When the path reaches **Cho La Glacier**, descend E along it, following metal posts.

8 4:40: At the bottom of the glacier, descend SE through a gully. After a while, the path bends right and descends steeply SW, through a cleft in cliffs (cairns; rocky and icy). At the valley floor, bear left and descend along it. Eventually, the path contours left around a ridge.

7 7:00: Shortly afterwards, reach the village of **Dzongla (4830m)**.

TP11 Dragnag/Gokyo

Gokyo & Gokyo Ri

Stage TP11 involves the short (but energy-sapping) crossing of Ngozumpa Glacier between Dragnag and Gokyo. The glacier's ice is almost completely covered with loose rock and the route winds its way through this barren wasteland. Although there are still beautiful snowy peaks on the horizon, you will need to focus much of your attention on trying to locate the well-camouflaged cairns and on keeping your balance on the uneven surface. However, at the end of the day, you will have the satisfaction of knowing that you have walked across the longest glacier in Nepal (36km long). Furthermore, for ACW trekkers, the arrival at spectacular Gokyo will be adequate reward for the hard work.

A stay in Gokyo is a highlight of any trip to the Khumbu. The colourful village has a stunning location on the shores of Dudh Pokhari (a magnificent turquoise lake), within sight of Cho Oyu (the 6th highest peak on the planet). In winter, Gokyo's lake freezes over completely and the ice does not clear until April. Gokyo has some comfortable lodges, with incredible views across the water, and is a great place to relax for a day or two. In particular, the wonderful Thanka Inn is easily our favourite lodge in the Khumbu: it is run by the friendly Pasang Tshering Sherpa and is many levels better than other lodges. In fact, it is so warm and homely that you will not want to leave: book in advance.

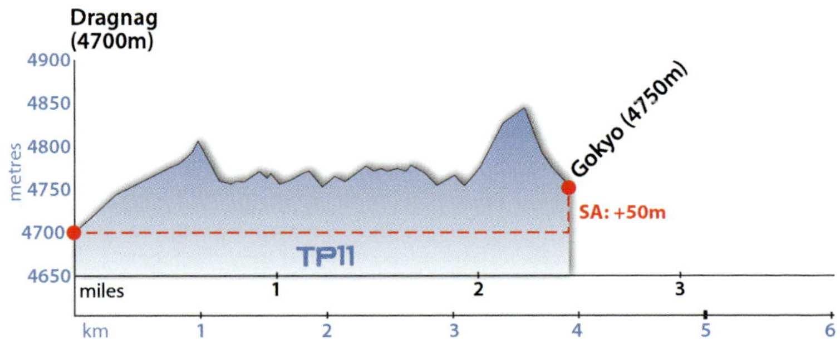

		Time	Distance	Ascent	Descent	SA Increase	Max Alt
TP11 (ACW)	Dragnag to Gokyo	2:00	3.9km 2.4miles	301m 988ft	251m 824ft	+50m +164ft	4836m 15867ft
TP11 (CW)	Gokyo to Dragnag	2:00	3.9km 2.4miles	251m 824ft	301m 988ft	-50m -164ft	4836m 15867ft

However, Gokyo's major drawcard is that it is the staging point for some of the best day-hikes in the region. The ascent of Gokyo Ri (SR5; p204) is most people's favourite: it is one of the finest Everest viewpoints accessible to trekkers. But there are other incredible hikes too: the lake at Gokyo is only one in a chain of lakes that have formed along the W side of the Ngozumpa Glacier and you can hike N to visit the others (SR6-8; p206): although fewer trekkers explore this wild landscape N of Gokyo, it can be one of the most rewarding parts of your trip. Look out for ruddy shelducks in the lakes and snowcocks on the shore.

Many CW trekkers will want to spend the night at Dragnag because starting the long climb to Cho La pass, immediately after the exertions on the Ngozumpa Glacier, is a daunting prospect. Furthermore, a night in Dragnag enables you to cross the pass earlier in the morning (when the weather is often better than later in the day) and allows more surplus time before nightfall in which to deal with any problems. Very fit hikers can hike all the way from Gokyo to Dzongla in one day but you would need to start very early.

Lodges (with accommodation, restaurant, & shop)	**Dragnag** (0km) » **Gokyo** (3.9km)
Terrain/ Navigation	The rocky path across the glacier is unstable and rock-falls are common: proceed carefully and move as quickly as safety allows through unstable sections. Occasionally, the path is re-routed due to the glacier's movements. Route-finding through the rubble can be tricky: cairns are difficult to spot.
Difficulty	**Hard.** Although the terrain is challenging, the stage is short.
Medical Assistance	**Gokyo International Health Care Centre:** beside Namaste Lodge; the old rescue post in Gokyo (run by the International Porter Protection Group) closed in 2019.
Points of Interest	**Ngozumpa Glacier:** Nepal's longest glacier **Views of Cho Oyu:** the world's 6th highest mountain **Gokyo:** 11

ACW

Stage TP11: Dragnag to Gokyo (See map on p203)

10 From **Dragnag**, follow a path NW up the ablation valley of **Ngozumpa Glacier**. Soon, the path climbs over the glacier's lateral moraine and then heads across the glacier itself. An undulating path winds (generally NW) through the rocky debris that covers the ice: cairns are difficult to spot. Eventually, at the W side of the glacier, climb across the lateral moraine: cross a saddle (with views of Gokyo's lake). Keep SH and soon climb again. 5min later, cross another small saddle and descend.

11 2:00: 5min later, reach **Gokyo (4750m)**.

CW

Stage TP11: Gokyo to Dragnag (See map on p203)

11 From **Gokyo**, climb SE. Soon, keep SH across a small saddle. Climb to another saddle and then descend the lateral moraine of **Ngozumpa Glacier**. An undulating path winds (generally SE) through the rocky debris that covers the glacier's ice: cairns are difficult to spot. At the E side of the glacier, climb across the lateral moraine. Then follow a path SE down the glacier's ablation valley.

10 2:00: Arrive at **Dragnag (4700m)**.

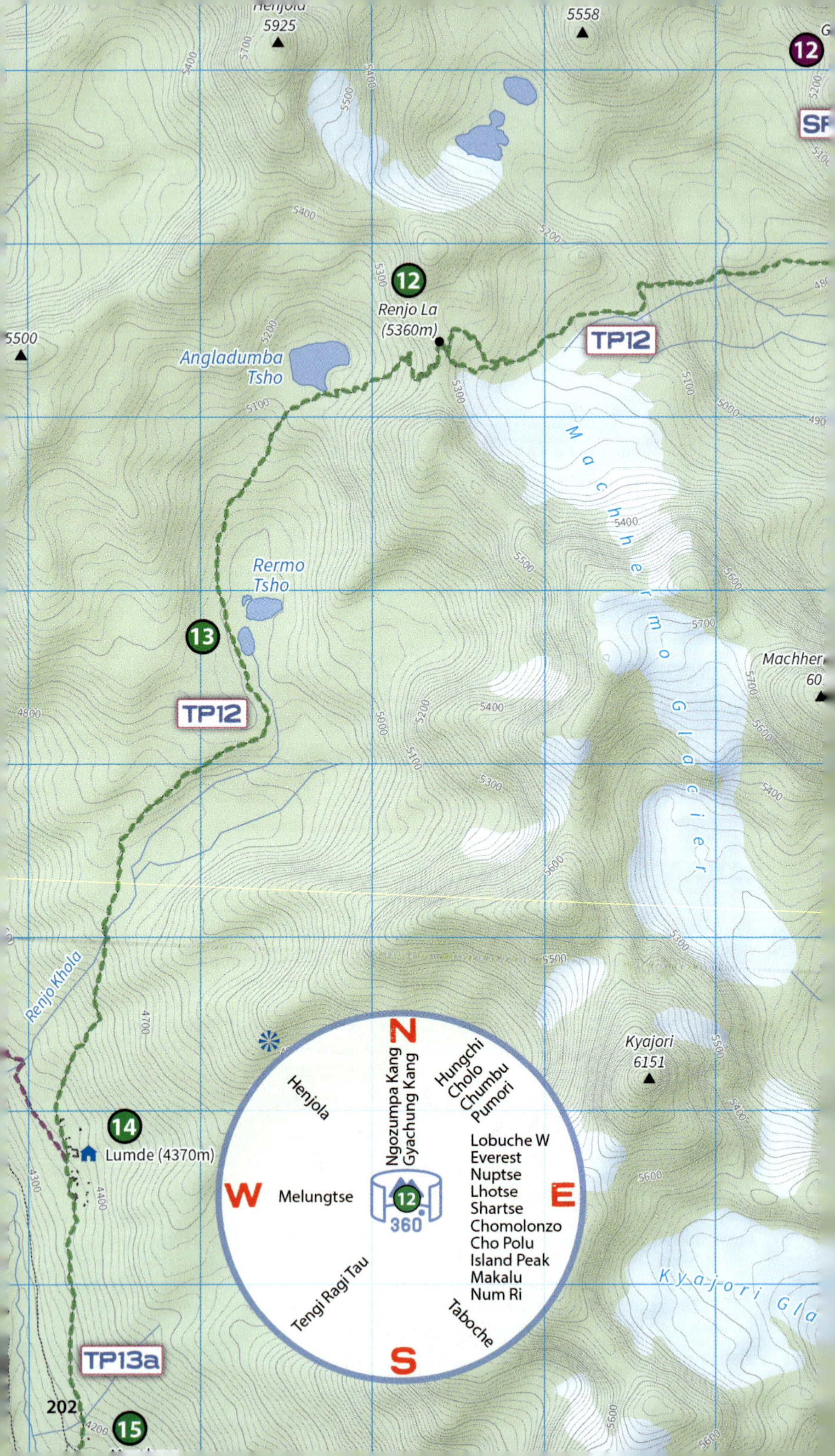

Henjola
5925
5558
12
Renjo La
(5360m)
TP12
Angladumba
Tsho
5500
Machhermo Glacier
Rermo
Tsho
13
TP12
Machhermo
Renjo Khola
Kyajori
6151
14
Lumde (4370m)
N
Ngozumpa Kang
Gyachung Kang
Hungchi
Cholo
Chumbu
Pumori
Henjola
Lobuche W
Everest
Nuptse
Lhotse
Shartse
Chomolonzo
Cho Polu
Island Peak
Makalu
Num Ri
W
Melungtse
E
12
360
Tengi Ragi Tau
Taboche
S
Kyajori Gla
TP13a
202
15

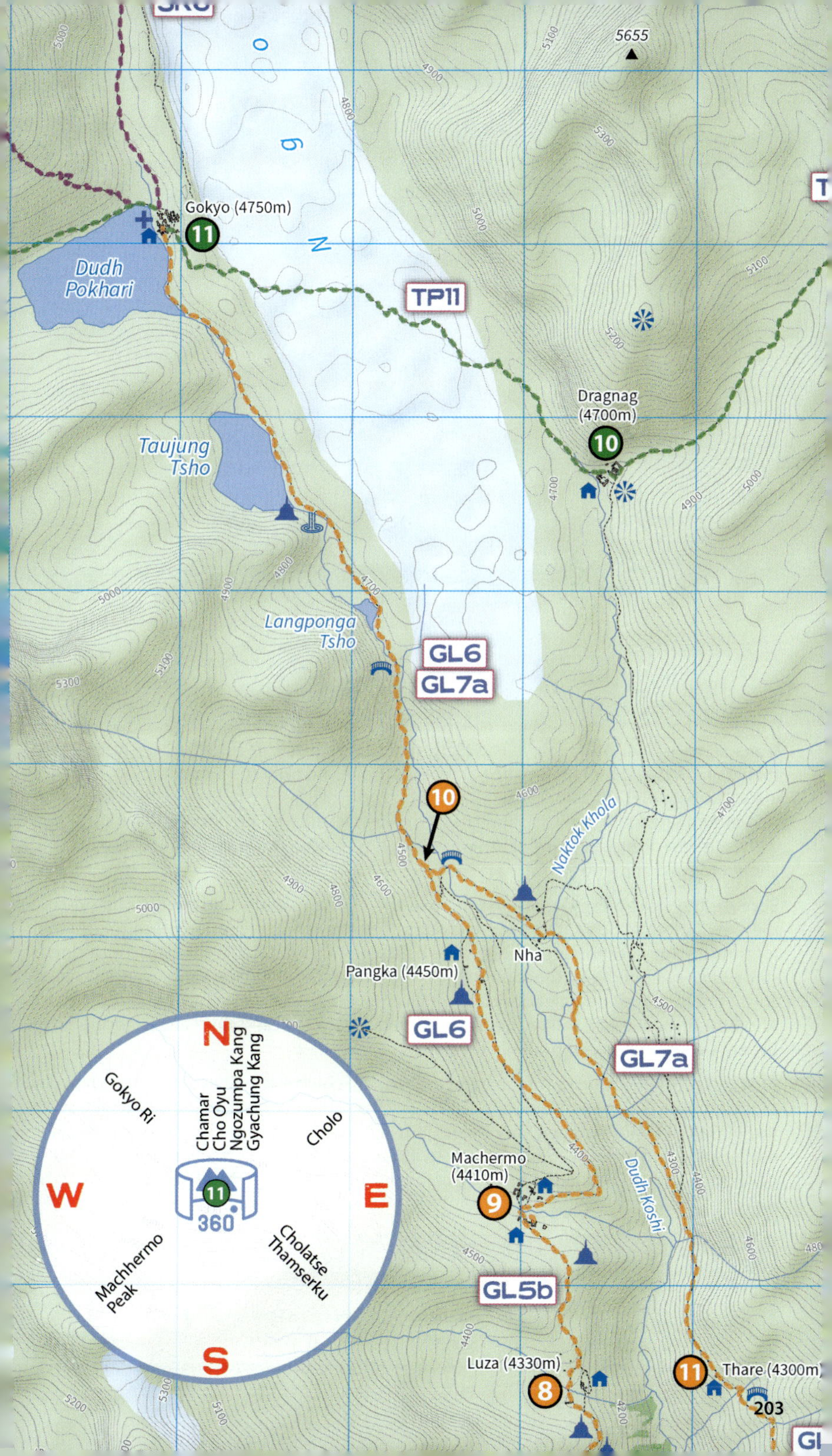

5655
Gokyo (4750m)
11
Dudh Pokhari
TP11
Taujung Tsho
Dragnag (4700m)
10
Langponga Tsho
GL6
GL7a
10
Naktok Khola
Nha
Pangka (4450m)
GL6
GL7a
N
Gokyo Ri
Chamar
Cho Oyu
Ngozumpa Kang
Gyachung Kang
Cholo
W
E
11
360
Machhermo Peak
Cholatse
Thamserku
S
Machermo (4410m)
9
Dudh Koshi
GL5b
Luza (4330m)
8
11
Thare (4300m)

SR5 Side Route: Gokyo Ri

Immediately N of Gokyo, there is a broad rounded summit known as Gokyo Ri (see image on p200). Although it is 5357m high, from below it appears less noteworthy than its higher and more dramatic neighbours. However, from the summit, its significance instantly becomes clear because Gokyo Ri is one of the great Everest viewpoints for non-mountaineers. From its summit, which is bedecked with colourful prayer flags, you witness a vast display of some of the world's highest peaks, including four 8000ers (Everest, Lhotse, Makalu and Cho Oyu).

Because the air is often clearer first thing in the morning, and clouds frequently obscure the view before midday, many trekkers start climbing very early; some reach the summit for sunrise. However, this is not always the best time to do it. Later in the morning, if clouds stay away, fewer of the surrounding slopes will be in shadow and the views are spectacular. Furthermore, sunset on a clear day is magnificent (with the setting sun lighting up Everest). Also bear in mind that it can be unpleasantly cold on Gokyo Ri at sunrise and it can therefore be more enjoyable to climb later in the day.

ACW trekkers (who have spent the night at Dragnag) could climb Gokyo Ri on the same day as hiking from Dragnag to Gokyo. Alternatively, you could undertake the climb on a spare day in Gokyo. Unless you are very strong, it is not feasible to climb Gokyo Ri on the same day as travelling to/from Lumde across Renjo La. CW trekkers could climb Gokyo Ri either on their AD in Gokyo or in the morning before hiking from Gokyo to Dragnag (to spend the night).

		Time	Distance	Ascent	Descent	SA Increase	Max Alt
SR5	Gokyo to Gokyo Ri (return)	3:30	3.2km 2.0miles	610m 2001ft	610m 2001ft	0m 0ft	5357m 17576ft

Gokyo Ri

It can be cold at the top, especially at sunrise and sunset: bring plenty of warm layers. To reach the top before sunrise, you have to get up very early: carry snacks with you and save breakfast for your return to Gokyo; bring a head-torch as it will be dark on the climb.

11 (See map on p209). From **Gokyo**, head N along the edge of the lake. After a few minutes, reach the N tip of the lake: TL and cross a shallow (often frozen) stream. Shortly afterwards, TR at a junction: the path on the left heads to Renjo La (TP12; p210). The path zigzags up the southern flank of the mountain.

12 2:15: Reach the summit of **Gokyo Ri (5357m)** which is marked by strings of prayer flags. Return by the same route.

11 3:30: Arrive back in **Gokyo (4750m)**.

Lodges (with accommodation, restaurant, & shop)	**Gokyo** (0km)
Terrain/ Navigation	The rocky trail is steep. Route-finding is straightforward: the path is well-trodden.
Difficulty	**Hard.** The steep, punchy climb is tough at such high altitude.
Medical Assistance	**Gokyo International Health Care Centre:** see p201
Points of Interest	**Extraordinary Himalayan viewpoint:** you can see (almost) everything!

SR6-8 Side Routes: Gokyo Lakes

Although many Gokyo visitors undertake the spectacular half-day hike to the top of Gokyo Ri (p204), far fewer people head further up the valley to visit the more remote lakes N of Gokyo. However, if you do make the effort, it will be one of the most unforgettable parts of your trip. You will find a wild and dramatic wonderland of high snowy peaks and there are no signs of human habitation (other than the path). The starkness of the rock and ice contrasts beautifully with the otherworldly turquoise of the lakes and there are numerous vantage points from which you can enjoy the display: the best of these is the curiously-named 'Scoundrel's Viewpoint', situated on the edge of the huge Ngozumpa Glacier.

The route to the 4th and 5th lakes and Scoundrel's Viewpoint is straightforward (with a clear path that is rarely too steep). However, fewer people venture N of the 5th lake and bringing a guide can be a good idea: set out early and carry food.

		Time	Distance	Ascent	Descent	SA Increase	Max Alt
SR6	Gokyo to 4th Lake (return)	1:30	4.4km 2.7miles	130m 426ft	130m 426ft	0m 0ft	4860m 15946ft
SR7	Gokyo to Scoundrel's View/5th Lake (return)	4:15	12.3km 7.6miles	360m 1181ft	360m 1181ft	0m 0ft	4980m 16339ft
SR8	Gokyo to Six Lakes (return)	7:00	18.7km 11.6miles	570m 1870ft	570m 1870ft	0m 0ft	5190m 17028ft

Ngozumpa Tsho, the 5th Lake

Lodges (with accommodation, restaurant, & shop)	**Gokyo** (0km)
Terrain/ Navigation	The paths are rocky and sometimes uneven. However, between Gokyo and Scoundrel's Viewpoint 15, the route is rarely steep, poses no technical difficulties and is simple to follow (in good conditions). However, between 15 and the Six Lakes 16, the route is rougher and less obvious. When snow covers the route (particularly in early season), route finding can be challenging.
Difficulty	**SR6/7:** medium **SR8:** hard
Medical Assistance	**Gokyo International Health Care Centre:** see p201
Points of Interest	Remote, tranquil lakes Scoundrels Viewpoint: 15 Close-up views of Cho Oyu The Ngozumpa glacier

N
Cho Oyu
Ngozumpa Kang
Gyachung Kang
Hungchi
Cholo
Chumbu
Pumori
Lunag Ri
Lobuche W
Everest
Nuptse
W
Henjola
12
360
Lhotse
E
Chomolonzo
Cho Polu
Island Peak
Makalu
Num Ri
Tengi Ragi Tau
Kyajori
Machermo
Cholatse
Taboche
Kangtega
Thamserku
S

Stage SR6: Thonak Tsho (the 4th Lake) (See map on p209)

11 From **Gokyo**, head N along the edge of the lake. After a few minutes, reach the N tip of the lake: keep SH (ignoring the path heading W to Gokyo Ri and Renjo La). Continue N along an obvious grassy footpath, which runs below the E face of Gokyo Ri.

13 0:50: Reach the S edge of **Thonak Tsho (the 4th Lake; 4860m)** at the base of black cliffs. To return to Gokyo, retrace your steps: alternatively, for the 5th Lake, continue N along Stage SR7.

Stage SR7: Ngozumpa Tsho (the 5th Lake) (See map on p209)

13 0:50: From the **4th Lake**, climb onto a low ridge, heading N through bleak terrain of rock and ice.

14 2:30: Arrive at the S end of **Ngozumpa Tsho (the 5th Lake; 4980m)** which is surrounded by massive boulders. Climb the moraine on the E side of the lake.

15 2:40: Reach **Scoundrel's Viewpoint** which is an undefined point on the moraine overlooking the enormous Ngozumpa glacier. To the N, the view of Cho Oyu (the world's 6th highest mountain) is breathtaking: you can also see Everest, Lhotse and Nuptse to the E. To return to Gokyo, retrace your steps: alternatively, for Gyazumpa Tsho, continue N along Stage SR8.

Stage SR8: Gyazumpa Tsho (the Six Lakes) (See map on p209)

15 2:40: From **Scoundrel's Viewpoint**, a faint path continues N up the valley. Pass between the glacier and **Ngozumpa Tse** (a minor summit to the W): if you had energy, you could scramble up the S flank to an obvious ridge: however, more technical skills are required to reach the summit. Later, the trail bends left, heading W.

16 4:00: Reach **Gyazumpa Tsho**, the largest of **six lakes** located beneath Cho Oyu. To return to Gokyo, retrace your steps.

11 7:00: Arrive back at **Gokyo (4750m)**.

Gyazumpa Tsho
16
Ngozumpa Tse
5553
SR8
Ngozumpa Tsho
14
15
Scoundrel's Viewpoint
5767
SR7
5335
Ngozumpa Glacier
Thonak Tsho / 4th Lake
13
5483
SR6
5558
Gokyo Ri
5357
12
SR5
Gokyo (4750m)
11
Dudh Pokhari

TP12 Gokyo/Lumde (Lungden)

Stage TP12 involves the crossing of Renjo La, the lowest of the TPT's three passes and probably the easiest of them. Nevertheless, the panorama from the top is so fine that it is many trekkers' favourite: there are exceptional views across the Dudh Pokhari lake towards Everest, Lhotse, Makalu, Nuptse and plenty more of the world's highest mountains. For ACW trekkers (starting the climb from Gokyo), the altitude gain is less than that endured on the previous two passes and most ACW travellers should be well acclimatised by now. However, once over the top, there is a knee-jerkingly long descent all the way to Lumde. The scenery is stunning as you pass more exquisite lakes and drop into a remote corner of the Bhote Koshi valley which seems far removed from the Khumbu's busier honey-pots.

Most ACW trekkers finish the day at Lumde (Lungden), a small settlement located on the floor of the steep-sided Bhote Koshi valley: it is a peaceful place with a handful of lodges

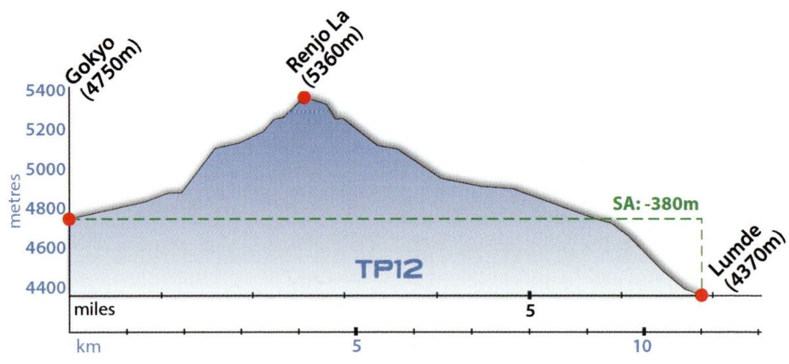

		Time	Distance	Ascent	Descent	SA Increase	Max Alt
TP12 (ACW)	Gokyo to Lumde	6:15	11.0km 6.8miles	635m 2083ft	1015m 3330ft	-380m -1247ft	5360m 17586ft
TP12 (CW)	Lumde to Gokyo	7:30	11.0km 6.8miles	1015m 3330ft	635m 2083ft	+380m +1247ft	5360m 17586ft

Renjo La: Everest, Nuptse, Lhotse (centre); Makalu, Cholatse, Taboche (right); Hungchi, Cholo, Chumbu, Pumori (left)

but it is cold when the sun disappears. However, if you are in good shape, it is possible to continue down to Thame (after a late lunch in Lumde): this is a long day but it could mean that you can spend the following morning relaxing in lovely Thame.

For CW trekkers, this is the first of the three passes and your body will still be acclimatising. Remember that Lumde to Renjo La is a huge jump in altitude for those who were in Namche only a few days previously. Take it slowly and head back down immediately if you feel unwell. For CW acclimatisation strategy, see p20 and p48. CW trekkers will stay at Gokyo (p200).

Whichever direction you are travelling, start early to give yourself plenty of time and to increase your chances of clear weather on the pass. Between Gokyo and Lumde, there are no facilities: bring plenty of food.

Lodges (with accommodation, restaurant, & shop)	**Gokyo** (0km) » **Lumde** (11.0km)
Terrain/ Navigation	High altitude mountainous route with steep, challenging terrain. The climb to the pass is long, particularly if travelling CW. On either side of the pass, the route is rocky. Some sections are very steep and exposed, especially on the W side of the pass. Snow lies around Renjo La until well into the spring and the high altitude means that fresh falls are always a possibility. In icy conditions, the steep paths near the pass can be treacherous and spikes/crampons may be required. The trail is generally easy to follow in good conditions. However, snow conceals the paths, making walking more challenging and route-finding more difficult. Navigation is also difficult in low visibility. In such conditions, do not leave without a guide.
Difficulty	Very hard in both directions, although it is more difficult travelling CW.
Medical Assistance	**Gokyo International Health Care Centre:** see p201
Points of Interest	Spectacular views from Renjo La: 12 Peaceful alpine lakes Village of Lumde in the wild Bhote Koshi valley: 14

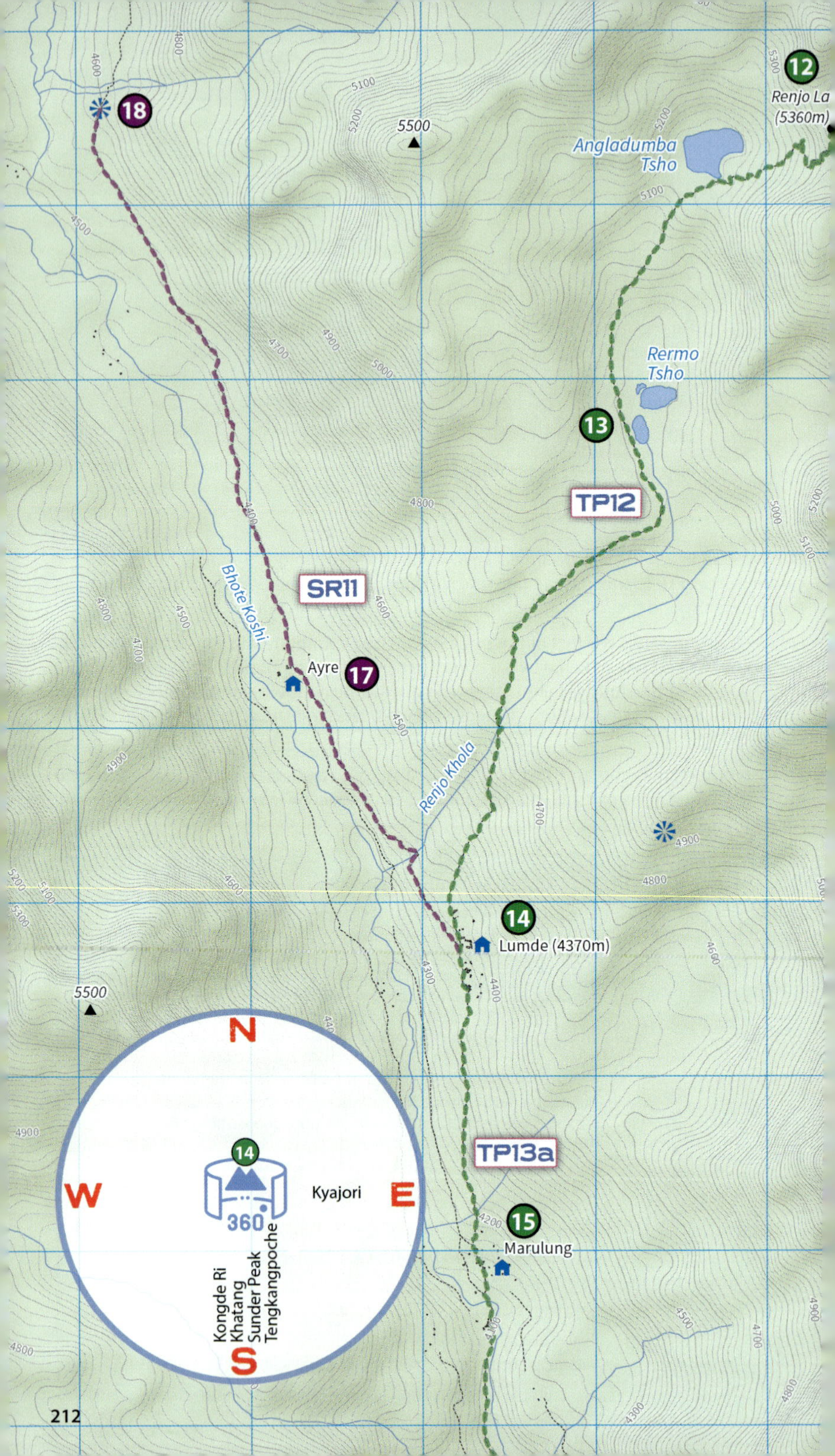

12
Renjo La
(5360m)
Angladumba
Tsho
5500
18
13
Rermo
Tsho
TP12
SR11
Bhote Koshi
Ayre
17
Renjo Khola
14
Lumde (4370m)
5500
N
W
E
S
14
360
Kyajori
Kongde Ri
Khatang
Sunder Peak
Tengkangpoche
TP13a
15
Marulung

ACW

Stage TP12: Gokyo to Lumde (See map on p203)

11 From **Gokyo**, head N along the edge of the lake. After a few minutes, reach the N tip of the lake: TL and cross a stream. Shortly afterwards, TL at a junction: the path on the right climbs to Gokyo Ri (SR5; p204). The trail climbs W and becomes increasingly steep. Cairns guide the way. Zigzag up to a rock face. Then climb steeply.

12 3:30: Reach **Renjo La pass (5360m)** which is decorated with prayer flags. The staggering views are as fantastic as anywhere else on the TPT. Cross the pass and descend steeply W on rock slabs: treacherous in icy conditions. Head along the S shore of **Angladumba Tsho lake (5130m)**. Afterwards, an obvious trail descends more gently (S) and the slopes become more grassy.

13 4:45 Pass to the W of the **Rermo Tsho** lakes. Follow the **Renjo Khola** stream downwards, soon bending right to head SW: the route can be slippery. Later cross the Renjo Khola and descend S.

14 6:15: Reach **Lumde (4370m)**, a small yak herders' village.

CW

Stage TP12: Lumde to Gokyo (See map on p203)

14 From Lumde, climb N up the flank of the Bhote Koshi valley. Cross the **Renjo Khola** stream and continue N. Follow the Renjo Khola when it bends right to head NE. Later, it bends left and climbs N again.

13 3:00: Pass to the W of the **Rermo Tsho** lakes. The terrain becomes increasingly rocky and barren. Head along the S shore of **Angladumba Tsho lake (5130m)**. Afterwards, climb a steep rocky slope.

12 5:00 Reach **Renjo La pass (5360m)** which is decorated with prayer flags. Descend steeply (E), enjoying your first proper views of Everest in the distance. The trail descends quickly: follow cairns closely. The gradient eases along N shore of **Dudh Pokhari** lake. At the N tip of the lake, keep SH at a junction. Just afterwards, cross a shallow (often frozen) stream and TR along the E shore of the lake.

11 7:30: After a few minutes, reach **Gokyo (4750m)**.

Renjo La: view W towards Angladumba Tsho lake

SR11 Side Route: Ayre & the Bhote Koshi valley

Kongde Ri (SR11)

For CW trekkers, an AD in Lumde is highly recommended and this beautiful side-route will help fill your time and aid acclimatisation. From Lumde, a path heads N up the Bhote Koshi valley, keeping to the E of the river: it travels an ancient trade route to the Nangpa La pass (across which Sherpas used to carry goods to and from Tibet). A few km from Lumde, you will find the village of Ayre which is simply a small collection of buildings used by yak-herders during the summer: there is one basic trekking lodge. It is a scenic and peaceful place but if you continue further up the valley, the views are even better. However, we would not recommend that you continue further than the viewpoint at 18 and keep well away from the Nepal/Tibet border: in the past, people have been shot crossing the frontier.

		Time	Distance	Ascent	Descent	SA Increase	Max Alt
SR11	Ayre & Bhote Koshi Valley (return)	3:30	10.9km 6.8miles	380m 1247ft	380m 1247ft	0m 0ft	4635m 15207ft

Lodges (with accommodation, restaurant, & shop)	**Lumde** (0km) » **Ayre** (2km; lodge has irregular opening hours)
Terrain/ Navigation	The path is rocky and sometimes faint, however, route-finding is rarely problematic. The gradient is rarely steep. This is very remote terrain and few people visit.
Difficulty	**Medium**
Medical Assistance	**Thame Health Clinic:** see p217.
Points of Interest	**Village of Ayre** **Upper Bhote Koshi valley:** probably the wildest part of the Khumbu

14 **(See map on p212).** From **Lumde**, follow a path N up the **Bhote Koshi** valley.

17 0:30: Pass the village of **Ayre (4340m)**. From Ayre, many trekkers simply return to Lumde but, if you wish to explore further, continue N up the valley: keep to the E side of the river. Continue N past a side valley (to the W): in the base of the valley, there are remote pastures and herders' cabins.

18 2:00: Shortly afterwards, reach a **viewpoint** (just before the path crosses a stream); you can see Cho Oyu (the world's 6th highest mountain). Retrace your steps.

14 3:30: Arrive back at **Lumde (4370m)**.

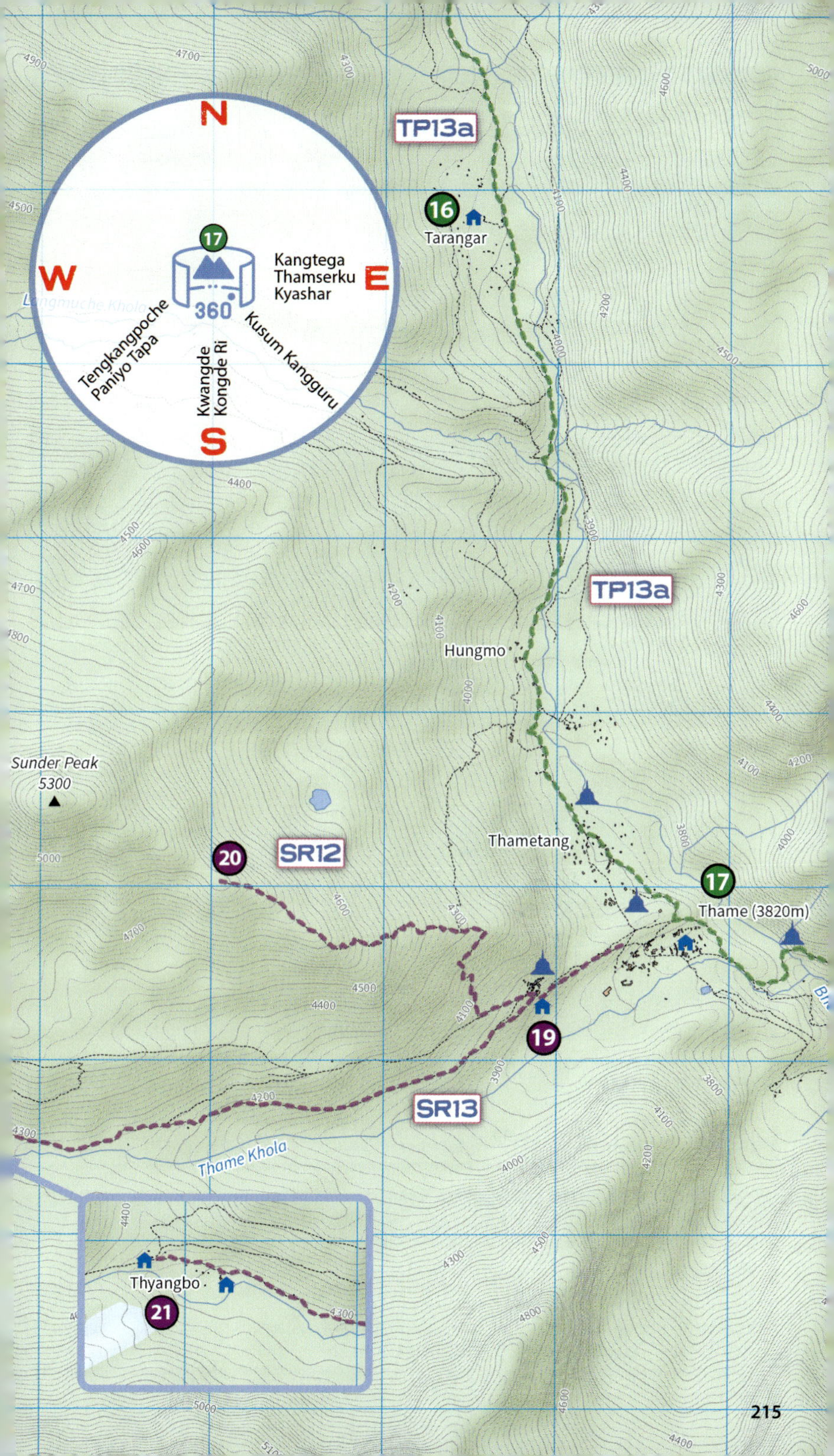
N
W
E
S
17
360
Kangtega
Thamserku
Kyashar
Kusum Kangguru
Kwangde
Kongde Ri
Tengkangpoche
Paniyo Tapa
TP13a
16
Tarangar
TP13a
Hungmo
Sunder Peak
5300
20
SR12
Thametang
17
Thame (3820m)
19
SR13
Thame Khola
Thyangbo
21

TP13 Lumde/Namche

Thame Gompa

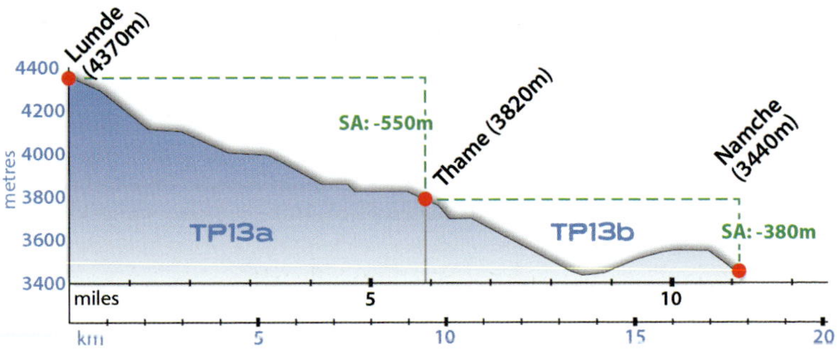

ACW		Time	Distance	Ascent	Descent	SA Increase	Max Alt
TP13a (ACW)	Lumde to Thame	3:30	9.4km 5.8miles	45m 148ft	595m 1952ft	-550m -1805ft	4370m 14338ft
TP13b (ACW)	Thame to Namche	3:30	8.4km 5.2miles	276m 906ft	656m 2152ft	-380m -1247ft	3820m 12533ft

CW		Time	Distance	Ascent	Descent	SA Increase	Max Alt
TP13b (CW)	Namche to Thame	4:15	8.4km 5.2miles	656m 2152ft	276m 906ft	+380m +1247ft	3820m 12533ft
TP13a (CW)	Thame to Lumde	5:00	9.4km 5.8miles	595m 1952ft	45m 148ft	+550m +1805ft	4370m 14338ft

For ACW trekkers, TP13 is largely downhill all the way to Namche. The scenery in the high reaches of the remote Bhote Koshi valley is wonderful, with the fabulous Kongde Ri (to the S) dominating your attention. However, the very finest views are behind you and the real joy of this part of the trek is being immersed deeply in Sherpa culture: trekking has less importance here than in the E part of the Khumbu and you will be treated to a more authentic display of local culture. Most of the villages, small and largely untouched, are surrounded by alpine pastures and are the abode of yak-herders. Marulung and Tarangar are typical settlements: they each have a lodge or two but facilities are more basic than elsewhere; although few ACW trekkers stop in these villages, they are useful if you want to push on a little further immediately after arriving at Lumde. Marulung and Tarangar are also useful overnight stops for CW trekkers wishing to ascend slowly.

About halfway between Lumde and Namche, you will reach Thame, an attractive, stone village wedged between mountains and surrounded by potato and barley fields. It is located at the foot of the peaceful Thame Khola valley (where it joins the larger Bhote Koshi valley). Both the Thame Khola and the Bhote Koshi remain wonderfully traditional and together have probably the finest collection of religious buildings in the Khumbu: there are dozens of monasteries, shrines and stupas scattered around the hillsides. The village of Thame has one of the largest and most interesting monasteries in the region (p220) and there are plenty more to visit between Thame and Namche: many of them are rarely visited by foreign trekkers. Many of Thame's buildings were badly damaged during the 2015 earthquake but most had been re-built. However, in 2024, the village was hit by another natural disaster, this time a glacial outburst flood, and many buildings were destroyed: at the date of press, re-building was underway.

Many ACW trekkers, eager to get back to Namche, pass quickly through Thame, merely stopping for lunch and a hasty look around the monastery before pushing on. This is a shame, however, because Thame (with its many Buddhist sites) is a cultural highlight of the TPT. We prefer to hike Section 13 over two days, spending a leisurely afternoon and a night at Thame. In fact, there is so much to do in Thame that you could spend several days visiting monasteries and doing some of the excellent day-hikes: this is highly recommended for CW trekkers because it will significantly reduce the risk of AMS further up the valley.

Between Thame and Namche, you will pass more villages including Samde, Thamo and Phurte. They each have lodges and there are Buddhist structures seemingly everywhere. If you had time, there are monasteries in the surrounding hills too (which few trekkers ever bother to visit). The terrain changes as you approach Namche and there are more trees covering the slopes. The arrival into Namche from this side is fabulous and it will put you in the mood for a celebration!

Lodges (with accommodation, restaurant, & shop)	**Lumde** (0km) » **Marulung** (2.1km) » **Taranga** (4.7km) » **Thame** (9.4km) » **Samde** (11.4km) » **Thamo** (12.8km) » **Theso** (14.1km) » **Phurte** (14.8km) » **Namche** (17.8km)
Terrain/ Navigation	Undulating paths which are generally easy to follow.
Difficulty	**ACW:** Medium **CW:** Hard
Medical Assistance	**Thame Health Clinic:** destroyed in the 2024 flood (see above). At the date of press, it was not clear if, or when, this would be re-built. **Khunde Hospital:** 2.7km N of Namche
Points of Interest	Views of the Rolwaling Himal The remote villages of Marulung 15 and Tarangar 16 Thame village and monastery 17. A joyful return to Namche (for ACW trekkers) 9

ACW

Stage TP13a: Lumde to Thame (See map on p212)

14 From **Lumde**, the trail heads S down the E flank of the **Bhote Koshi** valley.

15 0:35: Reach **Marulung (4160m)**, a small gathering of herders' huts with a few lodges. Continue S and cross a bridge over the river.

16 1:15: (See map on p215). Pass the village of **Tarangar**. Afterwards, the path continues S through fertile terrain, passing stupas and mani walls. Between **Hungmo** and **Thametang**, the ancient **Kyaro Kerok Gompa** sits on the hillside to the W: with spare time, you could visit it. At the S end of **Thametang**, pass a large stupa. Continue S over a ridge and pass some stone stupas: you will see Thame resting in a bowl below.

17 3:30: Arrive in **Thame (3820m)**.

Stage TP13b: Thame to Namche (See map on p220)

17 From **Thame**, head SE down the **Bhote Koshi** valley. At some murals, cross the river. The trail climbs briefly and then descends through the village of **Samde (3650m)**.

18 2:00: Pass **Thamo (3520m)**, a larger village with several lodges. After 5-10min, keep SH at a junction: the path on the left climbs N to Mende and the wonderful Lawudo Gompa. After **Theso**, cross a stream and go through an archway. Shortly, pass a stupa.

19 2:50 Arrive at the village of **Phurte (3500m)** which has a stupa. Continue SE through rhododendron forest. About halfway between Phurte and Namche, TR at a junction: the path on the left heads to Syangboche (to connect with GL3; p224). Eventually, the trail emerges from the trees and bends left around the corner: just below you will see Namche.

9 3:30 Pass **Namche Gompa** and head into the village of **Namche (3440m)**.

CW

Stage TP13b: Namche to Thame (See map on p220)

9 From **Namche Gompa**, climb SW. Soon, TR around a corner and head NW through rhododendron forest: look out for pheasants here.

19 1:15 Pass **Phurte (3500m)** which has a stupa. Then continue NW. Just after an archway, cross a stream: then pass through **Theso**. Soon, ignore a path on the right which climbs N to Mende and the wonderful Lawudo Gompa.

18 2:40: Head NW through **Thamo**, a larger village with several lodges. Continue NW through the small village of Samde. Cross the river next to some murals.

17 4:15: Arrive in **Thame (3820m)**.

Stage TP13a: Thame to Lumde (See map on p215)

17 From **Thame**, climb NE over a ridge, passing some stupas. At the S end of Thametang, pass another stupa. Head N through **Thametang**. Between Thametang and Hungmo, the ancient **Kyaro Kerok Gompa** sits on the hillside to the W: with spare time, you could visit it. The path continues N, rising slowly through pastures.

16 2:50 Pass the village of **Tarangar**, another small farming village (which has a lodge). Continue N. At around 4100m, cross the **Bhote Koshi** river on a small bridge.

15 4:10: (See map on p212). Reach **Marulung (4160m)**, a small gathering of herders' huts with a few lodges. Continue N up the E flank of the valley.

14 5:00 Reach **Lumde (4370m)**, a small yak herders' village.

Cho Oyu and the Bhote Koshi valley viewed from Sunder Peak (see p222)

Alternative Trail to Kongde

From Thame, most ACW trekkers follow the main trail (TP13b) and visit Namche for the second time. However, there is an alternative route that follows a little-used path from Thame directly to Toc Toc (avoiding Namche). It is a beautiful wilderness trail that passes the small settlement of Kongde (4140m) where you can stay at Yeti Mountain Home: surprisingly, for such a remote location, this is one of the most upmarket lodges in the Khumbu. The views here are jaw-dropping. Advance reservations are essential.

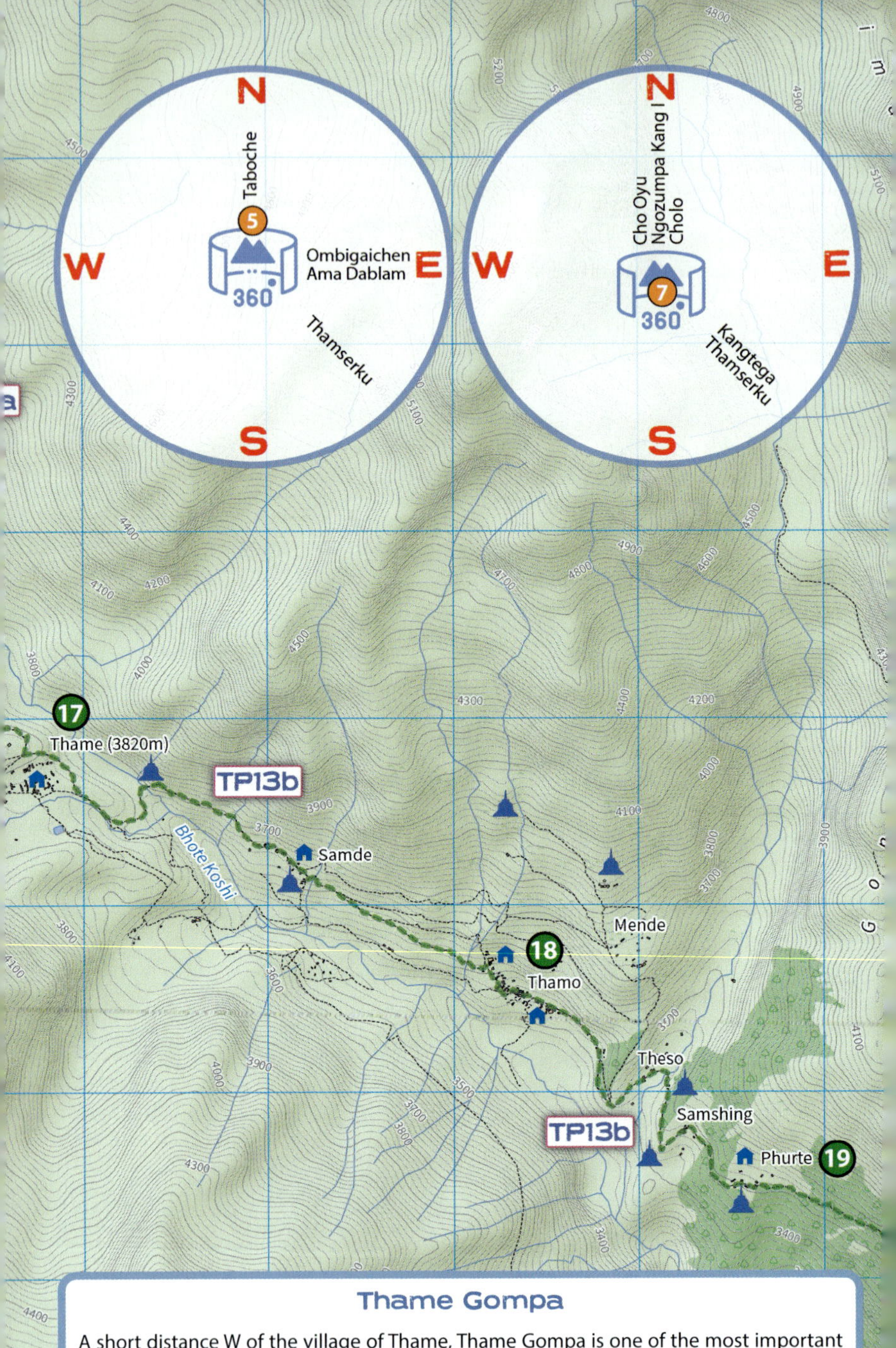

Thame Gompa

A short distance W of the village of Thame, Thame Gompa is one of the most important monasteries in the Everest region. It was founded, in the 18th century, by Lama Rolpa Dorje who was said to have had magical powers: on display in the monastery, there is an iron bar which apparently, he bent with his bare hands. There are also some excellent murals on the gompa's walls and many of the books inside are hundreds of years old.

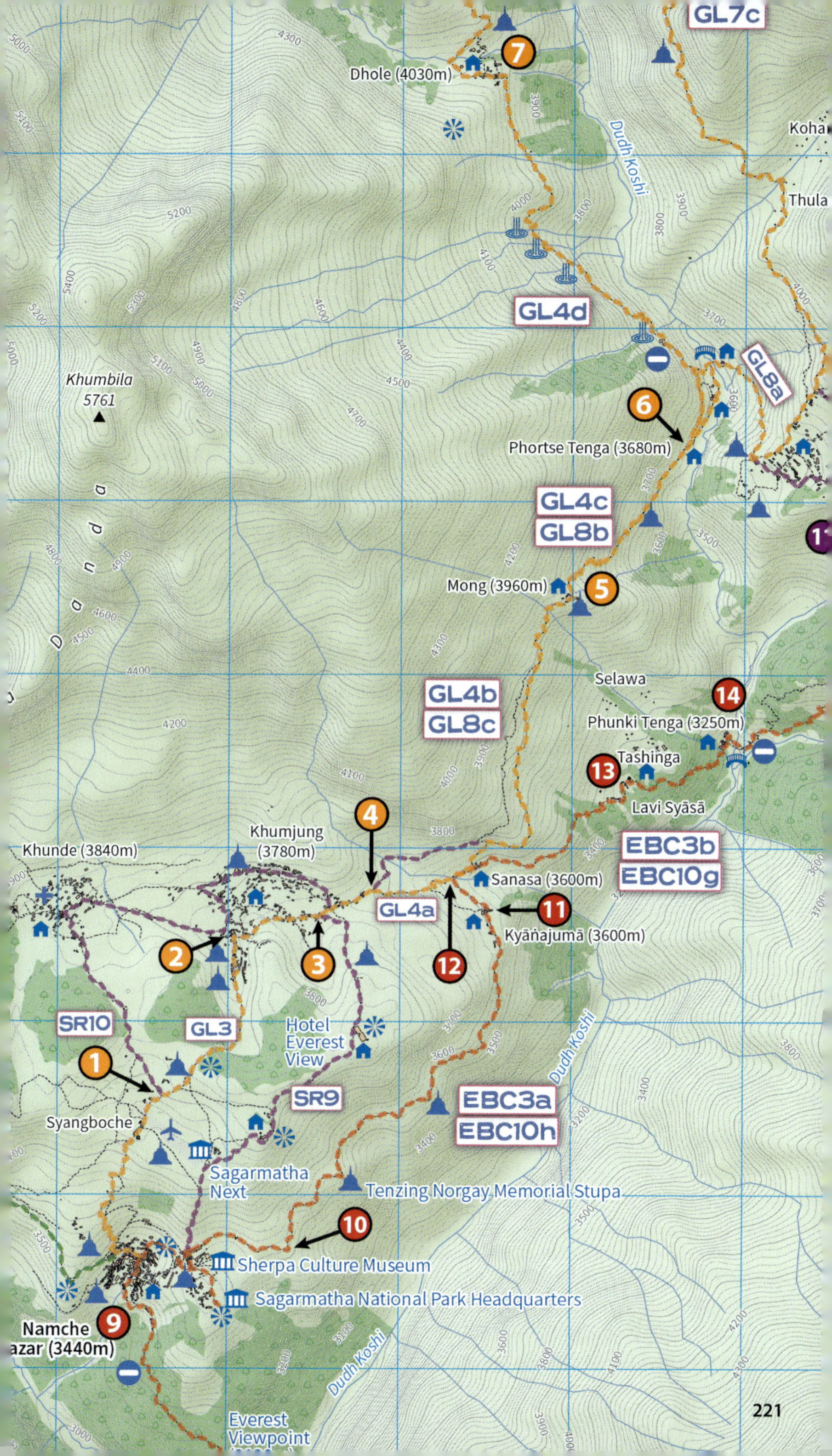
Dhole (4030m)
GL7c
Koha
Thula
Dudh Koshi
GL4d
GL8a
Khumbila
5761
Phortse Tenga (3680m)
GL4c
GL8b
Mong (3960m)
GL4b
GL8c
Selawa
Phunki Tenga (3250m)
Tashinga
Lavi Syāsā
EBC3b
EBC10g
Khunde (3840m)
Khumjung
(3780m)
Sanasa (3600m)
GL4a
Kyāñajumā (3600m)
SR10
GL3
Hotel
Everest
View
SR9
EBC3a
EBC10h
Syangboche
Sagarmatha
Next
Tenzing Norgay Memorial Stupa
Sherpa Culture Museum
Sagarmatha National Park Headquarters
Namche
azar (3440m)
Everest
Viewpoint

SR12 Side Route: Sunder Peak's SE Spur

The climb to Sunder Peak

Although tough, this is Thame's best side-trip: it is a useful acclimatisation hike for TPT (CW) trekkers. Sunder Peak is the mountain immediately to the W of Thame and the 360° panorama from the summit is mind-blowing: there are uninterrupted views of the region's main peaks including Everest, Lhotse, Nuptse, Cho Oyu, Makalu and Ama Dablam. However, you do not even need to reach the top to make your jaw drop: most trekkers are happy to stop on top of the spur on the ridge at about 4950m (20). The path to the spur is easy to follow (if a little rough further up): however, above it, the route is very rough, exposed and very steep; we do not recommend climbing to the summit without a guide.

		Time	Distance	Ascent	Descent	SA Increase	Max Alt
SR12	Thame to Sunder Peak Spur (return)	5:30	8.3km 5.2miles	1130m 3708ft	1130m 3708ft	0m 0ft	4950m 16241ft

Lodges (with accommodation, restaurant, & shop)	**Thame** (0km)
Terrain/ Navigation	The rocky trail is steep. Route-finding is straightforward: the path is generally well-trodden but becomes more rocky further up.
Difficulty	**Very Hard.** The steep, punchy climb is tough at such high altitude.
Medical Assistance	**Thame Health Clinic:** see p217.
Points of Interest	**Extraordinary Himalayan viewpoint:** you can see (almost) everything!

17 **(See map on p215).** From **Thame**, climb SW to **Thame Monastery** (19). Behind the monastery, pick up a path climbing SW. Soon, the path turns N and climbs more steeply. At around **4300m**, the route bends to the W again. Shortly afterwards, keep SH at a junction (still climbing W).

20 3:30: Reach the **spur on the ridge** (about 4950m) where most people stop. Retrace your steps back down the mountain.

17 5:30: Arrive back in **Thame (3820m)**.

SR13 Side Route: Thyangbo

From Thame, a clear path runs W up the wild and beautiful Thame Khola valley to the tiny village of Thyangbo. The gradient is rarely steep and the path is easy to follow through the remote terrain so this makes for an excellent day-hike (which is significantly less strenuous than Sunder Peak). There are two lodges in Thyangbo where you could in theory eat or sleep, however, in practice they are not always open: enquire in Thame in advance and make sure that you carry some snacks in case they are closed when you arrive.

		Time	Distance	Ascent	Descent	SA Increase	Max Alt
SR13	Thame to Thyangbo (return)	4:15	10.4km 6.5miles	530m 1739ft	530m 1739ft	0m 0ft	4350m 14272ft

Lodges (with accommodation, restaurant, & shop)	**Thame** (0km) » **Thyangbo** (5.2km; lodges not always open)
Terrain/ Navigation	The rocky trail is clear and rarely steep. Route-finding is straightforward
Difficulty	**Medium**
Medical Assistance	**Thame Health Clinic:** see p217.
Points of Interest	The remote and peaceful Thame Khola valley

(17) **(See map on p215).** From **Thame**, climb SW to **Thame Monastery** ((19)). From there, pick up a path climbing W along the valley.

(21) 2:45: Arrive at the village of **Thyangbo (4350m)**. Retrace your steps.

(17) 4:15: Arrive back in **Thame (3820m)**.

Gokyo Lakes Trek Stages

GL3 Namche/Khumjung

Stupa at Khumjung La

Our version of the GLT crosses the hill N of Namche, passing Syangboche Airstrip on the way to Khumjung: there are some incredible vantage points and photogenic stupas. However, in fact, this is just one of three different (equally fantastic) routes between Namche and Khumjung and you could use any one of them: all three routes offer fabulous views of Thamserku and Kongde Ri; the other two routes are SR9 (p112) and SR10 (p118).

Green-roofed Khumjung is a highlight of the Namche area. On arrival at (2) on the S fringe of the village, you can either follow GL3 east through the village (orange on the map) or an alternative route around the N of the village which passes the gompa (purple on the map).

Acclimatisation options: although this is a short stage, Khumjung (3780m) is 340m higher than Namche, making it a sensible overnight acclimatisation stop: furthermore, there is plenty to do around Khumjung (see p112). However, If you decide to continue upwards (without overnighting at Khumjung), then we recommend sleeping at Sanasa (3600m) or Phortse Tenga (3680m) instead: Mong (3960m) is too high to be a sensible overnight stop for most trekkers, straight after Namche. The downside to sleeping at Phortse Tenga is that your subsequent day would be very short because it would not be wise to continue higher than Dhole (4030m) that day: the next villages above Dhole are Luza (4330m) and Machermo (4410m) which are too high. Our preference is to be cautious and live with the short day from Namche to Khumjung, jumping to Dhole the following day.

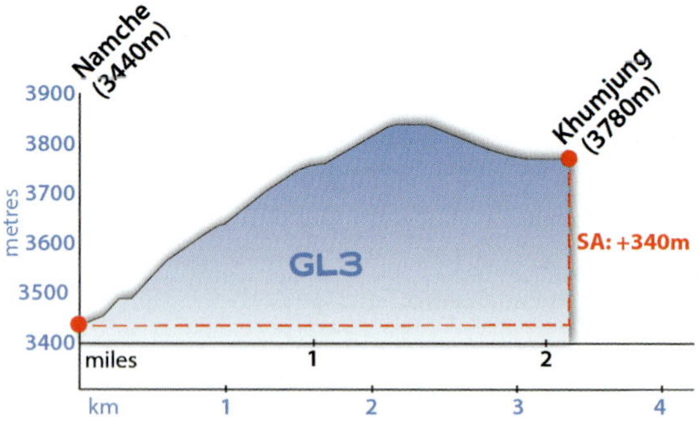

		Time	Distance	Ascent	Descent	SA Increase	Max Alt
GL3 (S-N)	Namche to Khumjung	2:10	3.4km 2.1miles	425m 1394ft	85m 279ft	+340m +1116ft	3840m 12599ft
GL3 (N-S)	Khumjung to Namche	1:30	3.4km 2.1miles	85m 279ft	425m 1394ft	-340m -1116ft	3840m 12599ft

S-N

Stage GL3: Namche to Khumjung (See map on p220)

9 Head to **Namche Gompa**. From there, zigzag steeply up to the N: the path splits but the branches soon converge. After 1hr, keep SH at a junction: the path on the left goes to Thame. Shortly afterwards, cross **Syangboche Airstrip**.

1 1:20: A few minutes later, keep SH at a junction: the path on the left heads to Khunde (SR10; p118). Pass a stupa. Soon, keep SH (NE) across a pass with another stupa **(Khumjung La; 3840m)**. Descend N towards Khumjung. Walk along the left side of the region's longest mani wall: pass **Edmund Hillary School**.

2 2:00: Arrive at the twin stupas at the S edge of **Khumjung (3780m)**. TR and head E through the village: alternatively, keep SH (N) for the route around the N side of the village.

3 2:10: Reach a junction at the **E side of Khumjung**. Head E for GL4a (p227) or S for SR9 (p112).

N-S

Stage GL3: Khumjung to Namche (See map on p220)

3 From the junction at the **E side of Khumjung**, head W.

2 0:10: From the N side of **Edmund Hillary School**, walk S along the left side of the region's longest mani wall. Afterwards, climb on a path ('Namche'). Cross a pass with a stupa **(Khumjung La; 3840m)**. After passing another stupa and a mani wall, reach a junction: descend SW.

1 0:45: A few minutes later, keep SH at a junction ('Namche'): the path on the right heads to Khunde (SR10; p118). Shortly afterwards, cross **Syangboche Airstrip**: then continue descending on a path. Shortly after that, keep SH at a junction: the path on the right goes to Thame. Soon, the path descends steeply in zigzags: it splits a few times but the branches soon converge.

9 1:30: Arrive at **Namche Gompa**.

Lodges (with accommodation, restaurant, & shop)	**Namche** (0km) » **Khumjung** (3.4km)
Terrain/ Navigation	The rocky paths are generally well-maintained and easy to follow. The route between Namche and Syangboche Airstrip is very steep. Route-finding is mostly straightforward.
Difficulty	**Medium**
Medical Assistance	**Khunde Hospital:** 1km W of Khumjung
Points of Interest	**Syangboche Airstrip** **Spectacularly situated stupas** **Khumjung:** monastery with 'yeti scalp' (p114); Edmund Hillary School; longest mani wall in the Khumbu

GL4 Khumjung to Dhole

Sanasa

The GLT heads N up the W side of the Dudh Koshi valley which is coated with pine, birch and rhododendron. N of Sanasa, the paths are noticeably less busy because the majority of trekkers continue E instead (along the CEBC). After gaining height, you should spot Cho Oyu (the world's 6th highest peak) for the first time: the views of it are even better over the coming days. To the E and W, the scenery is lovely but the views are often limited by the high valley walls. However, the vista to the SE, involving Kangtega and Thamserku, is sublime.

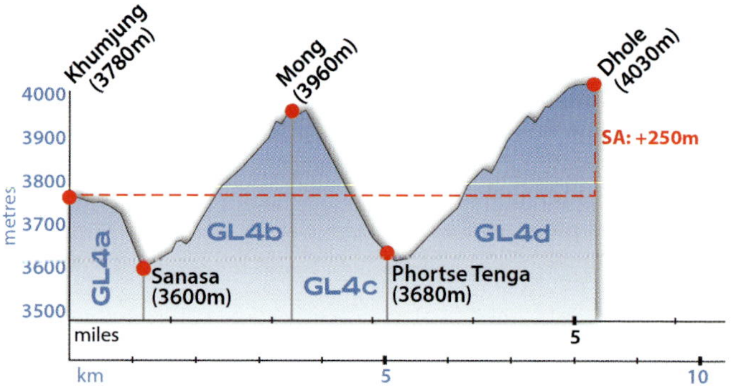

S-N (CW)		Time	Distance	Ascent	Descent	SA Increase	Max Alt
GL4a	Khumjung to Sanasa	0:20	1.2km 0.7miles	0m 0ft	180m 591ft	-180m -591ft	3780m 12402ft
GL4b	Sanasa to Mong	1:45	2.3km 1.4miles	400m 1312ft	40m 131ft	+360m +1181ft	3960m 12993ft
GL4c	Mong to Phortse Tenga	0:30	1.5km 0.9miles	25m 82ft	305m 1001ft	-280m -919ft	3960m 12993ft
GL4d	Phortse Tenga to Dhole	2:20	3.3km 2.1miles	444m 1457ft	94m 308ft	+350m +1148ft	4030m 13222ft

At the N end of GL4, you reach the village of Dhole which rests at the foot of a side-valley created by one of the many tributaries flowing into the Dudh Koshi. If your previous sleep stop was at Khumjung, it is not advisable to continue higher without sleeping at Dhole: the subsequent accommodation at Luza is another 300m higher. Dhole is a lovely place with great views and good lodges, making it perfect for an overnight stop. Alternatively, you could stop for the night before reaching Dhole: there are lodges at Sanasa, Mong and Phortse Tenga. However, bear in mind that, heading N, the trail rises significantly between Sanasa and Mong and then drops back down between Mong and Phortse Tenga: accordingly, be wary about spending the night at Mong (3960m) if your previous night was at Namche because that is a jump of 520m (which breaks the acclimatisation rules).

Lodges (with accommodation, restaurant, & shop)	**Khumjung** (0km) » **Sanasa** (1.2km) » **Mong** (3.5km) » **Phortse Tenga** (5km) » **Dhole** (8.3km)
Terrain/ Navigation	The rocky paths are generally well-maintained and easy to follow. Some steep and/or sustained climbs and descents. Route-finding is mostly straightforward.
Difficulty	**Medium:** the distance travelled is fairly short. However remember that the altitude reaches 3960m and you will still be acclimatising.
Medical Assistance	**Khunde Hospital:** 1km W of Khumjung
Points of Interest	Villages of Mong 5 and Dhole 7 First sighting of Cho Oyu Superb views of Kangtega & Thamserku

S-N

Stage GL4a: Khumjung to Sanasa (See map on p220)

3 From the junction at the **E side of Khumjung**, take the path descending E.

4 0:10: At another junction, TR for Sanasa: alternatively, TL to head directly to Mong (without passing Sanasa).

12 0:20: Reach a junction at **Sanasa (3600m)**; for Mong, TL and soon head N (GL4b); alternatively, head E for Phunki Tenga (EBC3b; p122) or S for Namche (EBC3a).

Stage GL4b: Sanasa to Mong (See map on p220)

12 From the junction at **Sanasa**, climb NE through trees ('Gokyo'). At a junction, TR on a clear path heading E: it soon bends left and climbs N across the slope.

5 1:45: Arrive at the small village of **Mong (3960m)**.

Stage GL4c: Mong to Phortse Tenga (See map on p220)

5 From **Mong**, the path descends NE across the partially wooded slope.

6 0:30: Arrive at **Phortse Tenga Guest House (3680m)** where there is a junction: keep SH for Dhole (GL4d). Alternatively, TR and descend for Phortse (GL8a; p238): a short distance along that trail, there are more lodges.

Stage GL4d: Phortse Tenga to Dhole (See map on p220)

6 From **Phortse Tenga Guest House**, the main path heads N: it undulates, gradually gaining height, as it contours around the slopes. There are a few steeper sections which are slippery when wet. 5-10min from the guest house, keep SH at a junction: the path descending to the right heads to Phortse (GL8a).

7 2:20: Arrive at **Dhole (4030m)**.

GL5 Dhole to Machermo

The GLT continues N up the W side of the Dudh Koshi, leading you above 4000m. With greater height comes bigger skies and, from the ridge S of Machermo, you should have an uninterrupted view of Cho Oyu and its gargantuan neighbours: in particular, look out for Gyachung Kang (the 15th highest mountain on earth and the highest peak under 8000m).

Machermo is a sprawling village, set in the base of a broad valley, with a variety of lodges. Because it is almost 1000m higher than Namche, the generally accepted principles of altitude acclimatisation recommend that trekkers who have walked from Namche (in three days or less) should stop at Machermo for two nights. However, in practice, many trekkers do not do this because Gokyo is only another 340m further up and they plan to acclimatise there instead (over two or three nights): we do not recommend that approach. In any case, if you are feeling unwell at Machermo, it is unwise to proceed higher and a second night there will greatly aid acclimatisation. Alternatively, sleep lower down in the small village of Luza which is normally very peaceful.

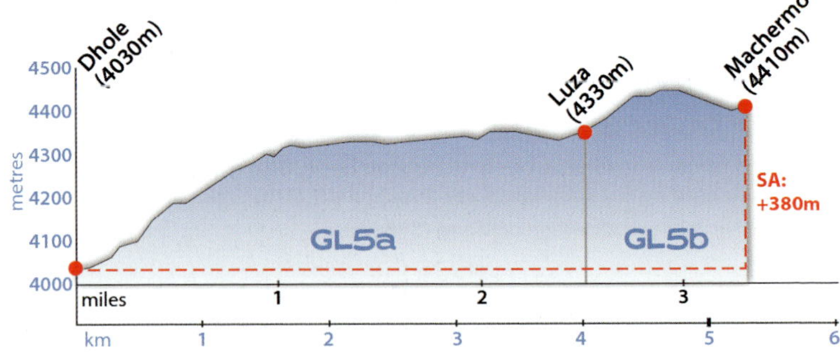

S-N (CW)		Time	Distance	Ascent	Descent	SA Increase	Max Alt
GL5a	Dhole to Luza	2:20	4.1km 2.5miles	340m 1116ft	40m 131ft	+300m +984ft	4330m 14207ft
GL5b	Luza to Machermo	0:45	1.2km 0.7miles	125m 410ft	45m 148ft	+80m +262ft	4430m 14535ft

The path near Machermo

Lodges (with accommodation, restaurant, & shop)	**Dhole** (0km) » **Mountain View Top Hill Lodge** (1.6km) » **Luza** (4.1km) » **Machermo** (5.3km)
Terrain/ Navigation	The rocky paths are generally well-maintained and easy to follow. Some steep and/or sustained climbs and descents. Route-finding is mostly straightforward.
Difficulty	**Medium:** although the stage is short, most trekkers will be feeling the high altitude
Medical Assistance	**Khunde Hospital:** 1km W of Khumjung **Gokyo International Health Care Centre:** see p201
Points of Interest	Villages of Luza (8) and Machermo (9) Great views of Cho Oyu

S-N

Stage GL5a: Dhole to Luza (See map on p230)

(7) From **Dhole**, the path climbs around the slopes to the N: as you rise above the tree-line, the views are excellent. At about **4300m**, pass **Mountain View Top Hill Lodge**. Afterwards the gradient eases and the path contours more gently around the slopes.

(8) 2:20: Arrive at **Luza (4330m)**.

Stage GL5b: Luza to Machermo (See map on p230)

(8) From **Luza**, climb N. Cross a ridge and then descend NW.

(9) 0:45: Arrive at **Machermo (4410m)**.

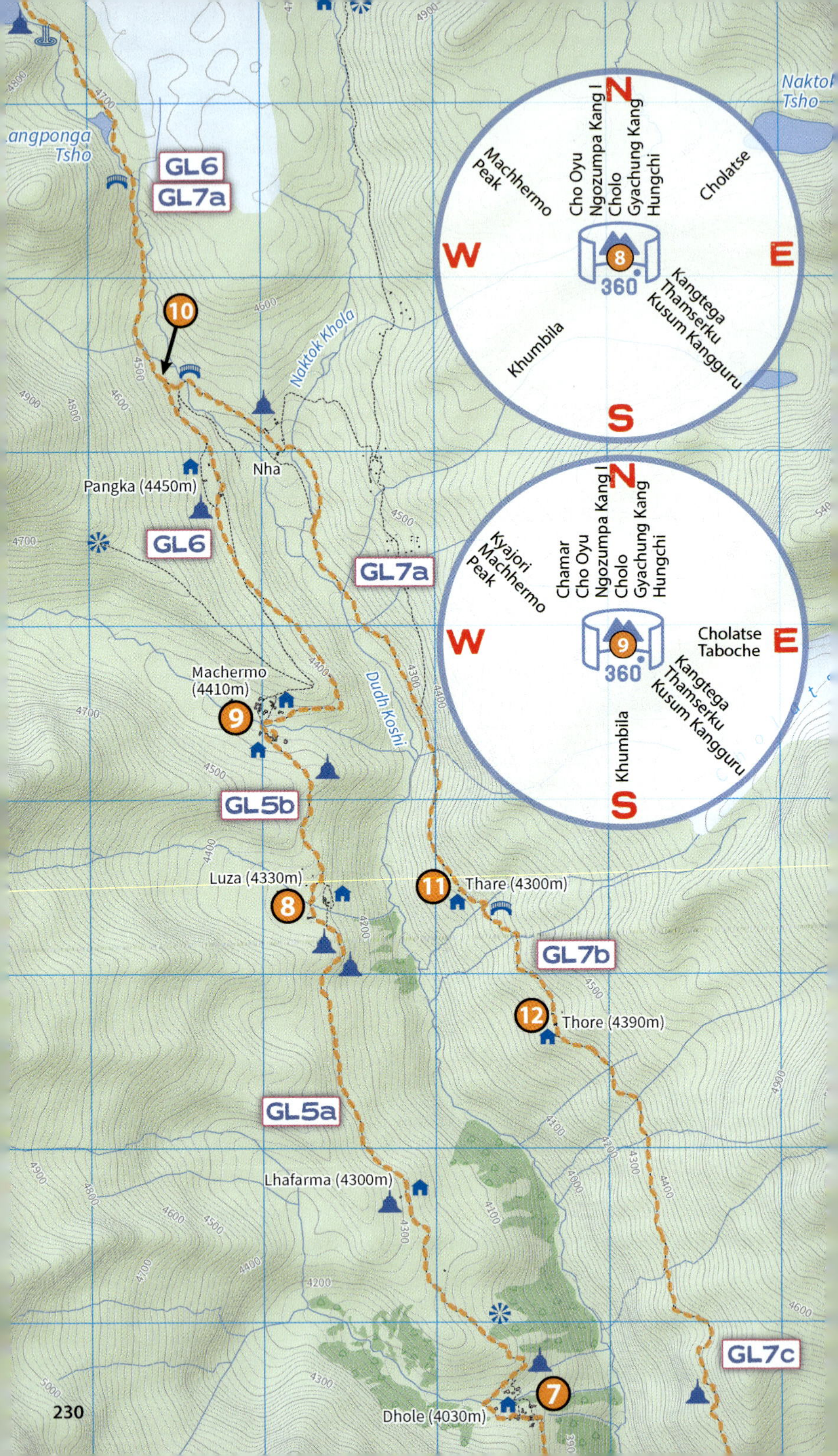

Langponga Tsho
Naktok Tsho
GL6
GL7a
Naktok Khola
Nha
Pangka (4450m)
GL6
GL7a
Machermo (4410m)
Dudh Koshi
GL5b
Luza (4330m)
Thare (4300m)
GL7b
Thore (4390m)
GL5a
Lhafarma (4300m)
GL7c
Dhole (4030m)
N
Cho Oyu
Ngozumpa Kang I
Cholo
Gyachung Kang
Hungchi
Machhermo Peak
Cholatse
W
E
360
Kangtega
Thamserku
Kusum Kangguru
Khumbila
S
N
Kyajori
Machhermo Peak
Chamar
Cho Oyu
Ngozumpa Kang I
Cholo
Gyachung Kang
Hungchi
Cholatse
Taboche
W
E
360
Kangtega
Thamserku
Kusum Kangguru
Khumbila
S

One of the Khumbu's many stupas

GL6 Machermo to Gokyo

Dudh Pokhari (the 3rd lake)

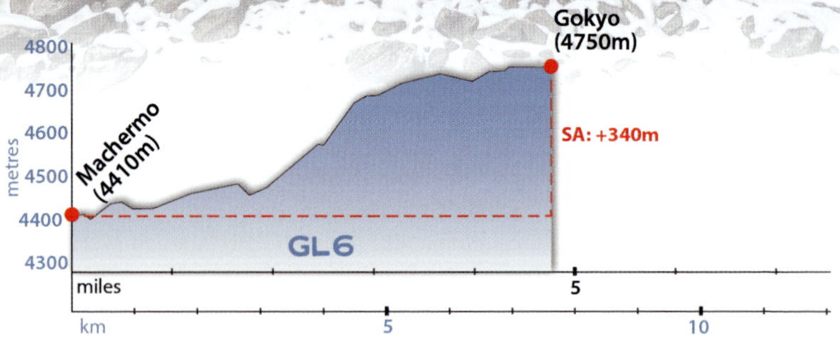

S-N (CW)		Time	Distance	Ascent	Descent	SA Increase	Max Alt
GL6	Machermo to Gokyo	3:20	7.6km 4.7miles	443m 1453ft	103m 338ft	+340m +1116ft	4750m 15585ft

Continuing N up the Dudh Koshi valley, the scenery is wonderful. After leaving Machermo, you approach a prominent hill (to the N) in the middle of the valley which is, in fact, the terminal moraine of the Ngozumpa Glacier: the trail heads up the narrow ablation valley on the W side of it. After a steep ascent, the first of Gokyo's famous lakes appears: this one is small but beautiful nonetheless. The second lake is bigger and more dramatic but the stage does not reach its crescendo until the third lake (with the village of Gokyo on its shores). For information on Gokyo, see p200.

Between Machermo and Gokyo, there is only one lodge: it is located at Pangka (4450m) and, if you slept at Machermo, you will pass it well before lunchtime; many trekkers grab a drink here and push on to Gokyo for lunch.

Lodges (with accommodation, restaurant, & shop)	**Machermo** (0km) » **Pangka** (2.4km) » **Gokyo** (7.6km)
Terrain/ Navigation	The paths are generally well-maintained and easy to follow. The climb N of (10) is long and steep. Route-finding is mostly straightforward.
Difficulty	**Hard:** the climb is tiring and the altitude is very high.
Medical Assistance	**Gokyo International Health Care Centre:** see p201
Points of Interest	Pangka (see below) Ngozumpa Glacier's terminal moraine Three beautiful lakes The village of Gokyo (11) Views of Cho Oyu, the world's 6th highest mountain

S-N

Stage GL6: Machermo to Gokyo (See map on p230)

(9) From **Machermo**, head E and climb the ridge to the N. Then continue N up the valley. Continue N past **Pangka (4450m)**.

(10) 1:20: Keep SH at a junction: the path to the right goes to Thare (GL7a; p234). The valley narrows as you climb beside the river (on a steep path cut into the hillside). Cross a bridge over the river and continue N. Soon pass to the E of **Langponga Tsho (the 1st lake; 4680m)**. (See map on p203). 15min later, pass the peaceful **Taujung Tsho (the 2nd lake; 4720m)**. 10-15min later, reach **Dudh Pokhari (the 3rd lake)**: the hill SH is the famous Gokyo Ri (SR5; p204).

(11) 3:20: Reach the village of **Gokyo (4750m)** at the NE corner of the 3rd lake.

The Pangka Avalanche

In November 1995, a huge cyclone in the Bay of Bengal caused severe storms across the Nepal Himalaya. Two metres of snow fell in only a few days, triggering avalanches on the slopes above the village of Pangka. The avalanches completely covered many of the village's lodges, killing 26 people including 13 Japanese trekkers and 11 guides/porters. Today, only one lodge remains in the village: it is apparently, far removed from the avalanche zone.

GL7 Gokyo to Phortse

You will spend much of this magnificent section on an unforgettable balcony path beneath the summits of Cholatse and Taboche. If you yearn to stay off the beaten track, then this is the route for you: the paths on the E side of the Dudh Koshi valley are noticeably more quiet than those to the W although they are also more challenging. Between Nha and Phortse, there are only a handful of lodges (at Thare and Thore): although basic, they have fabulous positions on the W facing slopes and lose the sun relatively late in the day; it is cold in the morning though. There is little to choose between Thare and Thore (both in name and nature): perhaps the views are marginally better at Thore (where you can see Cho Oyu) but that is splitting hairs.

At the S end of the route, Phortse rests on a lofty terrace, on the S slopes of Taboche, above the confluence of the Dudh Koshi and Imja Khola rivers. Away from the CEBC, it sees fewer trekkers and has an authentic feel. There are plenty of lodges, scattered between potato fields, and a monastery at the top of the village.

From Phortse, there are three options:

- **GL8:** the main GLT route to Sanasa via Phortse Tenga (p238)
- **AR1:** an alternative route which heads to Tengboche (p124). From there, you can return to Namche (via Sanasa) using EBC10f (p172).
- **AR2:** an alternative route which heads to Pangboche (p126). From there, you can return to Namche (via Tengboche and Sanasa) using EBC10d (p172).

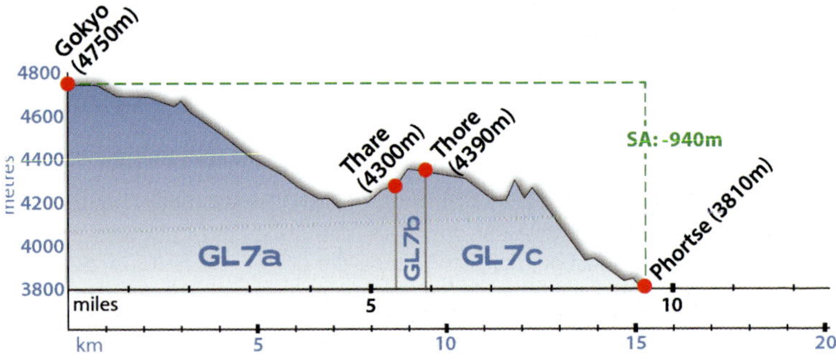

N-S (CW)		Time	Distance	Ascent	Descent	SA Increase	Max Alt
GL7a	Gokyo to Thare	2:45	8.3km 5.2miles	140m 459ft	590m 1936ft	-450m -1476ft	4750m 15585ft
GL7b	Thare to Thore	0:45	1.2km 0.7miles	120m 394ft	30m 98ft	+90m +295ft	4390m 14404ft
GL7c	Thore to Phortse	2:15	5.6km 3.5miles	107m 351ft	687m 2254ft	-580m -1903ft	4390m 14404ft

N-S

Stage GL7a: Gokyo to Thare (See map on p203)

11 From **Gokyo**, head S along the E side of the lake. 10-15min later, pass **Taujung Tsho (the 2nd lake; 4720m)**. 10-15min afterwards, pass to the E of **Langponga Tsho (the 1st lake; 4680m)**. Cross a bridge over the river and descend steeply S (on a path cut into the hillside).

10 1:05: TL at a junction and descend into the valley. Soon the path bends left and crosses a bridge over the river: on the other side, a rocky path heads SE. 10-15min later, after the buildings at **Nha**, TL and head briefly E. Shortly afterwards, ford a stream on rocks. Then descend S on a path. After a while, the path climbs above the river.

11 2:45: Reach the lodge at **Thare (4300m)**.

Stage GL7b: Thare to Thore (See map on p230)

11 From **Thare**, climb SE on a path. Soon cross a bridge over a stream. Then continue climbing on an amazing balcony, high above the river.

12 0:45: Reach **Thore (4390m)**.

Stage GL7c: Thore to Phortse (See map on p236)

12 From **Thore**, an undulating balcony path heads S, gradually descending. Eventually, after passing a stupa, descend more steeply. Cross a stream bed at **Thulang** and continue S.

13 2:15: Arrive at a junction at the top of **Phortse (3810m)**, close to the monastery. To head directly to Phortse Tenga, TR and descend SW along the tree-line at the N edge of the village. Alternatively, to go through the centre of Phortse (where most lodges are located), head S from 13: soon, TR at a second junction and descend SW. For Tengboche/Pangboche (AR1/AR2), stay high at the second junction and head S along the top of the village.

Lodges (with accommodation, restaurant, & shop)	**Gokyo** (0km) » **Thare** (8.3km) » **Thore** (9.5km) » **Phortse** (15.1km)
Terrain/ Navigation	Paths are often narrow and rocky but generally straightforward to follow. However, at Nha, make sure that you do not take the path heading N by mistake. The descent from the first lake to 10 is steep. The balcony path on the E side of the Dudh Koshi is exposed in places: take care. Between Thore and Phortse, there is a long, steep descent.
Difficulty	**Hard:** this section is long with much descent. The narrow, rocky paths are tiring.
Medical Assistance	**Gokyo International Health Care Centre:** see p201 **Khunde Hospital:** 1km from Khumjung
Points of Interest	Three of the Gokyo lakes Ngozumpa Glacier's terminal moraine Villages of Thare 11, Thore 12 and Phortse 13

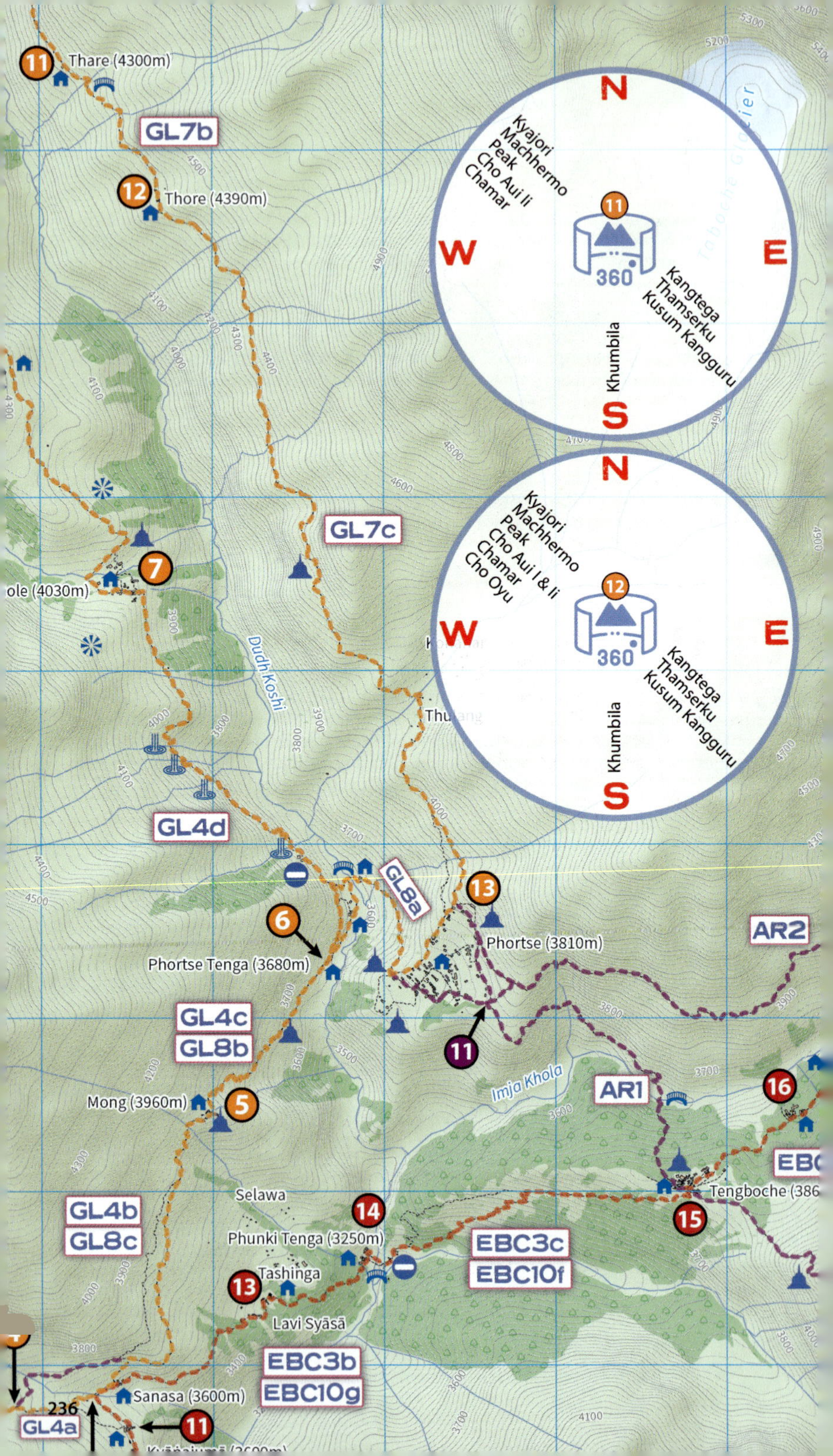

Thare (4300m)
GL7b
Thore (4390m)
ole (4030m)
GL7c
Dudh Koshi
GL4d
GL8a
Phortse Tenga (3680m)
Phortse (3810m)
AR2
GL4c
GL8b
Imja Khola
AR1
Mong (3960m)
Selawa
GL4b
GL8c
Phunki Tenga (3250m)
EBC3c
EBC10f
Tashinga
Lavi Syāsā
Tengboche (386
EBC3b
EBC10g
Sanasa (3600m)
GL4a
236
N
W
E
S
Kyajori
Machhermo
Peak
Cho Aui li
Chamar
Kangtega
Thamserku
Kusum Kangguru
Khumbila
360
N
W
E
S
Kyajori
Machhermo
Peak
Cho Aui I & Ii
Chamar
Cho Oyu
Kangtega
Thamserku
Kusum Kangguru
Khumbila
360

Phortse
N
Cho Aui I
Machhermo Peak
W
Khumbila
13
360
E
Thamserku
S

GL8 Phortse to Sanasa

Yaks on the trail near Sanasa

N-S (CW)		Time	Distance	Ascent	Descent	SA Increase	Max Alt
GL8a	Phortse to Phortse Tenga	0:40	1.9km 1.2miles	85m 279ft	215m 705ft	-130m -427ft	3680m 12074ft
GL8b	Phortse Tenga to Mong	1:20	1.5km 0.9miles	305m 1001ft	25m 82ft	+280m +919ft	3960m 12993ft
GL8c	Mong to Sanasa	0:40	2.3km 1.4miles	40m 131ft	400m 1312ft	-360m -1181ft	3960m 12993ft

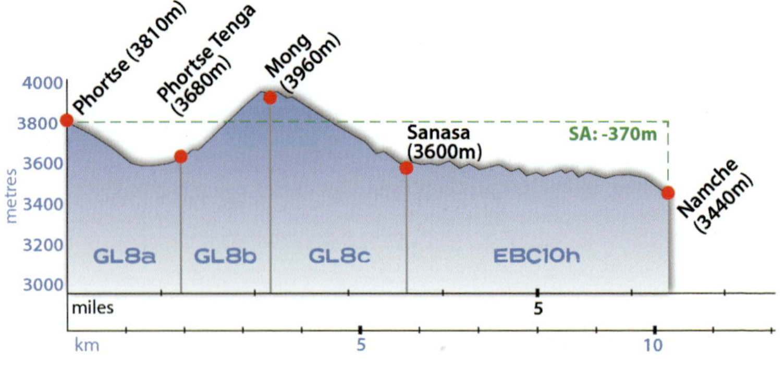

From Phortse, the GLT crosses the Dudh Koshi to Phortse Tenga. Then it climbs steeply to Mong using the path travelled previously on Section GL4 (p226). By the time you leave Mong, you need to have decided upon your route back to Namche because you are not far from the junctions near Sanasa. There are four ways to hike from Sanasa to Namche:

- **Main CEBC route** (Stage EBC10h; p173): this is the route used in our GLT itinerary.
- **Namche via Everest View Hotel** (Stages GL4a & SR9; p227 & p112).
- **Namche via Khumjung** (GL4a & GL3; p227 & p224).
- **Namche via Khumjung and Khunde** (GL4a & SR10; p227 & p118).

They are all incredibly scenic and it makes sense to return using a different route from that used on the ascent.

Lodges (with accommodation, restaurant, & shop)	**Phortse** (0km) » **Phortse Tenga** (1.9km) » **Mong** (3.4km) » **Sanasa** (5.7km) » **Kyanajuma** (6.2km) » **Namche** (10.2km)
Terrain/ Navigation	The rocky paths are generally well-maintained and easy to follow. Some steep and/or sustained climbs and descents. Route-finding is mostly straightforward.
Difficulty	**Medium:** the climb between Phortse Tenga and Mong is tiring but it comes early in the day. Afterwards, the route is largely downhill.
Medical Assistance	**Khunde Hospital:** 1km W of Khumjung.
Points of Interest	Village of Mong (5) Superb views of Everest, Lhotse, Nuptse and Ama Dablam Tenzing Norgay Memorial Stupa (near (10))

N-S

Stage GL8a: Phortse to Phortse Tenga (See map on p236)

(13) From the **Everest Lodge** (at the **W side of Phortse**), descend N through forest. Just after a lodge, cross a bridge over the **Dudh Koshi** river. Immediately afterwards, TL at a junction (and head S): the path climbing W heads to Dhole (GL4d; p226). Pass a few more lodges.

(6) 0:40: Arrive at **Phortse Tenga Guest House (3680m)**. There is a junction here: head SW for Mong (GL8b).

Stage GL8b: Phortse Tenga to Mong (See map on p236)

(6) From **Phortse Tenga**, the path climbs SW across partially wooded slopes.

(5) 1:20: Arrive at the small village of **Mong (3960m)**.

Stage GL8c: Mong to Sanasa (See map on p220)

(5) From **Mong**, the path heads briefly SW and then descends S across the slope. Soon, TL at a fork. After a while, the path bends right to head W. Shortly afterwards, reach a junction: TL for Sanasa (GL8c) and descend through trees; alternatively, TR at the junction for an alternative route to Khumjung (which avoids Sanasa; shown in purple on map).

(12) 0:40: Reach the junction at **Sanasa (3600m)**: for the main route to Namche, head S (Stage EBC10h; p173); for Khumjung, head W (Stage GL4a; p227).

Stage EBC10h: Sanasa to Namche (See map on p220)

For route description, see p173.

Hiking into the Khumbu

W1 Bhandar to Sete

Bhandar Gompa

An enjoyable start to the journey through the middle hills of the Solukhumbu. You will see few other trekkers and the normal daily life of rural Nepalese communities will unfold before you. Immediately after leaving Bhandar, with its ramshackle shops and houses, Buddhist culture is apparent: after a few prayer wheels, reach the village gompa which has two bright white stupas bedecked in colourful prayer flags. However, unlike the higher regions closer to Everest, you will see evidence of Hindu culture too.

A long traverse through villages and fertile slopes brings you to the village of Kinja where the damage caused during the 2015 earthquake is still visible: despite the dearth of trekkers, Kinja still has around four guesthouses. Afterwards, there is a long, steep climb to the village of Sete which is beautifully nestled in the terraced slopes: there are some excellent mani walls and superb views S to Pikey Peak. It a lovely place to stop for the night and, at 2570m, is a better location for acclimatisation than Kinja.

W-E		Time	Distance	Ascent	Descent	SA Increase	Max Alt
W1a	Bhandar to Kinja	3:00	10.4km 6.5miles	152m 499ft	782m 2566ft	-630m -2067ft	2240m 7349ft
W1b	Kinja to Sete	3:30	4.9km 3.0miles	960m 3150ft	0m 0ft	+960m +3150ft	2570m 8432ft

Lodges (with accommodation, restaurant, & shop)	**Bhandar** (0km) » **Korem** » **Kinja** (10.4km) » **Sete** (15.3km)
Terrain/ Navigation	Path and tracks are generally clear and well-maintained. The climb from Kinja to Sete is steep and tough: the path is muddy after rain. Route-finding can be tricky: there are only a few signposts.
Difficulty	**Hard:** the 1000m climb is a tough start to the trek.
Medical Assistance	Hospitals in Jiri (OR)
Points of Interest	Villages of Bhandar, Kinja (1) and Sete (2) Views of Pikey Peak

Stage W1a: Bhandar to Kinja

S From the square at the W side of **Bhandar** (where jeeps arrive from Kathmandu), descend E through the village. At the bottom of the village, TL and head NE. Shortly afterwards, TL at a fork (ignoring the signposted route to Dokharpa). At the next few junctions, head E: soon pass the **monastery** and descend SE. 15min later, TL between buildings. Shortly after crossing a bridge, TL and head E on an undulating track. About 30min later, the route starts to descend E, gradually getting closer to the river: there are a few short-cuts across the track's hairpins. At the base of the valley, pass through the village of **Korem** where there is one lodge. Continue E. 10min later, pass through a yellow archway: immediately afterwards, TR ('Everest'). Immediately after that, TL and climb ('Kinja').

(1) 3:00: Shortly afterwards, TL on a path (white arrows) and climb through the village of **Kinja (1610m)**.

Stage W1b: Kinja to Sete

(1) From the top of **Kinja**, follow a path that climbs steeply E ('Sete'). Notice the wooden logs affixed to buildings with a single small hole in the front: these are beehives. At about 2400m, TL and climb on a path. 15-20min later, TR onto a grassy track. Shortly afterwards, climb E past **Sunrise Lodge** (on the W side of Sete). Pass some mani walls.

(2) 3:30: Reach the village of **Sete (2570m)**.

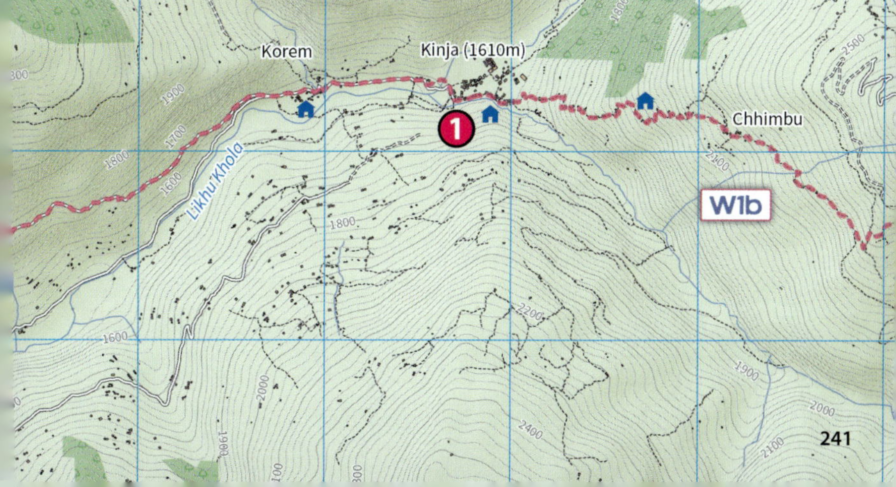

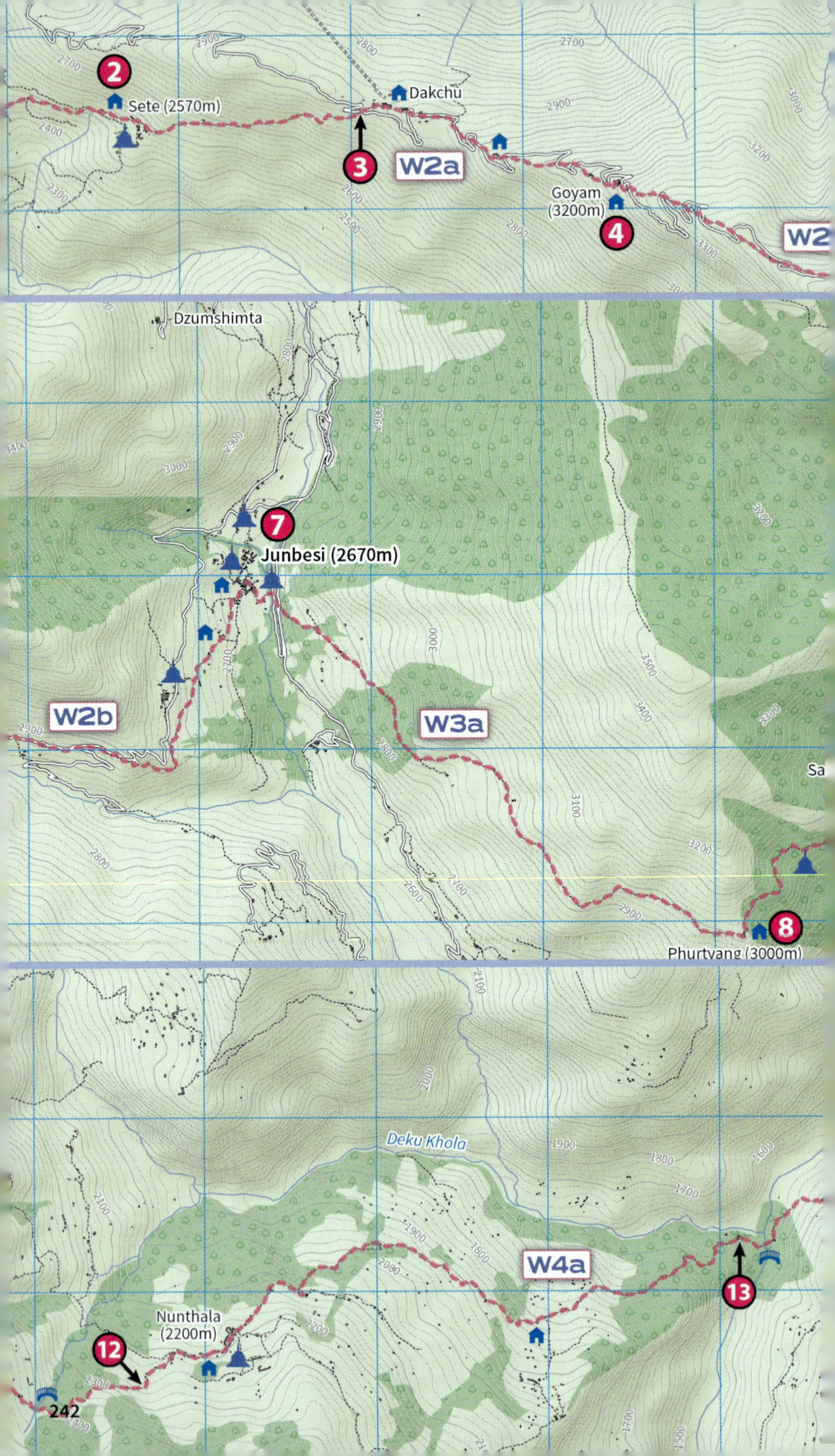

2
Sete (2570m)
3
Dakchu
W2a
Goyam
(3200m)
4
W2
Dzumshimta
7
Junbesi (2670m)
W2b
W3a
Sa
8
Phurtyang (3000m)
Deku Khola
W4a
13
Nunthala
(2200m)
12
242

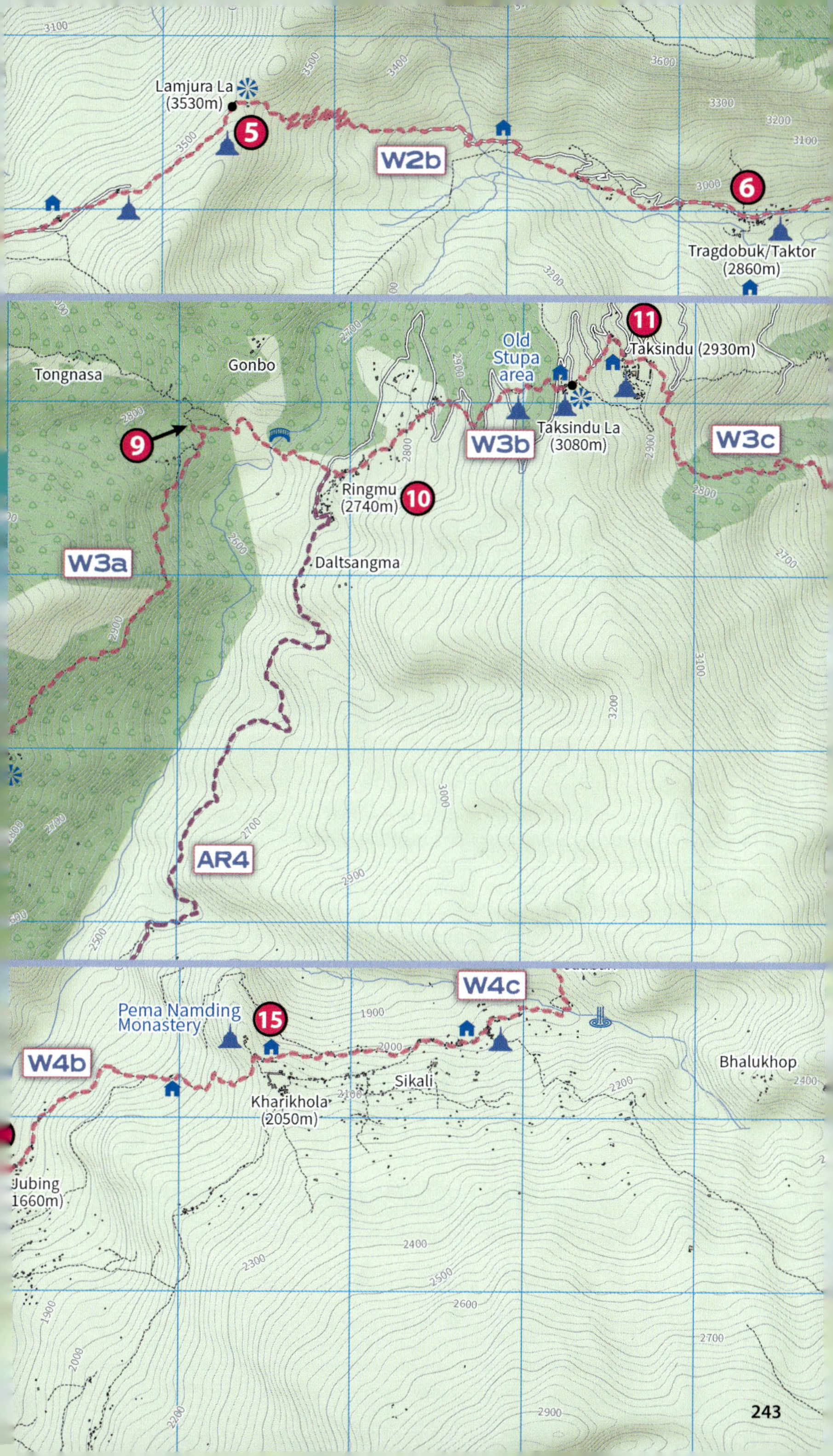

Lamjura La
(3530m)
5
W2b
6
Tragdobuk/Taktor
(2860m)
11
Taksindu (2930m)
Old
Stupa
area
Tongnasa
Gonbo
9
W3b
Taksindu La
(3080m)
W3c
Ringmu
(2740m)
10
W3a
Daltsangma
AR4
W4c
Pema Namding
Monastery
15
W4b
Sikali
Kharikhola
(2050m)
Bhalukhop
Jubing
1660m)

W2 Sete to Junbesi

Forested slopes near Sete

A beautiful hike through Nepal's middle hills with more superb views of Pikey Peak: the scenery is particularly fine in spring when the rhododendrons are in bloom. There are also plenty of mani walls, stupas and monasteries to enjoy along the way. However, the highlight is the crossing of Lamjura La pass (if you are lucky enough to reach it before the afternoon clouds roll in). Although the views at Lamjura La are normally best in the morning, it is hard to get there early enough if you slept at Sete the previous night. Staying at Goyam (instead of Sete) solves this problem but it makes it difficult to structure the previous days: Sete to Goyam is a very short day; however, Kinja to Goyam would involve a mammoth 1600m climb in a single day. Furthermore, the altitude at Goyam is 3200m which might be problematic for some people so early in the trek. The views at Goyam are excellent.

Junbesi is a lovely overnight stop with lodges and shops for resupply. The stupa at the bottom of the village is one of the region's most beautiful: it is completely encircled by prayer wheels and adorned with colourful prayer flags; the spire is finished with bright gold paint.

W-E		Time	Distance	Ascent	Descent	SA Increase	Max Alt
W2a	Sete to Goyam	2:45	3.8km 2.4miles	630m 2067ft	0m 0ft	+630m +2067ft	3200m 10499ft
W2b	Goyam to Junbesi	4:00	11.7km 7.3miles	395m 1296ft	925m 3035ft	-530m -1739ft	3530m 11582ft

Lodges (with accommodation, restaurant, & shop)	**Sete** (0km) » **Dakchu** (1.9km) » **Goyam** (3.8km) » **lodges W of Lamjura La** (6.7km; currently closed) » **Tragdobuk/Thaktok** (13km) » **Junbesi** (15.5km)
Terrain/ Navigation	Path and tracks are generally clear but can be muddy. The climb from Sete to Lamjura La is long and sometimes steep. The descent from the pass is long, steep and often muddy. Route-finding can be tricky: there are only a few signs.
Difficulty	**Hard:** 1000m of climbing followed by 900m of descent. Lamjura La sits at 3530m and it is normal to feel the altitude (so soon after leaving Kathmandu).
Medical Assistance	Hospitals in Jiri (OR)
Points of Interest	Views of Pikey Peak Lamjura La 5 Tragdobuk/Taktor gompa 6 Village of Junbesi 7

Stage W2a: Sete to Goyam

2 From **Sete**, climb E.

3 1:20: Cross a track and pick up a path on the left of a mani wall. Shortly afterwards, at the top of the ridge, reach **Dakchu** (where there are some lodges). Head E along the ridge: just after **Sonam Lodge**, TL and climb on a track. 5-10min later, TL and climb a steep path through rhododendron forest: the path crosses the track several times. Pass some mani walls and watch for deer in the forest.

4 2:45: Reach **Tashi Delek Lodge** at **Goyam (3200m)**, a beautiful place to stop for a drink.

Stage W2b: Goyam to Junbesi

4 From **Tashi Delek Lodge**, head E: keep SH across a track and climb on a path. The path crosses the track several more times. 20min from the start, there are several lodges (currently closed). 20min later, keep SH up the track (which climbs the left side of the ridge): shortly afterwards, ignore a path on the right ('Lamjura'). Pass a large stupa (above the path).

5 1:45: Reach **Lamjura La pass (3530m)**; the lodge here has closed. TR and head between rocks to descend on a path: soon, enter trees. Cross a track several times. At the time of writing, tree-felling had blocked the path and it was necessary to descend on the track. Shortly after the **Shanti Chetra Lodge**, TR on a path. Soon, head down the track again.

6 3:10: Pass the village of **Tragdobuk/Taktor (2860m)**; there are lodges, a gompa and a stupa. Just before a large outcrop, TR on a path, leaving the track. Soon, the path bends left around the outcrop (colourfully painted) and heads N. Shortly afterwards, notice **Serlo Gompa** above on the left. Descend N. Pass **Namaste Lodge**.

7 4:00: Arrive in **Junbesi (2670m)**.

W3 Junbesi to Nunthala

The balcony path above Junbesi

Climbing around the slopes E of Junbesi, the route travels a spectacular balcony path that provides the best scenery of the trek so far: if skies are clear, you can see Everest for the first time (far away to the NE). Large stupas give the landscape an unmistakably Nepalese flavour and, if your trek coincides with the blooming of the rhododendrons and magnolias, you are in for a colourful treat.

Ringmu is a good place to break for lunch because afterwards, there is another climb followed by a relentless descent all the way to Nunthala. Crossing Taksindu La pass, you can spot many of the Khumbu's high peaks including Kusum Kanguru, Thamserku and Kangtega. The views at the pass are often best in the morning and it can be lovely to spend the night at the lodge there; however, most trekkers continue to Nunthala where there is a better choice of accommodation.

W-E		Time	Distance	Ascent	Descent	SA Increase	Max Alt
W3a	Junbesi to Ringmu	4:15	10.8km 6.7miles	650m 2133ft	580m 1903ft	+70m +230ft	3020m 9909ft
W3b	Ringmu to Taksindu	1:30	2.9km 1.8miles	352m 1155ft	162m 532ft	+190m +623ft	3080m 10105ft
W3c	Taksindu to Nunthala	1:00	4.2km 2.6miles	11m 36ft	741m 2431ft	-730m -2395ft	2930m 9613ft

Lodges (with accommodation, restaurant, & shop)	**Junbesi** (0km) » **Phurtyang** (4.8km) » **Salung** (6.6km) » **Ringmu** (10.8km) » **Taksindu La** (13.4km) » **Taksindu** (13.7km) » **Nunthala** (17.9km)
Terrain/ Navigation	Path/tracks are generally clear but can be muddy. The climb from Junbesi to Phurtyang is long and tiring. The climb from Ringmu to Taksindu La is steep. The descent from Taksindu La to Nunthala is a long knee-jerker. Route-finding can be tricky because there are only a few signs. In particular, navigation between Salung and Ringmu is difficult because the path splinters.
Difficulty	**Hard:** a long section with plenty of climbing/descent.
Medical Assistance	Hospital in Phaplu (OR)
Points of Interest	**Beautiful stupa at Junbesi** 7 **Everest Views on Stage W3a** **Village of Ringmu** 10 **Taksindu La pass:** large stupas and good views **Taksindu Gompa** 11 **Village of Nunthala** 12

Stage W3a: Junbesi to Ringmu

7 Descend SE through **Junbesi**. From the stupa, descend steps: at the bottom, TL and cross a bridge over the river. Then TR. Shortly afterwards, TL and climb on a path: there are super views of the monasteries on the far side of the valley. Above the tree-line, the path contours around the magnificent open slopes.

8 2:15: Pass the beautifully situated **Everest View Sherpa Lodge** at **Phurtyang (3000m)**: you can see Everest on a clear day. Afterwards, continue contouring around the slopes. Pass a large stupa perched on the edge of the hillside. Continue through the village of **Salung**. Then descend NE: route-finding is tricky as the path splinters.

9 3:45: Approaching the valley floor, TR and descend on a path (orange waymarks; easy to miss). Cross to the other side of the valley using a suspension bridge. Then keep SH up a cobbled track. A few minutes later, TL and climb on a steep path ('Lukla').

10 4:15: Arrive at **Ringmu (2740m)**.

Stage W3b: Ringmu to Taksindu

10 From **Ringmu**, climb NE on a cobbled path. Keep SH across a track ('Lukla'). TR after a mani wall, climbing on a cobbled path. Cross the track a few more times. Pass a large walled stupa (bedecked with prayer flags). Then climb on a cobbled path. Keep SH past the lodge and stupa at **Taksindu La (3080m)**: go through an archway to cross the pass. Then descend through rhododendron forest. Soon, cross a track and continue on a path.

11 1:30: Arrive at the village of **Taksindu (2930m)** which has a large monastery and some lodges: **Home Stay Lodge** was the home of Babu Chhiri Sherpa, a local hero who climbed Everest 10 times and spent 21hr on the summit without supplementary oxygen (a record which still stands).

Stage W3c: Taksindu to Nunthala

11 Head through **Taksindu**, keeping to the N of the gompa. Initially, descend S: the path gradually bends to the E. 30min from Taksindu, TL at a fork. Later, cross a suspension bridge. When you meet a track, head down it until the path resumes.

12 1:00: Shortly afterwards, reach a track at a fork: head N and descend into the sprawling village of **Nunthala (2200m)**.

W4 Nunthala to Bupsa

Kharikhola Gompa

Leaving Nunthala, a long descent through forest leads to a suspension bridge over the Dudh Koshi river (which is fed by the glaciers below Everest): 'Dudh Koshi' means 'milk river'; you will become familiar with the river's milky waters over the coming days because you will follow it at least as far as Phunki Tenga (on Stage EBC3b). After crossing the river, the first climb of the day leads you through the sprawling village of Jubing and up to the pass at Kharikhola. Jubing is a pleasant place to take a break and it has a number of lodges: unusually for this region, it is inhabited by Rai people rather than Sherpas. However, the views are better at Kharikhola: Hill Top Guest House is superbly located on the pass beside Pema Namding Monastery; to access the monastery, climb a long and colourful set of steps which are flanked by prayer wheels.

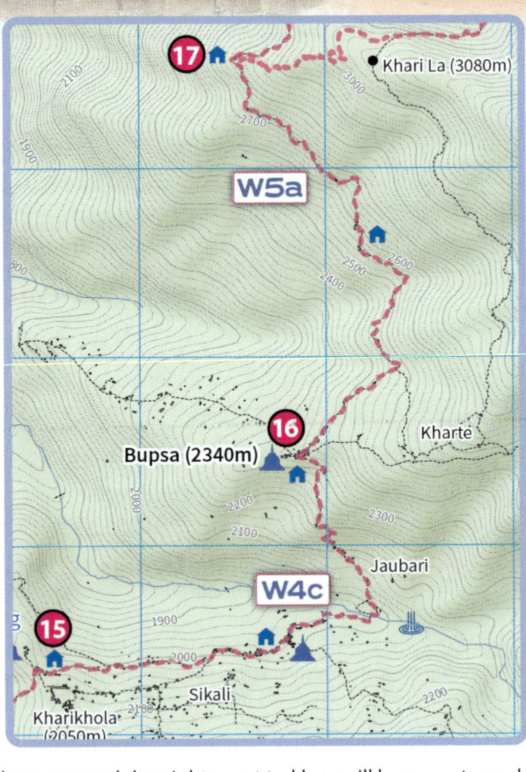

Although Kharikhola is a great place to spend the night, most trekkers will be eager to push on. About 2km E of the village, the path crosses a tributary of the Dudh Koshi: this marks a general change in direction of the trek; the journey E is over and now you head N to Namche and beyond; the following day, you will join the route of the CEBC. From the tributary, a steep climb brings you to Bupsa which is perched on a ridge and has a small monastery. The lodges are well positioned to enjoy the excellent views.

W-E		Time	Distance	Ascent	Descent	SA Increase	Max Alt
W4a	Nunthala to Jubing	1:40	5.4km 3.4miles	190m 623ft	730m 2395ft	-540m -1772ft	2200m 7218ft
W4b	Jubing to Kharikhola	1:30	3.2km 2.0miles	390m 1280ft	0m 0ft	+390m +1280ft	2050m 6726ft
W4c	Kharikhola to Bupsa	2:00	4.0km 2.5miles	391m 1283ft	101m 331ft	+290m +951ft	2340m 7678ft

Lodges (with accommodation, restaurant, & shop)	**Nunthala** (0km) » **Bijoy Lodge** (2.9km) » **Jubing** (5.4km) » **Kharikhola** (8.6km) » **Bupsa** (12.6km)
Terrain/ Navigation	Path and tracks are generally clear but can be muddy. The descent from Nunthala to the Dudh Koshi is long and tiring. Route-finding can be tricky: there are few signs.
Difficulty	**Hard:** 1000m of climbing and plenty of descent.
Medical Assistance	Hospitals in Phaplu (OR) and Lukla
Points of Interest	**Dudh Koshi river** 13 **Village of Jubing** 14 **Pema Namding Monastery in Kharikhola** 15 **Village of Bupsa** 16: small monastery

Stage W4a: Nunthala to Jubing

12 Head NE through **Nunthala**. At the far side of the village, descend NE on a steep path. 35min from Nunthala, cross a track and pick up a path to the left of **Bijoy Lodge**. Afterwards, the path crosses the track a few more times ('Lukla').

13 1:15: TR down a track. Shortly afterwards, TR at a fork onto a path. Then cross a suspension bridge over the **Dudh Koshi river**: afterwards, TL and climb on a track. Shortly afterwards, TR and climb steep steps.

14 1:40: Reach the village of **Jubing (1660m)**.

Stage W4b: Jubing to Kharikhola

14 Climb NE through **Jubing**. Continue NE out of the village. Shortly after **Quiet View Lodge**, TR at a junction and continue climbing E.

15 1:30: Arrive at **Hill Top Guest House** in **Kharikhola (2050m)**. The guesthouse is superbly located on the pass beside **Pema Namding Monastery** (visitors welcome).

Stage W4c: Kharikhola to Bupsa

15 From **Hill Top Guest House**, continue E. Just afterwards, TR at a fork: alternatively, TL for other lodges. Shortly afterwards, TL at a junction and descend. TR onto a broad track. Cross a bridge near a large waterfall. Then bear left to head NW. A few minutes later, TR and climb.

16 2:00: Reach the village of **Bupsa (2340m)**.

W5 Bupsa to Cheplung

Khumbila seen from Chutok La

Heading N, the excitement is palpable because, at the end of this section, you will finally join the main trail to EBC. However, to get there, you still have to complete a challenging hike with lots of climbing and descent. The first (and hardest) part of the route involves a long climb, from Bupsa to Puiya, through rhododendron forest: it can be muddy and slippery. From Puiya, an undulating balcony path heads NW to Chutok La pass which is the finest viewpoint of the trek so far: the biggest mountains are tangibly closer and you should see Lukla for the first time.

After descending to Surke, the most direct route to Namche heads N along W5d (avoiding Lukla): it meets the CEBC at Cheplung (1). However, there is also an alternative route (AR3; p252) which connects Surke with Lukla (the official start of the CEBC).

Because this section is so hard, some trekkers prefer to split it, sleeping at Puiya, Chheubas or Surke. The following day, you could push on beyond Cheplung, perhaps to Phakding or further: you will have already spent many days between 2000m and 3000m so, from an acclimatisation point of view, there is no reason why you could not even go as far up as Jorsale that day.

As you approach the CEBC, you will notice an increase in the number of porters and pack-animals on the trail. When pack-animals are passing, remain on the safe inside of the trail: do not stand on the exposed outside of the path because trekkers are sometimes knocked off the edge by the animals.

W-E		Time	Distance	Ascent	Descent	SA Increase	Max Alt
W5a	Bupsa to Puiya	3:45	8.1km 5.0miles	700m 2297ft	349m 1145ft	+440m +1444ft	2900m 9515ft
W5b	Puiya to Chheubas	1:00	2.7km 1.7miles	85m 279ft	145m 476ft	-60m -197ft	2810m 9220ft
W5c	Chheubas to Surke	1:00	3.8km 2.4miles	89m 292ft	529m 1736ft	-440m -1444ft	2775m 9105ft
W5d	Surke to Cheplung	2:00	4.6km 2.9miles	410m 1345ft	30m 98ft	+380m +1247ft	2660m 8727ft

Lodges (with accommodation, restaurant, & shop)	**Bupsa** (0km) » **Sonam Lodge** (17; 3.5km) » **Puiya** (8.1km) » **Paiya** (9.3km) » **Chheubas** (10.8km) » **Surke** (14.6km) » **Chaurikharka** (18km) » **Cheplung** (19.2km)
Terrain/ Navigation	Because of the large numbers of pack-animals, paths are muddy and slippery. At the time of writing, the original route between 17 and 18 was closed: the alternative route via Khari La is steep and muddy. Route-finding is straightforward except that the alternative route between 17 and 18 is tricky to follow.
Difficulty	**Hard:** significant climbing/descent
Medical Assistance	Hospital in Lukla
Points of Interest	**Chutok La pass:** views of Khumbila and Gyachung Kang (the world's 15th highest mountain) **Village of Surke** 20 **Mani walls and prayer wheels at Chaurikharka/Cheplung** 1

Stage W5a: Bupsa to Puiya

16 From **Bupsa**, climb initially NE on a path: ignore the path that descends past the monastery. Soon the route bends left and climbs generally N, contouring around the slopes. 1hr from the start, pass two lodges. Then climb steep steps.

17 2:00: Just after a mani wall, reach **Sonam Lodge**. From there, there are two routes. At the time of writing, the original route (which contoured NE around the ridge) was closed because a new dirt road was being constructed: it is not clear whether this route will reopen. The harder alternative route (which may become permanent) climbs steeply E up the ridge towards **Khari La pass** and then descends steeply E to rejoin the original route: route-finding is tricky on the climb; if in doubt, head up the main track.

18 3:45: Reach the village of **Puiya (2780m)**.

Stage W5b: Puiya to Chheubas

18 From **Puiya**, head NW on a path which undulates across the slopes. Pass through the village of **Paiya**: there is a police **checkpoint** where you should show your passport.

19 1:00: Reach **Chheubas (2720m)**.

Stage W5c: Chheubas to Surke

19 From **Chheubas**, head N on a lovely balcony path which contours around the slopes. Pass beautiful mani walls and **Chutok La (2775m)**. Afterwards, there are superb views of Khumbila and Gyachung Kang. The path now descends.

20 1:00: Cross a bridge at the village of **Surke (2280m)**.

Stage W5d: Surke to Cheplung

20 From **Surke**, the path climbs N.

21 0:20: Reach a junction at a round mani wall; for Cheplung, keep SH (W5d); alternatively, TR for Lukla and climb steps (AR3; p252). The clear path to Cheplung climbs N. After 20min, cross a bridge. Head N through the village of **Chaurikharka** which has a long series of mani walls and prayer wheels. TL at a fork, ignoring the path on the right which heads to Lukla.

1 2:00: Reach a junction at the village of **Cheplung (2660m)**. This is where you meet the CEBC: head N for Namche (EBC1b; p105) or S for Lukla (EBC11d; p176).

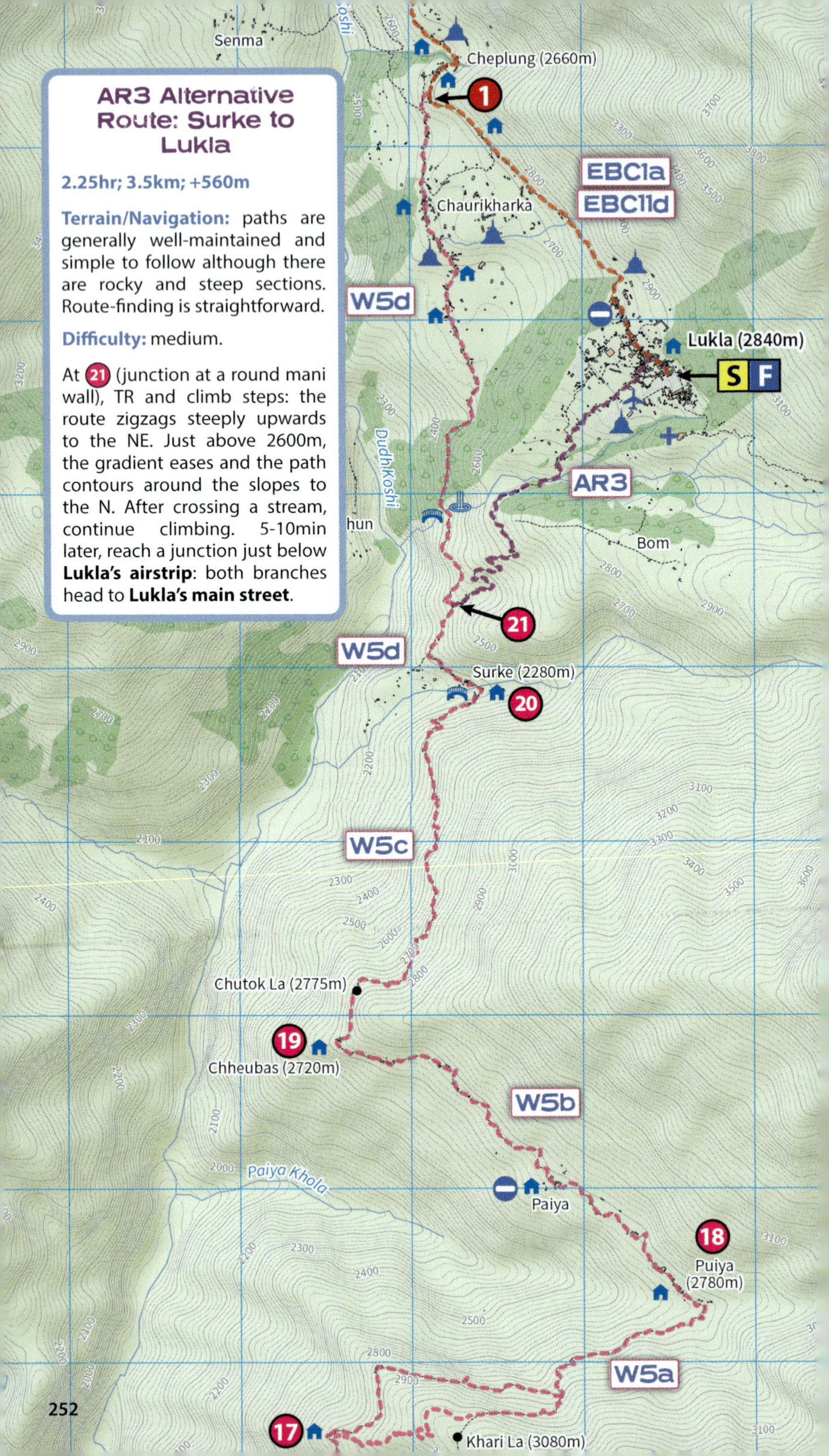

AR3 Alternative Route: Surke to Lukla

2.25hr; 3.5km; +560m

Terrain/Navigation: paths are generally well-maintained and simple to follow although there are rocky and steep sections. Route-finding is straightforward.

Difficulty: medium.

At 21 (junction at a round mani wall), TR and climb steps: the route zigzags steeply upwards to the NE. Just above 2600m, the gradient eases and the path contours around the slopes to the N. After crossing a stream, continue climbing. 5-10min later, reach a junction just below **Lukla's airstrip**: both branches head to **Lukla's main street**.

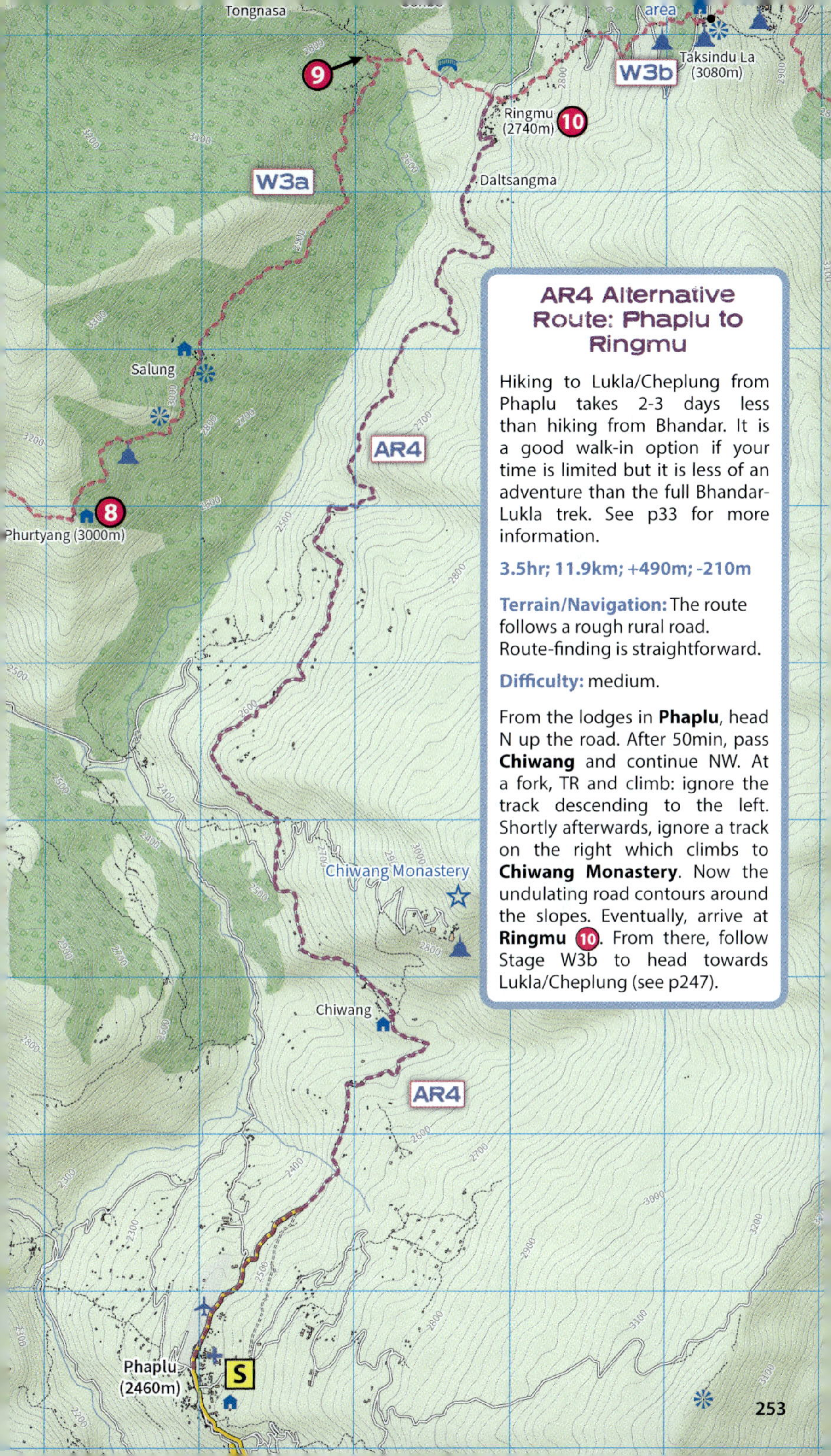

Tongnasa
9
W3b
Taksindu La
(3080m)
Ringmu
(2740m)
10
Daltsangma
W3a
Salung
AR4
8
Phurtyang (3000m)
AR4 Alternative Route: Phaplu to Ringmu
Hiking to Lukla/Cheplung from Phaplu takes 2-3 days less than hiking from Bhandar. It is a good walk-in option if your time is limited but it is less of an adventure than the full Bhandar-Lukla trek. See p33 for more information.
3.5hr; 11.9km; +490m; -210m
Terrain/Navigation: The route follows a rough rural road. Route-finding is straightforward.
Difficulty: medium.
From the lodges in Phaplu, head N up the road. After 50min, pass Chiwang and continue NW. At a fork, TR and climb: ignore the track descending to the left. Shortly afterwards, ignore a track on the right which climbs to Chiwang Monastery. Now the undulating road contours around the slopes. Eventually, arrive at Ringmu 10. From there, follow Stage W3b to head towards Lukla/Cheplung (see p247).
Chiwang Monastery
Chiwang
AR4
Phaplu
(2460m)
S

Makalu viewed from Kongma La (TP7)

Further Reading & Bibliography

- A Definitive Guide to Sagarmatha National Park by Margaret Jefferies (Pilgrims Publishing; 2006)
- A Photographic Guide to Birds of the Himalayas by Bikram Grewal & Otto Pfister (New Holland; 2004)
- Birds of Nepal by Richard Grimmett et al (Bloomsbury; 2016)
- Buddhism for Dummies by Jonathan Landaw, Stephen Bodian & Gundrun Bühnemann
- Everest: Summit of Achievement by Stephen Venables et al (Royal Geographical Society; 2003)
- Flowers of the Himalaya by Adam Stainton (Oxford India Paperbacks; 2010)
- Himalayan Flowers, Trees and Animals by Tej Kumar Shrestha et al (2011)
- Into Thin Air by Jon Krakauer (Pan Books; 1998)
- Life and Death on Mt. Everest by Sherry B. Ortner (Princeton University Press; 1999)
- Natural History of the Wild Side of Everest by Frances Klatzel (Mera Publications; 2022)
- Nepal by Bradley Mayhew et al (Lonely Planet; 2023)
- Mount Everest National Park: Sagarmatha Mother of the Universe by Margaret Jefferies (The Mountaineers; 1991)
- The Rough Guide to Nepal by Stuart Butler et al (Rough Guides; 2018)

Our guide and porter on the way to Kongma La (TP7)

Lhotse viewed from Chukhung (TP6/7)

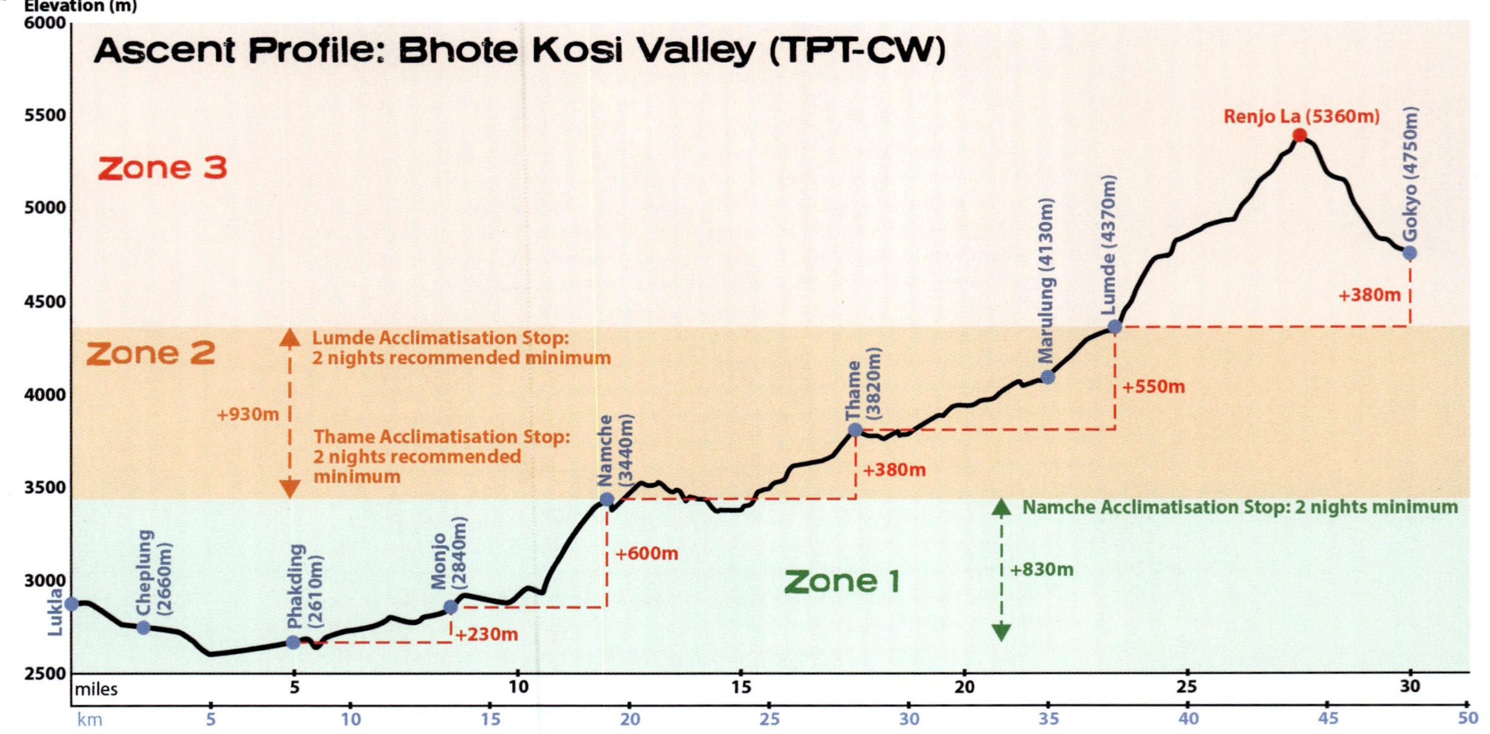

Ascent Profile: Bhote Kosi Valley (TPT-CW)
Elevation (m)
6000
5500
5000
4500
4000
3500
3000
2500
Zone 3
Zone 2
Zone 1
Lumde Acclimatisation Stop: 2 nights recommended minimum
+930m
Thame Acclimatisation Stop: 2 nights recommended minimum
Namche Acclimatisation Stop: 2 nights minimum
+830m
Lukla
Cheplung (2660m)
Phakding (2610m)
Monjo (2840m)
Namche (3440m)
Thame (3820m)
Marulung (4130m)
Lumde (4370m)
Renjo La (5360m)
Gokyo (4750m)
+230m
+600m
+380m
+550m
+380m
miles
5
10
15
20
25
30
km
5
10
15
20
25
30
35
40
45
50

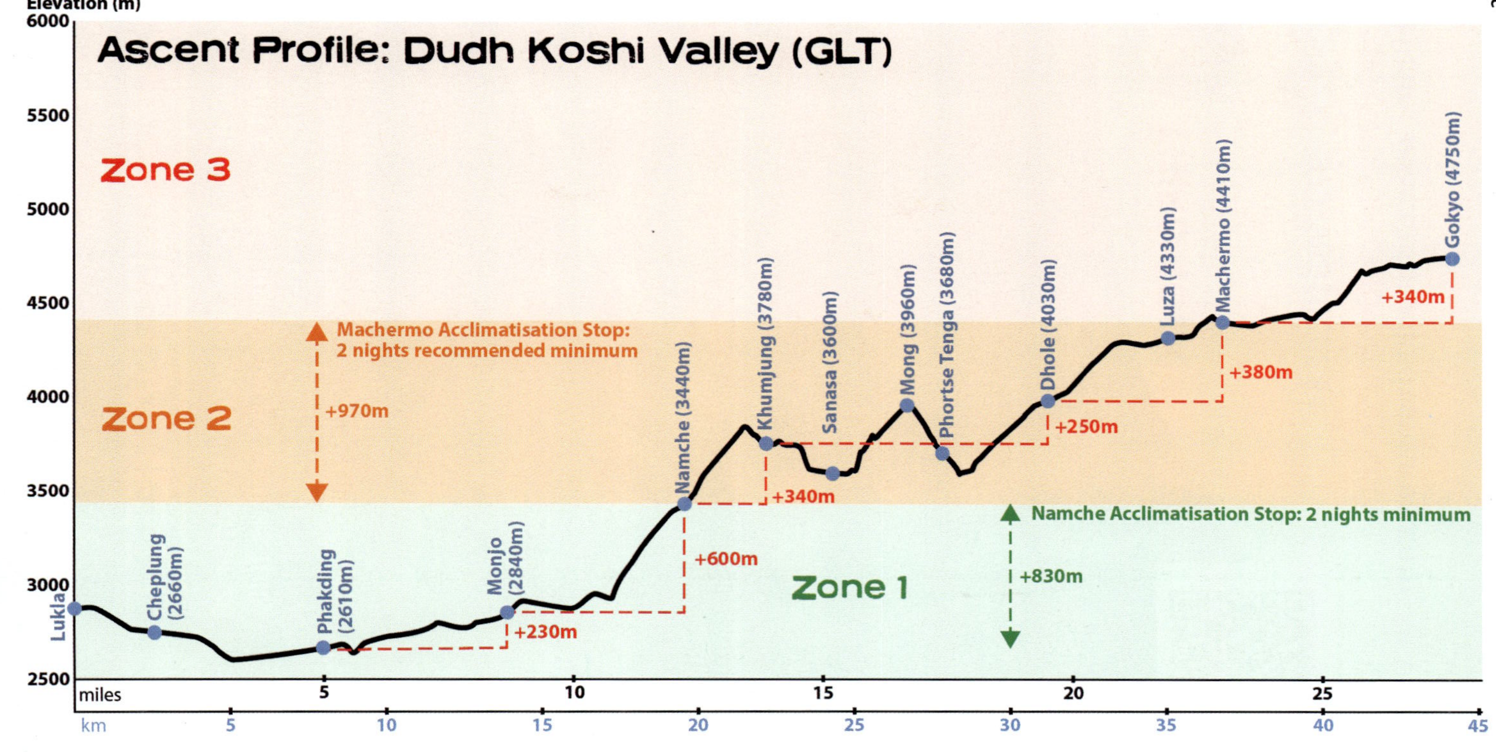
Ascent Profile: Dudh Koshi Valley (GLT)
Elevation (m)
6000
5500
5000
4500
4000
3500
3000
2500
Zone 3
Zone 2
Zone 1
Machermo Acclimatisation Stop:
2 nights recommended minimum
+970m
Namche Acclimatisation Stop: 2 nights minimum
+830m
Lukla
Cheplung (2660m)
Phakding (2610m)
Monjo (2840m)
Namche (3440m)
Khumjung (3780m)
Sanasa (3600m)
Mong (3960m)
Phortse Tenga (3680m)
Dhole (4030m)
Luza (4330m)
Machermo (4410m)
Gokyo (4750m)
+230m
+600m
+340m
+250m
+380m
+340m
miles
5
10
15
20
25
km
5
10
15
20
25
30
35
40
45

Explore Nepal

Reach New heights !

EXPERIENCE EVEREST !

Join us at the top of the world! We offer 20 different Everest itineraries as well as fully customisable trekking packages for all levels. Create memories that last a lifetime. Adventure awaits - don't wait any longer!

  +977-9851055684

contact@thirdrockadventures.com

Website: www.thirdrockadventures.com